Chronicles
Pre-Celtic Europe

(Survivors of the Great Tsunami)

by
Alewyn J. Raubenheimer

Chronicles from Pre-Celtic Europe
(Survivors of the Great Tsunami)
By Alewyn J. Raubenheimer

ISBN-13: 978-1496168771
ISBN-10: 1496168771

Previously published under the title "Survivors of the Great Tsunami" by the same author (© 2010, © 2011)

First Edition: March 2010
Second Edition:: August 2011
Third Edition: March 2014

Web Site: www.impactsurvivors.com
Email: info@impactsurvivors.com

Dedicated to
Beulah

Acknowledgements

If there is one person whose hand I would have liked to shake, it is Dr. J.G. Ottema who died in 1879. He was right all along.

What should have made him world famous, destroyed him; a disillusioned and embittered old man. In the end, he took his own life; shunned by friends, discredited by colleagues and ridiculed by the press. Like a Vincent van Gogh, he was denied his rightful place in the sun. I trust this book will set the record straight.

A special word of thanks goes to my brother Connie and my son Werner for their ongoing encouragement. To my other children and their spouses, Dean, Janet, Jeanette, Stefan and Christel for acting as sounding boards: Thank you for your hours of listening to my monologues.

Preface

Chronicles from Pre-Celtic Europe was first published in 2010 under the title *Survivors of the Great Tsunami*. The book proves beyond reasonable doubt that the *Oera Linda Manuscript* discovered in the Netherlands during the mid-19th century is authentic and indeed the oldest writing on European Pre-History. This captivating manuscript shows that West European Civilization pre-dates Greek And Roman Societies by millennia and that many milestones which were previously attributed to the Greeks, Romans, Phoenicians, Egyptians and others should, in fact, be accredited to North-Western Europe.

Research subsequent to the 2011 publication made it necessary to add the additional evidence uncovered and to select a more appropriate title for this work. The revision also presented an opportunity to clarify certain topics and to re-arrange others in a more logical order. In addition to the earlier irrefutable facts, further evidence is presented here to prove that the 2500 year old *Oera Linda Manuscript* is authentic and a true reflection of certain key events in West European and world pre-history going back some 4200 years, to 2193 BC. The Oera Linda manuscript is appended here as Annexure 2 in order to enable the reader to better understand this investigation.

The Oera Linda document came to light in the Netherlands in 1867. Some considered it one of the most sensational finds in the history of Western Civilisation; others declared it a hoax. Over the next 145 years the latter venomously attacked and tried to discredit the manuscript. The opponents of the manuscript went beyond all reason, objectivity and logic to brand it the work of one or more, until now, unidentified pranksters. The perplexing aspect of the whole saga is that it was not an historian, an archaeologist or even a linguist who rejected the manuscript as a hoax in the first place, but a physician, Johan Winkler. Strange as it may sound, the egoistic Winkler's ill conceived and amateurish ideas still form the basis of the *Hoax Theorists'* arguments to this day. One would have thought that it should be obvious to any rational investigator that he did not have the credentials to make a pronouncement on such an important issue. Once Winkler had solicited the support of his friends and colleagues in the highly esteemed *Frisian Society for History and Culture*, though, many did not consider it worth their while or social standing to go against the Society or to persist in their views that the manuscript was authentic. The quite substantial number of scholars who dared to suggest that the manuscript was not a hoax, were so ridiculed and discredited that they were (and still are) driven out of the ranks of mainstream academia. Although the burden of proof remains with those who believe in the authenticity of the manuscript, the case has been declared closed by the *hoax theorists* a very long time ago and no more evidence or arguments in favour of the Oera Linda Book are allowed. By the implied reasoning of these adherents to the hoax theory, they themselves, therefore, do not have to produce any tangible evidence to support their stance that the manuscript is a falsification, nor do they have to entertain any opposing arguments. Whenever these hoax conspiracy theorists themselves did try to prove the manuscript a fraud, they could not do so. The reason is simple: The *Oera Linda Book* is not a hoax; it is one of the most important documents available today on European pre-history. In fact, without the Oera Linda Book it is impossible to piece together or understand Europe's socio-political development over the last 4200 years.

I did not address the many and varied theories flaunted by the advocates of the *Hoax Conspiracy* but rather left it to the facts to prove that the Oera Linda Book is indeed what it claims to be; a true reflection of certain key events in European pre-history. These events dramatically and irrevocably changed the course of Europe, the Middle East and South Asia.

I have spent many hours in debate, research and the translation of a number of letters, reports and affidavits from the late 19th century and early 20th century Netherlands. From these documents it is abundantly clear that that the three main suspects in the hoax theory, namely Cornelis over de Linden, Eelco Verwijs and Francois Haverschmidt could not and did not conspire to create the Oera Linda Book. A number of Dutch authors such as E. Molenaar (1949) have reached the same conclusions in the past after in-depth studies and research. Their findings, however, are still ignored in the Netherlands.

The second important addition to this edition is an expansion on the influence of, and references to the Frisians, Celts and other social groupings and tribes in the Oera Linda Book. This is particularly important in light of the rapid advancement of our understanding of *Continental Celtic society*[1] brought on by a plethora of archaeological finds over the last number of years. Archaeologists and historians are increasingly coming to the realisation that the stereotype *Celt* portrayed by ancient scribes was the product of prejudice, ignorance and Roman propaganda. *Celtic Society* was, in fact, much more refined, affluent and developed than thought until recently. They were certainly not more villainous than the Romans and in certain respects, were on a much higher level of sophistication; such as in their social norms, decorum and responsibilities within their own society.

In my research, I visited a number of Celtic archaeological sites and museums in the Netherlands, France and Germany. Amongst these were De Hamert, Oss, Glauberg, Hochdorf, Heuneberg and the European Archaeological Park at Bliesbruck-Reinheim. I was struck by the resemblance between archaeologists' reconstruction of *Celtic Society* and the descriptions given in the Oera Linda Book. These insights were not available in the 19th century. The Oera Linda Book also lifts the veil on some aspects of *Celtic Society* that still perplex archaeologists. One unexpected revelation is the rank of the mysterious *Princesses* or *Priestesses* found in sumptuous burial chambers at many archaeological sites.

The first section of The Oera Linda Book, *The Book of Adela's Followers*, was compiled in the present day Netherlands in 558 BC when *Celtic* civilization is thought to have been at its hight in South-Western Europe. This was contemporaneous with the *Hallstatt Culture* (ca 800 to 450 BC). The book is not confined to the Hallstatt period, though, but gives us valuable insights into the time frames defined by the *Únětice Culture* (ca 2300 to 1600 BC), the *Tumulus Culture* (ca 1600 to

---

1 Unlike Insular Celts, many Continental Celts have incorrectly been identified as such by archaeologists. Whilst most West- and North-West Europeans shared a common ancestry, culture and religion, not all were Celts. At this stage archaeology alone is not able to make the distinction between Celts and non-Celts.

1300 BC) and the *Urnfield Culture* (ca 1300 to 800 BC). Writings in the Oera Linda Book subsequent to the Book of Adela's Followers were mostly done during the *La Tène Period*. (ca 450 BC to the start of the Christian era). The terms culture and period is used interchangeably here. This is not strictly correct as different cultures probably shared the same periods.

Ancient Roman writers sometimes used the terms *Gauls* and *Celts* as synonyms; an error that has precipitated to the present day amongst many. Gallic culture was essentially an external religious movement that infiltrated southern Europe from the Middle East from 2000 BC to 1600 BC. The name Gaul appears to be a demonym for the Golan Heights on the present day border of Syria and Israel. The Celts, on the other hand, were an internal socio-political group that broke away from the main proto-Frisian group in 1628 BC. Whilst the Celts initially held sway over Gallic territories, Gallic religion with their Druid priests never gained a meaningful foothold north of the Alps.

The second misconception today is that the Celts occupied most of Western and Central Europe during the Hallstatt and La Tène Periods. The Celts, Germans, Saxons, Danes and Frisians all had the same ancestry and shared a common culture. It is therefore almost impossible to distinguish between Celtic Society and, say, Saxons or Frisians from archaeology only. As late as 200 BC the Frisian authors of the Oera Linda Manuscript still saw the lands north of the Rhine right up to Lake Constance as their domain and not belonging to the Celts.

A further crucial conclusion reached here is that the Oera Linda Book was most likely kept up to date or added to right up to the latter part of the Frankish Empire. We know that the last Frisians to lose their independence to Charles the Great in AD 772 were those who held out in Groningen east of the Lauwers River. After 772 Charles turned his attention to the Saxons, the Frisians' closest allies for millennia. The Frisian-Frankish Wars ended with the final Frisian uprising in AD 793. The Saxon-Frankish Wars lasted until 804 when the last rebellion of disaffected Saxon tribes was crushed.

In a bloody campaign, both Frisians and Saxons were forced to accept the Roman Catholic Faith. In only one incident, at the *Massacre of Verden* in AD 782, some 4500 captive Saxons were beheaded for practicing paganism after supposedly having converted to Roman

Catholicism. As proof of Charles' fanatic resolve to force the Saxons into Roman Catholicism, he issued a legal code in 785 AD, the *Capitulatio de partibus Saxoniae*, which included the death sentence for any Saxon who refused to convert from their native Germanic paganism to Christianity.

Liko ovira Linda's letter of 803 AD, which came with the Oera Linda manuscript, was written shortly before the perceived, at the time, final demise of Frisian and Saxon independence at the hands of the Franks in 804 AD. The Frisian's fight for freedom and their resistance to Christianity, in fact, continued for centuries afterwards. Liko ovira Linda, though, thought he saw the writing on the wall and his letter must be seen as a last desperate plea to his descendants to preserve some of their history, customs and religion. The reason for the missing sections from *The Writings of Beden* and at the end of the Oera Linda Book can, therefore, most likely be laid at the door of Charles the Great's savage Christianization campaign against the Frisians and Saxons. In fact, it is very likely that Liko ovira Linda himself removed all references to the Romans, the Holy Roman Empire and the Franks from the Oera Linda Book. In the light of the Frisians' and Saxons' fanatical resistance against Roman Catholicism, it is most likely that these missing chapters contained derogatory references to, and incriminating evidence against certain individuals and/or associations. Had this information fallen into the wrong hands, Liko and his family would most likely have had to pay with their lives. The whole episode is reminiscent of the obliteration of Celtic Societies by the Romans 800 years before and the bloody destruction of the Inca Civilisation, Codices and history by the Spanish Conquistadors in Mesoamerica 800 years later.

It is unfortunate that the zealous *Crusaders* to Northern and North-Western Europe destroyed all records of Germanic Paganism. We are left with the impression that the religions of all Europeans north of the Rhine were almost indivisible and that all were polytheists and idol worshippers since the dawn of time. The Oera Linda Book, however, describe Europe's oldest religion as monotheistic and older, but very similar to Judaism. Polytheism and idolatry was only introduced after 2092 BC with the arrival of migrants from Central Asia and the Far East. From Liko ovira Linda's reference to *Wralda* in his letter of AD 803, and the fact that the Oera Linda Book describes their religion in detail, leaves one with the impression that their form of monotheism was still practised by some right up to the end of the Early Middle Ages. It is therefore quite possible that several copies of the Oera Linda Book may still have existed up to the 8th century AD.

The notion that Western Europe attained literacy only after the Roman Occupation is dispelled and the reference to Greek-type letters found in Gaul in Julius Caesars' account of the Gallic Wars acquires a totally new significance. The Oera Linda Manuscript clearly describes how the Greeks received their alphabet from Western Europe. A large number of West Europeans, however, regressed into illiteracy and barbarism after the 1628 BC *Celtic Revolution*. In the modern vernacular, some may even have called it the *European Spring*.

The Oera Linda manuscript is undoubtedly one of the most important and captivating insights into the pre-history of Europe available to us today – an insight which archaeologists and historians should best take heed of, or ignore to the continued detriment of their respective fields of study.

Alewyn J Raubenheimer.
Johannesburg, March 2014.

Contents

LIST OF TABLES

LIST OF FIGURES

The Letters

AD 1256

Okke my Son,

You must protect these books with body and soul. They contain the history of all our people, as well as of our forefathers. Last year I saved them from the flood with you and your mother; but they got wet and began to perish. In order not to lose them, I copied them on imported[2] paper. Should you inherit them, you must also copy them. Your children must do so too so that they may never be lost.

Written at Liuwert[3]. After Atland[4] sank, it is the three thousand, four hundred and forty-ninth year; that is, by the Christian calculation, the twelve hundred and fifty sixth year[5].

Hidde, surnamed oera Linda. – Watch!

AD 803[6]

Beloved Heirs,

For the sake of our dear forefathers, and for the sake of our dear freedom, I beg you a thousand times: Oh Beloved, never let the eye of a monk glance over these writings. They speak sweet words but they secretly tamper with everything that relates to us Frisians[7]. To gain rich endowments they conspire with puppet kings. These know that we are their greatest enemies because we speak to their people of liberty, rights, and the duties of rulers.

---

[2] Lit. Foreign Paper, i.e. expensive paper, signifying the importance of the manuscript to Hidde oera Linda.

[3] Leeuwarden, capital of the province of Friesland in the Netherlands.

[4] Aldland or Atland, Old Land.

[5] Atland, therefore, disappeared in 3449 – 1256 = 2193 BC.

[6] Written after the conquest of the Frisians and shortly before the final defeat of the Saxons by the Frankish Armies of Charles the Great in AD 804. By AD 803 Liko ovira Linda had all but lost hope that Frisian independence could ever be regained.

[7] In the original text, Liko ovira Linda actually uses the term Frias.

They, therefore, seek to destroy all that we derive from our forefathers, and all that is left of our old customs.

Oh Beloved, I have been in their courts. If Wralda wills it and do not strengthen us, they will altogether exterminate us.

Written at Liudwerd.[8] (In the) Eight hundredth and third year by the Christian concept.

Liko, surnamed ovira[9] Linda.

---

[8] Leeuwarden, capital of the province of Friesland in the Netherlands. As with other places in the Oera Linda Book, the name and/or spelling changed several times as the book was written by different authors who lived centuries apart.

[9] The family name had changed from *overa Linda* in 530 BC, to *ovira Linda* in AD 803, to *Oera Linda* in AD 1256 and to *over de Linden* by the 19th century.

Introduction

> *So between malice on one side and servility on the other,*
> *the interests of posterity were neglected. But historians*
> *find that a tone of flattery soon incurs the stigma of*
> *servility and earns for them the contempt of their readers,*
> *whereas people readily open their ears to the criticisms of*
> *envy, <u>since malice makes a show of independence.</u>*
> Publius Cornelius Tacitus (*c.* AD 56 – 117)

 *ae Victis!*[10]

With these words of utter contempt for the Romans, Brennus, the Gaulish chieftain, threw his sword on the weights of the scale. The consular tribune of Rome, Q. Sulpicius, had negotiated a ransom of 1000 pounds of gold with the victorious Gauls and now he dared question the weights used by these barbarians.

It was the year 387 BC. For the first time in 360 years, the legions of Rome were crushed and the city sacked - by an enemy never seen or heard of before[11]. The Romans realised that they had brought the disaster upon themselves by underestimating these strangers; both in terms of their military prowess and their reverence for international protocol. The Romans had killed one of the Gaulish headmen and had ridiculed their envoys.

All that was known of these invaders is that they came from beyond the Po and the Alps and that the Romans' neighbours and

---

[10] Woe to the vanquished!
[11] Titus Livius Patavinus (59 BC – AD 17), *The History of Rome*, Book 5.

adversaries to the north, the Etruscans and Umbrians, are said to have been embroiled in conflict with them for hundreds of years.

Over almost four centuries since descendants of Trojan survivors had founded Rome, the city had build up a reputation as the most formidable military power on the Italian Peninsula. Now, at the battle of the Allia, they were humiliated by a rabble of undisciplined tribesmen. The Romans took revenge soon after and went on to expand their power base in Italy. Later they triumphed over Carthage and made inroads into Greek territories weakened by Alexander's Eastern exploits.

The next time the Romans engaged a people from beyond the Alps, however, they again suffered crushing defeats; this time at the hands of the Cimbrians and Teutones. At the Battle of Noreia in 112 BC, some 24 000 Roman soldiers of a 30 000 strong army were killed despite having led the enemy into an ambush. Roman propagandists claimed they were overwhelmed by a force ten times bigger than their own. The Senate had to be pacified.

The Romans had learned dear lessons from these North-Western Europeans and introduced the *Marian Reforms* in 107 BC. Instead of a volunteer army, they now had a professional salaried army with standard issue weapons and year-round training. All citizens could now enroll; not only the nobility. New fighting tactics such as the maniple were introduced to counter the agility of their new-found foes. They were now ready for the *barbarians*.

In 105 BC the Romans again engaged the Cimbrians and Teutones in the Battle of Arausio. The result was a third crushing defeat and the virtual annihilation of the Roman army of 80,000 troops and 40,000 auxiliaries; the largest army the Romans had ever sent into and lost in battle. This time Roman sources claimed that they were defeated by a 200 000 strong enemy – twice the size of the defeated Roman army. Rome's only saving grace after the defeat was the fact that the Cimbrians and Teutones had no designs towards invading the Italian Peninsula; something which has intrigued historians right up to the present.

After Arausio, internal strive caused the Cimbrian and Teutone coalition to break up into smaller groups. This allowed the

Romans to gain the upper hand and, eventually, destroy this threat to the Roman Republic.

Who were these people from north of the Alps and how did they manage to inflict such humiliating defeats on the mighty Roman army of the time? Where did they get their weapons from? Their command structures? Their knowledge of military tactics, strategy and logistics?

For centuries historians believed that European civilisation evolved from the ancient Egyptians, Akkadians, Sumerians, Assyrians, Phoenicians and, lastly, the Babylonians and Persians. Out of the mists of time these communities mastered the human and natural sciences and built empires whose splendour is still evident thousands of years later. Some say that ancient mariners from China first circumnavigated the globe and man's consciousness reached its zenith at the feet of the Himalayas and Mount Fiji. This happened while primitive Neolithic or Stone Age hunter-gatherers still inhabited Europe.

Over millennia these highly developed civilisations vied with one another for dominance. In time, some of their knowledge and achievements crossed the Aegean, then the Adriatic and, at long last, over the Alps. Why did it take more than three thousand years for civilisation to penetrate the dark forests of Europe? Why did the ancients elect to build their empires in North Africa and the Middle East where, apart from some rivers, they were surrounded by an arid and barren landscape? Why did they avoid the forests and fertile plains of Europe? Did they know something that we do not? Is it not conceivable that some other civilised people, or at least an advanced culture, already held the title deeds to Central-, Western- and Northern Europe and, equally important, the means to retain such possession?

The idea of the simple linear development of society from the culture of the Paleolithic (Old Stone Age) through the successive stages of the Neolithic (New Stone Age), Bronze and Iron Ages must be given up. Today we find primitive cultures co-existing with advanced modern society on all the continents – the Bushmen of Australia, the Bushmen of South Africa, truly primitive peoples in South America and in New Guinea; some tribal people in the United States. We shall assume now that, some 20 000 years or more ago, while Paleolithic peoples held out in Europe, more advanced cultures existed elsewhere on the earth, and that we inherited a part of what they once possessed, passed down from people to people[12].

This statement by Dr. Charles Hapgood may ring true, but for one aspect. What if an advanced civilisation did exist in Europe some 20 000 years ago or, at least, 4000 years ago? To be even more blunt: Is it not time we consider the possibility that our civilisation actually originated and developed in Europe and, more precisely, in Western Europe and not *elsewhere on earth*?

In these early years of the 21st century, historians are still mystified by ancient Egyptian references to *Sea Peoples*. Who compiled the amazingly accurate maps in antiquity? Who were the Minoans? Where did our modern alphabet and numerals come from? Who were the ancient Britons and Europeans? Where did the Celts, the Gauls and the Druids come from? Who founded Athens and Rome and when? What set the Cimbrian migration in motion and what caused the Roman-Cimbrian Wars? Who are the mysterious *princesses* or *priestesses* found in Celtic hill graves? What are the origins of monotheism, democracy, capitalism, free enterprise and human rights? Why did these concepts take hold in Europe earlier than anywhere else? What caused the demise of the Old Kingdom of Egypt in ca 2200 BC and the Akkadian Empire in 2193 BC?

Astonishingly, the answers to these questions and many more have been in the public domain for more than 145 years in the form of an ancient Frisian manuscript. The document, which is a collection of pre-historic writings and memoirs dating from the third millennium BC, is the oldest known record of European history. Certain chapters in the manuscript, in fact, are older than the Bible.

On 15th April 1820, Andries over de Linden, aged 61, died at Enkhuizen, some 50 kilometres north-east of Amsterdam. Shortly before his death he handed over some old documents to his daughter, Aafje Reuvers. Andries and his wife had shared the same house with his daughter and her husband, Hendrik Reuvers, for many years and

---

[12] Dr. Charles Hapgood in Maps of the Ancient Sea Kings; Evidence of Advanced Civilisation in the Ice Age, 1966.

he trusted her, but not so his irresponsible son, Jan. Aafje was charged with the safekeeping of the documents for his grandson and Aafje's nephew, Cornelis over the Linden, aged 9, until he had grown up.

Aafje kept the documents for the next 28 years. For whatever reason, Hendrik would not allow her to hand the parcel over to Cornelis. It was only after Hendrik had died and Aafje had remarried Koos Meijlhof that she again remembered this family heirloom. In 1848 she handed the documents over to her brother's 37 year old son. She died the following year.

> *"This is a family book", she said on handing it over. "The language is Old Fries and has been preserved by the family for centuries, therefore, I must impress upon you that you must value it very highly."*[13]

By his own words, Cornelis over de Linden was not too impressed with his inheritance. He could not even read it; yet, it intrigued him. Over the next 18 years he would occasionally page through the book and try to make sense of the strange letters. He even bought an Old Frisian dictionary and some books on rune script, but to no avail. In the meantime his successful career took up most of his time. He had become Chief Superintendant of the Royal Dockyard at De Helder in the Netherlands. This left little time for the old manuscript.

> *Educated friends, who could have helped me with my further investigations, I did not have, and to call on somebody through the press who would have translated it for a sum, I could not afford.*

In ca May 1867, whilst on leave, Cornelis met a Mr. Siderius in Amsterdam. Later at Siderius' home in Harlingen, Friesland, Cornelis mentioned the old manuscript and the fact that he could not read it. Siderius told Cornelis that they had a schoolmaster, a Mr. Jansen, in Harlingen who was well versed in Old Frisian and that Cornelis

---

[13] Essay by Cornelis over de Linden (Addressed to grandson Cornelis III (Oct 1872 – Feb 1874).

should send him some pages of the manuscript. Once home, Cornelis copied 4 pages and mailed them to Siderius.

On 11th June 1867, Cornelis over de Linden received an enthusiastic letter from Siderius. In his letter Siderius stated that Cornelis' manuscript contained some very Old Frisian laws and that he would visit Cornelis in eight days and would like to get a further consignment of copies. Cornelis duly traced more pages and handed these over to Siderius. He also showed Siderius the original manuscript.

After some months, Cornelis wrote to Siderius enquiring about progress on the translation. Siderius replied that Jansen could not do the translation and he had forwarded the copied portions to the archivist of Friesland, Dr. Eelco Verwijs. They, however, now thought the manuscript was the work of a practical joker as the language *was too modern.*

On 7 October 1867 Cornelis over de Linden wrote directly to Eelco Verwijs despite knowing full well that Verwijs and others had already rejected the manuscript as a hoax. With his letter he included some pages of the original manuscript to prove that the manuscript was indeed authentic. All he wanted was a translation for his own benefit. He clearly had no designs towards material gain or to fool anybody. Verwijs' pompous reply and subsequent actions, however, showed that he had other intentions. Over the next two years he tried to intimidate Cornelis in handing over the original. It is obvious that Verwijs was in it for personal gain. Fortunately, over de Linden saw through his ruse.

Despite Cornelis having sent a full copy of the manuscript to Verwijs, he was only rewarded with one translated page. Two years later, and unbeknown to Cornelis, Verwijs tabled the manuscript at a meeting of the *Frisian Society for History and Culture* - on 24 November 1869. By this time Cornelis over de Linden had resigned himself to the fact he will never learn the contents of his manuscript.

On a proposal from Verwijs, the Frisian Society requested one of their executive members, the physician Johan Winkler, to evaluate the copied manuscript. For some inexplicable reason the egoistic Winkler had convinced the Society that, although he had no formal training in linguistics, he was a self-taught authority on Old Frisian.

What is even more astonishing is that he was not an historian either, yet his pronouncement on the manuscript is still regarded as infallible by some. How did he manage to deceive a nation for more than a century? Lesser men would have been caught out, but not so Winkler. Thirteen months later, on 24 December 1870, Johan Winkler tabled his very brief verdict: *The Oera Linda Book is a hoax! Case closed.*

It is remarkable how Winkler's conclusion mirrored Verwijs' views from previous correspondence from Verwijs to Winkler. It is not difficult to suspect that Winkler could hardly read or interpret the manuscript; let alone translate it. He used all Verwijs' misgivings to declare the manuscript a fraud. Even more remarkable is that Winkler, years later, pointed to Verwijs as a possible participant in the *hoax* or so-called *conspiracy*.

Had it not been for the highly qualified and respected linguist, Dr. Jan Gerhardus Ottema, who was in the meeting when Winkler tabled his report, the copied manuscript would most likely have been relegated to the dustbin. After the meeting had accepted Winkler's verdict, Dr. Ottema, nevertheless, asked permission to take the manuscript home for perusal. Two months later, in February 1871, J. G. Ottema tabled a lengthy and detailed report: *The Oera Linda Book,* as it became known, was authentic!

Oh, horror upon horror! The highly esteemed members of the distinguished Frisian Society for History and Culture had made an unthinkable mistake - and that blue blooded Frisian, Johan Winkler, was a fraud! This information and the ramifications to the society could never be put up with. The 67 year old introvert, Jan Ottema, had to learn a lesson: Regardless of how meritorious a cause, never show off your colleagues and peers.

Despite the most convincing arguments, Ottema could not persuade the Society to retract their initial verdict, let alone fund the publishing of the translated Oera Linda Book. He had drawn a line in the sand and almost immediately old friends became adversaries. The controversy was not restricted to the inner chambers of the Society, but had soon engulfed most all of the Netherlands and the Dutch press. He had to go it alone and in 1872 he personally funded the publishing of *Thet Oera Linda Bok* and later a second edition in 1876. William Sandbach also published an English translation in 1876.

Even before publication, some Dutch academics and theologians went out of their (and truth's) way to prove that the Oera Linda Book was a hoax. As a case in point, the Oera Linda Book described an ancient people who had their dwellings on stilts on the Swiss lakes. In 1854 the water in Lake Zurich dropped to record lows and exposed ancient pile dwellings - exactly as mentioned in the Oera Linda Book. Before 1854 nobody knew about these. When Dr Ottema pointed this out, his opponents merely retorted that the manuscript was then written after 1854. All evidence pointing to the Oera Linda Book having existed before 1854 were conveniently ignored. Even as late as 2004 a very prominent Dutch academic had to admit that there is overwhelming evidence pointing to the existence of the manuscript as early as 1830. He explains, however, that the original manuscript had *disappeared* and *a new old manuscript* (sic!) was compiled after 1854!

Despite their spurious conjecture, the adherents of the Hoax Conspiracy were, and still are, nevertheless, so successful with their campaign that no serious academic in the Netherlands want to be associated with the book. My own investigations and those of others showed that none of the so-called suspects who may have committed the fraud as suggested by them, were capable of compiling such an elaborate *hoax*. Even the allegations that the language of the Oera Linda Book is gibberish (Dutch: *Wartaal*), with no precedent in ancient Frisian, is unfounded. In fact, the language shows a remarkable resemblance to the Old West-Frisian dialect and, to lesser extent, to the old Rustringer dialect of Northern Frisia (in Germany). Dr Ottema, in his paper delivered to the Frisian Society for History and Culture in February 1871, stated:

> The language is very old Frisian, still older and purer than the Frisian Rjuchtboek or old Frisian laws, differing from those both in form and spelling, so that it appears to be an entirely distinct dialect, and shows that the locality of the language must have been (as it was spoken) between the Vlie and the Scheldt.

Other academics such as Dr. A. T. Reitsma and Prof. Dr. Vitringa concurred with Ottema's findings. This however did not deter the Hoax Theorists. They merely added more voices to their choir.

In his preface to his second edition in 1876, Dr Ottema addressed the arguments of the adherents to the Hoax Theory of his day. His evidence, however, was and still is conveniently ignored. Today it almost seems as if the book only has value for New Age, pagan and occult groups – in stark contrast to the intentions and beliefs of the original prudish authors.

As to my allegation that the Oera Linda Book is forcibly suppressed in the Netherlands, one only needs to go to the Dutch website *Semafoor.net* of the academic study group, *SEM*.

SEM is an acronym for *Studiekring Eerste Millennium* (Study Circle First Millennium) and has as its aim a renewed investigation into the first millennium history of the Low Countries between the Somme River in Northern France and the Elbe River in Northern Germany for the period 100 BC to 1200 AD. Herewith some translated extracts from the website (my emphasis):

*1. Some 15 years ago I received a typed text of Albert Delahaye sent by the Albert Delahaye Foundation wherein the Oera Linda Book **was secretly used** to support his views on the history of the Low Countries in the first millennium. It took many telephone calls to convince the then secretary H. Jochems that this edition of the work would be to the detriment of Delahaye, rather than to his advantage.*

*2. He, who, however, tries to put forward a new perspective on the history of the first millennium and uses the Oera Linda Book as an authentic (13th century) source, **is wrong from the outset.** In the SEM it was more or less agreed some years ago not to do this in publications under the auspices of the SEM [sic]. **Not everybody was satisfied with this unwritten rule.** To them this was a form of self-censure. Jensma, in his dissertation, tended somewhat strongly in the direction of, amongst others, Albert Delahaye and Joël Vandemaele;*

*3. Jensma alleges the following (P.188): '**Neither Molenaar nor Vleer dared, and it typified the Netherland situation, declare the book outright authentic'.***

4. The truth is that the work of Delahaye was absolutely not based on the OLB; that he indeed did see the OLB as a supporting work for a time, that he also produced a typed manuscript about it and that he decided himself (sic) not to publish it. The publishers of the posthumous editions of Delahaye's work also did not do so (gave it up).

In 1985 the archivist, W.A. Fasel, wrote to Delahaye that Delahaye 'is not only destroying his hard earned credibility, but is <u>**making himself ridiculous in perpetuity**</u> (undying)'

5. *What was at first seen as pseudoscience and called as such, can nevertheless lead to changes in scientific approaches and views. Of this, however*<u>*, there is no such possibility with the Oera Linda Book.*</u>

So much for academic freedom and objectivity.

Despite all efforts to discredit the Oera Linda Book since 1867, subsequent discoveries have increasingly vindicated the book. Many of its claims, which were not known in the 19th century, have now been either proven correct or, in a few cases, at least probable. Conversely, **none of the historical facts mentioned in the book have ever been proven wrong**. If the Oera Linda book was a 19th century hoax, the author(s) must have had an unparalleled knowledge of ancient history and an extraordinary insight into human behaviour. In addition, he or they must have been brilliant linguists to have been able to invent an ancient dialect and script. Are we to believe that this genius was reserved for a single anonymous writing, without any clear motive and not to be repeated anywhere else? To be realistic, the claims and facts in the Oera Linda Book were impossible for anyone to have forged in the 19th century or even during the preceding 4000 years.

Perhaps one of the most startling revelations in the Oera Linda Book comes from the graphic description of a cataclysmic natural disaster in 2193 BC. The catastrophe virtually destroyed an advanced monotheistic and democratic maritime civilization in Western and Northern Europe. This is precisely what scientists are now concluding for several countries from Asia, through the Mediterranean to the North Sea and beyond. What is equally remarkable is that the book gives exact dates and accurately describes a number of other important historical events. Some of these were only discovered or verified in the late 20th and early 21st centuries by archaeologists and advanced dating methods.

During the latter half of the 20th century archaeologists concluded that legendary Troy (Troy VIIa) was destroyed in ca 1188 BC. Yet, a hundred years earlier, the Oera Linda Book mentioned the destruction of Troy in that year. Towards the end of the 19th century the story of Troy was still regarded as a myth.

Another one of many claims made in the Oera Linda Book is that ancient Frisians (or rather, Proto-Frisians) landed on Crete in ca 1600 BC under the leadership of a Sea King or, in today's terms, an admiral, by the name of Minnos. The Frisians built a harbour and introduced far-reaching reforms on the island. After an assassination attempt on his life, Minnos fled back to the present day Netherlands, leaving his compatriots behind.

During the opening years of the 20th century, archaeologists unearthed a previously unknown Bronze Age civilisation on the island of Crete. Sir Arthur Evans named it the Minoan Civilisation after the mythic King Minos in Greek Mythology. Towards the end of the 20th century archaeologists had concluded that the Minoans reached the apex of their civilisation during the Neopalatial Period (1700 BC – 1425 BC). After a catastrophe in 1600 BC, the palaces, or rather administrative buildings, were rebuilt greater than ever before (LMIA period – 1600 BC to 1480 BC).

If the Oera Linda Book is a 19th century hoax, how did the author(s) manage to pick this key date of 1600 BC in Minoan history more than a century before scientists established it? In the 19th century nobody knew that a Minoan Civilisation ever existed. Somebody may have deduced the civilization from Greek mythology but most certainly not the date.

The Oera Linda Book describes episodes from the life of one of their respected matriarchs, Nyhellenia, who lived in 1630 BC. In 1970, a Dutch fishing boat found a stone votive dedicated to her near the East Schelde estuary of the Netherlands in the flooded sites of Domberg and Colijnsplaat. Subsequent dredging operations in the area produced some 160 similar artefacts. The Oera Linda Book tells us that Nyhellenia and Minerva, the Roman goddess of wisdom, arts, trade, and defense was one and the same person.

Ancient scribes from the Middle East, Egypt, Greece, Rome and India all substantiate the claims made by this manuscript from antiquity, whilst modern sciences from archaeology to genetics and linguistics confirm its authenticity. The evidence provided here does not only prove beyond reasonable doubt that the Oera Linda Book is true but, even more astonishing, that the cradle of Western Civilisation lay in Europe.

The pioneers from Europe's western seaboard founded civilisations from Greece to Persia. They led the world out of the Stone and Bronze ages into the Iron Age. They gave the world the *Greek alphabet* and *Indo-Arabian numerals*, democracy and free enterprise. They were partial progenitors of the Phoenicians, the Pelasgians, the Minoans, the Hyksos, the Philistines, the Sea People and the Aryans. They taught the Jews about monotheism and they themselves were the *gods* in Greek mythology and Hinduism; deified by the superstitious and polytheistic natives of their host countries.

The Oera Linda Book not only fills critical gaps since the Early Holocene[14] in European and world history, but it also led me to the discovery of a previously inhabited land the size of Ireland which now lies submerged around the Faroe Islands. Irrefutable evidence of this sunken island was found north-west of the British Isles beneath the cold waters of the Atlantic. What is alarming is that the fundamentals of the event that destroyed this land, devastated Western Europe and killed hundreds of thousands, are still in place. The mechanisms at work are the same as those that caused the March 2011 earthquake and tsunami in Japan. It happened before and it will happen again.

It is hoped that this book will renew interest in the Oera Linda Book and that it will provide some pointers to historians and archaeologists alike in their quest to unravel Europe's pre-historic past. The last word on this ancient manuscript has not been spoken and until it is taken seriously, we shall continue to grope in the dark.

We owe it to the memory of the millions of people, our ancestors, who perished under the most terrible conditions 4200 years ago.

---

[14] The Holocene is the last approximately 12 000 years of earth's history starting with the end of the last Ice Age.

Chapter 1

Apocalypse

The Oera Linda Chronology

T he first book in the Oera Linda Manuscript is the

Book of Adela's Followers. The book was hastily compiled in 558 BC on recommendation by the highly esteemed *Adela ovira Linda*. She had previously been nominated to the position of *Volksmoeder*[15] but had declined the position. Now the country was under thread of war and the General Assembly accepted her proposal to gather as much of their history as possible into a single book lest this was lost in the impending conflict with the Fins.

In the second book, *The Writings of Adelbrost and Appolonia* the authors, in addition to their own memoirs, added more ancient writings which were omitted from the *Book of Adela's Followers*. Subsequent authors also interspersed their recollections with those from other times and places. A first cursory look at the Oera Linda Book can, therefore, be somewhat confusing. This book is an attempt to examine the historical facts in chronological order.

The start of the Oera Linda Book's calendar is 2193 BC; the date of the demise of *Aldland* (Old Land) or *Atland* (Naval slang) mentioned by Hidde Oera Linda in his letter of AD 1256. This date of 2193 BC, or the rounded date of 2200 BC, is not only of relevance to the Oera Linda Book, but is quoted numerous times in connection with

---

[15] Lit. "Folk Mother", Mother Superior, Supreme Matron, i.e. National Leader

historical and archaeological research into ancient civilisations. In scientific circles reference is made to the *4.2 ka BP Event* (4.2 kilo annum or 4200 years Before Present) which denotes a global event defined by severe and very rapid climate change. The date, or rather the events surrounding it, is of such great significance to the Oera Linda Book and World history that we need to examine it very closely before we proceed with the rest of the Oera Linda narrative.

In the 19th century Netherlands, the date of 2193 BC was not unique to the Oera Linda Book. The date also appeared in the Frisian *Volksalmanak* (National Calendar) as the date of the Biblical Deluge or *Noah's Flood* The calendar was widely circulated long before Cornelis over de Linden received the manuscript from his aunt, Mrs. Aafje Meylhoff, in August 1848.

Proponents of the Hoax Theory claim that the so-called perpetrators of the *hoax* merely quoted this date from Frisian tradition which, in turn, was derived from Biblical chronology. This date for the Biblical Flood, however, is not used anywhere else in Christian or Jewish literature. If one accepts that the Bible was the source of the Oera Linda Book's date for the Deluge, one would then also expect the author(s) to have used the Biblical description of the disaster. This, however, is not the case. The description of the Deluge in the Bible is remarkably different from that in the Oera Linda Book. Why would the creators of this *elaborate hoax* have used a Biblical date but then ignored the description in their primary reference? Where, then, did the Frisians get this date from if not from the Bible?

It is a well-researched and documented fact that a cataclysmic event happened in the Near-, Middle- and Far East some 4200 years ago. From the Aegean and Turkey to Egypt and across the Middle East to India and the Far East, archaeologists found traces of the sudden collapse of whole cities and civilisations. The notion that the decline of these societies was very rapid is supported by ice core analyses from Antarctica, Greenland, Mount Kilimanjaro and the Himalayas. Deep-sea core drilling in the North Atlantic and tree rings in North America all point to a sudden climate change in the latter half of the Holocene. It is also remarkable that most civilisations older than, say, 4200 years were remote from any oceans or seas; contrary to what one would expect. There appear to have been relatively little coastal development during these earlier years or, more than likely, very little remained thereof.

A number of ancient scribes described an epic disaster, or a series of disasters, that ravaged earth for years and perhaps even decades. From their accounts and from archaeological finds we glean that many civilizations were destroyed and arts, sciences and technologies wiped out. Countless people perished in the carnage and many more died in the resultant outbreaks of disease, pestilence, and famine. Governments, social, religious and educational systems and infrastructure that were developed and refined over millennia, collapsed. Production, agriculture, trade and commerce came to an abrupt end. In the aftermath, traumatized and starving survivors fled the scenes of destruction and the world experienced the greatest mass migration in the history of man.

Human endeavours were reduced to the most basic needs for survival. In the void left by the collapse of institutionalized security and military structures, anarchy reigned. Looting, pillaging, murder, rape and every conceivable atrocity became a way of life. Strength lay in numbers. Rulers, leaders, the wealthy, the intelligentsia and academics became the targets of anger and hate.

It was survival of the strongest. Tens of thousands more died in the violence. Who would have survived to record the ghastly events in the midst of such misery, destruction and devastation? Indeed, who would have had the inclination or the means to do so? For all intent and purposes man's collective memory was wiped out - deleted. It would take another 4000 years before we would be able to pick up the fragments and attempt to understand the extent of this most horrible catastrophe of all times.

Some ancient historians tried to chronicle their intense but localised experiences. In time, however, their tales became just that – tales, legends, fables, and myth. Only now at the start of the 21st century are we able to verify and understand what these ancient scribes tried to tell us. Through forensics, geology, oceanography, ice- and deep-sea core drilling, climatology, sedimentology, astronomy, human genetics, philology, anthropology, archaeology, history and many more fields of study, the door is slowly opening. By combining and cross-referencing all these diverse fields of study, we can finally begin to connect the dots. In the light of modern day scientific discoveries from all over the world, we shall have a fresh look here at how ancient scholars described the events that unfolded 4200 years ago.

The controversial British archaeologist to Turkey, James Mellaart (1925 -2012) proposed that drought and migrations could have been primary causes of the collapse. Many share his opinion. Whilst archaeological evidence points to widespread famine and a resultant mass migration after ca 2200 BC, however, climate change and the much-hypothesized resultant drought alone cannot explain the almost instantaneous destruction of these ancient cities. The ruination brought on by a drought-induced famine would have been substantially slower. In fact, the French archaeologist, Claude FA Schaeffer, suggested as early as 1948 that the initial collapse was brought on by earthquakes throughout the region; a very sudden end, therefore.

Let us begin by looking at the Oera Linda Book's account of the disaster and then compare this with what other sources tell us about the event.

The European Disaster

The Oera Linda Book is arguably the most realistic record we have today of a catastrophe that hit planet earth and, more specifically, Europe and Britain towards the end of the third millennium BC. From more than 4000 years ago the pain, anguish and despair of that unknown author lamenting the lot of Frya's People (Proto-Frisians), are quite evident. This is possibly as close as we shall ever get to an eyewitness report of this most devastating event to have assailed man:

How the Bad times came.

The whole summer the sun hid behind the clouds, as if it did not want to see the earth. The wind rested in its place causing smoke and mist to hang like sails above the houses and marshes. The air was dreary and dull, and in the hearts of people, there were neither joy nor happiness.

In the midst of this stillness, the earth began to tremble as if she was dying. The mountains split open to spew out fire and ash, others sank into her bowels, and where there were fields, mountains rose up. Aldland, called Atland by the sailors, sank down and the wild waves went so high over mountain and dale that everything was submerged. Many people were buried in the earth and many who had escaped the fire perished in the water. Not only in Finda's Land[16] did the mountains spew fire but also in Twiskland[17]. Forests were burned one after the other, and when the wind came from there our land was covered with ash. Rivers changed their course, and at their mouths, new islands were formed of sand and floating animals.

Three years earth suffered, but when it improved, the forests could be seen. Many countries were submerged, others had risen out of the sea and in Twiskland half of the forests were destroyed. Bands of Finda's people came and settled in the empty spaces. Our dispersed people were exterminated or became their slaves. Then watchfulness was doubly impressed upon us, and time taught us that unity is our best fortress.[18]

Mountains, bow your heads; clouds and streams, weep. Yes. Skenland[19] blush, Slavic nations trample on your cloak. O, Frya![20]

This account is not only of relevance to Europe, but also helps us to better understand what happened elsewhere. It is important that we take note of the description of the disaster; however improbable it may seem at this stage: the overcast sky (the sun did not shine), the smoke cover, the lack of wind, volcanic eruptions, widespread fires, earthquakes, floods and sea floods, rivers changed their courses, general despondency and multiple deaths. The catastrophe lasted for three years, followed by anarchy and an inability to defend themselves against marauding bands of displaced people from Eastern Europe. Finally, Frya's Land was invaded by migrants from central Asia and Mongolia:

---

[16] The East
[17] Tyskland, Deutchland, Germany
[18] OLB: The Book of Adela's Followers, Chapter 21
[19] Scandinavia
[20] OLB: The Book of Adela's Followers, Chapter 22

One hundred and one years after Aldland sank, a people came out of the East. That people was driven out by another nation. Beyond our Twiskland they fell into dispute, divided into two groups, and each went its own way.

Of the one group no account came to us, but the other group went to the back of our Skenland. Skenland was sparsely populated and the back the least of all. Therefore they were able to conquer it without contest, and as they did no other harm, we did not wish to make war.[21]

The migrants mentioned here in the Oera Linda Book was part of the post-2200 BC mass migration identified by archaeologists. This was not known in the 19th century.

Harvey Weiss, professor in Near Eastern Archaeology at Yale University in New Haven, Connecticut, has been involved for many years in archaeological work at Tell Leilan; a city of the Bronze Age Akkadian Empire on the Habur Plains of Northern Mesopotamia in modern day Syria. He writes:

Whether at Tell Leilan or Tell Taya, Chagar Bazar or Tell al-Hawa, the results told the same story: between 2200 and 1900 BC people fled the Habur and Assyrian plains en masse.

Elsewhere he compares his conclusions with other archaeological work:

In Egypt, the Old Kingdom, during which the great pyramids were built, gave way to the turmoil of the First Intermediate Period; in Palestine, Early Bronze Age towns were abandoned; in Mesopotamia Akkad collapsed and nomadic people made strange movements across and down the Euphrates and Tigris valleys.[22]

The late Finnish climatologist, Dr. Timo Niroma from Helsinki, Finland, mentioned on his website *The Third Millennium BC (3100-2100*

---

[21] OLB: The Book of Adela's Followers, Chapter 23
[22] *The Sciences*, May/June 1996, p.34

BC) that the population of Finland dropped to about 33 % from 2400 BC to 2000 BC.

The Akkadian Disaster

The city of Akkad (Biblical: Accad; Sumerian: Agade) was the capital of the Akkadian Empire. To date archaeologists have been unable to find the exact location of Akkad although it is believed to have been somewhere within in the city limits of modern-day Baghdad. One of the most prominent theories today is that barbarians from the North, known as Gutians, sacked the city and caused the demise of the empire when it was already on the decline as a result of years of weakening political leadership. The much hypothesized drought only occurred later and was the final straw in the collapse of the empire. The Akkadian empire is believed to have been at least as big as the later Sumerian empire.

Professor Weiss concluded that the city of Akkad was suddenly abandoned in 2193 BC – exactly the same year in which the Oera Linda Book claims that the old Fryan Civilization in Western Europe was destroyed.

The Sumerian King List[23], describing the Akkadian Empire after the death of king Shar-kali-shari (ca 2217 – 2193 BC), gives us some idea of the chaos that followed after 2193 BC:

> *Who was king? Who was not king? Irgigi the king; Nanum the king; Imi the king; Ilulu the king – the four of them were kings but reigned only three years. Dudu reigned 21 years; Shu-Turul, the son of Dudu, reigned 15 years. ... Agade was defeated and its kingship carried off to Uruk. In Uruk, Ur-ningin reigned 7 years; Ur-gigir, son of Ur-ningin reigned 6 years; Kuda reigned 6 years; Puzur-ili reigned 5 years; Ur-Utu reigned 6 years. Uruk was smitten with weapons and its kingship carried off by the Gutian hordes.*

---

[23] First studied and published in the earl 1900's.

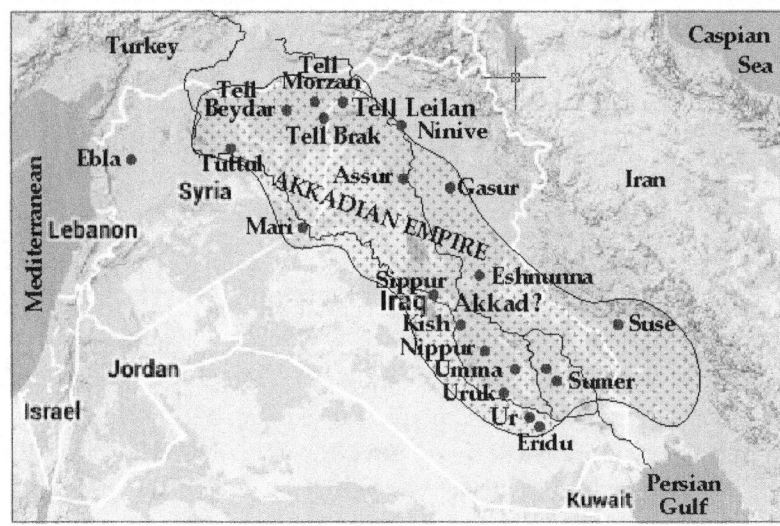

Figure 1: The Bronze Age Akkadian Empire

From the King List we can see that the Gutians only overran Southern Mesopotamia 69 years after 2193 BC. They were, therefore, not the cause of the initial collapse as many would have us believe. It is important that we bear this in mind because this is the same sequence of events that took place in Europe as explained by the Oera Linda Book: a disaster of epic proportions followed by chaos, looting and pillaging. In the aftermath we find the mass migration of displaced and starving survivors which, in turn, led to invasions and sacking of the once powerful, but now weakened, empires of antiquity. We find exactly the same consequences in Egypt after the collapse of the Old Kingdom. Remember that very little, if anything, was known about the Akkadian empire in the 19th century.

The *Curse of Akkad* (ca 2100 BC), was translated from cuneiform in the early 20th century. For many years Assyriologists considered *The Curse* to be purely fictional. Recent findings at Tell Leilan, however, led archaeologists to believe that the tablet was, in fact, based on real events and provides further insights into the aftermath of the disaster:

- *For the first time since cities were built and founded, the large fields produced no grain.*
- *The flooded fields produced no fish.*

- *The watered gardens produced no honey and wine,*
- *The heavy clouds did not rain.*

Note the *flooded fields* and *watered gardens* described above. Here we have clear evidence of a famine which was brought on by floods and not by drought. Could this point to massive sea-floods which could have stripped away the fertile topsoil? We can take this conjecture one step further: Perhaps the flood was caused by a huge tsunami from the Persian Gulf which left behind large shallow lakes of salt water. Such an inundation of seawater would have contaminated every fresh water source from rivers to wells, causing an immediate lack of drinking water, killed all crops and created an acute famine. This would explain the very sudden mass migration of the survivors as described by archaeologists. The large shallow lakes of stagnant water with decaying bodies and animal carcasses would have been the sources of diseases and pestilence.

Dr. Timo Niroma provided us with the answer on his website. He stated:

> *The Third Dynasty of Ur was the last attempt to revive Sumer, after a chaos of 100 years beginning with the destruction of Akkadian Sumer around 2200 BC. During the Akkadian period, wheat was the most important cereal and its share of the harvest was about 20%. During the years 2200-2100 BC the saltiness of the soil rose markedly, possibly because of sea floods and, after them, because of the following dryness that evaporated the water leaving the salt behind. In the northern Mesopotamia, the wheat share dropped to 2% and in the southern part to zero. This change seems to coincide with the period when there was no central authority.*

As in the case of Egypt, which will be shown later, we see a collapse of the central government while archaeological findings point to civil disorder and a flood of refugees. The Curse of Akkad mentions one more detail that is worth noting:

> *He who slept on the roof, died on the roof.*
> *He who slept in the house, had no burial.*

Could this be a reference to people who were killed and swept away by the flood? It would further appear that some tried to find refuge on the roofs of their houses. Dr. Niroma spread the disaster much wider than the Middle East:

> Mesopotamia and other above-mentioned places were not the only victims of the 2200 BC event. As far away as in China, the Hongsan culture fell in pieces at this same time. This, if not anything else, is an indication of the mighty character of the event, and bolsters us to consider it as global.[24]

In his paper, Desert Storm, Professor Weiss says the following (my emphasis):

> Only decades after the city's massive walls were raised, its religious quarter renovated and its grain production reorganized, Tell Leilan was **suddenly abandoned**. In our excavations, the collapsed remains of Akkadian buildings are covered with erosion deposits that show no trace of human activity.[25]

Were these erosion deposits caused by wind and/or water? Elsewhere Prof. Weiss concluded that it would appear that some building projects were even abandoned before completion. One can only assume that these projects were started in prosperous times but, they were never finished. It would appear that in the midst of this prosperity something happened which caused a sudden cessation of construction activities.

In collaboration with soil scientist and archaeologist Marie-Agnés Courty of the *National Centre for Scientific Research in Paris*, Harvey Weiss noted that the remains of the city was covered with a thin layer of volcanic ash followed by some 200 mm of fine sand. Dr. Courty found very little evidence of earthworm activity, which pointed to a prolonged period of aridity. It may well be that this absence of

---

[24] Timo Niroma, Helsinki, Finland: *The Third Millennium BC (3100-2100 BC)*
[25] *The Sciences*, May/June 1996, p. 33

earthworm activity, however, can rather be ascribed to the fertile topsoil having been washed away by disastrous floods.

We have thus far seen that the 2193 BC collapse was very sudden and most likely accompanied by earthquakes and volcanic activity. From Professor Weiss and Dr. Courty's observations it was shown that we should not rule out the possibility of devastating floods as well. In the aftermath of the disaster, we find the whole region in turmoil with survivors fleeing in all directions.

The Lament for Urim

Four thousand two hundred years ago Urim, or Ur as it is also known, was a coastal city on the Persian Gulf at the Euphrates River Delta. It was one of the largest cities in the old Akkadian Empire with population of some 65 000. Today the remains of Ur are 250 km from the Gulf and 10 km south of the Euphrates. Research seems to indicate that the city was devastated by drought and nomads between 2200 and 2000 BC when the population dropped by as much as 93%.

From thousands of cuneiform tablets discovered and translated by Assyriologists, we are able to gain valuable insights into the civilisations of ancient Mesopotamia. Amongst these records we find lamentations for five cities whose destruction was bewailed after having been devastated in ca 2200 BC. These are: the Laments for Ur, for Sumer and Ur, for Nippur, for Eridu and for Uruk. We shall only look at one of them: *The Lament for Urim* (Ur) and compare this to the Oera Linda Book's account.

The Oera Linda Book tells us that the 2193 BC disaster lasted for three years. This meant that people had to find food and shelter for the duration of three summers and three winters whilst their world was shaken by earthquakes, inundated by floods and scorched by fire; presumably from volcanic activity but, perhaps also from meteorite showers. From our own modern day experiences, we know that certain elements in society resort to pillaging and looting at the first inkling of chaos. Now imagine the havoc that would have been caused by desperate people over an extended period – especially if there is no security system in place to restrain them.

The Lament for Urim was most likely written as an ancient form of Greek tragedy or narrative poetry and not as a strict historical record as we know it today. The reader is asked to bear with the following somewhat lengthy extract from the lamentation. This is unfortunate but very necessary when one challenges entrenched ideas. The summary is placed under sub-headings to show the similarities with the Oera Linda Book:

1. Floods

- *...and my city was destroyed in its foundations; and Urim perished where it lay. Because the hand of the storm appeared above, I screamed and cried to it 'Return, O storm, to the plain'.*
- *My house founded by the righteous was pushed over on its side like a garden fence.*
- *Wind and rain have been made to fall on it, as onto a tent, as onto a shelter on the denuded harvest ground. Urim, my all-surpassing chamber, the house and the smitten city, all have been uprooted. Like a shepherd's sheepfold it has been uprooted. The swamp has swallowed my possessions accumulated in the city.*
- *The little ones lying in their mothers' arms were carried off like fish by the waters.*
- *O my brick-built Urim which has been flooded, which has been washed away, O my good house, my city which has been reduced to ruin mounds,*

2. Meteorite storm or shower

- *Enlil* (a chief deity) *brought Gibil* (god of fire) *as his aid. He called the great storm of heaven...*
- *The scorching potsherds made the dust glow.*
- *In all the storehouses abounding in the Land fires were kindled. In its ponds Gibil, the purifier, relentlessly did his work.*

- *On my ones coming from the south he (Enlil) hurled fire. Alas, my city has indeed been destroyed before me. On my ones coming from the highlands Enlil hurled flames.*

3. Denudation of lands by Fire and Floods

- *Wind and rain have been made to fall on it, as onto a tent, as onto a shelter on the denuded harvest ground.*
- *The great storm howls above. The storm that annihilates the Land roars below.*
- *It attacked the Land and devoured it completely.*
- *The storm ordered by Enlil in hate, the storm which wears away the Land, covered Urim like a garment*
- *In the fields of my city there is no grain, their farmer is gone. My fields, like fields from which the hoe has been kept away, have grown tangled weeds. My orchards and gardens that produced abundant syrup and wine have grown mountain thorn bushes. My plain that used to be covered in its luxurious verdure has become cracked like a kiln.*

4. River avulsion[26] (changing course)

- *In the river of my city dust has gathered, and the holes of foxes have been dug there. In its midst no flowing water is carried.*
- *My slave-girls and children have been carried off by boat* (but not where the river used to be).
- *The teme plants grow in the middle of your watercourses which were once suitable for barges, and mountain thorn bushes grow on your roads which had been constructed for wagons*

---

[26] In sedimentary geology, avulsion is the rapid abandonment of a river channel and the formation of a new channel. Avulsion typically occurs during large floods which carry the power necessary to rapidly change the landscape and are common in deltaic settings where the river enters the ocean and channel gradients are typically very small.

5. Government / central authority destroyed

- *The Land's judgment disappeared. The Land's counsel was swallowed by a swamp.*

6. Famine

- *The weak and the strong of Urim perished from hunger.*

7. Results of the Floods and *Firestorm*

- *Then the storm was removed from the city, that city reduced to ruin mounds.*
- *Its people littered its outskirts just as if they might have been broken potsherds. Breaches had been made in its walls. On its lofty city-gates where walks had been taken, corpses were piled. On its boulevards where festivals had been held, heads lay scattered (?). In all its streets where walks had been taken, corpses were piled. In its places where the dances of the Land had taken place, people were stacked in heaps. They made the blood of the Land flow down the wadis like copper or tin. Its corpses, like fat left in the sun, melted away of themselves.*

8. Looting and People attempting to fend off plunderers.

- *The heads of its men slain by the axe were not covered.*
- *Men struck down by the spear were not bound with bandages; its men who were finished off by the battle-mace were not bandaged. He who stood up to the weapon was crushed by the weapon. He who ran away from it was overwhelmed by the storm.*
- *All the treasures accumulated in the Land were defiled.*
- *The good house of the lofty untouchable mountain, E-kic-nu-jal, was entirely devoured by large axes. The people of Cimacki and Elam, the destroyers, counted its worth as*

- *only thirty shekels. They broke up the good house with pickaxes. They reduced the city to ruin mounds.* (pillaging and searching for treasure)
- *Enlil has indeed transformed my house* (Temple); *it has been smitten by pickaxes.*
- *He who came from the south has carried my possessions off to the south. He who came from the highlands has carried my possessions off to the highlands. My silver, gems and lapis lazuli have been scattered about. The swamp has swallowed my treasures. Men ignorant of silver have filled their hands with my silver. Men ignorant of gems have fastened my gems around their necks. My small birds and fowl have flown away. My slave-girls and children have been carried off by boat. Woe is me; my slave-girls bear strange emblems in a strange city. My young men mourn in a desert they do not know.* (Denuded landscape which was once fertile fields).

9. Cloud and smoke cover

- *In the Land he did not let the bright sun rise; it shone like the evening star.*

It is noticeable that the lamentation makes no mention of the Gutians. The only plunderers mentioned by name are the Chimacki and those from Elam. The Elamites were close neighbours and vassals of the Akkadians after they have been subjugated some time before. It would not be unreasonable to suspect that the Elamites resented the Akkadians and that they would have exploited any misfortune the Akkadians may have suffered.

The Egyptian Disaster

The First Intermediate period of ancient Egypt is typically the initial 100 years after the demise of the Old Kingdom. The Kingdom came to an end with the reign of Pepi II; the longest ruling pharaoh in Egyptian history and the last major ruler of the 6th dynasty.

It is noteworthy that both Assyriologists and Egyptologists give the same reasons for the demise of Akkad and Egypt at exactly the same time. In both cases we are told that the centralised monarchies grew weak. This would have caused some decadence to set in and led to increased rivalry and succession squabbles between provincial rulers and heirs. Of late, it has also been suggested that severe regional droughts contributed to the weakening of the long serving monarchs' power bases. In both cases we find that these long established and highly developed empires entered a period of anarchy & famine for no clear reason other than a possible drought.

From what we have thus far seen from *The Oera Linda Book*, *The Lament for Urim*, *The Curse of Akkad* and archaeological discoveries, the question must also be asked for Egyptian history: *Are we interpreting the evidence correctly?*

Let us now take a closer look at the works of some ancient Egyptian scribes, starting with *The Admonitions of Ipuwer*; a work which should rather be called *The Lament of Ipuwer*.

The Admonitions of Ipuwer.

There do not seem to be consensus as to when Ipuwer[27] lived. Some believe he lived during the First Intermediate period whilst others favour the Middle Kingdom or perhaps even as late as the Second Intermediate Period of Ancient Egypt. In his Admonitions, he laments the collapse of his country in ca 2200 BC. One modern researcher, whose work is widely quoted, however, concluded that:

> *The Admonitions of Ipuwer has not only no bearing whatever on the long past First Intermediate Period, it also does not derive from any other historical situation. It is the last, fullest, most exaggerated and hence least successful, composition on the theme 'order versus chaos'.*[28]

---

[27] Andre Dollinger: Ancient Egyptian didactic Literature: The admonitions of Ipuwer
[28] M. Lichtheim: 1973-80, *Ancient Egyptian Literature*, Vol. I, p.150, University of California Press.

This view is still shared by many Egyptologists today and sounds surprisingly similar to the judgments passed on *The Oera Linda Book* and the initial verdict on *The Curse of Akkad*. Perhaps it is a normal first reaction to reject anything that challenges our paradigms; also known as paradigm paralysis.

It would be reasonable to assume that ancient scribes were intelligent and educated people who wrote for a sophisticated audience. Given the high profile of their commissions and the social standing of these early scholars, it is unlikely that substandard work or fallacies would have been tolerated. Literacy in ancient Egypt was ostensibly not for the commoners or the masses and hence the written word was not used for mass communication and sensationalism, as we know it today. As we continue in our quest to connect the dots, we shall hopefully find out whether Ipuwer's writings had any foundation in facts or whether it was indeed exaggerated.

In the light of what we know today of the 4.2ka BP Event[29] we shall for the time being give Ipuwer the benefit of the doubt. Let us now look at his tale:

Closely examining his Admonitions, it would appear that Ipuwer was an eyewitness to a natural disaster that happened very suddenly and killed scores of people. He described the results of a series of events that his readers seemed to have been familiar with. Although he also referred to a famine, it is evident that, initially at least, this was not because of a drought – the Nile was overflowing!

As time went on foreign refugees from the East overran Egypt in search of food and water. The country, which was already reeling from the effects of the disaster, now descended into anarchy and civil disorder. When compared to other authors the most probable causes for his lamentations were the following:

---

[29] 4 200 years Before Present (1950) or 2200 BC - one of the *Bond Events* as postulated by professor Gerard C Bond of Columbia University.

1. Floods

- *Behold, Egypt is fallen to pouring of water, and he who poured water on the ground has carried off the strong man in misery.* (Note: Swept away by a flood.)
- *When men send a servant for humble folk, he goes on the road until he sees the flood; the road is washed out and he stands worried.*
- *Indeed many dead are buried in the river; the stream is a grave (tomb) and the place of embalmment has become a stream.* (Note: People drowned. They would not have buried people intentionally in their only source of drinking water.)
- *[…] his children who are witnesses of the surging of the flood*
- *Indeed, the desert is throughout the land, the nomes (districts) are laid waste.* (Note: Submersion and / or denudation from floods?)
- *... those who were on their husbands' beds, let them lie on rafts.* (Note: rafts – not boats. This would indicate unexpected floods)
- *Behold, noble ladies are now on rafts...*

2. Contaminated water

- *Indeed the Nile overflows, yet non plough for it.* (Note: Not a drought)
- *Indeed the river is blood yet men drink of it.* (Note: Muddy, salty and decaying bodies of people and animal carcasses?)
- *Men shrink from human beings and thirst after water.* (Note: Bodies decaying in water sources)

3. Earthquakes

- *Indeed, the land turns around as does a potter's wheel, towns are destroyed and Upper Egypt has become an empty waste.*

- (Note: also refers to floods and the resultant denudation of arable lands)
- *Indeed, those who were in the place of embalmment are laid out on the high ground, and the secrets of the embalmers are thrown down because of it.* (Note: Tombs destroyed by earthquakes. It seems unlikely that tomb robbers, as some would have it, would have removed dead bodies from their graves just to dump them outside.)
- *Behold, the secret of the land whose limits were unknown is divulged, and the Residence is thrown down in a moment.* (Earthquakes)

4. Fire

- *Indeed, doors, columns and walls are burnt up.*
- *Behold, the fire has gone up on high, and its burning go forth against the enemies of the land.* (Note: Asteroids streaking across the sky)

5. Multiple Deaths

- *…and there is no man of yesterday.*
- *Indeed, men are few, and he who places his brother in the ground is everywhere.* (Note: The greater proportion of the population killed and people being buried in the ground – not in the river)

6. Disease and Pestilence

- *Indeed, hearts are violent, pestilence is throughout the land, blood is everywhere, death is not lacking, and the mummy cloth speaks even before one come near it.*

Throughout Ipuwer's lamentations, he recorded how hordes of refugees streamed into Egypt and ravaged and pillaged the country. He described scenes of social disorder and anarchy where the rulers and upper classes were deposed of by the working classes and wandering bandits. Special mention is made of the killing of scribes and the destruction of their work. Some modern researchers estimate that Egypt lost as much as 30% of her population. It is suggested here that the figure may have been much higher.

The similarities between Ipuwer's work and those of others such as the Oera Linda Book and the Lament for Urim, can only lead to one conclusion: Ipuwer not only described a real event in Egyptian history, but he was most likely an eyewitness to the cataclysm.

The Prophecy of Neferti

The *Prophecy of Neferti*[30] was written after the demise of the Old Kingdom of Egypt and is therefore not a prophecy but rather a description of actual events. As with *The Lament for Urim* it is suspected that this *prophecy* may have been written as a theatrical work which was performed on stage or in the theatre. The lead actor would have taken the role of a prophet pronouncing judgement over Egypt as a lesson to future generations. The account is one of dejection albeit not as graphic as that of Ipuwer. There are a few facts, however, that stand out:

1. The country was not defeated in war as there was, initially at least, still some semblance of a national administration in place. A military conflict would not have been so curtly described or so readily accepted without tales of battles, heroism, etc:

- *See, there are great men in the governance of the land, yet what has been done is as though it had never been done.*

2. Descriptions of devastation and lack of manpower and other resources to rebuild the country:

---

[30] M. Lichtheim, *Ancient Egyptian Literature*, Vol.1 pp.139ff

- *Re must begin by refounding* (rebuilding) *the land which is utterly ruined, and nothing remains.*
- *This land is destroyed and there are none who care for it; there are none who speak and there are none who act.*

3. Neferti describes the lack of sunlight, which could have been caused by dust storms as postulated by some. He, however, also describes an absence of wind, which would rather imply a cloud, or smoke cover as recorded by other authors of the time.

- *the sun is veiled, and will not shine when the people would see; none will live when the sun is veiled by a cloud, and everyone are dulled by the lack of it.*
  The Oera Linda Book said: *the sun hid behind the clouds* and *The Lament for Urim* said that *the sun shone like the evening star.*
- *...the south wind will oppose the north wind, and the sky will not be with one single wind.*
  The "Oera Linda Book" said "The wind rested in its place".
- *Re separates himself from men; he shines, that the hour may be told, but no one knows when noon occurs, for no one can discern his shadow, no one is dazzled when he is seen; there are non whose eyes stream with water, for he is like the moon in the sky, though his accustomed time do not go astray, and his rays are in men's sight as on former occasions.*

4. Neferti described the Nile without water, which sounds like a severe drought:

- *The river of Egypt is dry and men cross the water on foot;*
- He continued, however:
  ...men will seek water for ships in order to navigate it, for their course has become the riverbank, and the bank serves for water; the place of water has become a riverbank...

Here we see the exact same avulsion of the Nile as we find for the Euphrates in The Lament for Urim. The Oera Linda Book stated it thus: Rivers changed their course and at their mouths new islands were formed of sand and floating animals.

The Biblical Deluge

The Bible does not give us a lot of detail except to say that the water came from both the sky and the ground. Again, we get the hint of a possible tsunami, but otherwise there are no similarities with the Oera Linda Book's description.

Genesis 7: 11,12

(11) *In the six hundredth year of Noah's life, in the second month, the seventeenth day of the month, on that day all the fountains of the great deep were broken up, and the windows of heaven were opened. (12) And the rain was on the earth forty days and forty nights.*[31]

In the Hebrew calendar, the 17th day of the 2nd month is *17 Cheshvan*. If we now apply a calendar converter and combine the year 2193 BC on the Gregorian calendar and 17 Cheshvan on the Hebrew calendar, the Biblical Deluge, the destruction of the Fryan Atland and the world at large would have commenced on **Wednesday, 21 October 2193 BC**[32].

Some ancient Jewish scriptures give the date of the Deluge, or Noah's Flood, as 2105 BC. This is some 88 years later than the date of 2193 BC but is still within an acceptable margin of error over a period of 4200 years, especially given the extent of the damage, death and trauma described earlier.

All over the world, we find legends of floods and other disasters that have elements of the event described above, such as the Epics of Gilgamesh and folklore from South America. It is quite likely that they all refer to the same event.

---

[31] The New King James Version. 1996, c. 1982. Thomas Nelson: Nashville
[32] Some calendar converters give this date as Monday, 10 October 2193 BC

At a first glance, it would appear that mention of the many survivors from all over the world contradicts the Bible. In the book of Genesis, it seems to state categorically that all life apart from the eight persons and the animals on Noah's ark were wiped off the face of the earth. This, however, is not the case. The problem does not lie with the Bible or with the ancient scribes, but rather with the interpreters and translators of the Bible. The hereto-accepted translation of Genesis 7:23 read:

(23) So He (God) destroyed all living things which were on the face of the ground: both man and cattle, creeping things and birds of the air. They were destroyed from the earth. Only Noah and those who were with him in the ark remained alive.

The words, *the earth*, which signifies the whole planet, was translated from the Hebrew word *erets* (eh·rets).[33] The word *erets* appears 2504 times in the Bible. In 1543 cases, the word was translated to signify *land*, 712 times as *earth*, 140 times as *country* and 98 times as *ground*. Other lesser meanings included *world*, *way*, *common*, *field*, *nations* and *wilderness*. An example of a different meaning given to *erets* was when God called Abram in Genesis 12:1:

Now the Lord had said to Abram:
Get out of your country (erets), *from your family and from your father's house, to a land* (erets) *that I will show you.*

Obviously, God did not tell Abram to leave this planet for another planet.

In light of the overwhelming evidence of the numerous survivors from sources outside the Bible, it is thus reasonable to assume that the Bible does not say that all life was wiped out on planet earth (*erets*). I would suggest that the Bible rather meant all those living creatures in a specific land (*erets*), country (*erets*), or perhaps the known world (*erets*) of the author of Genesis. Although the disaster was

---

[33] The New Strong's Dictionary of Hebrew and Greek Words.

worldwide, not everybody and everything were destroyed. The Bible is right, but not our interpretation.

Scientific evidence of a global disaster

Thus far we have had a look at what ancient scribes had to say about the 2200 BC event. We have also taken note of archaeological evidence that point to a sudden and widespread collapse of many towns, cities and civilizations from China (Hongsan Culture) to Europe, the Middle East (Akkadian Empire) and Egypt (Old Kingdom) – all around circa 2200 BC. In India the Harappan Urban Society collapsed at the same time.

The dominant theory today is that the demise of these ancient cultures was the result of a hereto-unexplained change in global climate. We have seen, however, that none of the old scribes attributed their misery to drought. On the contrary, the one common denominator to all these old legends is floods. It would be reasonable, therefore, to speculate that the proposed climate change, droughts and famines were not primary causes of the catastrophe, but rather that these were outcomes of the initial event.

Following are only a few randomly selected scientific articles of global floods that happened about 4200 years ago. Please note that there are much more evidence of this event and of many other paleo-tsunamis. The aim of this investigation, however, is merely to illustrate that there is sufficient evidence to support the Oera Linda Book's claim of a catastrophe in 2193 BC. None of this evidence was available in the 19th century.

China

The extract of a paper written by Chun Chang Huang and others from the Department of Geography, Shaanxi Normal University, Xi'an, Shaanxi in the People's Republic of China in 2010, *Extraordinary floods related to the climatic event at 4200 a*[34] *BP on the*

---

[34] annum

Qishuihe River, middle reaches of the Yellow River, China, gives evidence of these floods:

> *A paleo-hydrological study was carried out in the Qishuihe River valley in the middle reaches of the Yellow River.*
>
> *The results show that successive floods occurred between 4300 and 4000 a BP in association with the abrupt climatic event of 4200 a BP. These overbank floods had the riverbank settlement inundated repeatedly.*
>
> *The climatic event of 4200 a BP and the climatic decline at 3100 a BP were believed to be characterized by droughts previously. This work provides solid evidence that both severe droughts and extreme floods were parts of the climatic variability during abrupt climatic event and climatic decline in the semi-arid to sub-humid zones over the world.*

North Africa

Arguably the most compelling evidence for the 4200 years Before Present (BP) Event can be found in North Africa and the Sahara Desert. Archaeologists and Paleoclimatologists have established that, more than 4500 years ago, North Africa consisted of grassland, thorn bush savannas and the largest fresh water lakes on earth. Lake Meggafezzan and Lake Megachad, in fact, were comparable in size to Great Britain and the Black Sea respectively. The region teemed with wild life.

The *Potsdam-Institut fuer Klimafolgenforschung* (Potsdam Institute for Climate Impact Research) in Germany, headed by Prof. Dr. Martin Claussen, analyzed climate feedbacks from the last several thousand years as reported in ScienceDaily.[35]

- *Before that time, the Sahara was covered by annual grasses and low shrubs, as evidenced by fossilized pollen.*

---

[35] *Sahara's Abrupt Desertification Started By Changes in Earth's Orbit, Accelerated By Atmospheric and Vegetation Feedbacks.* ScienceDaily, Washington, July 12, 1999.

- *The transition to today's arid climate was not gradual, but occurred in two specific episodes. The first, which was less severe, occurred between 6,700 and 5,500 years ago. The second, which was brutal, lasted from 4,000 to 3,600 years ago. Summer temperatures increased sharply, and precipitation decreased, according to carbon-14 dating. This event devastated ancient civilizations and their socio-economic systems.*

- ***The change from the mid-Holocene climate to that of today was initiated by changes in the Earth's orbit and the tilt of Earth's axis.*** (my emphasis)

Scientists are uncertain whether these changes in the Earth's orbit and the tilt of Earth's axis happened gradually (over millennia), or suddenly (over a few centuries). Perhaps we should ask the unthinkable: Could these changes not have happened instantaneously, such as over a period of, say, 0 to 3 years?

In pre-historic times, Lake Yoa in North Eastern Chad was part of the greater Lake Megachad and then, about 4000 years ago, its waters suddenly turned salty[36]. This happened around the same time when the salt content of the ground increased at Tell Leilan in Syria, more than 2500 kilometres away. Scientists speculate that the cessation of fresh water recharge to the lake from rain or rivers and subsequent evaporation would have dramatically increased the salt content over the ensuing millennia. Archaeologists, however, noted that the salinity suddenly increased 4000 years ago. This was not a gradual process. Many of the lakes in North Africa today are salt-water lakes. This sudden increase in salinity could only have taken place by a massive inundation of sea water.

---

[36] Scientific American, May 9, 2008: *From Bountiful to Barren: Rainfall Decrease Left the Sahara Out to Dry - How a once-wet landscape became one of the world's great deserts.* By Adam Hadhazy

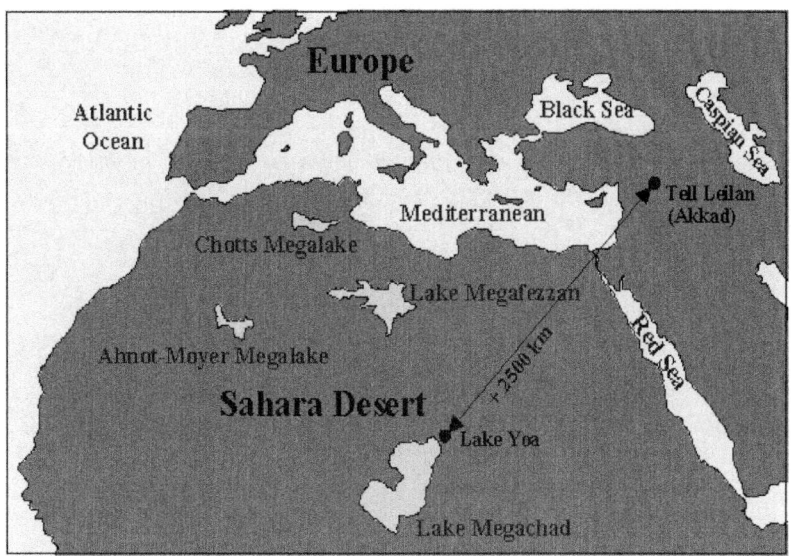

Figure 2: The Great Lakes of North Africa.
(During the Mid- Holocene)

As an aside, we can safely infer from the above findings that the great pyramids of Egypt were not built in the desert, but in a land of plenty.

The Caribbean

Dr. Sander R. Scheffers of the School for Environmental Management and Science at Southern Cross University, NSW, Australia, and others, in an article, *Tsunamis, hurricanes, the demise of coral reefs and shifts in pre-historic human populations in the Caribbean*[37], noted:

> *Three extreme impacts with different magnitudes can be clearly distinguished. The youngest event occurred at approximately 500 BP, a second event at 3,100 BP, and the oldest at 4,200 BP (Scheffers, 2002; Scheffers et al. 2006).*

---

[37] *Quaternary International*, Volume 195, 15 February 2009, Pages 69-87.

The Netherlands

Otto S. Knottnerus from Zuidbroek in the Netherlands wrote an article, *Sea Level Rise as a Threat to Cultural Heritage*, in the Wadden Sea Newsletter[38] 2000 (No. 2). Of note was the following statement in the article:

Near Delfzijl (Netherlands), Neolithic settlers built a megalithic-chambered tomb about 3350 BC. After 2200 BC, the site disappeared under several feet of clay and peat

In the Oera Linda book's account of the 2193 BC disaster that struck the west coast of Europe, we read:

Rivers changed their course, and at their mouths, new islands were formed of sand and floating animals.[39]

Spain

Francisco Ruiz   from the Department of Geodynamics and Palaeontology, University of Huelva, Avda, Spain, and others, noted in the research article, *Evidence of high-energy events in the geological record: Mid-Holocene evolution of the south-western Doñana National Park (SW Spain)*[40] :

This was followed by a renewed phase of instability (4200–4100 cal. years BP) indicated by the presence of fine storm-lain deposits and thicker, probably tsunami-induced shelly deposits.

---

[38] *The Wadden Sea Newsletter* is a periodical of the Trilateral Wadden Sea Governmental Council's Secretariat to inform scientific-, nature management- and policy-making institutions in Denmark, the Federal Republic of Germany and The Netherlands about research in the Wadden Sea area.

[39] OLB: The book of Adela's followers, Chapter 21

[40] *Palaeogeography, Palaeoclimatology, Palaeoecology*, Volume 229, Issue 3, 20 December 2005, Pages 212-229

Sri Lanka

Ranasinghage, P. N et al in *Signatures of Paleo-coastal Hazards in Back-barrier Environments of Eastern and South-eastern Sri Lanka*[41] :

> *The most recent pre-2004 tsunami event likely occurred around 1000 yrs BP with the older events around 4200 yrs BP and 4900 yrs BP.*
> *The ~ 4200 and ~ 4900 yrs BP events were recorded in multiple cores from Kirind and Vakarai as well as in cores from Hambantota by Jackson (2008).*

South Africa

Since the 2004 Sumatra-Andaman earthquake off the west coast of Indonesia, and the ensuing tsunami that killed some 230,000 people in fourteen countries, new interest was aroused in the study of ancient tsunamis. The importance of tsunamis was given further impetus by the March 2011 tsunami that struck the east coast of Japan killing some 23,000 people. I did not view any research that focused specifically on paleo-tsunamis in South Africa. There would appear, however, to be ample evidence of these tsunamis along the South African coast, notably at archaeological sites.

Over many years archaeologists have been investigating pre-historic cave habitats along the southern sea board of the Western Cape Province. Some of the more prominent sites are *Klasies River*, *Pinnacle Point*, *Blombos* and *Die Kelders*. The focus of archaeologists was primarily on the examining and dating of Middle Stone Age[42] tools and artefacts.

In 1991 Professor Christopher Henshilwood from the University of Bergen in Norway discovered the Blombos Cave which

---

[41] The Smithsonian/NASA Astrophysics Data System: American Geophysical Union, Fall Meeting 2010, abstract #NH21A-1397
[42] More than 32 000 years ago.

lies some 100 m from the coast and 35 m above sea level. Under his direction, the cave has been excavated many times.

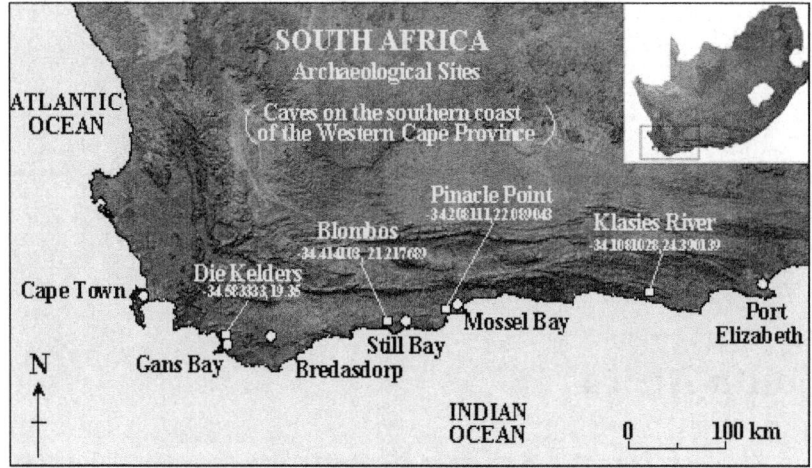

Figure 3: Some archaeological sites.
(South Africa's South Coast.)

The Blombos Project Team recorded the following:

When excavations at BBC commenced in 1991 the cave entrance was almost totally sealed by dune sand, also c. 20 cm of undisturbed aeolian sand overlay the surface of the Later Stone Age indicating no disturbance of the cave's contents since the final LSA occupation c. 290 years ago.

The LSA deposits are less than 2 000 years old, not as deep as the Middle Stone Age, and are more massively bedded and undistorted.

Sterile yellow dune sand 10 – 60 cm thick named BBC Hiatus blew into the unoccupied cave during lowered sea levels about 70 000 years ago. Shortly afterwards the cave entrance was blocked by a > 40 m dune. It is likely that the cave only re-opened after the mid-Holocene (c. 5000 - 3000 years ago) when high sea levels eroded the base of this dune 30 m below the cave causing the dune at the entrance to subside. BBC Hiatus separates the LSA and MSA across > 95% of the excavated area and provides visible evidence that the LSA occupation did not disturb the underlying MSA deposits.

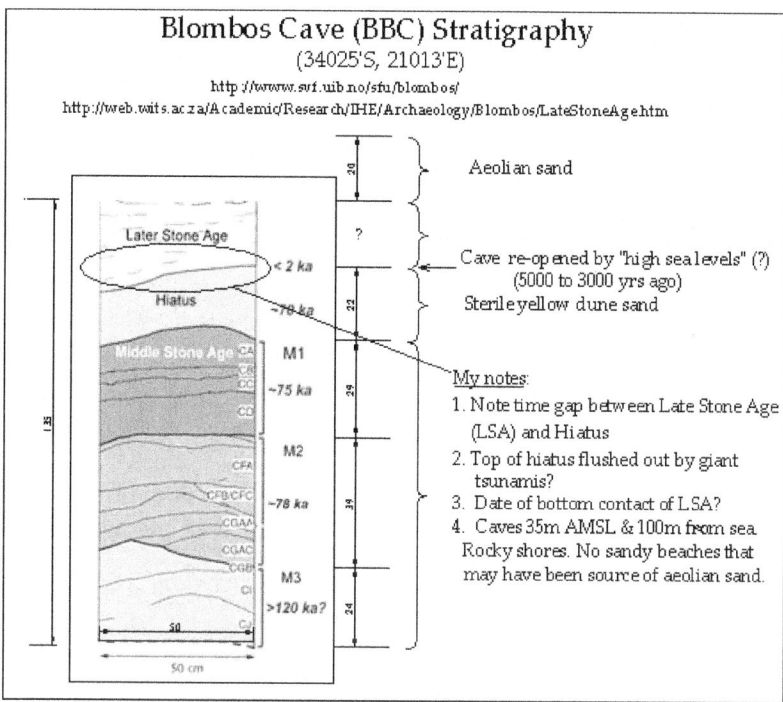

Figure 4: Blombos Cave Stratigraphy
(With acknowledgement to The Blombos Cave Project)

Current Sea levels are at their highest in the last 120 000 years. Some 10 000 years ago sea levels were approximately 10 meters below the present and, since about 8000 years ago, mean sea levels remained fairly static. The fact that the caves re-opened between 5000 to 3000 years ago can thus not be ascribed to rising sea levels. Between the Middle and Late Stone Ages we find a gap of some 70 000 years in the cave; filled in only with an (undated) hiatus of sterile dune sand.

The evidence rather suggests that the cave was flushed out by a massive tsunami some 5000 to 3000 years ago and not by rising sea levels – a possibility which archaeologists also acknowledge at the Klasies River Caves. Again, we see a hint of the 4200 year BP event.

The Klasies River Caves are situated approximately 300 kilometres east of the Blombos caves. Dr. D.M. Avery of the South African Museum noted:

> *Late Pleistocene occupation appears to have terminated some time around 70,000 BP (Deacon & Geleijnse, 1988; Thackeray, 1992) after a period, towards the top of the sequence in shelter 1A, when non-occupation horizons become more prominent.*
>
> *The Upper member is itself capped by an undated "scree" apparently devoid of archaeological remains (Deacon & Geleijnse, 1988). At some subsequent stage slumping removed a major proportion of the deposits (Deacon & Gileijnse, 1988) but this seems to have been a proportion of the entire sequence rather than differential removal from the top. Later Stone Age deposits, dated between about 4800 and 2500 BP, topped the sequence in cave 1 (Singer & Wymer, 1982).*[43]

The caves at Klasies River lie at 18, 6 and 0 meters above sea level, whereas Blombos is 35 meters above sea level. Yet, the formation and dating of the stratigraphy within these caves are remarkably similar.

> *Around 75,000 years ago during cave remodeling the stratigraphic sediments were moved out into external middens. Other scenarios for the discontinuous stratigraphy suggest natural factors like **megatsunami** washout or inconsistent dating.* (my emphasis)

The following photographs of possible paleo-tsunami depositions were taken in the Overberg district in the Southern Cape Province. They have not been dated or evaluated by any scientific methods or persons and are merely included here as examples of possible tsunami footprints.

The first photograph was taken some 50 metres from the coast and some 20 metres above sea level. The sequence is protected by the overlying calcrete which formed an impermeable layer when the fossil dunes became cemented by the interaction of rainwater with the acidic soils.

---

[43] *Journal of Archaeological Science* (1995) 22, 343–353, *Physical Environment and Site Choice in South Africa* by Dr D Margaret Avery, Honorary Associate at Iziko South African Museum, Vice President, International Union for Quaternary Research (INQUA), with the portfolios: *Africa, and Commission for Palaeoecology & Human Evolution*

Immediately below the breccia we find the suggested tsunami layer which in turn was deposited on previous sand dunes. The finess of the underlying dunes would suggest that they were of aelion origin.

Both Figures 5 and 6 following display layers of unstratifed, angular fragments of various sizes and composition as one would expect from tsunami-like deposits. Note that the clayish-type material in Figure 6 overlying the stone layer is very similar to the material underlying the tsunami layer. This would suggest that the mode of deposition of these layers is the same and was interrupted only by the event that created the layer of rocks.

Figure 5: Apparent Tsunami evidence.

(Photo taken of a road cutting near Cape Agulhas, the most Southern point of Africa.)

Figure 6: Apparent Tsunami evidence.
Photo taken in a road cutting some 35 kilometres from the ocean and some 120 metre above mean sea level near the town of Napier. Note the matchbox for scale (±2,5cm).

In researching archaeological and geological literature regarding coastal formations around the South African coast, it would appear that many of these boulder and stone layers are ascribed to rising and falling sea levels; very often in excess of 100 metres over the last 18 000 years. This seems very unlikely, as rising and falling sea levels, if this occurred, would have been a relatively slow and ongoing process. The resulting layering would have been more stratified, continuous and would have consisted of more rounded pebbles or rocks. One would also not expect such distinct boundaries between vastly different depositions such as clay and stone, or aelion sands and stone.

From all the aforementioned historical, archaeological and geological evidence, it should be clear that the 2200 BC event was global, catastrophic and violent. Much of the liberated material and other evidence of the time would have been churned up and mixed with older material, making identification and dating more difficult. Land and glacier evidence would largely have been washed off by the multitude of tsunamis and floods that were, in all probability, part of the larger event. Distinct markers such as volcanic telltales in ice cores or in sedimentary records may thus be fairly obscure. In more sheltered locations, this mixing of layers of different ages would have been less severe, but then, so would have been the effects of the disaster.

There should be little doubt that the cataclysm was global and it is suggested that researchers should eventually be able to identify this as a marker or datum line all around the world.

A New Epoch

The causes of the 4.2ka BP event have been debated in scientific circles for some time. The theories vary from climate change as a result of the slowdown, or even shutdown, of the oceans' thermohaline circulation, to solar activity; from changes in earths orbit and axial tilt to bolide impacts and everything in between. Perhaps they all contributed. Even the cyclical nature of Bond Events could be ascribed to the periodic and predictable appearances of comets in their cosmic orbits.

An important piece of evidence as to a possible cause, the severity and outcome of the event is locked up in the Oera Linda Book. In the description of Frya's Land before the 2193 BC disaster, we note:

> Before the bad time came our land was the most beautiful in the World. The sun rose higher and there was seldom frost. The trees and shrubs produced various fruits, which are now lost. In the fields we had not only barley, oats, and rye, but also wheat which shone like gold, and which could be baked in the sun's rays. The years were not counted, for one was as happy as another[44]. (My underlining).

The observation that the sun rose higher is a clear indication that earth's orientation relative to the sun had changed after the catastrophe. This statement cannot be interpreted any other way. It is also obvious that this happened very suddenly and not over millennia

---

[44] OLB: The book of Adela's followers, Chapter 20

or even centuries as some are suggesting. The description is supported by the observation made by scientists from the *Potsdam Institute for Climate Impact Research* in Germany:

> *The change from the mid-Holocene climate to that of today was initiated by changes in the Earth's orbit and the tilt of Earth's axis.*

This information was not available in the 19th century and is compelling evidence that the Oera Linda Book is authentic. The statement that their land was warmer before the disaster is also borne out by what climatologists are now concluding for mid-Holocene Europe. Neither the original authors nor any so-called forger in the 19th century could have realised the enormity of these seemingly unimportant observations. Again, this is undeniable evidence that the Oera Linda Book is authentic and based on factual information. Even the best deceiver in the 19th century could not have foreseen the late 20th century AD discovery of a change in Earth's orbit and a pronounced climate change some 4200 years ago. Earth may have vibrated or shook for a while after the event whilst settling in her new orbit. The Oera Linda Book states that the *Bad Times* lasted three years.

In addition to the references to the sun's orientation and the change in Europe's climate, the book left us a third clue in the description of their boundaries:

> *On one side we were bounded by Wralda's Sea, on which no nation but us might or could sail; on the other side we were hedged in by the broad Twiskland, through which the Finda's people dared not come on account of the thick forests and the wild beasts.*
>
> *At the morning boundary, we went over the extremity of the Aster[45] Sea, at the evening to the Middle Sea[46].*

---

[45] Baltic Sea, also known as the East Sea in German
[46] Mediterranean.

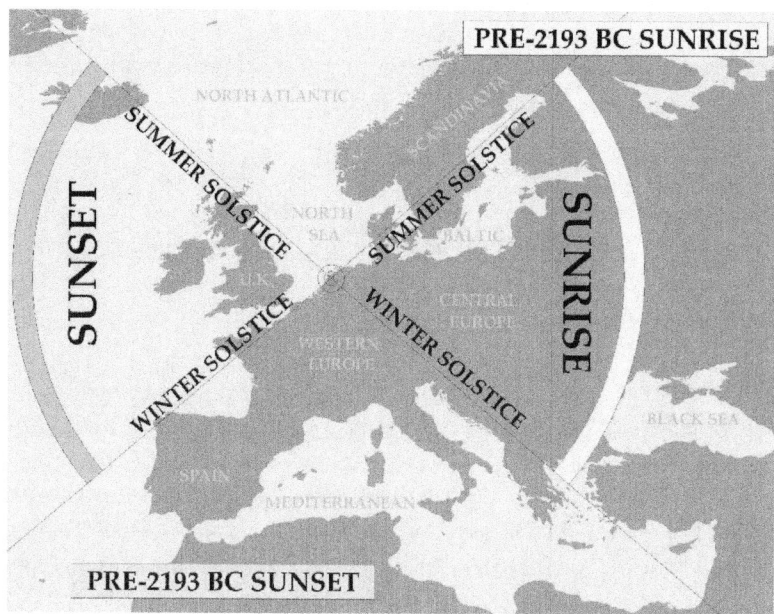

Figure 7: Sunset and Sunrise in Amsterdam.
Present day positions of Sunset and Sunrise in the Netherlands
compared to the Oera Linda Book's description.

The previous figure shows the approximate pre-2193 BC positions of sunrise and sunset in Europe as described in the Oera Linda Book. This is compared to the present positions between the summer and winter solstices as observed from Amsterdam in the Netherlands.

The morning boundary, or sunrise, was over the Baltic Sea (north-northeast) and the evening boundary, or sunset, over the Mediterranean (south to south-southwest). The closest that sunrise comes to this description today is at the summer solstice when the sun rises in a north-easterly direction. The nearest sunset is in a south-westerly direction at the winter solstice.

Another ancient document which describes changes in the earth's orientation is the Book of Enoch[47]; an ancient Jewish work

---

[47] [47] A work ascribed to Enoch, the great-grandfather of Noah and son of Jared (Genesis 5:18). Translated from the Ge'ez language (Ethiopic) by Richard Laurence, London, 1883.

which is thought to have been written before 300 BC. The book is considered non-canonical and pseudepigraphical (falsely attributed) in all Christian churches except the Ethiopian Coptic Church:

Chapter 55
*(4) And when that agitation took place; the saints out of heaven perceived it; **the pillar of the earth shook from its foundation**; and the sound was heard from the extremities of the earth unto the extremities of heaven at the same time.*

Chapter 64
*In those days Noah saw that **the earth became inclined**, and that destruction approached. (2) Then he lifted up his feet, and went to the ends of the earth, to the dwelling of his great-grandfather Enoch. (3) And Noah cried with a bitter voice, "Hear me; hear me; hear me": three times. And he said, "Tell me what is transacting upon the earth; for **the earth labours, and is violently shaken.** Surely I shall perish with it". (4) After this there was a great perturbation on earth, and a voice was heard from heaven. I fell down on my face, when my great-grandfather Enoch came and stood by me.*

It would appear logical to assume that the statements: *the pillar* (axis?) *of the earth shook from its foundation* and, *Noah saw that the earth became inclined,* confirm the Oera Linda Book's *the sun rose higher*. Again, we see that Earth's orientation changed suddenly and dramatically.

We may speculate as to what may have caused a change in earth's orbit and axial tilt, but it should be clear to the reader that, whatever the cause, this would have given rise to massive climate changes all over the world as reported by various scientific disciplines. If we accept this model, it would explain why Europe suddenly became colder and why North Africa turned to desert after ca 2200 BC. It would also clarify the sequence of events as described by ancient scribes, namely:

The sudden collapse of cities and civilizations,
Dramatic Climate Change,

Drought & Famine,
Chaos and disorder,
Mass Migrations and, finally
Invasions and conquests.

The following sketch serves to show the possible effects of a simultaneous change in Earth's orbit and axial tilt as described by the Oera Linda Book, The Book of Enoch and the findings of paleo-climatologists.

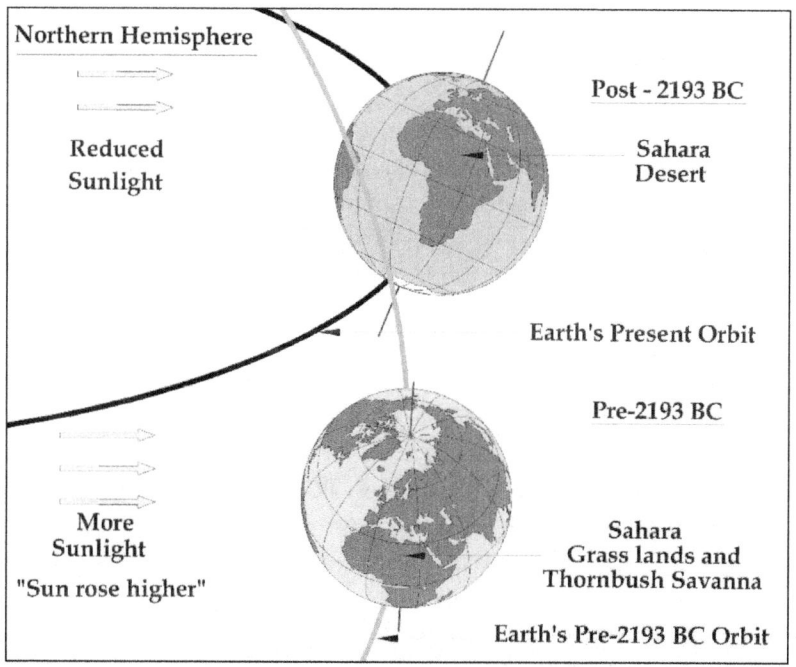

Figure 8: Earth's orbital change.
A speculative sketch showing a possible change in Earths pre-2200 BC orientation relative to the sun. After the event, Europe and the Northern Hemisphere received less sunlight and hence became colder.

A Cosmic Impact?

Many scientists, such as Dr. Dallas Abbott of the Lamont-Doherty Earth Observatory of Columbia University and Dr. Sharad Master of the University of the Witwatersrand in South Africa, have tried to link the 4.2 ka BP Event to specific bolide impact sites. Whilst the event was most likely triggered by an asteroid impact or perhaps a number of impacts, their views cannot be regarded as much more than speculation at this stage. Identification of possible impact sites from satellite images is simply not enough. These sites need to be examined up close and dated by scientific means before they can be labelled as the *smoking gun*.

We have gathered from the work of Professor Weiss and Doctor Courty that the topsoil of Akkad was virtually barren and Dr. Niroma described the high salt content of the ground. The ancient scribes from Egypt, Akkad, Western Europe, the Bible and other sources all refer to, inter alia, a flood. We have seen that the desertification of North Africa started some 4200 years ago and the water of Lake Yoa turned salty around the same time. Fossil evidence indicates that the Moeris (Birket Qarun) saltwater lake in Egypt used to be a fresh water lake in ancient times. The combined evidence suggests tsunamis and sea floods on a global scale which severely affected many, if not all, coastal and relatively low-lying areas. In addition, ancient scribes mentioned falling stars, earthquakes and volcanoes. German scientists found that the change from the mid-Holocene climate to that of today was initiated by changes in the Earth's orbit and the tilt of Earth's axis.

Whilst Dr. Abbott and her colleague, Dr. W. Bruce Masse of the Near Earth Object study group have not yet been able to date their *Flood Comet*, the Burckle Impact, it may nevertheless be worth our while to have a look at it. It may just give a logical explanation as to what may have happened.

Dr Abbott investigated chevron dunes on the island of Madagascar in 2005[48]. She found that the chevrons consist of deep

---

[48] The Geological Society of America: 2006 Philadelphia Annual Meeting (22–25 October 2006)

ocean sediments and cosmic impact debris. She postulated that the 200-metre-high dunes might have been caused by an asteroid or comet which struck earth some 4500 years ago. The same phenomenon was observed on the west coast of Australia. By projecting the direction and distance of the possible source of the dunes and with the assistance of satellite imagery, Dr. Abbott located the 30 kilometre diameter Burckle impact crater at a depth of more than 3800 metres on the bottom of the Indian Ocean; some 1500 km south-east of Madagascar. The event has already been dubbed the *Flood Comet*. Dr. Masse tentatively placed a date of ca 4900 years Before Present on the event.

Figure 9: Fenambosy Chevron, Madagascar.
The chevron, one of four, is 200 metres high and five kilometres from the ocean. (Photo: With acknowledgement to The New York Times: November 14, 2006)

Judging from the Madagascar dunes, the Burckle Impact must have been massive. There is no doubt that an event which may have caused ocean sediments to be deposited 200 metres high would have caused mega tsunamis hundreds of metres high.

The force of the impact would have been the equivalent of several million nuclear bombs exploding in quick succession. Such tsunamis, caused by the massive shockwaves from the impact in the Indian Ocean, would have raced up the red sea to the Gulf of Suez and up the Gulf of Aqaba via the Wadi al-Jayb rift valley to the Dead Sea in Palestine. The mega-wave would have spilled from the Gulf of Suez, through the Bitter lakes and right into the Mediterranean. At the same time, the tsunami would also have advanced up the Indus Valley and via the Persian Gulf into Mesopotamia, causing the disaster as described.

It must also be pointed out that the chevron dunes on Madagascar are still 200 metres high after more than 4000 years of erosion. Initially they could have been much higher. It must be borne in mind that the dunes would have been deposited by the initial impact. Subsequent waves from the disturbance would have reduced the height of the dunes immediately after. The sediments in these dunes, however, did not come from the impact site, but rather from much closer to Madagascar. As the seismic impulse caused by the impact approached shallower waters near land, the wave slowed down but the wave height increased and thereby it's destructive power. These waves would then have liberated sediments from the shallower continental shelve and beach and deposited these on land.

The Burckle Impact could have caused vast quantities of seawater and superheated steam to be projected into the upper atmosphere. The resultant salt rain would have precipitated in areas beyond the reach of these massive tsunamis and would have contaminated even more fresh water sources.

If scientists are correct in suggesting that the impact occurred in the third millennium BC, it is highly unlikely that it could have happened any time other than 2200 BC. We have seen ample historical, archaeological and geological evidence that a devastating global disaster happened in ca 2200 BC. We do not have the same evidence for 2500 BC or even 2900 BC. Had the Burckle Impact struck earth some 300 to 700 years before the 4.2 ka BP event, the ancient civilizations of Egypt, Akkad, Harappa, etc. would have been destroyed then and not in 2200 BC as all the evidence suggest. There would have been insufficient time for these ancient civilizations to have recovered and reached an advanced level of development in such a short space of time.

Some scientists suggest that the chevron dunes are of aeolian (wind) origin. Should this be the case, one would expect the process to be ongoing. What we do find, however, is that the dunes are overgrown with vegetation and they lay at almost right angles to the prevailing wind direction. One should also expect to find stratification in the dunes that would reflect climatic fluctuations over time. The profile of the dunes and the footprint observed from satellite images do not match those of wind-blown dunes. Aeolian dunes typically have an angle of repose of about 34° on the leeward side whereas the Fenambosy chevrons are substantially steeper at 42°. The question should also be asked as to how one explain the deep ocean sediments in the dunes? In the absence of core drilling and definitive dating, the impact hypothesis may tentatively be accepted as a plausible cause for the dunes.

The Burckle crater is not the only impact that dates from this time. The Rio Cuarto and Campo Del Cielo impact crater fields in Argentina are evidence of asteroids that exploded in the Earth's atmosphere during the same period, creating massive air blasts and meteorite showers.

We have observed the results of the relatively minor comet air blast that hit Tunguska in Russia in 1908. The explosion flattened an estimated 80 million trees over an area of 2150 km^2 and is believed to have been caused by the air blast of a comet or asteroid exploding and disintegrating about 5 to 10 km above the earth. The blast was estimated to have been about 1000 times more powerful than the Hiroshima bomb. In comparison to the Burckle Crater, though, the Tunguska event is insignificant

Figure 10: Tunguska Explosion, Siberia, June 1908

While numerous chevrons, meteorite impacts and related phenomena have been discovered, very few have been dated. It is quite likely, though, that the earth may have moved through an asteroid belt, tail or cloud around 4200 years ago which may have caused the planet to be bombarded by asteroids, comets, air blasts and perhaps several Burckle size impacts. Depending on the severity of these impacts, earthquakes and aftershocks, tectonic-plate movements and volcanic eruptions may have resulted and continued for as much as three years after the event as stated in the Oera Linda Book.

The last evidence we will consider here are the findings of Professor Lonnie Thompson, professor of geological sciences at Ohio State University and leader of an expedition in 2000 to retrieve ice cores from Mount Kilimanjaro in Tanzania.[49] From the analysis of these ice cores he found that Africa had suffered a severe 300 year drought from about 2000 BC. It is suggested here that this drought was exacerbated by widespread forest and grassland fires as described for Europe in the Oera Linda Book and which might have been brought on by meteorite showers. In addition, denudation of the land by severe floods and contamination by saltwater rain could have resulted in a

---

[49] *Glaciology: Ice Man: Lonnie Thompson Scales the Peaks for Science*: Science Magazine, 18 October 2002

very arid and dusty landscape that affected the continent for centuries, even during times of normal rainfall.

The extent of acid or other forms of toxic rain and gasses that would have resulted from all these fires or meteorite explosions is a question that will be left to persons more knowledgeable on the subject. This would surely have had a compounding effect and would have increased the Albedo, or reflection coefficient, in North Africa to beyond the point of no return.

We have seen that all of the ancient scribes described a mysterious cloud or smoke cover but no wind or rain. This would have obscured much of the meteorite activities. Ipuwer may have referred to such activities when he stated:

> *Behold, the fire has gone up on high, and its burning goes forth against the enemies of the land.*

He also mentioned trees that were stripped bare and made reference to a lot of noise. Could this have been caused by air blasts and shock waves? Again, the 1908 Russian event comes to mind.

The Oera Linda Book states that the earth vomited fire and Dr. Courty recorded a layer of volcanic ash at Tell Leilan. The book mentioned that forests throughout Europe were destroyed by fire. Was this from volcanoes or might it have been from asteroid impacts and air blasts? It is only fair to assume that such young volcanoes would still have been very evident today; so, where are they? Again, the Oera Linda Book left some clues. In the description of the disaster we read:

> *Not only in Finda's Land did the mountains spew fire but also in Twiskland.*

Finda's Land is what we call Asia, and might have included Eastern Europe and Russia. Twiskland is Germany - also known as Tyskland in German.

A cursory search on the internet shows that some thirty extinct or dormant volcanoes have been discovered in Germany alone. Whilst the latest eruptions from a few have been dated to between the early and mid-Holocene, most have (apparently) not been dated yet. Many extinct volcanoes have also been discovered in Russia, but their last eruptions are merely given as *Holocene*. It would appear that volcanologists are concentrating on the more active and high-profile volcanoes such as Vesuvius, Edna, Santorini, Krakatoa, Mount St Helens, etc. The Oera Linda Book, however, tells us that some of the extinct volcanoes in Germany erupted as little as 4200 years ago. This begs the question:

> *If the Oera Linda Book is a hoax, why would they have included this information – especially at a time when they either did not know about these volcanoes in Germany, or when they had no means by which they could determine the age of the volcanoes even if they were aware of them.*

In the 19th century, all these volcanoes would have appeared to be millions of years old. Yet, many, if not most of them, are now dated to have erupted during the Holocene like the Oera Linda Book suggests.

In this chapter, we compared the 2193 BC claims of the Oera Linda Book to other ancient scribes as well as measured these against modern scientific discoveries. While a number of other hereto unknown and startling historical facts will be dealt with in this book, it is hoped that the reader will already start to gain an appreciation for the authenticity and importance of the Oera Linda Book. Without fear of contradiction it can be stated that the book is a treasure trove of information for historians, anthropologists, archaeologists and others.

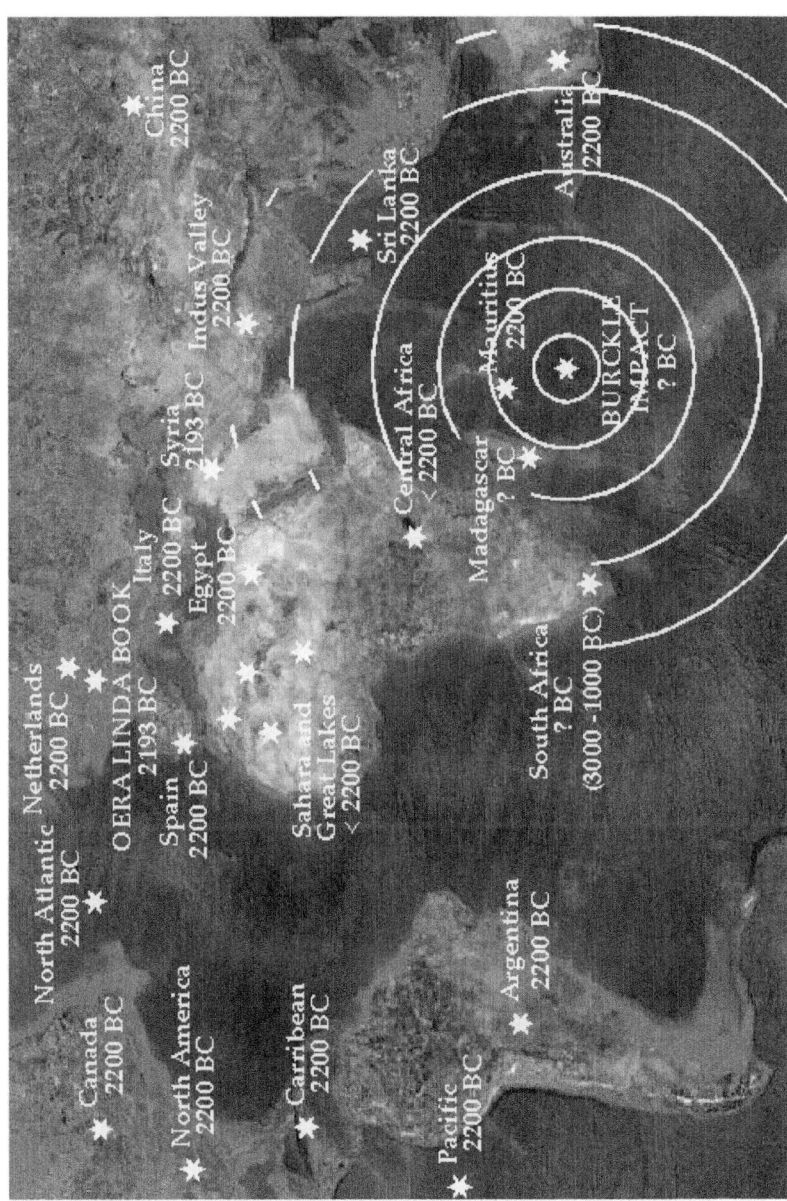

Figure 11: Evidence of events around 2200 BC

Chapter 2

The Fryan Federation

The Commission

T hrow this bitch overboard! [50]

These were the last words the mortally wounded Frana heard before she plunged to her watery grave. An institution that served the nation since the dawn of time died with her. Shortly after, the eternal lamp was extinguished. The cords linking Frya's People to the past had been cut and the bonds of unity broken. A single murder changed the course of Europe irrevocably.

The Fins and Danes were subsequently repelled and seven months later, in 589 BC, the General Assembly convened. The threat from the North was temporarily checked and a new Folk Mother[51] had to be chosen. The lot fell on *Adela ovira Linda*; a popular choice had she not had her designs on marriage.

An Honorary Mother ought to be as pure in her conscience as she appears outwardly and care equally for all her children. Now, as I love Apol more than anything else in the world, I cannot be such a mother[52].

---

[50] OLB, The Book of Adela's Followers, Chapter 31.
[51] *Folk Mother* or *Matriarch*. Her primary duty (and that of the Matrons) was not governance, but to guard over the morals of the nation.
[52] OLB, The writings of Adelbrost and Appolonia, Chapter 1.

New nominations were invited but this time every constituency backed its own candidate; nobody would yield. The impasse lasted for the next 30 years. Without clear and unifying leadership, distrust and division increased whilst national issues of security were neglected. It was now everyone for themselves. In Lower Saxony the Fins had once again penetrated up to the Weser River; in the South the Gauls and Celts, their former compatriots, invaded their realm right up to the Schelde.

In 559 BC the General Assembly convened, as so many times before, to elect a new leader; this time under the cloud of war. Frya's Land[53], or The Fryan Federation, a term of choice that will later become clearer, was by now a shadow of the former union that controlled all of Europe some 1700 years earlier. There were now only 13 Burgh Matrons[54] left amongst Frya's People. The degenerate Celts still had their Matrons but those ties had been cut more than a millennium before.

Adela Ovira Linda, who was still a highly respected councillor, recommended her husband's niece, Tuntia, to the position of Folk Mother. The nomination, however, was again vetoed and no leader chosen. The next Folk Mother would only be elected 254 years later, in 305 BC.

In her second proposal to the General Assembly, Adela recommended that a commission[55] be established to collect all their historical writings in a single book lest these were destroyed in the impending war. Her recommendation resulted in the *Book of Adela's Followers* and later, *The Oera Linda Book*; the *Rosetta Stone* of European history and the only explicit proof of a benign world power that disappeared. History, however, is littered with references to this civilization, as we shall see.

The farsightedness of Adela's recommendation and the subsequent work under the guidance of the 5-man commission allow

---

[53] The *Land of Frya* (Earth Mother) or *Land of the Free* (people).
[54] The original term used in Old Fries is *Burchfâm*. This was variously translated as *Femmes, Burghmaids, Priestesses*, etc. From the description of their functions and duties in the Oera Linda Book, however, it would appear that they are best described as *Matrons*.
[55] OLB: The book of Adela's followers, Chapter 1

us today, almost 2600 years later, to gain an insight into this forgotten society; the most advanced culture in antiquity (by Western Standards).

As with all societies who suffered the devastation of the 2193 BC Event, most of their records and, in fact, the very fibre of this ancient civilization was largely destroyed. They had to start afresh. We therefore find mostly post-2193 BC history in the Oera Linda Book. There are some references, though, to *the good old days* that allow us to reconstruct the extent of their pre-disaster dominion. Their system of government, laws, religious beliefs and ethical norms are fairly well documented.

In order to understand the Oera Linda Book and the history of Frya's People we need to have a closer look at their country, their religion and social norms. This will also shed light on the vast extend of *Celtic Society*, both Insular and Continental, that archaeologists have been uncovering over the last number of decades.

It must be pointed out that the terms *Celts* and *Celtic Society* are applied in this chapter as archaeologists understand these at present. The Celts and Frisians shared a common heritage and culture and it is therefore quite difficult to distinguish between the two from archaeological finds only. In fact, most of the Celtic citadels, hill forts and graves such as Heuneberg, Hallstatt, Hochdorf and others discovered in Germany, Austria and France were not Celtic by the Oera Linda Book's definition. This should become clearer later.

Boundaries

Although the cataclysm that destroyed their world in 2193 BC was now 1634 years in the distant past, the memory of that bygone era was kept alive in their schools and on their buildings. Every town and village that representatives of the 589 BC Commission approached could relay the pre-disaster boundaries of their realm:

This stands inscribed on all burghs. Before the Bad Time came...[56]

The Oera Linda Book claims that their land extended from Britain in the west to somewhere near the present western border of Poland, including Italy, the Balkans and Greece as well as Austria, Hungary and parts of the Czech Republic (Bohemia); from Spain in the south to Norway, Sweden and Finland in the north. Scandinavia was called *Skenland*, meaning *Beautiful Land*. The older portions of the Oera Linda Book refer to the Baltic Sea as the *Aster Sea* (East Sea). It is still known today as the East Sea in Dutch, German, Norwegian, Swedish, etc. From about 300 BC the book also refers to the Baltic as the *Balda Sea*. The Mediterranean was called the *Middle Sea*.[57] The description seems to include the greater part of the modern day European Union. They also had colonies in North Africa.

Convicted criminals were exiled to Britain, which was used as a penal colony where inmates had to work in the tin mines. This arrangement lasted until the appearance of the Celts after the Celtic Revolution which was triggered by a brief but brutal civil war in ca 1628 BC. There are no references to Ireland.

Mention is made that, apart from all the small rivers, they had 12 large rivers on which they could sail to the sea. These could have included the Oder or even the Vistula, both of which discharge into the Baltic Sea in the north. It would seem logical to assume that either of these rivers could have formed a natural eastern boundary.

The book states that *Twiskland*[58] with her dense forests and wild animals formed a barrier between Frya's Land and any would-be invaders from the East; perhaps more specifically the Slavic nations from Eastern Europe and Asia. *Twiskland* means *Between Land* (Dutch: Tusschenland) and denotes Germany; still known today as Tyskland in German.

Atland or *Aldland* means the *Old Land* that suddenly disappeared in 2193 BC; 4200 years ago. There is very little indication

---

[56] OLB: The book of Adela's followers, Chapter 20
[57] German: Mittelmeer, Afrikaans: Middellandse See.
[58] Compare with *twixt* as in *betwixt and between*. From Old English and Old Frisian: *Betweox*: between, among, amidst, meanwhile.

as to where this old land might have been. It is clear, however, that Atland was not part of mainland Europe and it may possibly have been somewhere to the west or north-west – perhaps even in the North Atlantic. Some try to link Atland with *Doggerland*, a former landmass in the southern North Sea that gradually sank below the waves some 8000 years ago. Neither the time frame nor the description in the Oera Linda Book shows any resemblance between Atland and Doggerland.

The pre-2193 BC Federation, therefore, seems to have comprised both Europe as well as Atland somewhere to the west. The fact that they referred to the *Old Land* could imply that this submerged land could have been their country of origin from where they colonised Europe in the distant past. This, quite possibly, could still have been the location of their capital and the seat of central government at the time of the 2193 BC event.

Rear Admiral Inka sailed west in ca 2000 BC in search of remnants of the Old Land[59]; that is, some 193 years after the event that destroyed their world. If Atland were part of Europe or Doggerland in the North Sea, he would have known whether there was anything left. He would not have had to go in search of it. We can therefore only assume that this part of their federation was a fair distance away.

The book makes no further mention of Inka, unlike the incorrect observation from some modern commentators that the Frisians claimed to have founded the Inca Civilisation in South America. Admittedly, there is this suggestion, but it may also mean that the Incas derived their name from someone in their ancient past that crossed paths with them and whom they may have deified and taken their name from. This is another reason why the book was rejected in the 19th and 20th centuries. Even DNA profiling does not appear to provide us with evidence of a European incursion into the Americas at the time. The Oera Linda Book do, however, mention that most of Inka's crew consisted of Fins of eastern descends (Slavic / Chinese / Mongolian).

Wr-alda's Sea means *God's Sea*, which, since time immemorial, has been known to us as the Atlantic Ocean. Herodotus mentioned it in his *Histories* written in the 5th century BC. The hereto-assumed origin

---

[59] OLB: The book of Adela's followers, Chapter 24.

of the word is that it is named after the mythical god Atlas. In light of the Oera Linda Book it now seems more logical that the name would rather mean the *Ocean of the Old Land, Atland Ocean* or *Atlantic Ocean* – a Greek term that came to be used long after the 2193 BC event.

The following map was compiled from the description given in the Oera Linda book:

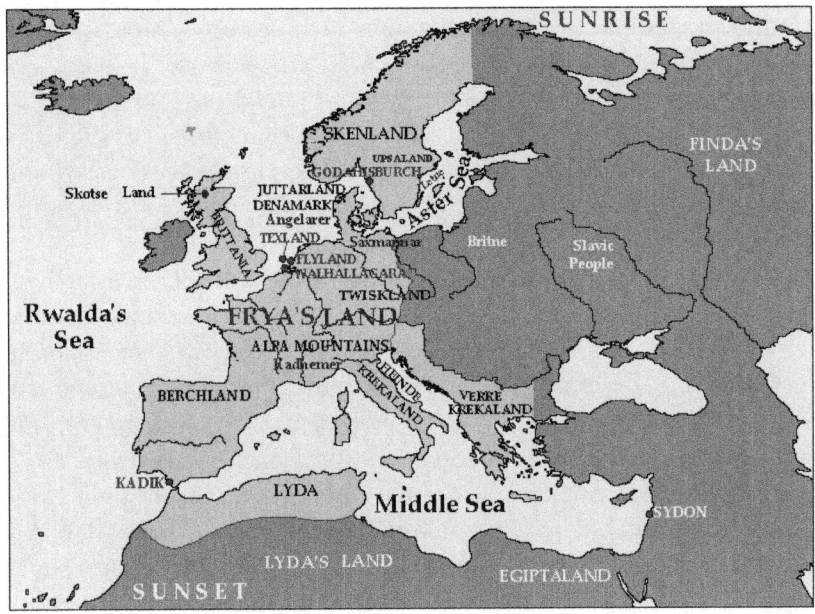

Figure 12: Frya's Land before 2193 BC

The account in the Oera Linda Book seems to describe a federation of ethno-religious states, or a *United States of Frya*, bound by a common ancestral heritage and religious affiliation. It would further appear that these Fryans, or proto-Frisians, were the dominant and most advanced tribe in Europe at the time.

At a first glance the extent of Frya's Land as described in the Book of Adela's Followers seems exaggerated until we take notice of archaeologists' present reconstruction of the *Celtic World* during the time of the Hallstatt and La Tène Cultures. The Celts, by present understanding, occupied most of the British Isles and Western Europe. The Oera Linda Book suggests that the same area had comprised the

Fryan Federation. The book later explains how the Celtic faction, or *Kaltaners*, broke away from Frya's People in 1628 BC. This extended sphere of *Celtic* influence was not known in the 19th century and is further proof of the book's authenticity.

This ancient and forgotten Frya's Land or Fryan Federation not only encompassed all of *Celtic Society* but also most of the 21st century AD European Union. In a certain sense, one could argue that it took the Fryan Federation 2600 years to reunify after the 1628 BC Celtic Revolution, or 4200 years after the 4.2 ka BP event.

The description of their land and their weaponry before the *bad time* came also shows that they were an Iron Age people more than 4200 years ago when most of the developed world of the time was still in the Bronze Age. They had tin mines in Britain (Wales) and iron and copper mines in Scandinavia.

They described their European states as these would have been before the disaster but we find that their influence around the Mediterranean had mostly dwindled to the point of non-existence by the time the Book of Adela's Followers was compiled. As was the case with Egypt, who took the better part of 300 years to overcome the utter devastation of the 4.2 ka BP Event, the Fryan Federation must have taken a few centuries as well.

As the smoke cleared and the water receded after the disaster, small bands of survivors started finding each other in the chaos. No sooner had they managed to establish rudimentary settlements when they had to defend themselves against bands of refugees and invaders from the East. One may safely assume that most of their maritime expertise and technology would have perished and that the survivors were those who resided further inland. It would have taken some time before they would have been able to start building new fleets to resume their commercial activities. By then very little memory and records would have existed of their previous holdings around the Mediterranean. These would also have been destroyed and by the time the Frisians returned, other migrants had filled the void left by their absence.

Government

Frya's Land, despite its size, was an exclusive society. Citizenship seems to have been defined by an ethnic nationalism which included a shared ethnic ancestry, a common faith, a common culture and a common language with, assumingly, dialectal variations. Whereas civic nationalism is inclusive and defines nationality by *jus soli* (law of the soil, or by birth in a country), the Frisians' ethnic nationalism was exclusive and defined citizenship by *jus sanguinis* (the law of blood or descent).

Uppermost in their world view was their attempts to prevent outside influences from affecting their national character. No outsider was allowed into their fold and if any of their own had been under the influence of external temptations for too long, he or she was not allowed back. Endogamy[60] was rigorously practiced. Exogamous[61] marriages were not allowed and once someone married a foreigner, he or she could never return.

> *Should any of them desire one of your daughters as a wife, and she is willing, explain to her foolishness; but if she still wants to follow her suitor, let her go in peace.*
>
> *If your son wishes for a daughter of theirs, you must do the same as with your daughter; but neither the one nor the other may ever return, for they would introduce foreign morals and customs...*[62]

The Fryan Federation seems to have had some form of Social Democracy. They opposed inequality, oppression, poverty and the concentration of wealth in the hands of a few. They had a centralised planned economy and community of goods and property.

> *Four things are given for your enjoyment, namely air, water, land, and fire. Wralda, though, is the sole possessor of them. Therefore I advise you, you should choose upright men who will fairly divide the*

---

[60] Marriage within a specific tribe or similar social unit.
[61] Marriage outside the tribe, family, clan, or other social unit.
[62] OLB, Book of Adela's Followers, Chapter 3

labour and the fruits, so that no-one shall be exempt from work or from the duty of defence[63].

If a man has taken a wife, he must be given a house and yard. If there is none, it must be built for him[64].

It is recommended that the reader look at chapters 3 to 12 in the Book of Adela's Followers to understand the socialist nature of Frya's People. Although there are notable differences, one may compare the Fryan Federation with some of the modern day Mennonite, Amish and Hutterite communities in North America. It should perhaps come as no surprise that the father of the Mennonite Church, Menno Simons (1496–1561), hailed from Friesland. The Fryan's were obviously not Christian and they were not pacifists. Although they preferred to settle disputes by diplomatic means, they were not averse to taking up arms.

If we find ourselves in a foreign market, be it near or far, and it happens that that nation wants to harm or rob us, we should immediately fall on them; for although we desire to do everything for the sake of peace, our neighbours should never underestimate us or think we are afraid.

They were ultra conservative in their moral and ethical codes and these were rigorously enforced. It is not difficult to imagine that some may have experienced their laws as oppressive and even invasive; especially once they have been exposed to outside influences. This may have provided fertile ground for the seeds of the 1628 BC Celtic revolution.

In my youth I sometimes grumbled at the strictness of the law but later I often thanked Frya for her Tex and our forefathers for the laws that they compiled from it[65].

---

[63] OLB, Book of Adela's Followers, Chapter 3
[64] OLB, Book of Adela's Followers, Chapter 7
[65] OLB: The book of Adela's Followers, Chapter 13.

The head of state or Folk Mother resided at Fryasburgh in Texland, known today as Den Burgh on the island of Texel in the Netherlands. We may assume that this was the capital of the Federation and this was also the education centre of choice for tertiary education.

Each state or district had a provincial capital or citadel where a female governor, or Burgh Matron, resided. We do not know how many burgh matrons or states there were originally, but mention is made of quite a few of them such as in Scandinavia, Britain, Spain, Swabia, Lower Saxony and others. As mentioned before, there were only thirteen of these matrons left towards the end of their dominance of Western Europe in 558 BC. They were democratically elected from female clerics who had completed an apprenticeship spanning several years. They were not allowed to marry or to have been married before. If they wished to marry, they had to relinquish their position, as it was felt that a conflict of interests could arise if they had to tend to both a family and to the governance of the land.

From the ranks of the burgh matrons, all the citizens with voting rights elected a federal leader or Folk Mother. Her appointment was for life, as was the appointment of the Burgh Matrons. The Folk Mother could nominate her successor but the constitution allowed for the Folk Mother and the Matrons to be removed from office if they violated the constitution or neglected their duties. In cases of gross misconduct they could be exiled or banished to the penal colony in Britannia[66], or even be sentenced to death. What is abundantly clear is that the Oera Linda Book does not ascribe any magical skills or occultist practices to the Folk Mother or the Burgh Matrons (apart from Kalta who severed all ties with their creed).

An important token of their civilisation was their perpetual flame or torch.[67] The Folk Mother and every Burgh Matron had a burning flame in their citadels, which dedicated maidens had to keep burning at all times. Whenever a new citadel was built or a new Burgh Matron appointed, her lamp had to be lighted from the folk mother's lamp in the capital. It would appear that the flame was seen as a token

---

[66] Formerly *Westland* (Wales).

[67] OLB: The book of Adela's Followers, Chapter 6.

of her legitimacy, her oath to uphold and defend their creed and as a symbol of their religion and civilization.

Some translations and commentators refer to these female clerics as priestesses, which may create the impression of some cultic or mysterious order. Nothing appears to be further from the truth. Their primary function was to ensure adherence to their very high moral code, laws and religion in all aspects of daily life and governance. It was incumbent on them to maintain the peace. Their other duties included education, welfare, medical care, housing, botanical research, farming, business ethics and the administration of justice in collaboration with the male Counts[68], Dukes[69] and magistrates. The appeal court resided with the Folk Mother. Some researchers in the past concluded that Frya's Land had a matriarchal system of governance. While it is true that the highest offices in the land seem to have been held by women, we find that they were primarily seen as the custodians of their creed. The folk mother and the burgh matrons had to ensure that all religious and secular activities conformed to their ethical and religious codes. This included social responsibilities and behaviour, legislation and administration, and even warfare. The men were responsible for the governance of the land and had to take care of defence, maritime affairs, trade, commerce, and the schooling of the youth in these disciplines. We find broadly the same system in Iran today where a Guardian Council of clerics oversee and monitor the administration of the democratically elected government (at least in theory). We shall later come back to the connection between Iran and Western Europe.

Despite the fact that the folk mother and burgh matrons held the highest positions of state and therefore the power of veto, the democratically elected General Assembly ruled. In numerous instances, we note that they governed the land without a folk mother for decades and in one instance for almost three centuries. Apart from

---

[68] The Oera Linda Book: *Gevretman*. A democratically elected chieftain of a district or state comprising several cities or *burghs*. He represented his electorate on the federal council or *General Assembly*. Danish, Norwegian, and Swedish: *Greve*; Dutch, Afrikaans: *Graaf*; German: *Graf*; English equivalent: *Count.*

[69] The Oera Linda Book: *Hertoga*. A democratically elected leader of a district or state. Answerable to the *Gevretman* or Count.

the counts and dukes, they also had magistrates and Burghomeisters, or mayors. The burghomeisters were responsible for the observance of municipal and building regulations and their duties included the maintenance of public amenities such as the market place, the commons, botanical gardens, parks, forests and yes, nature conservation.

The highest military rank was that of King; Warrior Kings in command of the infantry and cavalry, and Sea Kings in command of the Navy and sea soldiers, or marines. Admirals were in command of the fleets and resorted under the Sea Kings; the fleets being both merchant and military. The admirals mentioned in the Oera Linda Book would rather appear to have been closer to the modern day rank of Rear Admiral. (Dutch: *Schout-bij-Nacht*). The kings, in turn, came under the jurisdiction of an Alderman from the General Assembly – something like a modern Secretary of Defence or a Minister of Defence. The Folk Mother, as head of state, was the Commander in Chief of the armed forces thereby ensuring civilian control of the military as we see in Chapter 9 of The Book of Adela's Followers:

These are the rights of Mothers and Kings.

1. If war breaks out, the Mother sends her messengers to the King; the King sends messengers to the Counts to defend the country.

2. The Counts call all the citizens together and decide how many men shall be sent.

3. All the resolutions must immediately be sent to the Mother by messengers and witnesses.

4. The Mother lets all resolutions be gathered and gives an average number, that is, the middle number of all resolutions together, which the people as well as the King should be satisfied with for the time being.

5. If the armed forces are on campaign, the King only have to consult with his headmen (officers), *though there must always be three burghers without voice* (observers) *from the Mother sitting in front. These burghers must send daily messengers to the Mother so that she would know if anything is done contrary to the counsels of Frya.*

The title of king had a very different meaning from the modern concept. From the Oera Linda Book we can see that the role evolved from these purely military positions in antiquity to that of the hereditary monarchs of later times. It would seem that this was as a result of the influence of the autocratic patriarchal systems that invaded Europe from the East after 2193 BC. A further interesting fact was that kings were not allowed to bear arms in a conflict:

> 12. *Those that fight with weapons in their hands cannot think clearly and remain wise; therefore it follows that no king must bear arms in battle. His wisdom must be his weapon, and the love of his warriors must be his shield.*[70]

Kings were elected for a three-year term. Once his term had expired, he could only be elected again after an interval of seven years. This would appear to have been quite an effective way of preventing personality cults and military coups. The Fryan Federation pursued democracy to the full:

> *All Frya's children are born equal. Therefore, they must have equal rights on land and elsewhere, that is water, and in all that Wralda has given.*[71]

The following gives us an idea as to how far they took their democratic rights:

> 1. *All Frya's sons have equal rights, and therefore every stalwart youth may apply to the Olderman to become a seafarer, who may not refuse him as long as there is any vacancy.*
> 2. *Navigators may elect their own masters.*
> 3. *The merchants must be chosen and appointed by the community to whom the merchandise belongs and the navigators have no voice in their election.*

---

[70] OLB: The book of Adela's followers, Chapter 8.
[71] OLB: The book of Adela's followers, Chapter 7.

4. If during a voyage it is found that the king is bad or incompetent, another may be put in his place, and on return home, the king himself may lodge his complaint with the Olderman.[72]

5. If the armed forces are on campaign, the King only have to consult with his headmen (officers), though there must always be three burghers without voice (observers) from the Mother sitting in front. These burghers must send daily messengers to the Mother so that she would know if anything is done contrary to the counsels of Frya.

6. If the king wishes to do anything which his council opposes, he may not persist in it.

7. If an enemy appears unexpectedly, then the king's orders must be obeyed.

8. If the king is not present, the next in command must be obeyed, and so on in succession according to rank.

9. If there is no headman present, one must be chosen[73]

The fact that the troops and sailors could elect their own officers and commanders without the sanction of the General Assembly, could explain why sea kings and warrior kings were sometimes very young. We read about Wodin, Inca and Tunis who were generals before they were 25 years old. According to Fryan law, young men had to be married by the time they turned 25 and when they got married, the community had to give them a house. We can assume they were all young and single because they were still living with their parents or relatives when they were elected as generals.

The following diagram is a broad outline of how their administration appeared to have functioned:

---

[72] OLB: The book of Adela's followers, Chapter 12.
[73] OLB: The book of Adela's followers, Chapter 9

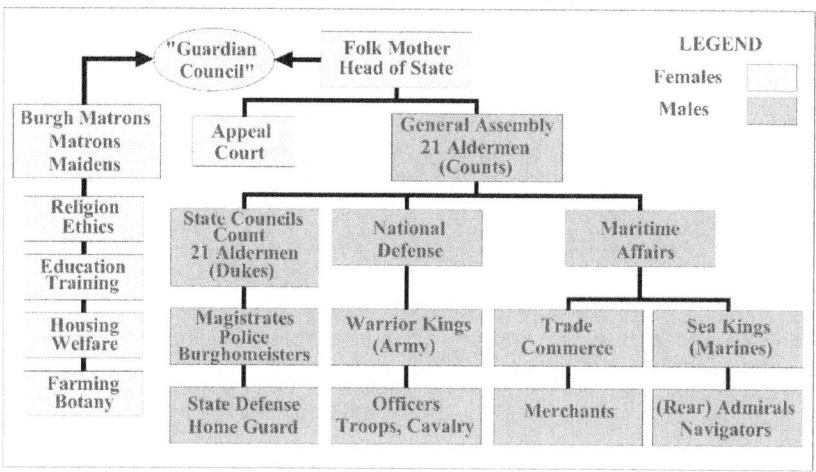

Figure 13: Administration of the Fryan Federation.

Whereas each state, comprising a number of towns, had a burgh matron at the state capital, the counts, magistrates or aldermen presided over as many as three states simultaneously. Under the auspices of the Folk Mother and General Assembly they were responsible for the general governance of the land, as well as for the Citizen Force and mobilisation in times of war.

Schooling was compulsory for all children. From the age of 12 boys had to spend one day a week on military training. Once they were considered skilled in the handling of weapons, they entered into either the military or the navy as warriors, sailors or marines. Their national conscription lasted for three years and only after they had completed their service period, were they allowed to vote in elections. A person had to be a voter for seven years before he could become a candidate for election himself.

An interesting stipulation stated that no person of distinction was allowed to vote in the election of burgh defenders – only the people. The burgh defenders referred to in this context were not the combatants in the army or navy, but rather officers who were responsible for maintaining law and order in the towns. Influential people could therefore not abuse their power by intimidating these officers, but equally, this arrangement protected the stature and integrity of the leaders. We read that each burgh matron could appoint up to 300 of these police officers and that they had to undergo training in law, defence and commerce.

Any person who declined a nomination for any public office lost his voting rights for life.

Religion

The Oera Linda Book describes the oldest religion in Europe. The Frisians and their ancestors practiced monotheism for more than 3000 years; from before the 4.2 ka BP event until ca AD 800 when they were forcibly Christianised by the Franks. Through the ages many of their compatriots adapted to the idolatry and cultic practices introduced by the Magyars from Central Asia and the Gauls from the Middle East. Pagan gods such as Thor and Wodin were latecomers on the scene. The Frisians, however, remained monotheists and, as some 20th century commentator noted, *Protestant at that*, without of course the third person of the Trinity, Jesus Christ. Throughout the book, one reads how they abhorred idolatry, witchcraft and the occults.

In trying to define the religion of Frya's People, one must first understand the four basic concepts as these appear in the Oera Linda Book:

1. Wralda means God; the most Ancient of Ancients, or the most Ancient Father. This was their name for God, the Creator.

2. Wralda also means world or everything in the Universe, in other words, all physical and metaphysical or spiritual things.

3. Wralda's Spirit means the spirit of God. This is obviously the very being of Wralda–God, but is quite separately identifiable from Wralda–World.

4. Irtha means the Earth, being an object created by Wralda. The Earth is not synonymous with The World, but merely part of it.

In the Oera Linda Book they use the same word for God (Creator) as for World (Creation). At a first glance, this sounds like pantheism:

Pantheism is the view that God is everything and everyone, and that everyone and everything is God. Pantheism is similar to polytheism (the belief in many gods), but goes beyond polytheism to teach that everything is God.[74]

In pantheism, it is quite acceptable to pray to all kinds of objects or creatures as they are all supposed to be part of God. Frya's folk were very much against worshipping idols, so they were clearly not pantheists. Let us then look at panentheism, which seems to be a bit closer:

Panentheism is essentially a combination of theism (God is the Supreme Being) and pantheism (God is everything). While pantheism says that God and the universe are coextensive, panentheism claims that God is greater than the universe and that the universe is contained within God. Panentheism holds that God is the "supreme effect" of the universe. God is everything in the universe, but God also is greater than the universe. Events and changes in the universe effect and change God. As the universe grows and learns, God also increases in knowledge and being.[75]

The Oera Linda Book clearly states that Wralda is all knowing and unchangeable:

Wralda is wisdom, and the laws that he has made are the books from which we learn, nor is any wisdom to be found or gathered, but in them. Men may see a great deal, but Wralda sees everything. Men may learn many things, but Wralda knows everything. Men may unlock many things, but to Wralda everything is open. Mankind is male and female, but Wralda created both. Mankind love and hate, but Wralda alone is just. Therefore, Wralda alone is good, and there is no good without him. In the progress of time all creation alters and

---

[74] http://www.gotquestions.org/pantheism.html
[75] http://www.gotquestions.org/panentheism.html

changes, but goodness alone is unalterable; and since Wralda is good, he cannot change.[76]

From the above quote, it is thus clear that the Oera Linda Book's religion does not fit in with panentheism either, as Wralda does not grow and learn. It would this seem that, although we have the problem with Wralda–God and Wralda–World, the Oera Linda Book's religion, nevertheless, comes very close to monotheism as we find it in Judaism and Christianity. The following few quotes out of many illustrate the essence of this oldest recorded monotheistic religion in the world:

Hail to all the well-intentioned children of Frya! Through them the earth shall be blessed. Learn and announce to the nations.

Wralda is the ancient of ancients or the most ancient, for he created all things. Wr-alda is all in all, for he is eternal and everlasting. Wr-alda is omnipresent but invisible, and therefore his being is called a spirit. All that we can see of him are the created beings who came through his life and go back again, because from Wralda all things proceed and return to him. From Wralda comes the beginning and the end; all things are glorified through him. Wr-alda is the only almighty being, because from him all other power is borrowed and returns to him. From him come all crafts and all crafts return to him. Therefore, he alone is the creator, and nothing was created outside him.

Wralda established eternal principles that are law in all creation and there are no good laws or they must be established therein. But although everything is in Wralda, the wickedness of men is not from him. Wickedness comes from laziness, carelessness, and stupidity; therefore, they may well be injurious to men, but never to Wralda. Wralda is wisdom, and the laws that he has made are the books from which we learn, nor is any wisdom to be found or gathered, but in them. Men may see a great deal, but Wralda sees everything. Men may learn many things, but Wralda knows everything. Men may unlock many things, but to Wralda everything is open. Mankind is male and

---

[76] OLB, *The Writings of Adelbrost and Appolonia,* **Chapter 4**

female, but Wralda created both. Mankind love and hate, but Wralda alone is just. Therefore, Wralda alone is good, and there is no good without him. In the progress of time all creation alters and changes, but goodness alone is unalterable; and since Wralda is good, he cannot change. As he endures, he alone exists; everything else is show.[77]

Wralda, who alone is good and eternal, made the beginning, then came time. Time wrought all things, also the earth. The earth bore grass, herbs and trees, all beautiful animals and all bad animals. All that is good and beautiful she (Earth) brought forth by day, and all that is wicket and bad she brought forth by night.[78]

Wralda's spirit may only be thanked with bended knees, yes thrice fold; for what you have received from him, for what you enjoy, and for the hope he gives you in times of distress.
Let not your neighbour express his thanks to you on bended knees; that is for Wralda's spirit only. Envy would assail you, Wisdom would ridicule you, and my matrons would accuse you of sacrilege.[79]

The old Frisians were religious monotheists. Some commentators believe that in addition to Wralda, they also worshipped the earth as well as their First Earth Mother, Frya. It would appear that there might be some truth to this as far as Frya was concerned, even though they claimed to have only worshipped Wralda.

As for the allegation that the old Frisians worshipped the earth, this is a blatant, if not mischievous, misconception. Their so-called personification of *Mother Earth* is no different from our modern reference to earth by exactly the same term. We assuredly, however, do not worship *Mother Earth*.

The reader is again reminded of the commandment that stated that they must bare and bend their knees to Wralda's Spirit only. Nowhere do they mention Frya or the earth in this context.

---

[77] OLB, *The Writings of Adelbrost and Appolonia*, Chapter 4: Doctrine that was inscribed on the burgh tower of Liudwerd (Leeuwarden).
[78] OLB: The book of Adela's followers, Chapter 2.
[79] OLB: The book of Adela's followers, Chapter 3.

Myths

The 2193 BC disaster not only destroyed the Fryan Federation but also all memory and such records of their past as there may have been. It is possible that Frya was their Folk Mother before the disaster. She may have died in the flood.

After the disaster she appears to have been elevated to the position of Earth Mother or Founding Mother by her successor. Fasta claimed to have been nominated by nobody less than Frya, and in fact, received instructions from Frya, who was now watching over them from her *Watch Star*. This is the only incidence we find in the Oera Linda Book where the Fryans deified a person.

> *Exalted Frya. When she had thus spoken, the earth shook like Wralda's sea. The ground of Flyland sank beneath her feet, the sky became black and green from tears, and when they looked for their mother she had already risen to her watch star[80]; then at length thunder spoke from the clouds, and lightning wrote in the sky, "Watch!"*
>
> *Far-seeing Frya. The land from which she had risen was now a stream, and except her Tex, all was destroyed that came from her hand.[81]*

Fasta's obviously strengthened her own hand by convincing the nation that she enjoyed divine sanction and fellowship:

> *Upon my servant Fasta I have placed my hopes. Therefore, you must accept her as your Honorary Mother. If you follow my advice, she will hereafter remain my servant as well as all pious matrons who succeed her. Then shall the lamp that I have lighted for you never be extinguished. Its light shall always illuminate your*

---

[80] The Oera Linda Book has numerous references to *Watch Stars* and instructions to *Watch* over the morals of the people. This is reminiscent of the Watchers refered to in Daniel 4:13, 17, 23 in the Bible as well as the unfallen watchers in The Book of Enoch (3) and in the Book of Jubilees.

[81] OLB: The book of Adela's followers, Chapter 2.

intellect, and you shall always remain as free from foreign domination as the sweet river-water from the salt water of the boundless sea.[82]

She not only established or re-established a corpus of laws under the claimed guidance of Frya, but she also recreated their origins and ancient history:

> *This stands written on the walls of Fryasburgh in Texland. It also stands in Stavia and in Medeasblik:*
>
> *"It was Frya's day, and it was seven times seven years since Fasta was appointed as Folk Mother by Frya's desire. The burgh of Medeasblik was ready, and a Burgh Matron was chosen. Fasta would light the new lamp and this was done in the presence of all the people, when Frya called from her watch-star so that every one could hear it:*
>
> *"Fasta, take your stylus and write the things which I may not speak.'*
>
> *Fasta did as she was told. Thus we, Frya's children, discovered our earliest history"*

There is a strong suspicion that Fasta with her lamp and burgh matrons (Dutch: Burghmaagde, Lit.: Burgh Virgins) were the predecessors of the later Vestal Virgins in Roman religion.

According to this Fryan myth, which Fasta apparently invented, Wr-alda created three Earth Mothers in the beginning. Lyda was the mother of the black people; Finda was the mother of the yellow people and Frya the mother of the white people. From then on all the descendants were referred to as the children or people of Finda, Lyda or Frya. Frya was described as blonde-haired with blue eyes and a fair complexion. Her name meant Freedom.

Frya should possibly be compared to Lady Justice or Justitia, with her weighing scales and double-edged sword who often adorns our courthouses or courtrooms as an allegorical personification of the moral force that underlies our legal system. Likewise, Frya was

---

[82] OLB: The book of Adela's followers, Chapter 3 (12).

possibly seen as the embodiment of divine order, law, ethics and custom – at least during the earlier part of their history.

Legal System and Ethical Code

Throughout the book, one gets the impression of a pious people who were guided in their everyday lives by their religion and moral codes. They were quite tolerant towards foreigners. They regarded themselves as a step above the other races, but they also believed that Wralda would punish them if they exploited these peoples. They regarded it as their duty to educate and train outsiders in their laws and doctrines; the essence of which resonated in the battle cry of the French Revolution some 3 800 years later - Liberty, Equality and Fraternity!

> *Never meddle with the people of Lyda nor of Finda. Wralda would help them so that any violence that goes out from you would return on your own heads.*
>
> *Should it happen that they want advice or something else from you, you should help them. If they come to rob you, though, then fall upon them like a raging fire.*[83]

One of the strictest codes they had as the Children of Frya or Free People was the prohibition on slavery. They were not allowed to enslave any other human being. They believed that if they made slaves of other people, Wralda would make slaves of them. They would equally not accept to be enslaved themselves but would rather commit suicide. This principle explains a lot of their history, as we shall see later.

> *Sensible Frya. The first she taught her children was self-control, the second was the love of virtue and when they were grown she taught them the value of liberty; for she said, "Without liberty all*

---

[83] OLB: The book of Adela's followers, Chapter 3 (8-9).

other virtues serve to make you slaves, your origins to eternal disgrace.[84]
Frya has said we must not allow amongst us any but free people; but what have they done? They imitated our enemies and instead of executing their prisoners or letting them go free, they have despised Frya's advice and have made slaves of them. Because they have done so, Frya could no longer protect them: they took freedom away from others and that is certainly why they lost theirs.[85]

Their constitution demanded that prisoners of war be either executed or set free. They were not allowed to make slaves of them and by implication, also not allowed to imprison them. They describe how prisoners of war should be taken to remote places where they could be instructed in the ways of the Frisians so that when they are set free they would no longer see the Frisians as enemies but rather as friends.

6. If we take prisoners, they must be taken deep into the country and taught our free customs.
7. If they are afterwards set free, it must be done with kindness by the matrons, in order that we may gain comrades and friends, instead of haters and enemies.[86]

Throughout the Oera Linda Book we read how seriously they took their missionary work. Their efforts to convert everyone with whom they came into contact had a profound influence on world history, as we shall see later. The reader should bear this in mind as we retrace their journeys.

In The Oera Linda Book we find the origins of the Common Law, as it appeared millennia later in Roman-Dutch Law. The Frisians believed that Wr-alda placed the knowledge of right and wrong, good and evil into the soul of every person. They called this inherent knowledge Eva and described it thus:

---

[84] OLB: The book of Adela's followers, Chapter 2.
[85] OLB: The book of Adela's followers, Chapter 1.
[86] OLB: The book of Adela's followers, Chapter 10 (6-7).

The word "Eva" is too sacred for common use; therefore, men have learned to say "Evin." "Eva" means that knowledge which is implanted in the breast of every man in order that he may know what is right and wrong, and by which he is able to judge his own deeds and those of others; that is to say, if he has been well and not badly brought up.

There is also another meaning attached thereto. "Eva" also means tranquil, smooth like water that has not been disturbed by a strong wind or something else. If the water is disturbed, it becomes troubled, uneven but it always tends to become calm again. That is its nature, just as the inclination towards justice and freedom that exists in Frya's children.

This tendency we have through the spirit of Wralda, our father, which speaks strongly in Frya's children and, therefore, will eternally be with us.

Eva is also a symbol for Wralda's spirit, who remains eternally just and undisturbed even though the body may suffer. Eternal and unalterable are the signs of wisdom and righteousness, which must be sought by all pious people, and must be possessed by all judges.

If men want to make regulations and rules that will remain good and fair, they must be equal for everybody. The judges must pronounce their decisions according to these laws.

If any offence is committed for which there is no law, a general assembly of the people shall be called; the judgement shall be passed in accordance with the inspiration of Wralda's spirit so as to be fair and just. By doing this, our judgment will never be wrong.[87]

The Frisians' seamanship and navy allowed them to be international merchants and explorers. They traded from the heart of Europe via rivers to all around the West European and Mediterranean coasts to as far as Egypt, Sidon and Byblos in Phoenicia. They had tin, iron and copper mines in Scandinavia and Britain and factories in Italy, Spain and Africa. By all accounts, they were very prosperous. They jealously guarded their reputation as reliable and honest businessmen

---

[87] OLB: The book of Adela's followers, Chapter 13.

and did not tolerate any dubious transactions. Any Frisian or foreigner that was found to be in breach of their business or ethical codes was blacklisted throughout the Federation. In extreme cases, offending countries were subdued by military force. Their trade missions frequently consisted of fleets in excess of a hundred ships with crews that could have amounted to any number from 4 000 to 10 000 sailors and marines. This would obviously have allowed them to enforce their business ethics and rules of conduct.

Should a foreign merchant come to the open markets at Wyringen or at Almanland and he cheats, he must immediately be fined, and it must be made known by the matrons over the whole country. If he comes back, nobody must buy from him and he must return as he came. Thus, should merchants be chosen to go to market or to sail with a fleet, only those who are well known and in good standing with the matrons should be chosen. If it happens, nevertheless, that there is a bad man amongst them who wants to defraud others, he must be opposed. If he has already done so, it must be corrected and the criminal banished from the land so that our name will be held in honour everywhere.

If we find ourselves in a foreign market, be it near or far, and it happens that that nation wants to harm or rob us, we should immediately fall on them; for although we desire to do everything for the sake of peace, our neighbours should never underestimate us or think we are afraid.[88]

11. Those coming to market may not practice usury. Should any do so, it will be the Matrons' duty to disclose them throughout the land so that they may never be elected to any office because they have greedy hearts. For self-enrichment they will betray everybody; the people, the Mother, their family and lastly their own selves.

12. If any anybody is so wicket as to knowingly sell sick animals or other goods as though in good condition, the market keeper must expel him and the matrons must name him throughout the land.[89]

---

[88] OLB: The book of Adela's followers, Chapter 13 (Minno's writings).
[89] OLB: The book of Adela's followers, Chapter 7 (11-12).

Architecture and Lifestyle

Many books we read about pre-historic Western Europe describe a primitive, almost Neolithic people that resided to the north and west of the Alps. They are stereotyped as hunter-gatherers and near Stone Age nomads. Invariably we see them in television documentaries as dirty, unwashed and unkempt savages where the strongest ruled. The more advanced Europeans of 4200 years ago are at best credited for having mastered fire, stone tools and primitive subsistence farming. They lived in rudimentary shelters in small communities and their diet consisted of whatever they could find in nature. It is commonly proclaimed that they only became civilized after the Romans invaded and occupied their lands.

The Oera Linda Book paints an astonishingly different picture. Before I am accused of taking the book at face value or perpetuating the hoax, let us look at what an outsider wrote about the Frisians of 3200 years ago.

For centuries scholars have been speculating about the whereabouts of *Scheria* and the *Phaeacians* where Ulysses, also known as Odysseus, spent 10 years after the Trojan War in Homer's *Odyssey*. Various islands in the Aegean and Adriatic Seas have been proposed. The Oera Linda Book gives us the answer – the *Phaeacians* were the *Frisians* and *Scheria* is the modern day *Schelde* Estuary in the Netherlands – exactly where *Kalib* in the Oera Linda Book, or *Calypso* in Homer resided.

In book V of his Odyssey written in ca 800 BC, some 400 years after the Trojan War (1188 BC), Homer describes the Frisians as *near of kin to the gods*:

> *When he* (Jove) *had thus spoken, he said to his son Mercury, 'Mercury, you are our messenger, go therefore and tell Calypso we have decreed that poor Ulysses is to return home. He is to be convoyed neither by gods nor men, but after a perilous voyage of twenty days upon a raft he is to reach fertile Scheria, the land of the Phaeacians, who*

are near of kin to the gods, and will honour him as though he were one of ourselves.'[90]

The Oera Linda Book, on the other hand, described the incident as follows:

> *After we have not seen any Krekalandar[91] in Almanland for twelve years, there came three ships, more beautiful than any we had or had ever seen. On the largest of them was a king of the Ionhis Islands[92]. His name was Ulysus[93] and the claims about his wisdom were great.*
>
> *A priestess told this king that he would become king over all the Krekalanda, so the advice was to get a lamp that was lighted from the lamp in Texland[94]. To obtain this, he had brought great treasures with him, above all, jewels for women, none in the world made more beautiful.*
>
> *They came from Troy, a city that the Krekalandar had conquered. All these treasures he offered to the mother, but the mother did not want to know of it. At last, when he saw that he had nothing to gain, he went to Walhallagara. There was a matron in office whose name was Kat, though commonly called Kalip[95], because her lower lip stuck out like a masthead.*
>
> *Here he tarried for years, to the annoyance of all that knew it. According to the matrons' claims, he eventually got a lamp from her; but it did him no good, because when he got to sea his ship was lost and he was taken up naked and destitute by the other ships.[96]*

A bit further Homer described a normal day in the household of King Alcinous of the Phaeacians – 3200 years ago. There are no doubt some exaggerations, but however great these are, we cannot begin to think of the Phaeacians in terms of stone-age people or

---

[90] Homer: *Odyssey*, Book V, p.1.
[91] Greeks
[92] Ionian Islands
[93] Ulysses
[94] Island of Texel, Noord Holland, The Netherlands
[95] *Calypso* in Homer's *Odyssey*
[96] The Book of Adela's Followers, Chapter 30.

savages. The reader will hopefully bear with the following extensive quotes where we shall compare Homer's description of the Phaeacians with the Oera Linda Book. For those readers who may have visited archaeological sites and reconstructions of Continental Celtic societies, I would like to suggest that these be borne in mind while reading the following descriptions. It must be pointed out again, though, that Celts used in this context portrays archaeologists' current understanding of the term.

King Alcinous, whose counsels were inspired of heaven, was now reigning. To his house, then, did Minerva fly in furtherance of the return of Ulysses. She went straight to the beautifully decorated bedroom in which there slept a girl who was as lovely as a goddess, Nausicaa, daughter to King Alcinous. Two maidservants were sleeping near her, both very pretty, one on either side of the doorway, which was closed with well-made folding doors.

By and by morning came and woke Nausicaa, who began wondering about her dream; she therefore went to the other end of the house to tell her father and mother all about it, and found them in their own room. Her mother was sitting by the fireside spinning her purple yarn with her maids around her, and she happened to catch her father just as he was going out to attend a meeting of the town council, which the Phaeacian aldermen had convened. She stopped him and said:

"Papa dear, could you manage to let me have a good big wagon? I want to take all our dirty clothes to the river and wash them. You are the chief man here, so it is only right that you should have a clean shirt when you attend meetings of the council. Moreover, you have five sons at home, two of them married, while the other three are good-looking bachelors; you know they always like to have clean linen when they go to a dance, and I have been thinking about all this."

She did not say a word about her own wedding, for she did not like to, but her father knew and said, "You shall have the mules, my love, and whatever else you have a mind for. Be off with you, and the men shall get you a good strong wagon with a body to it that will hold all your clothes."

On this he gave his orders to the servants, who got the wagon out, harnessed the mules, and put them to, while the girl brought the clothes down from the linen room and placed them on the wagon. Her mother prepared her a basket of provisions with all sorts of good things, and a goat skin full of wine; the girl now got into the wagon, and her mother gave her also a golden cruse of oil, that she and her women might anoint themselves. Then she took the whip and reins and lashed the mules on, whereon they set off, and their hoofs clattered on the road. They pulled without flagging, and carried not only Nausicaa and her wash of clothes, but the maids also who were with her.

When they reached the waterside, they went to the washing-cisterns, through which there ran at all times enough pure water to wash any quantity of linen, no matter how dirty. Here they unharnessed the mules and turned them out to feed on the sweet juicy herbage that grew by the waterside. They took the clothes out of the wagon, put them in the water, and vied with one another in treading them in the pits to get the dirt out. After they had washed them and got them quite clean, they laid them out by the seaside, where the waves had raised a high beach of shingle, and set about washing themselves and anointing themselves with olive oil. Then they got their dinner by the side of the stream, and waited for the sun to finish drying the clothes. When they had done dinner, they threw off the veils that covered their heads and began to play at ball, while Nausicaa sang for them.[97]

In book VIII of the Odyssey, King Alcinous describes the Phaeacians to Ulysses:

We are not particularly remarkable for our boxing, nor yet as wrestlers, but we are singularly fleet of foot and are excellent sailors. We are extremely fond of good dinners, music, and dancing; we also like frequent changes of linen, warm baths, and good beds, so now, please, some of you who are the best dancers set about dancing, that our guest on his return home may be able to tell his friends how much we surpass all other nations as sailors, runners, dancers and minstrels.[98]

---

[97] Homer: *Odyssey*, Book VI, p.1-2
[98] Homer: *Odyssey*, Book VIII, p.5

Homer relates Ulysses' first impressions of Alcinous' house as follows:

> *As the Phaeacians are the best sailors in the world, so their women excel all others in weaving, for Minerva has taught them all manner of useful arts, and they are very intelligent.*
>
> *Outside the gate of the outer court, there is a large garden of about four acres with a wall all round it. It is full of beautiful trees – pears, pomegranates, and the most delicious apples. There are luscious figs also, and olives in full growth. The fruits never rot nor fail all the year round; neither winter nor summer, for the air is so soft that a new crop ripens before the old has dropped. Pear grows on pear, apple on apple, and fig on fig, and so also with the grapes, for there is an excellent vineyard: on the level ground of a part of this, the grapes are being made into raisins; in another part they are being gathered; some are being trodden in the wine tubs, others further on have shed their blossom and are beginning to show fruit, others again are just changing colour. In the furthest part of the ground, there are beautifully arranged beds of flowers that are in bloom all the year round. Two streams go through it, the one turned in ducts throughout the whole garden, while the other is carried under the ground of the outer court to the*
> *house itself, and the town's people draw water from it. Such, then, were the splendours with which the gods had endowed the house of king Alcinous.*[99]

Apollonia, the daughter of Adela to whom we owe the Oera Linda Book, described her village as follows in ca 556 BC:

> *Now I would like to write myself; first about my burgh, and then about what I have been able to see.*
>
> *My burgh lies near the north end of the Liudgarda. The tower has six sides. It is three times thirty feet high; flat on top, with a small house upon it from where they study the stars. On either side of the tower is a house <u>three hundred feet long</u>, three times seven feet wide*

---

[99] Homer: *Odyssey*, Book VII, p.3

and as high, apart from the roof which is round. All this is built of hard-baked bricks, and on the outside there is nothing else. Around the burgh is a ring dyke, with a moat three times seven feet deep and three times twelve feet wide. If one looks down from the tower, he sees the shape of the Yule.

On the ground among the southern houses all kinds of herbs from near and far grow, of which the maidens must study the qualities. Between the northern houses there are only fields. The three houses on the north are full of corn and other necessities; the two houses on the south are for the maidens for school and to live. The most southern house is the Burgh Matron's house. In the tower hangs the lamp. The walls of the tower are inlaid with costly stones. On the south wall the Tex is inscribed. On the right side of this are the ordinances, and on the other side the laws; the other matters are found upon the three other sides. Against the dyke, near the house of the burgh matron, stand the oven and the mill, worked by four oxen.

Outside our burgh wall is the place where the Burgtheeren (officers?) and the soldiers live. The ring dyke around is an hour long—not a seaman's hour, but an hour of the sun, of which two times twelve go to a day. Inside the dyke is a level five feet below the top. On it are three hundred crossbows covered with wood and leather.

Besides the houses of the inhabitants, there are along the inside of the dyke three times twelve refuge-houses for the people who live in the district. The field serves for a paddock and for a meadow. On the south side of the outer ring dyke is the Liudgarde, enclosed by the great Linda Forrest. Its shape is three-cornered, with the widest part outside, so that the sun may shine in it, for there are a great number of foreign trees and flowers brought by the seafarers.

All the other citadels are the same shape as ours, only not so large; but the largest of all is that of Texland. The tower of Fryasburgh[100] is so high that it rends the sky, and all the rest is in proportion to the tower.[101]

Let us now compare Appolonia's description of her burg with the pre-historic hillfort of Heuneburg overlooking the upper Danube.

---

[100] Den Burg, Texel, The Netherlands
[101] OLB: *The writings of Apollonia.*, Chapter 7.

The fortified citadel is in Baden-Württemberg in the southwestern part of Germany, some 12 km east of Sigmaringen. The area has been excavated systematically by archaeologists since the 1950's who found that it had been inhabited since the 15th century BC. The following photographs show reconstructions of sections of the citadel dating from the 7th to the 5th centuries BC; exactly the same time when Appolonia described her own citadel in the Netherlands. She also told us that she travelled all the way up the Rhine to Lake Constance on the border of Germany, Switzerland and Austria during her apprenticeship to become a Burgh Matron. At the time the present state of Baden-Württemberg was still part of the Fryan Federation and not part of the Celtic domain as archaeologists are speculating.

Figure 14: An artist's impression of the Heuneberg citadel

Appolonia tells us that her burgh was built of hard-baked bricks and archaeologists tell us that Heuneberg's outer wall was built of mud bricks.

Figure 15: Reconstructed battlements at Heuneberg.
Note the wooden tiled roofs.

The main difference between Appolonia's burg and Heuneberg is that Appolonia's burg had a ring dyke whereas Heuneberg was situated on a plateau with a 4 metre high wall along the perimeter. The wall was topped by a roofed walkway. From Appolonia's description we may assume that Heuneberg's perimeter battlements were also equipped with crossbows.

Figure 16: The 14m x 30m large *Herrenhaus* at Heuneberg

The very large house in the south-east corner of the citadel is thought to have been the house of a local ruler and is sometimes referred to as the *Herrenhaus*. From Appolonia's description, however, this was most likely the equivalent of her school building where the burgh matron or maidens (teachers) lived and which may also have served as a meeting place for the Town Council.

Figure 17: Pre-historic houses at Heuneberg.

Geoff Carter, structural archaeologist, tells us about the discovery and theoretical reconstruction of longhouses that were built in the Netherlands some 7000 years ago. On his website, Theoretical Structural Archaeology102, he gives us an impression of what these old longhouses, discovered at Elsloo near Maastricht in the Netherlands, looked like:

> *Built by some of the first farming communities, this kind of longhouse represents the beginnings of architecture in Northern Europe. It is argued that it has left a heritage in architectural form and function that is still evident in the historical and contemporary built environment.*

Evidence of these structures has been discovered all over Europe and Carter gives us some idea what they looked like:

---

[102](http://structuralarchaeology.blogspot.com/2009/08/33-elsloo-32-neolithic-longhouse-made.html)

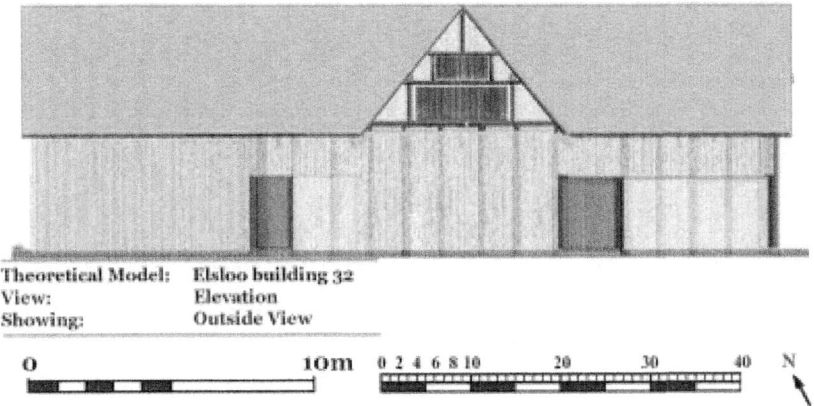

Figure 18: Reconstruction of 7000-year-old farmhouse
(by Geoff Carter)

Figure 19: Reconstruction of 7000-year-old farmhouse.
By Geoff Carter, from postholes discovered at Elsloo,
Netherlands.

Apollonia's account, which was written some 3000 years later, is thus quite believable and, once more, **this information was not available in the 19th century**. If the Oera Linda Book was a 19th century hoax, how could they have known that these buildings existed 2500 years ago and before?

David Keys, Archaeology Correspondent of *The Independent* wrote an article, *Found: Europe's oldest civilisation*, dated 11 June 2005, where he also mentions these longhouses discovered in Central Europe:

> Archaeologists have discovered Europe's oldest civilisation, a network of dozens of temples, 2,000 years older than Stonehenge and the Pyramids.
>
> More than 150 gigantic monuments have been located beneath the fields and cities of modern-day Germany, Austria and Slovakia. They were built 7,000 years ago, between 4800 BC and 4600 BC. Their discovery, revealed today by The Independent, will revolutionise the study of prehistoric Europe, where an appetite for monumental architecture was thought to have developed later than in Mesopotamia and Egypt.
>
> In all, more than 150 temples[103] have been identified. Constructed of earth and wood, they had ramparts and palisades that stretched for up to half a mile. They were built by a religious people who lived in communal <u>longhouses up to 50 metres long</u>, grouped around substantial villages. Evidence suggests their economy was based on cattle, sheep, goat and pig farming.

Apollonia described 300 feet (100 metre long) longhouses in her village. Compare this with David Key's article. This information was not available in the 19th century. In her account she also described the ringdyke and moat around her burgh. A paper written by H.A.C. Fermin and M. Groothedde, entitled *De Zutphense ringwalburg van de 9e tot de 14e eeuw* (The Zutphen Ringdyke Burgh from the 9th to the 14th Century)[104] describes the ringdyke burgh of Zutphen that was apparently founded in the 9th century AD. Zutphen is about 60 kilometres east south east of Amsterdam near Apeldoorn in the Netherlands.

---

[103] Could this not have been storehouses, community centers or communal dwellings? I am always intrigued by archaeologists' propensity towards *temples*.
[104] Zutphen Archaeological Publication No. 22

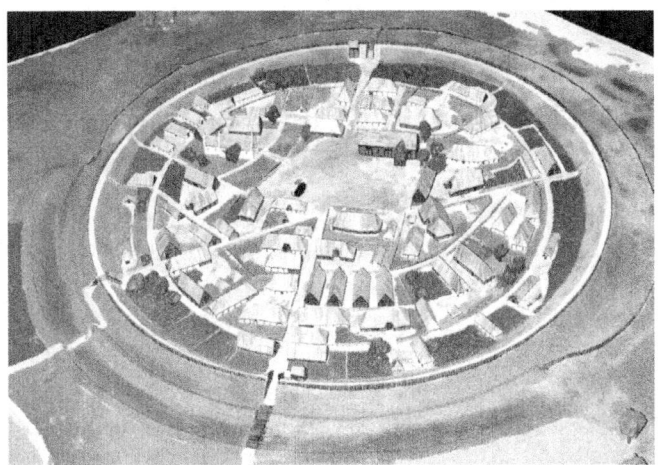

Figure 20: Ringdyke Burgh of Zutphen.
9th century AD (With acknowledgement to H.A.C. Fermin and M.
Groothedde)

The above figure gives us an idea what these ring dykes looked like. They are found all over Europe and Britain.

Fermin and Groothedde give a list of 42 fortified towns and burghs in the Netherlands that possibly existed in the 9th century. Of these, six are mentioned in the Oera Linda Book and dated back to at least the 6th century BC – 1500 years earlier. They are: Den Burgh on the island of Texel, Wieringen, Stavoren, Medemblik, Leiden and Middelburg.

From Apollonia's description we see that everyone except the commercial farmers lived inside the burghs. For those who were further away, townhouses were provided when they had to come to town for business or during times of hostility.

Besides the houses of the inhabitants, there are three times twelve refuge-houses along the inside of the dyke for the people who live in the district.[105]

---

[105] OLB: *The Writings of Adelbrost and Apollonia*, Chapter 7.

Throughout the book we gain the impression that materialism was not a prominent part of their creed which then poses the problem: What motivated them? Apparently their greatest ideals lay in the adventure of exploration, valour and community service, that is, acceptance, honour and status conferred on them by their fellow citizens. This was possibly the single most important factor that allowed them the extraordinary feats they accomplished. If one looks at the burghs they built with their protective walls, dykes or embattlements and moats, it may seem impossible to us that they could have achieved this without modern earthmoving equipment and machinery. They also did not employ slaves and therefore the building of these citadels had to be a collective effort that involved everybody.

Apollonia described the earthworks around her burgh thus:

> Around the burgh is a ring dyke, with a moat three times
> seven feet deep and three times twelve feet wide,
>   and
> The ring dyke around is an hour long — not a seaman's hour,
> but an hour of the sun, of which two times twelve go to a day.[106]

To understand their concept of expressing distance in terms of time, we have to find some means of converting a unit of time to a unit of length or distance. We know that the average person walking at a moderate pace covers about four kilometres per hour. When Apollonia stated that the fortification around her city was an hour long, it means that a person would have walked four kilometres in circumscribing the citadel. This would equate to a square with its sides all being one kilometre long, or one square kilometre.

This citadel, which Apollonia described as being larger than other citadels, was apparently not as big as the one at Walhallagara, the senior citadel. The citadel of Fryasburch, the capital where the Folk Mother resided, was the largest. Apollonia's citadel at the north end of the Liudgarda, if it was square, would have comprised an area of about one hundred hectares, and in the case of a circular shape, it could have

---

[106] OLB: The Writings of Adelbrost and Apollonia, Chapter 7.

been as much as 127 hectares. The moat alone would have been over 300 000 cubic metres, or about 600 000 metric tons, excavated.

Other incidences where they referred to distance in terms of time were, among others, the establishment of Athens. They built the city an hour, or four kilometres in our terms, from the harbour. In another place they say that Waraburch was three hours south of Medeasblik – by our reckoning then, 12 kilometres.

In the 19th century when the Oera Linda Book was discovered, nobody entertained any ideas of an advanced civilised people north of the Alps in pre-Roman times. We now know, however, that Appolonia's description matches modern day archaeological finds all over Europe. This is undeniable evidence that the Oera Linda Book is based on facts.

Textiles and Jewelry

On page 3 of book VII of his *Odyssey*, Homer mentioned the weaving abilities of the Phaeacian women:

> As the Phaeacians are the best sailors in the world, so <u>their women excel all others in weaving</u>, for Minerva has taught them all manner of useful arts, and they are very intelligent.

In the Writings of Adelbrost and Appolonia, the following eulogy in honour of Adela also mentions their textile manufacturing:

> <u>Her blouse is linen, her tunic[107] wool</u>; these <u>she spun and wove herself.</u> How could she add to her beauty? Not with pearls, for her teeth were whiter; not with gold, for her tresses were more brilliant; not with precious stones, for her eyes, though soft as those of a lamb, were so lustrous that you could scarcely look into them.
>
> Come, distant-living[108] friend. The birds of the forest fled before the numerous visitors. Come friend, you must hear her wisdom.

---

[107] Old Frisian: *Tohnekka*; English: *To the neck, Tunic.*
[108] A *distance* of more than 2500 years!

*By the gravestone of which mention is made in her tribute, mom's body
is buried. Upon the stone they had written the following words:
"Do not pass in haste, for here lays Adela"*[109]

The textile manufacturing mentioned by both Homer in 1200
BC and by Appolonia in 530 BC here is typical of what archaeologists
have discovered. Please note the variety of colourful textiles on the
following photograph:

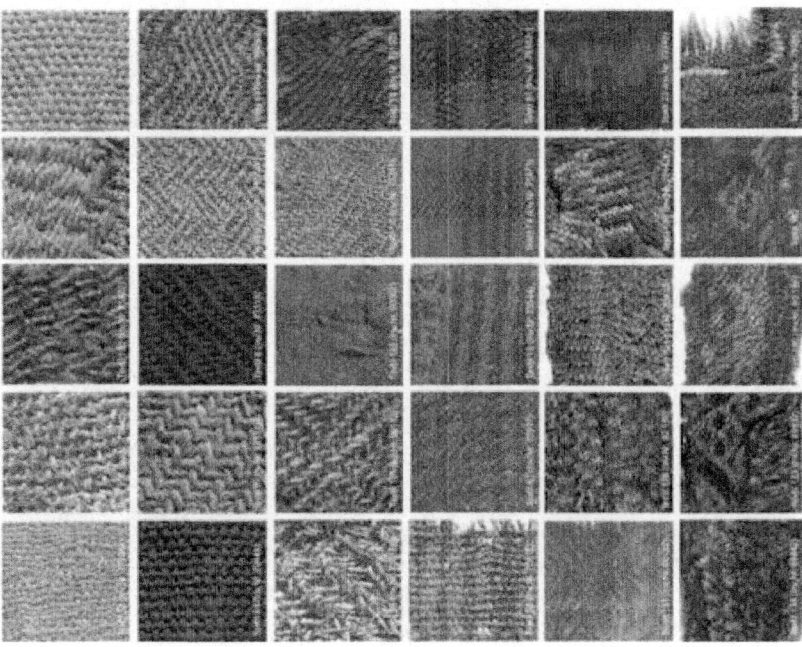

Figure 21: 10th to 9th c. BC textiles found at Hallstatt
(With acknowledgement to Heather Smith: *Celtic Clothing during the
Iron Age – a very broad and generic approach*[110])

---

[109] OLB: *The writings of Apollonia,* Chapter 3.
[110]http://www.academia.edu/1488040/Celtic_Clothing_During_the_Iron_Age-
_A_Very_Broad_and_Generic_Approach

Archaeologists are increasingly coming to the realization that the *West Europeans* were, by-and-large, a very affluent society. Numerous pieces of gold jewelry have been unearthed such as golden torques, bracelets and brooches. Appolonia testified to the same:

Just as at Staveren, the girls wore golden crowns on their heads, and rings on their arms and ankles[111]

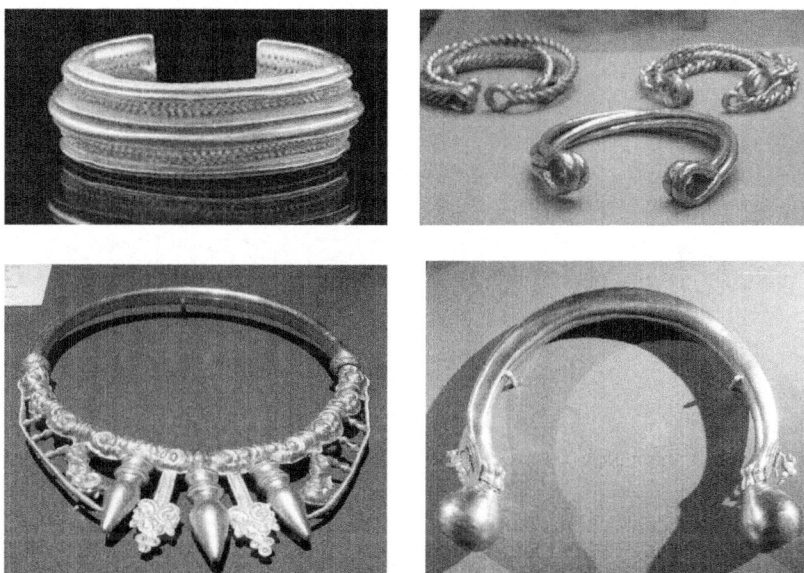

Figure 22: Celtic Gold Jewelry found at archaeological sites.

The Oera Linda Book describes the prominent roles that women played in their society. Their extensive training and leadership was highly respected. Now archaeology shows that women seem to have filled important positions in the Hallstatt and La Tène cultures. Nowhere else in history or archaeology do we find such an extensive display of females in high positions. If the Oera Linda Book was a 19th century fabrication, how did the author(s) manage to get this right?

---

111 OLB: The Writings of Adelbrost and Appolonia, Chapter 7.

In chapter four of the Writings of Konered in the Oera Linda Book (ca 250 BC), Konered tells the story of Adel Atharik's wife, Ifkja. She was sent from Suobaland (Swabia) in present day Baden-Württemberg by her father to Fryasburg in the Netherlands to be trained as a burgh matron. She thus hailed from the broader Heuneberg region.

In chapter three of the *Writings of Beden* (ca 200 BC) in the Oera Linda Book, we read about the travels of the burgh matron Reintja, who was famed for her wisdom. She travelled from the Netherlands to Denmark and then along the Baltic to Lithuania. From here she proceeded through the Twisklands (Poland, Czechia, Germany) to the Rhine and back to the Netherlands. All along her journey she made speeches in all the markets and in all the assemblies. From this it is obvious that she could travel freely and in relative safety. She may even have delivered her speeches in citadels or oppidums such as Manching, Heuneberg, Bliesbruck-Reinheim and Hochdorf. Beden made the following observation:

> *Among the Twisklanders many bad customs of the Tartars and Magyars have crept in, but likewise many of our laws have remained. Therefore, they still have matrons who teach the children and advise the old.*

From the above it seems quite reasonable to suspect that the female remains we find in many of the sumptuous grave mounds dating from the first millennium BC are those of the highly esteemed Burgh Matrons described in the Oera Linda Book.

Figure 23: Reconstruction of the Hochdorf *Celtic* Grave

So, there we have the Fryan Federation – the Federation of Free People. They wore clean linen shirts and had flowers in their gardens. They enjoyed hot baths and dressed up for dances. The girls used moisturizer for their skins. They had spacious houses with separate bedrooms for all, linen rooms, kitchens and reception areas. They had dedicated washing areas and cisterns (Laundromats!) for their laundry downstream from their towns. They buried their dead in graves and erected tombstones.

Their gardens and orchards were walled in with gates. They ploughed the fields and had cattle, horses, mules and sheep. Even today Friesland cows and horses are still much sought after. They had public parks and botanical gardens and practiced nature conservation. They appointed foresters to prevent indiscriminate destruction of woodlands and burghomeisters were responsible for overseeing the maintenance of public amenities.

The Frisian constitution, or Tex, as well as their laws, were displayed on public buildings. They had compulsory schooling with a curriculum that included reading, writing, history, arithmetic, religion, music, botany and social responsibilities. They had a Police Academy where dedicated officers received tuition in law, weapons training and commerce.

The Frisians had a social democracy and free elections. Frisian men and women attended council meetings. The women spun wool and made linen garments. They had strict rules for business and had factories all over Europe. Their ships traded in distant countries and circumnavigated the world while at home they had horse and mule-drawn carts. All this happened while marauding nomads inhabited the Asian Plains and in the Middle East people were living in tents and trekked after pastures for their livestock.

From Homer, archaeological finds and the Oera Linda Book we find a highly developed people with a lifestyle and values quite similar to our own. Even long before Homer, in 2200 BC, we read that the Frisians were already at this level - and in all probability long before that. We read that 4200 years ago West Europeans were using iron-age weapons and tools when the rest of humanity was still in the stone and bronze ages. Their Iron Age status will be examined later.

Literacy and the Yule

We have seen that every claim in the Oera Linda Book we have investigated thus far is supported by other ancient scribes, archaeology and/or other sciences; from the 2193 BC event to their lifestyle. Most of this information was not available in the 19th century. The very fact that the Oera Linda Book exists and accurately describes these should dispel any notion that the book is a hoax or that the ancient West Europeans were illiterate.

The Oera Linda Book's disclosures, however, do not stop there. The book also makes the preposterous claims that the Fryans invented the concept of the 24 hour day, the *Greek* Alphabet and *Hindu-Arabian* numerals. By now the reader should be accustomed to the fact that we should not reject the book's extravagant claims outright though.

As regards the origin of the 24-hour day, nobody seems to know for certain where this came from. Theories vary from the Egyptians having counted hours by their finger joints, to the lunar cycles in a year and even decan stars. In terms of our alphabet, we are taught that it originated from the Greeks even though the Greeks admit that they do not know where they received it from. Others sometimes give the credit to the Phoenicians, the Egyptians or the Sumerians. Our *Hindu-Arabic* numerals 1 to 9 supposedly evolved from the Brahmi system although neither the Arabs nor the Indians used these numbers. The Indian mathematician Aryabhatta is given the credit and Brahmagupta is said to have introduced the symbol zero 100 years later in the 6th century AD. Yet, for thousands of years before people were building pyramids, temples and palaces. They drew up bills of quantities for construction and purchase. International trade and commerce thrived and the logistics for massive military campaigns had to be calculated. Complex astronomical calculations and other scientific work were done. Without a proper system of numerals, these feats would not seem to have been possible.

The Oera Linda Book gives us the most credible answer to date. By deduction, we may conclude that time, the 24-hour day, our alphabet and our numerals are all based on the relationship between the radius and the circumference of a circle, which they called the Yule. In Chapter 20 in the Book of Adela's Followers, we read the following:

What is written hereunder is inscribed on the walls of Waraburch

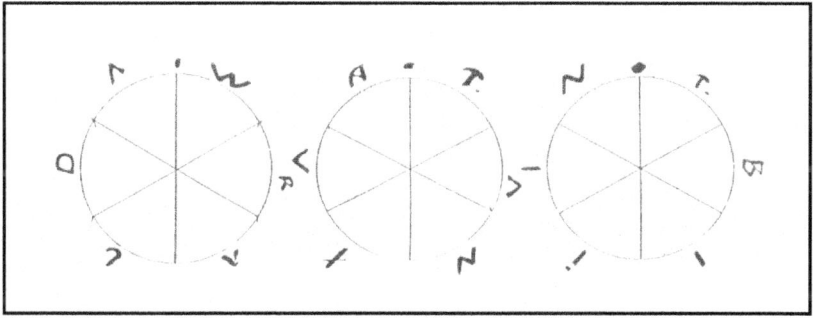

Figure 24: Signs of the Yule

What   appear above are the signs of the Yule. It is the first symbol of Wralda, also of the start or beginning from which time came, that is, the carrier, which must forever go around with the Yule.

From this Frya formed the set hand which she used for her Tex. When Fasta was Honorary Mother, she made running or continuous script from it. The Witking, that is Sea King, Godfreiath the Old, made separate numbers for both set and running script. It is therefore not too much that we have an annual festival to celebrate it.

We must eternally bring thanks to Wralda that he let his spirit flow so strongly over our forefathers.

In her time, Finda also invented a script but it was so pompous and full of flourishes and curls that her descendants soon lost the meaning of it. Afterwards they learned our writing, namely the Finns, the Thyrians and the Krekalander. But, they did not understand fully that it was taken from the Yule and that it always had to be written round like the sun. They also wanted their script to be illegible to other nations because they always had secrets. In doing this, they went quite astray, to the extend that the children could barely read and understand the writings of their elders; whilst our most ancient writings can be read as though it was written yesterday.

Here is the set script, under that the running script, followed by the numbers for both:

Figure 25: The Frisian Alphabet

In ca 550 BC, Apollonia, the daughter of Adela, wrote:

Outside our burgh wall is the place where the Burgtheeren (officers?) and the soldiers live. The ringdyke around is an hour long—

not a seaman's hour, but an hour of the sun, of which two times twelve go to a day.[112]

To the Frisians the circle was the perfect geometrical shape and the first symbol they received from an unalterable God. From the above we can see that a circle, or Yule, represented the cyclical nature of time, and time was called the carrier. Apollonia tells us that they had 24 hours in a day. The question now is why 24? Why not 20, or 32, or whatever? To understand this we first have to look at how they derived their writing system from this *holy* symbol, the circle.

They realised that there was an unalterable relationship between a circle and its radius. This is best explained by means of the following diagrams:

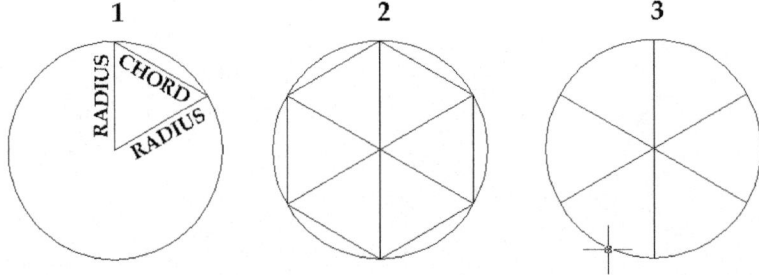

Figure 26: Origins of the Yule

Diagram 1 shows an equilateral triangle drawn from the centre of a circle with the three sides being equal to the radius. In diagram 2, we then show that there are six such equilateral triangles in a circle. From this, we get to diagram 3, which is what the Frisians called the sign of the Yule around which they designed their whole alphabet and numerals – including the figure 0.

The following figure shows the Oera Linda Book's ciphers, including the number 0, which were designed around the Yule. These

---

[112] OLB: *The writings of Adelbrost and Apollonia,* Chapter 7.

are compared to the ciphers found in the Moorish palace of Alhambra in Spain[113] which exclude the number 0.

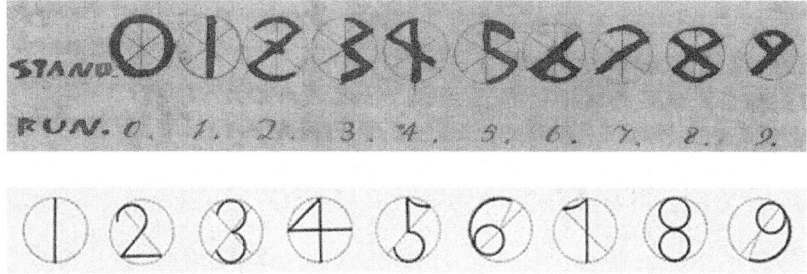
Figure 27: Oera Linda Book and Alhambra numerals

Many seem to take these numerals in the Alhambra Palace as proof that these ciphers were invented by the Muslims. The fact, however, is that the 700 year sojourn of the Moors in Spain meant that they were quite isolated from the rest of the Muslim world and more subjected to European influences. The unique numerals and especially the unique artwork are not repeated anywhere else in Muslim palaces and mosques. Clearly this uniqueness can only be ascribed to European artisans in the employ of the Spanish Moslems at the time.

What is even more astonishing is that our modern Western alphabet and numerals, with a base 10 system of calculation, are older than 4200 years. It did not come from the Greeks or the Phoenicians or the Arabians, Indians or whoever. No doubt, this will create a lot of controversy but, as with most of the facts in the Oera Linda Book, this description is the most credible.

To represent time the Frisians also turned to this holy, unalterable, or God-given symbol:

---

[113] *The Arabian antiquities of Spain,* by James Cavanah Murphy, London 1813

4   **5**

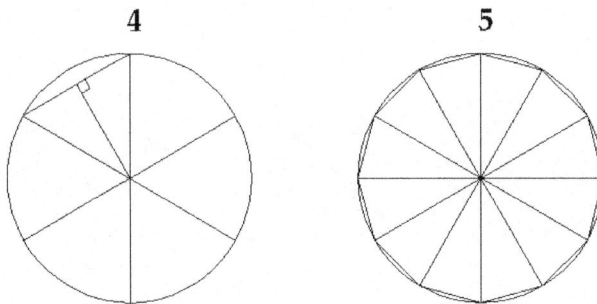

Figure 28: Dividing the Yule into 12 segments

From the sign of the Yule, they now drew a line from the centre of the circle perpendicular to the opposite chord as shown in diagram 4. This obviously halves the equilateral triangle. By doing this to all the triangles we now derive 12 segments in the circle as shown in diagram 5. Could this be the origin of the Egyptian base 12 System? Even in western societies the number twelve has a prominent role e.g. a dozen, a gross (12x12), 12 inches to a foot, 12 times tables, etc. The old Frisians, although they had a base ten system of numerals, often counted in multiples of twelve. We read for example that the Gertmanne stayed in India for twelve times a hundred years and two times ten years.

Having only 12 hours, that is six during the day and six at night, however, would have been impractical. Each of these segments are therefore halved again in exactly the same way as before and now we have 24 segments or 12 hours in a day and 12 hours in a night as shown in diagrams 6 and 7. They started counting their hours from when the sun was exactly overhead, or noon, which was the only fixed point that did not change by the seasons.

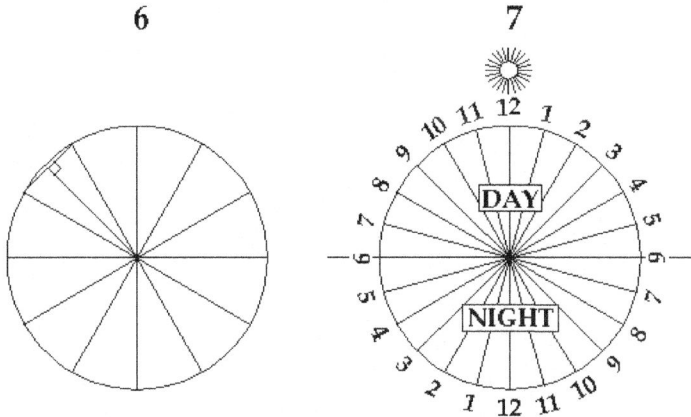

Figure 29: The 24-hour day

There we have the 24-hour day based on trigonometry - more than 4200 years old!

A note on Welsh Tin Mining

We know that tin mining had been practiced in Wales for more than four millennia. Popular belief has it that the industry was started by the Phoenicians from the Eastern Mediterranean in ca 2000 BC. The Oera Linda Book, however, claims that the Fryans were mining tin in Westland or Wales since time immemorial. The Phoenicians were merely traders in the metal. We do not have any evidence from anywhere in the world that the Phoenicians ever mastered the intricacies of mining and geology. The Oera Linda Book's account seems much more credible. The book also states that Britannia was their penal colony where the inmates were sentenced to hard labour in the tin mines. Millennia later the British, in much the same way, used Australia as a penal colony.

Shortly after 2000 BC, the exiled Sea King Tunis went into partnership with the Phoenicians. He introduced them to international trade and, more importantly, the skills to navigate and sail on the open seas. No doubt they were also introduced to the supply of tin from Wales. If we accept the Oera Linda Book's account, it is quite possible that this was the first time that the Phoenicians were exposed to the Fryans' numerals.

It is interesting to note that the mining practices and technology developed over thousands of years by these ancient Frisians were applied in South Africa during the late 19th and early 20th centuries AD, when tin and coal miners were imported from Wales to develop the coal, diamond and gold mining industries. In the South African mining industry these miners from Cornwall became known as the *Cousin Jacks*.

The claims of the Oera Linda Book sound incredible, but let us examine their story further. Once we know what to look for, the picture that emerges is quite unbelievable.

Chapter 3

Legacy of the Outcasts

Foreigners from the East[114]

One hundred and one years (2092 BC) after the global disaster that caused the submersion of the Oera Linda Book's *Aldland*, migrants from the East moved into North Eastern Scandinavia, or *Skenland*, as the Frisians called it. They were the descendants of the refugees who fled central Asia and Mongolia during and after the 2193 BC event and had adapted to a nomadic lifestyle.

Although the north-eastern parts of Finland were part of the Fryan Federation, these Fryans or Proto-Frisians hardly had a presence there and were not prepared to go to war over the matter. They were the second, third and fourth generations after the Deluge. The oldest of them had only heard the tales of the disaster from their grandfathers. As with north-western Europe, Scandinavia was now much colder than before the 4.2 ka BP Event and the north-eastern parts of Finland were much more inhospitable. These Proto-Frisians had already lost most of their dominion around the Mediterranean from the scourge of a hundred years earlier and smaller groups of roving bandits nearer to home kept them occupied. A political settlement or denial of this new

---

[114] OLB: The Book of Adela's followers, Chapter 23

threat in the Far North must, therefore, have seemed much more attractive.

The leader of the nomads who arrived in Finland was a despotic Priest-King with the title of *Magi*. The rest of the ruling classes, or oligarchy, was called *Magyarar*. While the Magyarar possessed bronze weapons, their Neolithic subordinates or slaves were equipped with stone weapons. The latter were kept in check by the Magyarar through superstition and witchcraft. They were named *Finnar* by the Frisians. This was because they were regarded as Asians, otherwise known as descendants of Finda. Mention is made of a third group of *Wild Shepherds* who were continuously *snapping at the heels* of the Magyarar.

Let us compare the Oera Linda account with our modern theories:

> *One hundred and one years after Aldland sank, a people came out of the East. That people was driven out by another nation. Beyond our Twiskland* <u>*they fell into dispute, divided into two groups, and each went its own way.*</u>
>
> *Of the one group no account came to us, but the other group went to the back of our Skenland. Skenland was sparsely populated and the back the least of all. Therefore they were able to conquer it without contest, and as they did no other harm, we did not wish to make war.*
>
> *Now that we have learned to know them, we want to write about their customs, and after that how matters went between us. They were not wild people, like many of Finda's race but, they are like the Egiptalandar; they have priests like them and in their churches they also have statues.*
>
> *The priests are the only masters; they call themselves Magyarar, and their headman is known as Magy. He is high priest and king in one. The rest of the people are of no account, and under their rule. These people do not even have a name but we call them Finna[115] because although their festivals are all melancholic and bloody, they are so formal that we are inferior to them in that respect. They are not to be envied, though, because they are slaves to their priests, and much more*

---

[115] Fins

to their creeds. They believe that evil spirits are everywhere and enter into people and animals, but of Wralda's spirit they know nothing. They have stone weapons, the Magyarar of copper. The Magyarar claims that they can exorcise and recall evil spirits. The people are always in dreadful fear and there is never any joy to be seen on their faces.[116]

Modern linguists tell us that the Finnish language, which belongs to the Finno-Permic language group, is the most closely related language to Estonian and Hungarian. Hungary, though, is some 1200 kilometres away. The Hungarian language belongs to the Ugric group which has developed in parallel with the Finno-Permic languages some 4000 years ago. The Finno-Permic and Ugric groups, both of the Uralic language family, would appear <u>to have parted ways west of the Ural Mountains</u> – precisely what the Oera Linda Book tells us. The book even tells us that the split happened 4000 years ago; again, precisely what modern researchers are proposing. Must we believe that this is another wild guess of the nineteenth century authors? Neither of these language groups is related to the Indo-European languages.

The Hungarians still refer to themselves as Magyar, a name which, according to the Oera Linda Book, goes back to more than 4000 years to what used to be a priestly order called the Magyarar. Present-day scholars believe that the name Magyar might have been derived from the name or title *Muageris* or *Mugel.* This would then be the Oera Linda Book's *Magy.*

The Oera Linda Book mentions a dispute between two groups beyond Twiskland after which they separated. The one group migrated to Finland and the other group disappeared. It would be reasonable to assume that this second group eventually settled in the region of Hungary and further south into the Balkans and Greece. This split is precisely what researchers find in their studies and would answer the Frisians' 4000 year old question as to what happened to the second group.

---

[116] OLB: Book of Adela's followers, Chapter 23.

The Altai Mountains in central Asia where Russia, China, Mongolia and Kazakhstan come together have been identified by scientists as the point of origin of a rapid and massive migration of peoples into distant parts of Europe and Asia at the start of the second millennium BC. Again we find the suggestion of the 2193 BC event and once more it corresponds with the Oera Linda Book. It is noteworthy that the region continues to experience periodic seismic activity.

The traditional religion of the indigenous Altaians is called Shamanism. This is a set of beliefs and practices whereby practioners communicate with the supernatural. A shamanist priest is known as a shaman who acts as an intermediary between the human and spirit worlds. They are supposedly capable of entering supernatural realms to provide answers for humans and to treat illnesses. Shamanism dates back to the Neolithic period and perhaps even as far back as the Paleolithic. The religion was practiced throughout the Iron Age by the Fino-Baltic peoples and also infiltrated the various Teutonic tribes.

In later Greek Mythology we find aspects of Shamanism, especially in their symbolic and mystic practices, having blended with elements of Greek paganism and Frisian monotheism. Shamanic practices later merged into Roman religion. The Oera Linda Book's description of the Magyarar's religion is an exact match of that of Shamanism.

In terms of DNA mapping, we find that the Y-chromosome haplogroup R1a seems to have its highest concentration (+50%) in the Altai mountain region. From there it reduces towards Russia (±45%) and further still to central Europe (±40%) and Scandinavia (±20%). In Poland we find R1a to be more than 50% of the DNA profile of the general population, and in Hungary about 40%. In Greece the number drops to about 10%. Another major branch of R1a is found through Kyrgyzstan into India.

In light of the aforementioned it may be reasonable to suspect that the Magyarar were the carriers of this R1a haplogroup and that they originated from central Asia. Altai means *Gold Mountain* and the Oera Linda Book mentions that the Magyarar possessed substantial quantities of the metal. Gold is still mined in the Altai region.

The second group we need to look at here is what the Oera Linda Book calls the Finna. It is evident that they were not merely a lower social order of the Magyarar, but a distinctly different ethnic group as their stone weaponry would suggest. They may well have been members of what archaeologists call the *Comb Ceramic Culture*; a group of settlers from the East that settled in Scandinavia at the same time as the Magyarars. There is a strong suspicion that they may have been related to the Yakuts (Haplogroup N) who originated from the Baikal Lake area north of Mongolia. The Yakuts practiced shamanism and also has genetic ties with the Nenets in northern Russia. The general population of the Sami in Scandinavia has about 40% of this haplogroup.

This episode is further proof that the Oera Linda Book is a credible document.

The influx of migrants from the East was part of the mass migration we saw in the Middle East and Egypt after the catastrophe of 2193 BC. It is interesting to note that we here find two distinctly different groups of people, originally being refugees, banding together for mutual support and protection. As we have seen, and from the description in the Oera Linda Book, the pagan Magyarar were very militant and regimental in their lifestyle and they dabbled in the occult. This sounds quite similar to the Hittites who settled in Anatolia at about the same time.

The Oera Linda Book mentions that the *People of Finda* experienced a similar catastrophe in the East in 2193 BC. In addition, the book claims that the Easterners' country was also submerged:

> In earlier times most of Finda's people lived together in their motherland, namely[117] Aldland, which now lies under the sea. They were thus far away and therefore we had no need for wars. When they were driven away and came hither to plunder, national defence, commanders, kings and war followed.[118]

---

[117] Could also be translated to mean: *Called (also?) Aldland.* This quotation creates quite a difference of opinion. Did the Fryans and the Findas each have their own Aldland or was there only one?

[118] OLB: The book of Adela's followers, Chapter 7.

The Outcasts

For the next 80 years the Magy kept his subjects under control but in 2012 BC they attacked the Fryan Colony in Skenland. The Magyarar and Finnar advance was brought to a halt by the Skenland citizen force close to its provincial capital Godahisburch – possibly present-day Gothenburg in Sweden. When the Fryan Federal Government was finally notified of the attack, they responded with a combined force of ships, marines and the army. With their superior iron weaponry the Frisians defeated the Magyarar decisively and the Magy begged for a truce. It would appear that he quite literally offered a peace pipe – stuffed with marijuana, opium or the likes. He enticed the young army general or Warrior King Wodin of the Fryan army to become king of the Magyarar. Wodin duly accepted. Under Fryan law he would have held the position of general for three years only but under the Magyarar his monarchy would have been for life. Instead of an electorate he would now have had subjects and slaves.

When Wodin returned, the Magi gave him his daughter to wife. Thereupon he was smoked with herbs, but they were magic herbs because he gradually became so audacious that he disavowed and ridiculed the spirits of Frya and Wralda whilst bending his free head before the false monstrous statues.[119]

Wodin subsequently defeated the Magyarar's other enemies, the *wild shepherds*, who led their charges on horseback. He then married the Magy's daughter. From this union a son was born and seven years later Wodin disappeared. The pagan Magy declared that Wodin had ascended to the gods and would therefore continue to be their ruler. His grandson, being the direct descendant of a deity, would be the undisputed future king of the Magyarar. The Magy would be steward of the crown, or regent, until the future monarch would have become of age. Thus the mythological Wodin or Odin, the Norse god

---

[119] OLB: The book of Adela's followers, Chapter 23

of war, came into being – possibly with the assistance of a drug overdose.

This acceptance of the crown of their enemy by Wodin went completely against the Frisian creed but neither the general of the marines, Sea King Tunis, nor his brother, Admiral Inka, did anything to stop Wodin from continuing with what must have been tantamount to high treason. Perhaps with the wisdom they obtained from drugs they saw this as a political solution to the Magyarar problem. It would appear that although individual states enjoyed a fair amount of autonomy, the Federal Government would have had to sanction such a far-reaching departure from their constitution. It is near impossible to imagine that such a sanction would have been forthcoming in any event. Not only did they not drive out the Magyarar after defeating them in battle, they in effect legitimized a foreign government within their own boundaries. By not arresting Wodin, who was their cousin, the two brothers became accomplices to the fact. In centuries to come this foothold of the Magyarar and their subordinate Finnar proved to be a major factor in the demise of the Fryan Federation.

Tunis and Inka stayed in Skenland for a total of 12 years ostensibly as a peacekeeping force. This in itself must have been a further contravention of Frisian law as their election to the positions was only for three years. With the disappearance of their cousin Wodin, the good life at the Magyarar court was over. They wanted to elect a new king but the Magy would have nothing of the sort. He must have realized that Tunis and Inka's positions had weakened substantially. They had not only lost a number of their ships and combatants who went back to Frisia but also lost the support of the Fryan Federation. They would not be able to call for reinforcements.

We do not know what other misdeeds the impetuous brothers committed in Skenland but when they wanted to return to Frisia in 2000 BC, the Folk Mother, Minna, refused to let them set foot on land anywhere in Denmark and along the west coast of Frisia. It is most likely that they would have been arrested and banished to the tin mines in Britannia or they would have been executed for treason. Thus they became outcasts.

It is clear that drugs played a significant role in the Fryan Federation's loss of Sweden. This may further explain why Tunis and

Inka did not take action against Wodin. The Magy would have kept them in supply as well.

It is strange that they were allowed to get away with a fleet of Fryan ships. Perhaps they now possessed the greater part of the Fryan Fleet or the main fleet was not available to accost them being on some trade mission elsewhere. In any event, the renegades were not captured.

Tunis and Inka proceeded with their fleet, which by now had a number of Finnar and Magyarar in their crews, (and possibly also wives) to *Kadik*, known to us today as *Cadiz* in Spain. The Burgh Matron of Kadik, Tutia, allowed them to replenish their supplies but, being refugees, she would not give them asylum. The two brothers in arms and in blood now realized that they had lost their last chance of redeeming themselves in the Federation.

Cadiz is regarded as one of the oldest inhabited towns in Europe. In his Jewish Antiquities, Book 1, Chapter 6.1, written in ca 90 AD, Flavius Josephus mentions Cadiz as one of the destinations of Noah's grandchildren:

> *Japheth, the son of Noah, had seven sons: they inhabited so, that, beginning at the mountains Taurus and Amanus, they proceeded along Asia, as far as the river Tanais (Tanis), and along Europe to Cadiz;*

The Taurus Mountains are in Turkey and the Tanais is today known as the River Don in Russia.

The Founding of Tyre

The Oera Linda Book continues with the history of Nef (Cousin) Tunis and the founding of Tyre in Phoenicia:

> *Thus sailing along the coast they came at last to the colony of Kadik[120], so called because the harbour was formed by a stone quay*

---

[120] Cadiz, Spain

(stone dyke). Here they bought all kinds of supplies but Tutia the Burgh Matron, would not allow them to settle there. When they were ready, they began to quarrel.

Tunis wanted to sail through the straits of the Middle Sea to enter the service of the rich king of Egiptalandum as he had done before, but Inka said he had had enough of all those Finda's people. Inka thought that perchance some high-lying part of Atland might have remained as an island, where he and his people might live in peace.

As the two cousins could not agree, Tunis planted a red flag on the beach, and Inka a blue one. Then every one could choose whom he wanted to follow, and amazingly, most of the Finna and Magyarar walked over to Inka, who had refused to serve the kings of Finda's people. When they had counted the people and divided the ships accordingly, the fleets separated. We heard of Nef Tunis afterwards, but nothing ever of Inka.

Nef Tunis sailed along the coast through the gateway of the Middle Sea. When Atland was submerged there was also much suffering on the shores of the Middle Sea. As a result many people from Finda's land came to our Heinde- and Fere Krekalanda and also many from Lyda's land. There were also many of our people that went to Lyda's land[121]. The result of all this was that the Heinde- and Fere Krekalanda were lost to the rule of the Mother. Tunis had counted on this. He therefore wished to choose a good harbour from which he might go and sail for the rich rulers but, as his fleet and his people looked so dilapidated, the Kadhemer (coastal people) thought they were pirates, and everywhere drove them away.

At last they came to the Phonisius coast, one hundred and ninety-three years after Atland was submerged.[122] Near the coast he found an island with two deep bays, so that there appeared to be three islands. On the middle one they established their hideout, and afterwards built a rampart around it.

When they wanted to give it a name, they were in disagreement; some wanted to call it Fryasburch or Neftunia, but the Magyarar and the Finna begged that it be called Thyrhisburch. Thyr

---

[121] The progenitors of the Berbers in North Africa.
[122] 2000 BC

was the name of one of their idols and it was on his day of commemoration that they landed there. In return they would for ever recognize Tunis as their king. Tunis let himself be persuaded and the others did not want to go to war about it.[123]

In time, *Thyrhisburch* (*Thor-his-Burgh* or the *Burgh of Thor*) became *Tyre*. Modern day teaching has it that Tyre means Rock.

In Ezekiel 26:17 in the Bible, written some 1420 years later in ca 580 BC, we read the following in the prophecy Ezekiel pronounced over Tyre:

(17) And they will take up a lamentation for you (Tyre) and say to you: "How you have perished, O one inhabited by seafaring men, O renowned city, who was strong at sea.[124]

A direct translation of the same verse in the Afrikaans Bible is even more revealing:

How did you come to your end, O most famous city? You who have been inhabited from across the sea.

Both these Bibles have been translated from the original Greek and Hebrew texts. Tyre is the only city in the Middle East mentioned by the Bible to have been founded by a people from over the sea. This is exactly what the Oera Linda Book tells us and is clearly more vindication of the Oera Linda Book. This verse in the Bible clearly shows that the Phoenicians were introduced to maritime trade by a people from across the sea; exactly what the Oera Linda Book tells us. The Phoenicians, therefore, were not the instigators of international sea trade as everybody have been and are still taught.

The resourceful and entrepreneurial Sea King Tunis found himself on a barren island off the Phoenician coast with a decrepit fleet and an understaffed crew that was so haggard they looked like pirates. In order to survive, they had to get a share of the lucrative maritime

---

[123] OLB: The book of Adela's followers, Chapter 24.
[124] The New King James Version. 1996, c. 1982. Thomas Nelson: Nashville

trade. He therefore negotiated a partnership with the inhabitants of nearby Sidon, filled 12 ships with merchandise and set out on his first sales trip back to Frya's Land. So successful was Tunis in his endeavours that we read in other later accounts that the famous city of Tyre was sought after and attacked by virtually every great empire for almost three millennia, including Alexander the Great and the Romans. The ancient island city of Tyre was eventually sacked by the Muslims in 590 AD – almost 2600 years after Sea King Tunis had built his burgh there. Mainland Tyre, however, exists to this day as the city of Sūr in Southern Lebanon.

When this prodigal son of Frya returned to Frisia with a fleet laden with luxury goods, all was forgiven. Perhaps this was because he presented an opportunity for the Frisians to rekindle their glorious merchant status of bygone days. He was given a free trade concession and warehouse facilities in his old country and his business venture was set to take off. This also says a lot about Tunis' diplomatic and business acumen. In fact, so successful was his undertaking that it placed a stranglehold on the Fryan merchants who was subsequently given only temporary respite through state intervention – the merchants from Tyre were then only allowed seven ships a year to Flyland[125]:

> When they were well established, they set some old seamen and Magyarar ashore and onwards to the burgh Sidon, but at first the coastal people did not want to know anything about them.
>
> "You are only foreign drifters" they said, "whom we do not respect".
>
> When we wanted to sell them some of our iron weapons, however, it at last went well. They also greatly desired our amber and their inquiries about it had no end. But Tunis, who was far-sighted, pretended that he had no more iron weapons or amber. Then merchants came and begged him to let them have twenty vessels[126], which they would freight with the finest goods, and they would provide as many people to row as he would require. Twelve ships were then laden with

---

[125] Present day Flevoland around the Ijsselmeer and Markermeer in the Netherlands
[126] From this it is very clear that the Phoenicians did not have their own ships.

wine, honey and tanned leather, and in addition saddles and bridles mounted in gold, such as had never been seen before.

With all this treasure Tunis sailed into the Flymar. The count from West Flyland was so impressed with all these goods that he arranged that Tunis be allowed to have a warehouse at the mouth of the Flymar. Later the site was known as Almanaland and the market at Wyrringa where they bartered, the Toletmark.

The Mother advised that they should sell anything except iron weapons but nobody paid attention to her. As the Tyriar now had a free hand, they came to transport our goods near and far to the detriment of our own sailors. It was subsequently decided at a general assembly to allow only seven Thyriar ships per year and no more.[127]

Here we have possibly the first recorded attempt at arms control.

More than a thousand years after Tunis founded Tyre, in ca 856 BC, we find a further interesting account in the Bible. King Solomon of the Jews approached King Hiram of Tyre, an old friend of his late father, King David, to assist with the building of the Jewish Temple in Jerusalem:

1 Kings 5:18
So Solomon's builders, Hirams builders, and the Gebalites quarried them; and they prepared timber and stones to build the temple.[128]

2 Chronicles 2:11-13
(11) Then Hiram king of Tyre answered in writing, which he sent to Solomon: Because the Lord loves His people, He has made you king over them. (12) Hiram also said: "Blessed be the God of Israel, who made heaven and earth, for He has given King David a wise son, endowed with prudence and understanding, who will build a temple for the Lord and a royal house for himself.

---

[127] OLB: The book of Adela's followers, Chapter 24
[128] The New King James Version. 1996, c. 1982. Thomas Nelson: Nashville.

(13) And now I have sent a skilful man, endowed with understanding, Huram my master craftsman, the son of a woman of the daughters of Dan, and his father was a man of Tyre, skilled to work in gold and silver, bronze and iron, stone and wood, purple and blue, fine linen and crimson, and to make any engraving and to accomplish any plan which may be given to him, with your skilful men and with the skilful men of my lord David your father

2 Chronicles 4:11-16

(11) Then Huram made the pots and the shovels and the bowls.. So Huram finished doing the work that he was to do for King Solomon for the house of God: (12) The two pillars and the bowl-shaped capitals that were on top of the pillars; the two networks covering the bowl-shaped capitals which were on top of the pillars; (13) four hundred pomegranates for the two networks (two rows of pomegranates for each network to cover the two bowl-shaped capitals that were on the pillars); (14) he also made carts and the lavers on the carts; (15) one Sea and twelve oxen under it; (16) also the pots, the shovels, the forks – and all their articles Huram his master craftsman made of burnished for King Solomon for the house of the Lord.

Solomon mentioned that the Tyrians were exceptional artisans when it came to wood and stonework. From this account it is clear that Solomon's temple was built and decorated by means of West European technology and with the help of craftsmen of Frisian descent.

Almost 900 years later Jesus reprimanded the degenerated Jewish monotheists and compared them with the descendants of another previously monotheistic society:

Matthew 11;20-22

(20) Then He began to rebuke the cities in which most of His mighty works had been done because they did not repent: (21) "Woe to you Chorazin! Woe to you Bethsaida! For if the mighty works which were done in you had been done in Tyre and Sidon hey would have repented long ago in sackcloth and ashes. (22) But I say to you, it will be more tolerable for Tyre and Sidon in the Day of Judgement than for you.

It is also interesting to note that nearby Sidon never achieved the fame and splendour of the Fryan-found Tyre. The Phoenicians could not quite make it without the north-west European influence.

In his e-book *From Goddess to King*, Anthony Radford makes the observation that it would have been unlikely for the Phoenicians to have become a sea faring nation of note without hard European oak and riverside building facilities. The quantity and quality of the Lebanon cedars would not have sufficed. It must be borne in mind that they not only acquired ships for themselves, but also sold large numbers to the Egyptians. The Oera Linda Book's account of how they obtained these, and the skills, from the sea kings and ship builders from the Rhine, seems more than just credible.

The founding of Marseille

As the Tyrian trade relationship with Frya's Land improved, they approached the Folk Mother with a seemingly harmless request – to sell to them some small islands four kilometres off the European coast in the North Western Mediterranean to serve as a halfway station on the long sea voyages from Phoenicia to Frisia. The Fryan General Assembly debated the request, the folk mother granted permission and a harbour was built. Tunis now had bases in both the Eastern and Western Mediterranean, both of which were destined to become world famous cities.

The Tyrians, however, did not keep this new harbour all to themselves but also allowed their pagan Sidonese partners to use the facilities thereby strengthening their Mediterranean monopoly against the Frisian merchants. The disillusioned Frisians soon realized their error and called the decision of their political leaders, to grant the Tyrians and Sidonese permission to build a harbour, a dung sale – in ancient Fries, Misselia. The four small islands are known today as the Frioul archipelago and Misselia as the city of Marseille. The motto of the city of Marseille, 4000 years later, still refers to this ancient name:

Actibus immensis urbs fulget Massiliensis – By her great deeds, the city of Massilia shines.

We may assume that the ancient Fryan meaning was lost over time. Writing some 1500 years later in the 5th century BC, the Greek historian, Thucydides, referred to Massalia as having been founded in 600 BC by Ionian Greeks from Phocaea, an ancient city on the west coast of Anatolia. Not only was he wrong about the founders of Marseilles, but his timing was also out by 1400 years. We shall come back to the Ionians a little later.

The Hyksos

We have to digress from Sea King Tunis and the Oera Linda Book to create a greater understanding of later developments. A very fascinating sequel to the deployment of Tunis's merchant navy in the Mediterranean relates to the mysterious Hyksos Rulers of Lower Egypt during the Second Intermediate Period. This period followed the Middle Kingdom in ancient Egypt. Hyksos is *Heqa Khasewet* in Egyptian and means *Foreign Rulers* or *Sheppard-kings*.

Whilst Egyptian chronology may sometimes seem quite complicated, the following table reflects a fairly accurate picture. The Fifteenth Dynasty of the Hyksos foreigners ruled between the indigenous Twelfth and Eighteenth Dynasties in Lower Egypt. The Twelfth Dynasty ruled from 1991 BC to 1803 BC towards the end of the Middle Kingdom and is regarded by subsequent Egyptians as their most affluent indigenous dynasty. Senusret III (Sesostris III), who ruled from 1878 to 1860 BC, was the greatest of these pharaohs. His success is attributed to the expansion of trade outside Egypt's borders which appears to have commenced from ca. 1998 BC onwards.

Table 1: Hyksos in Egyptian Chronology

Pharaohs/Kings	Reign (BC)			Remarks
	From	To	Period	
Eleventh Dynasty (Middle Kingdom - Indigenous Egyptians)				
Nebhetepre	2060	2010	50	
Sankhkare Mentuhotep III	2010	1998	12	
Nebtawyre Mentuhotep IV	1997	1991	6	
Twelfth Dynasty (One of greatest indigenous dynasties)				
Amenemhat I	1991	1962	29	
Senusret I (Sesostris I)	1971	1926	45	
Amenemhat II	1929	1895	34	
Senusret II (Sesostris II)	1897	1878	19	Tyre Founded 2000 BC
Senusret III (Sesostris III)	1878	1860	18	
Amenemhat III	1860	1815	45	
Amenemhat IV	1815	1807	8	
Sobekneferu	1807	1803	4	Female
Fifteenth Dynasty - Hyksos (Foreign Rulers - Manetho) 254 yrs				
Salatis	1779	1766	13	
Bnon (Beon)	1766	1722	44	Note Germanic type names
Apachnar (Khyan)	1722	1685	37	
Ianas	1685	1635	50	
Apophis	1635	1574	61	
Assis	1574	1525	49	
Eighteenth Dynasty (New Kingdom - Indigenous Egyptians)				
Ahmose I (Nebpehtyre)	1550	1525	25	
Ahmenhotep	1525	1504	21	

It should come as no surprise to us that the commencement of Egypt's international trade in 1998 BC happened at almost exactly the same time as the Tyrian or ex-Fryan merchants appeared in the area in ca 2000 BC as described in the Oera Linda Book. Again, how could a 19th century prankster have guessed this if the Oera Linda Book was a hoax? When Tunis and Inca parted ways in Kadik in 2000 BC, Tunis mentioned that he intended to go and work for the Egyptians with whom he had dealings before:

> *Tunis wanted to sail through the straits of the Middle Sea to enter the service of (sail for) the rich king of Egiptalandum as he had done before, but Inka said he had had enough of all those Finda's people.*[129]

It thus seems reasonable to suspect that Tunis indeed went to trade with or for the Pharaohs of Egypt. We have seen how the Tyrians acquired Misselia from the Fryans. The Tyrians may have approached the Pharaoh with an equally innocent request: A merchant navy needs a harbour and dry-docks or workshops for ship repairs. Their buyers, sellers and other administrative staff need offices. They need warehouses for imports and exports as well as accommodation for their crews and housing for their staff and their families. They need schools and community centres. No doubt, *Hyksos International Trading Company (HITCO)*[130] negotiated these arrangements with the Egyptian authorities to their mutual benefit. As the story unfolds it will become clear why the claim is made here that the Hyksos were of West European origins.

Apart from normal food and consumer commodities, luxury goods became popular and in a short while trade expanded to include products from the steel foundries and armament industries in Western Europe – swords, axes, composite bows, shields, helmets and, yes, chariots, horses and even ships. Before the Hyksos and Tyrians none of these were known in the Eastern Mediterranean theatre.

> *The Mother advised that they should sell anything except iron weapons but nobody paid attention to her. As the Tyriar now had a free hand, they came to transport our goods near and far to the detriment of our own sailors. It was subsequently decided at a general assembly to allow only seven Thyriar ships per year and no more.*[131]

---

[129] OLB: The book of Adela's followers, Chapter 24.
[130] A *tongue-in-cheek* company I made up.
[131] OLB: The book of Adela's followers, Chapter 24.

As time went by business expanded and so did the expatriate community. It is only logical that other Fryan entrepreneurs would have opened up shops, businesses and factories which in turn would have attracted more immigrants. By 1779 BC, some 219 years later, there were so many influential foreign merchants in Northern Egypt that they took control of Memphis and fortified Avaris. They may have had to convince the Egyptians initially that they needed a private standing army to protect them from the Assyrians, but eventually they became too powerful for the Egyptians as well. There was no Hyksos invasion per sé, but rather the natural evolution from a trading post to an economic and political power hub. Millennia later, in AD 1652, we observed exactly the same process when the Dutch established a halfway station at the Cape of Good Hope at the southern tip of Africa on their sea route to India. Three hundred years later, by AD 1948, this halfway station had become the white ruled Republic of South Africa. By 1994, though, South Africa had reverted to indigenous rule; the same sequence of events that unfolded in North Africa 3500 years before. The influence of West European culture and technology, although not replicated exactly, once again left an indelible mark.

The Minoan-type artwork unearthed by archaeologists at Hyksos sites show that there seems to have been some relationship with the inhabitants of Crete. The Oera Linda Book's description of how Minnos colonised Crete explains the West European connection to Crete. The Minoan Art on Hyksos sites also shows that this West European influence extended to Lower Egypt.

The Hyksos, like all West Europeans, did their written communication on paper as is shown throughout this book. This, and the fact that they spoke a foreign language, are the main reasons why so little remained of them in the histories and folklore of their host nations. Wherever they were overthrown or expelled, their writings and script had no meaning to the locals and were therefore destroyed or discarded. What little evidence remained of the Hyksos is that which the Egyptians recorded on their tablets and from their viewpoints. Even the Frisian names and religion would have been Egyptianised.

In Chapter 2 we saw that the Frisians called God Wralda which meant Wra-the Elder. The Egyptians called their god Ra or Re which creates a strong suspicion that the Egyptian sun god was named after Wra-alda, pronounced or sounding like *Ra-alda*.

We do know that the Hyksos rule was very stable and prosperous. Egypt was modernised through new technologies and sciences such as medicine, mathematics and astronomy. They built irrigation canals like the West Europeans and introduced improved farming methods and imported cattle and horses. They introduced monotheism and did not erect votives or statues because, as we have seen, they abhorred these. In fact, Manetho[132] bewailed the fact that the Hyksos went out of their way to destroy the Egyptians' pagan temples. It would appear that their administration was reluctantly accepted by the indigenous Egyptians. The locals regarded them as foreigners and invaders but, as long as they had the stronger army, they remained in charge. It would have been reasonable to assume that the eventual eviction of the Hyksos in ca 1525 BC was driven by nationalism, envy and or greed. These, however, were not the reasons.

The Hyksos had a relatively peaceful sojourn in Lower Egypt for almost 500 years. The last 254 years they reigned from Memphis and Avaris and by all accounts they were tolerated by the locals and accepted by the rulers of Upper Egypt. They brought trade, prosperity and stability to the region. The cause of their demise, when it came, was the result of the most astonishing sequence of events. What follows proves once again that fact is indeed stranger than fiction.

All along historians speculated that the Biblical Joseph, an Israelite and a foreigner, would not have been appointed to the second highest position in Egypt under an indigenous pharaoh. An outsider would not have been tolerated let alone respected. It was, and still is believed that such a situation would have been most unlikely. Some scholars proposed that his appointment must have been made when Egypt was under the rule of a foreign power – possibly the Hyksos. They are quite right.

---

[132] Quoted by Josephus in his book *Against Apion.*

Genesis 41:39-41 (NKJV)

(39) Then Pharaoh said to Joseph, "Inasmuch as God has shown you all this, there is no one as discerning and wise as you (40) You shall be over my house, and all my people shall be ruled according to your word; only in regard to the throne will I be greater than you." (41) And Pharaoh said to Joseph, " See, I have set you over all the land of Egypt."

From the above it is clear that the Pharaoh placed a lot of trust in Joseph. He therefore had a free hand to do whatever he thought best.

From Table 1 we can see that the 15th Dynasty or Hyksos Rule in Lower Egypt lasted from 1779 BC to 1525 BC. By using the 2193 BC event as our base date and the normal Bible timeline and genealogy, we see that Joseph was appointed Governor of Lower Egypt in 1560 BC; just 35 years before Hyksos Rule came to an end. Table 2 shows that Jacob Israel and his 70 followers entered Egypt in 1551 BC, nine years after Joseph's appointment and two years after the onset of a famine which the Bible described as worldwide.

The length of the Israelites stay in Egypt and the date of the Exodus remain problematic for Biblical Scholars. In Exodus 12:40 (New King James Version) the Bible seems to say very clearly that the Israelites were in Egypt for 430 years:

Now the sojourn of the children of Israel who lived in Egypt was four hundred and thirty years

Exodus 12:40 in the Samaritan Pentateuch[133], however, is different:

Now the sojourning of the children of Israel and fathers of them, who dwelt in Canaan and in Egypt, [was] four hundred and thirty years.

---

[133] The Samaritan Pentateuch is a version of the Hebrew language Pentateuch, the first five books of the Bible, traditionally written in the Samaritan alphabet and used by the Samaritans. It constitutes their entire biblical canon.

In Galatians 3:16-17, the apostle Paul agrees with the Samaritan version:

(16) Now to Abraham and his seed were the promises made...
(17) And this I say, that the Law, which was four hundred and thirty years later...

The Promises are given in Genesis 12:1-3

(1) Now the Lord had said to Abram: "Get out of your country, from your family and from your father's house, to a land that I will show you. (2) I will make you a great nation; I will bless you and make your name great; and you shall be a blessing. (3) I will bless those who bless you, and I will curse him who curses you; and in you all the families of the earth shall be blessed".

From the above we can now see that the time span from just before Abram left Haran for Canaan (The Promises) to the time when Moses received the Law (shortly after the Exodus), was 430 years. From Abram's exit from Haran to Jacob's entry into Egypt was 215 years. The Israelites' sojourn in Egypt, therefore, was also 215 years. In both the Judaic and Samaritan Pentateuchs we find that Moses was only the fourth generation from Jacob. This is further support for the 215 years.

Exodus 6:16
These are the names of the sons of Levi[134] according to their generations: Gershon, Kohath, and Merari. And the years of the life of Levi were one hundred and thirty-seven.

Exodus 6:18
And the sons of Kohath were Amram, Izhar, Hebron, and Uzziel. And the years of the life of Kohath were one hundred and thirty-three.

---

[134] Jacob's son.

Exodus 6:20
Now Amram took for himself Jochebed, his father's sister, as wife; and she bore him Aaron and Moses. And the years of the life of Amram were one hundred and thirty years.

If we now apply this 215 years to Table 2, the date for the Exodus would be 1336 BC. According to this date, Solomon's temple foundations would then have been laid in 856 BC, i.e. 480 years after the Exodus. The 2nd-century work, *Seder Olam Rabbah*, places construction in 832 BC, a difference of only 24 years. Even more important, though, is that the date of 2193 BC for the deluge is the only date in Biblical studies that tie in with the 4.2 ka BP Event. Except for the Oera Linda Book and the Old Frisian Calendar, this date is not used anywhere in Jewish or Christian literature. In the 19th century the 4.2 ka BP Event was yet to be discovered. Again, we must ask the question: Where did the Oera Linda Book or the Frisian Calendar get this date from?

Table 2: Biblical Chronology i.t.o. 2193 BC

Bible Reference	Yrs from previous	Name / Event	Date	
Date of Deluge (As per Chapter 1)			2193	BC
Gen. 11:10	2	Arpachshad	2191	BC
Gen. 11:12	35	Shelah	2156	BC
Gen. 11:14	30	Eber	2126	BC
Gen. 11:16	34	Peleg	2092	BC
Gen. 11:18	30	Reu	2062	BC
Gen. 11:20	32	Serug	2030	BC
Gen. 11:22	30	Nahor	2000	BC
Gen. 11:24	29	Terah (205 y. old @ death)	1971	BC
Gen. 12:4	130	Abram (75 y. old @ Terah's death)	1841	BC
Gen. 11:32	75	Promises; Abram to Canaan	1766	BC
Gen. 21:5	25	Isaac	1741	BC
Gen. 25:26	60	Jacob	1681	BC
Gen. 45:6	128	Famine start. (OLB Eartquake)	1553	BC
Gen. 47:9	2	Jacob to Egypt (130 y. old)	1551	BC
Gal. 3:16-17	215	Exodus / Law 430 y. after Promises	1336	BC
(Also see Exodus 12:40 in Samaritan Pentatech)				

Abram arrived in Canaan in ca. 1766 BC, some 234 years after the founding of Tyre and ±230 years after the commencement of Egyptian-Tyrian trade relations.

In his book Against Apion (1.14), Flavius Josephus writing towards the end of the first century AD, quoted the Egyptian historian Manetho when he referred to the Hyksos. Manetho himself lived during the 3rd century BC – more than 1600 years after the Hyksos first set foot on Egyptian soil. We may assume that by then he could only quote from Egyptian sources. His writings had a pro-Egyptian propaganda slant and he referred to the invaders as men of ignoble birth. This term would indicate that the Hyksos were a racially mixed group of Fryan, African, Phoenician and Egyptian descent – exactly as the Oera Linda Book described other North-Africans:

> *The people who live on the south side of the Mediterranean Sea, come for the most part from Phœnicia. The Phœnicians (Carthaginians) are a bastard race of the blood of Frya, Finda, and Lyda.*[135]

Manetho also had to ascribe various atrocities to the foreigners to justify the Egyptian uprising against the oppressors. Nevertheless, it is interesting that he recorded that the Hyksos took his country by force but without a battle:

> *(75) There was a king of ours whose name was Timaus. Under him it came to pass, I know not how, that God was averse to us, and there came, after a surprising manner, men of ignoble birth out of the eastern parts, and had boldness enough to make an expedition into our country, and with ease subdued it by force, yet without our hazarding a battle with them. (76) So when they had gotten those that governed us under their power, they afterwards burned down our cities, and demolished the temples of the gods, and used all the inhabitants after a most barbarous manner; nay, some they killed, and led their children and their wives into slavery. (77) At length they made one of themselves king, whose name was Salatis; he also lived at Memphis, and made both the upper and lower regions pay tribute, and left garrisons in places that were the most proper for them.*
> *(82) This whole nation was styled Hycsos, that is, Shepherd-Kings.*

Once we have accepted the previous table and especially the dates of the global disaster of 2193 BC and the entry of the Israelites into Egypt in 1551 BC, we can have a closer look at the administration of the Vice-Pharaoh, Joseph.

---

[135] OLB: The Writings of Beden, Chapter 3

Joseph, the ex-slave and convict, was appointed to the second highest position in Lower Egypt seven years before the onset of the famine. This would have been in 1560 BC when he was 30 years of age. His family joined him nine years later, in the second year of the famine when he was 39 years old – 22 years after his brothers sold him into slavery as a 17 year-old teenager.

The famine started two years before the Israelites came to Egypt, in other words 1553 BC. This date corresponds exactly with the demise of the Middle Minoan Civilization on Crete, which, archaeologists suggest, might have been caused by the eruption of the Thera volcano on Santorini. We therefore suggest that this eruption took place in 1553 BC and affected the climate around the Mediterranean to such an extent that it resulted in worldwide famine. The Oera Linda Book recorded a massive earthquake at the same time.

In terms of the Bible, the date 1553 BC is a straightforward calculation of Biblical chronology based on 2193 BC as the date for the Deluge. In terms of the Oera Linda Book, it is derived from a back calculation from Alexander the Great's campaign in India and specifically between 330 BC and 327 BC, 1224 years later. This will be explained in detail under the relevant section, but suffice to say at this stage that the dates match exactly.

Table 3: Joseph in Egypt & Exodus of Hyksos

EVENT	DATE	NOTES
Joseph born	1590 BC	Calculated from appointment as Governor of Egypt
Joseph sold into slavery (17 years old)	1573 BC	Genesis 37:2
Joseph appointed Governor (30 years old)	1560 BC	Genesis 41: 45-46 (7 years before famine)
Famine starts (See Table 2)	1553 BC	OLB reports earthquake (Thera 2nd eruption?)
Jacob to Egypt (See Table 2)	1551 BC	Two years after famine started
Famine ends	1546 BC	Famine lasted 7 years
Hyksos rule ends (Table 1) (Joseph 65 years old)	1525 BC	Conventional Hyksos chronology
Joseph died (110 years old)	1480 BC	Genesis 50:26 45 years after Hyksos
Exodus (See Table 2)	1336 BC	Israelites 189 years slaves under indigenous Pharoah

During the seven good years Joseph collected all the grain he could lay his hands on. When the famine started, he sold it back to the Egyptians, probably at inflated prices. We read in the Bible that by the end of the famine the indigenous Egyptians had no livestock and no property they could call their own. In addition, they were taxed 20% on all their produce for the favour granted them by the foreign Pharaoh to farm on *his lands*. Clearly this exploitation of the indigenous Egyptians could not continue. If our conventional Egyptian chronology is correct, this arrangement lasted for only 21 years after the famine when the Egyptians revolted and kicked the Hyksos out of Egypt. The Egyptian Leader, Ahmose I, may have been killed himself during the siege of Avaris.

Joseph, who died at age 110, would have been 65 and most likely in retirement at the time of the revolt. The Bible records that the new Pharaoh did not know Joseph. The Hyksos-Egyptian relationship, which lasted almost 500 years, came to an end when the Egyptians effectively became slaves in their own country – courtesy of Joseph and only 35 years after he had taken control of the Egyptian economy. Sensational as it may be, Joseph caused the downfall of his benefactors, the Hyksos Dynasty.

We shall come back to the Hyksos later to see what became of them after they left Egypt. Let us now return to ca. 2000 BC and Sea King Tunis.

The Gauls and Druids

The loss of the Fryans' market share in international trade, caused by the enterprising Nef Tunis[136] after 2000 BC, was just the beginning of their woes.

Tunis' Sidonese partners were not only interested in trade. As with certain twenty first century AD elements in the Middle East, their long-term goals were more ideological and global. It was then 200 years since the 2193 BC event and the Fryans still had not re-established their former dominance over Iberia and Southern France despite the presence of a Burgh Matron in Kadik. They sold the Frioul archipelago to the Tyrians, but did not have the means to protect the remainder of their southern lands or guard over the morals of the inhabitants. The Sidonese pagan missionaries, or *Gola* as they were called, soon realised this. They also realised that there was quite a fertile missionary field and a healthy demand for female companionship in the almost all-male penal colony of Britannia. From their bases in Sidon and Misselia the Gola actively spread their permissive pagan religion throughout the region. The need for the fairer sex in Britannia was met by abducting females from all around the Mediterranean. The Gola called themselves *Trowe Widena* or *Treow-Wits* (Adherents or knowers of the Truth). The Frisians did not trust

---

[136] Lit. *Cousin* Tunis

them at all and nicknamed them *Trowe Wendena* (truth avoiders) or *Truiwenden* in short.

The pagan religions from the East and Middle East now had the Fryan Federation in a pincher; the Magy and his Magyarar priests in the north and north-east and the *Treowit* priests with their Gola missionaries in the south and west. The Gola later become known as the Gauls and the name *Treowits* evolved into *Druids* – the mysterious leaders in ancient Gaul that destroyed Fryan monotheism in Southern and South Western Europe and held sway over the people in Gallic religion.

It is amazing to note how little tactics have changed over a 4000 year period. As we still see today, the Magyarar and the Gola realised back then that the permanent subduing of a people was not by force of arms, but rather by undermining their moral fibre. Where there are drugs involved, it also means the opening of new markets.

The ancient Gola priests from Sidon derived their name from the nearby Golan Heights; some 40 km south-east of Sidon. The Golan Heights are bordered by present-day Israel, Syria, Lebanon and Jordan. Golan means Captive in Hebrew. The refuge town Golan is mentioned in the Bible in Deuteronomy 4:41-43 (RSV). If this supposition is correct, it would mean that the ancient Gauls or French had ties with the Golan Heights, which was annexed by Israel in 1981.

This is how the Oera Linda Book described the sequel to Misselia:

> The Gola[137], as the missionary priests from Sidon were called, had noticed that the land there[138] was sparsely populated and far from the Mother. In order to make themselves look good, they had themselves called in our language "truth devotees" (trowe widena)[139]; but they had better have been called "truth avoiders" (trowe wendena) or in short, "Triuwenden," as our seafaring people afterwards called them.

---

[137] Gauls
[138] Southern France
[139] Druids: From *Treow+Wit*, literally meaning *Knower of the truth*.
See: *Treow* (Old English, Anglo Saxon), *Triuwi* (Old Frisian) = Truth, and *Wit* (Old English and Old Frisian) = Knowledge, understanding

When they were well settled, their merchants exchanged their beautiful copper weapons and all sorts of ornaments for our iron weapons and hides of wild animals, which were plentiful in our southern countries. The Gola, however, celebrated all kinds of vile monstrous festivals, which the coastal peoples promoted with their wanton girls and the sweetness of their potent wine.

If anyone of our nation had committed such a bad offence that his life was in danger, the Gola connived and sent him to Phonisia, that is, Palm land. When he was settled there, he had to write to his family and friends that the country was so good and the people so happy that no one could imagine it.

In Britannia, there were plenty of men, but few wives. When the Gola realised this, they abducted girls from everywhere and gave them to the Britne for nothing. All these girls, though, were their servants - children stolen from Wralda and given to false gods.[140]

It would take another 300 years for the Gola to realize their religious objectives in Southern Europe and then the changes were permanent. Their second attempt at European domination started in 1628 BC with the Celtic Revolution of which the Oera Linda Book also gives an account and which will be discussed later.

It is interesting to note that these incursions into Europe by Middle Eastern elements were, according to the Oera Linda Book, motivated by religious agendas.

These same Arabian peoples renewed their quest for world domination with the onset of Islam. Since AD 622 they have conquered the whole of the Arabian Peninsula, the Middle East and the Persian Empire up to India, Asia Minor, North Africa and large portions of Asia – mainly by ruthless military force. It is only in Europe where they were repelled although their influence, nevertheless, is permanent. A quest that was started 4000 years ago is still ongoing to this day, albeit under a different banner.

---

[140] OLB: The book of Adela's followers, Chapter 25.

King Neptune

Nef Tunis, the marine who became a general before he was 25, a fugitive from the law and an outcast by the age of 37, became a business tycoon in the best 21st century AD tradition. Some four thousand years ago he effectively controlled all European and Mediterranean trade. He founded Tyre and Marseille, and the Oera Linda Book has it that the country of Tunisia was named after him. It is also most likely that he was the progenitor of the much later Hyksos dynasty in Egypt. After his death he was deified by his Magyarar crews and the Golar priests with their druids. Nef Tunis eventually became known as Neptūnus in Latin or, as he is known today, Neptune, the mythological god of the sea. In life, King Neptune was quite a remarkable man.

Legends have it that Phoenicians settled on the coast of Tunisia ca. the 10th century BC and that the Tyrians founded Carthage in the 9th century BC. The legends could be out by a thousand years, but the other facts confirm what the Oera Linda Book states.

In book XIII of his Odyssey, Homer referred to Neptune and the Phaeacians and penned down these most revealing words:

> But Neptune did not forget the threats with which he had already threatened Ulysses, so he took counsel with Jove. "Father Jove", said he, "I shall no longer be held in any sort of respect among you gods, if mortals like the Phaeacians, <u>who are my own flesh and blood</u>, show such small regard for me.[141]

The Oera Linda Book tells us that Nef Tunis was a Frisian and Homer tells us that Neptūnus was a Phaeacian. Again we see that the Phaeacians were the Frisians (see Chapter 2). The fact that Homer states categorically that these mortal Frisians were Neptune's own flesh and blood means that King Neptune had to have been a mortal Frisian himself in the past – exactly what the Oera Linda Book says.

---

[141] Homer: *Odyssey*, Book XIII, p.3.

This account of Neptune's deification by the Phoenicians, therefore, means that the Greeks and Romans took their mythological god of the sea from the Middle East. Homer mentions Neptune in his Odyssey written before 800 BC. This indicates that Neptune was initially a Greek deity like the Greeks' other god of the sea, Poseidon. The Romans only adopted Neptūnus much later.

The Celtic Revolution

The Oera Linda Book tells us that in 1630 BC, some 370 years after Tunis founded Tyre, a Burgh Matron by the name of Minerva held office in the burgh of Walhallagara on the present day island of Walcheren in the province of Zeeland in the Netherlands. During her term of office an event took place which seems quite obscure in the narrative. We read of wild seas and that many a ship was lost. In addition, many of the Frisians' cattle died. The author, unlike the normal Fryan realism found throughout the book, ascribed the events to the witchcraft of another Burgh Matron, Syrhed (Beauty). The Sailors gave her the nickname of Kalta because she dabbled in the occult. Syrhed hailed from Flyburgh to the south of the Scheldt River estuary; possibly near present day Antwerp in Belgium.

> When Kalta saw that her scheme had failed, she went from bad to worst. She secretly sent for the Magyara to teach her sorcery. When she had had enough of this, she threw herself into the arms of the Golum[142], though, all her malpractices could not make her better.
> When she saw that the sailors avoided her more and more, she wanted to win them back by fear. When the moon was full and the sea stormy, she would walk in the wild surf, calling to the sailors that they would all perish if they did not worship her. Then she blinded their eyes, so that they mistook land for water and water for land causing many a ship to be lost with man and mouse.
> ...like all our cattle that died lately.[143]

---

[142] Also called *Gola* or *Golar* by different authors at different times.
[143] OLB: The book of Adela's followers, Chapter 26

One tends to gloss over this little piece of superstition or folklore until it is realised that another major event took place around the same time. Scientists found evidence of a climatic event around 1628 BC in the growth depression of European oaks in Ireland and Sweden. The same observation was made in North America for the period 1629 BC to 1628 BC. In addition, radiocarbon dating done on vegetative matter found in the lava on the Santorini Islands in the Aegean Sea indicated that the Thera volcano erupted violently between 1627 BC and 1613 BC with a 95% probability of accuracy. We shall come back to Thera later. Mention is made of the eruption only to serve as a method of confirming the dates of the events that followed.

In approximately 1628 BC a fight broke out between elements of the Frisian citizens' army on the one side, and the marines and navy on the other. The soldiers were followers of Syrhed whilst the sailors sided with Minerva. The incident was sparked during a military celebration in Flyburgh.

One of the main industries and sources of income in Flyburch was the manufacturing of paper from flax for the export market. Some entrepreneur in Walhallagara devised a method that replaced the flax from Flyburch with Yellow Water-lily leafs (Nuphar lutea) to make paper. This invention not only put the citizens of Flyburch out of business, but was also the first of a series of actions that dramatically altered the course of Fryan, European and world history – triggered by the humble water–lily leaf (Dutch: pompeblêden)!

Figure 30: Water-lily leafs in nature and on the Frisian Flag

We gather that the Fryan economy was already in recession for some time and, to make matters worse, some disease decimated their livestock. At a military celebration, Burgh Matron Syrhed of Flyburch incited her intoxicated citizen force soldiers by blaming their misfortunes on her colleague, Minerva, the Burgh Matron of Walhallagara. Syrhed claimed that Minerva was behind the collapse of their paper industry and the killing of their cattle. In a drunken stupor the soldiers attacked Minerva's burgh. The marines, under the command of Sea King Ion, retaliated. They saved Minerva, set fire to Flyburch, and in the ensuing fight a few thousand soldiers and marines perished.

The Folk Mother, Rosamund, declared a state of emergency, called up the citizen force, or Home Guard, from the surrounding towns, and quelled the uprising. Syrhed fled to Misselia and the soldiers were promptly dispatched to the penal colony in Britannia. The sailors, however, did not wait to be arrested and, together with Minerva and the maids from both burghs, they took refuge on the ships. They sailed away, ignoring a summons by their supreme commander or Secretary of Defence, Helprik. En-route they took some wives and children on board and departed with 127 ships fully laden with merchandise that was already loaded for a trade mission before the fight. As with Tunis some 373 years before, Ion and Minerva were now outcasts.

The sailors nicknamed Minerva *Nyhellenia* which was a term of endearment and meant *New Clarity*. They called Syrhed *Kalta* which had a derogatory connotation because she always spoke in riddles or cultic terms. From here on we shall call them by their nicknames for reasons that will become clearer.

We shall leave Ion and Nyhellenia for the moment and turn our attention to Kalta.

According to the Oera Linda Book, Syrhed, or Kalta, was an enchanting beauty. She was also very ambitious and with very few scruples. The book alleges that Kalta drugged the soldiers' beer before the Battle of the Scheldt River. This time, however, drugs did not merely cause a major setback to the Fryan Federation, but the harsh steps the Folk Mother and General Assembly took to punish the wrongdoers, split the whole country in two; a rift that the Federation would never recover from. Thousands were sent to the penal colony in Britannia.

The fighting landsmen were all caught, but Ion took refuge with his men on board his fleet, taking with him both the lamps, as well as Minerva and the matrons of both burghs. Helprik the chief had him banished, but while all the security forces were still on the other side of the Skelda, Ion sailed back to the Flymar, and then straight to our islands. His men and many of our people took women and children on board, and as Ion saw that he and his men would be punished like criminals, he secretly departed.

He did the right thing, because all our islanders and all the other Skelda people who had been fighting were taken to Britannia. This step was a mistake, for now came the beginning of the end.

After the Skelda debacle, Kalta found herself an exile in Misselia whilst her loyal ex-Fryan soldiers languished as convicts in Britannia. This oppressive punitive action by the Folk Mother, however, played right into the hands of Kalta. With the backing of the Gola in modern day Iberia and southern France, Kalta declared *UDI*. (Unilateral Declaration of Independence) and also annexed Britannia. She received all the support she needed to throw off the restrictive laws and creed of the Fryan Federation.

Now Kalta came and said: "You were born free, and for small offences you have been made outcasts, not for your own improvement, but to mine tin by your hands. If you wish to be free again and live under my council and care, come out then, you will be given weapons and I will watch over you."

Like lightning it went through the land and before the Carrier's Yule had made one revolution, she was mistress over all of them and the Thyriar from our southern states up to the Seiene[144].

She went even further and had herself declared Folk Mother of the new state. She built a citadel by the name of Kaltasburch which later became Keranak - *The Corner*. This may well have been the modern day coastal town of Carnac in south western France. Within a year her domain extended right up to the River Seine.

---

[144] Seine River

The Fryan Federation thus shrank further with the Gola backed Kalta now on their southern border and the aggressive Magyarar having taken possession of Finland and Sweden in the north.

In time the citizens of Kalta's state became known as the Kaltanar and eventually the Celts, a derivative of Cults – established ca 1627 BC.

In Chapter 26 of The Book of Adela's Followers, we find another interesting snippet:

> Over the Skelda at Flyburch, Syrhed presided. This matron was full of tricks, her face was beautiful, and her tongue was shrewd; but the advice that she gave was always in mysterious words. Therefore, the sailors called her Kalta[145], and the landsmen thought it was an honorary name.
>
> In order to give an impression of her great vigilance, she placed a rooster on her banner.

Here we have an explanation for the cockerel we find in ancient Celtic and Gaulish legends and myths. The rooster is still the unofficial emblem of France, 3600 years later. Julius Caesar encountered the Gaulish cock banners, the French revolutionaries used it as a motif in the 1700's and in World War II the French Resistance used it as their symbol.

It is noteworthy that the Gauls established themselves on the continent and in Britain some 350 to 370 years before the Celts. Neither group came into being as a result of an invasion or migration, but evolved from the same socio-political and religious dispensation introduced by foreigners from the Middle East and, of course, the political aspirations of Kalta. The Celtic language group still consists of continental Gaulish and its variants, Irish, Welsh, Cornish and Gaelic as spoken in the British Isles.

---

[145] From Cults, Cultic

The founding of Athens

Since the Gola went into partnership with Tunis some 373 years before, they extended their influence over most of the Mediterranean. It would appear as if even the prosperous, but small city-state of Tyre was now fully assimilated into their society if not their political dispensation. A significant number of the Tyrians, however, were still of Fryan descent and proud of it.

The Gola sided with the more liberal Kalta and the renegade fleet of Ion and Nyhellenia was not welcome anywhere. Even in Italy which the Frisians called Heinde Krekaland (near Greek Land) and which was part of the mighty pre-2193 BC Fryan Federation some 600 years before, word from the Gola had preceded them.

The fleet sailed to Tyre in the hope of finding refuge there. One may assume that they sent a scouting party ahead, because when they arrived at Tyre, they did not drop anchor but continued their voyage. Nyhellenia considered the Fryan religion in Tyre to have degenerated to the level of the pagan priests and she would not settle there.

As they sailed past, a small but significant incident occurred which may shed light on some of the questions we still ask today, some 3600 years later. The opportunistic Tyrians hijacked one of the ships towards the rear of the fleet. The Frisians, heavily laden with merchandise and families, could not retaliate, but the hot-headed Ion made a mental note for future reference.

After what must have been quite a few months of sailing through the Mediterranean, the fugitives from Frya's Land finally arrived in Attica in Verre Krekaland (Far Greek Land), or Greece. The surrounding countryside was barren and Ion was not impressed at all. Nyhellenia Minerva, however, thought that the desolation was exactly what they needed for a new beginning. At least the Gola would not be interested in such a godforsaken place. They found a natural harbour and dropped anchor. For Nyhellenia this was the end of their journey.

Ion decided that his fortunes, however, laid elsewhere. An impromptu referendum was held and some of the young adventurers and the remaining maids of Kalta decided to join Ion, but the majority elected to stay with Nyhellenia. Ion sailed away and Nyhellenia, with the consent and assistance of the local tribal chiefs, and her share of the cargo, stayed to build a stone fortress.

Thus, in ca 1627 BC, the same year that the Celts came into being, the City of Friends, Athenia, was founded. Burgh Matron Nyhellenia Minerva, who chose the name, had a citadel again.

> *When Minerva had examined the country, which the inhabitants called Attika, she saw that the people were all goatherds, and that they lived on meat, herbs, wild roots and honey. They were clothed in skins, and they had their shelters on the slopes (hellinga) of the mountains, wherefore we called them Hellinggars.*
>
> *At first they ran away, but when they saw that we were not after their possessions, they came back and showed great friendship. Minerva asked if we might settle there peacefully. This was agreed to on condition that we should help them fight against their neighbours who always came to abduct their children and steal their possessions.*
>
> *We then built a burgh at an hour's distance from the harbour. On Minerva's advice it was called Athenia, "because", she said, "those who come after us should know that we did not come here out of greed or by violence, but were received like friends."*[146]

The nickname Hellinggar, which the Frisians gave to these primitive residents of the slopes or hellings[147], stuck and today, 3600 years later, we still refer to them as the Hellenists or Hellenes. It is quite likely that they were still recovering from the Thera eruption a year or two before.

It is also interesting to note that this area, 3636 years ago and 566 years after the 2193 BC event, was inhabited by a Neolithic-type people under the control of pagan priests – exactly as was the case with the Magyarar and Finnar in Scandinavia.

It is necessary for us to pause here for a moment and also look at the impressive ex-Fryan fleet that now lay off the coast of Attica and the two main characters, Ion and Minerva.

---

[146] OLB: The book of Adela's followers, Chapter 28.
[147] The word still exists in Afrikaans and still has the same meaning.

As mentioned earlier, the fleet consisted of 126 ships (one was hijacked by the Tyrians) fully laden with merchandise for a trade mission. These refugees, therefore, were not poor. They had ample commodities for barter and to win over the locals. Secondly, these were not the quaint little boats we find among the Vikings some 2000 years later. They were heavy, long-distance, sea-going freighters that could accommodate upwards of 100 crew and passengers. If one works at only 40 persons per ship, the sailors, rowers, marines and some families could have numbered in excess of 5000 souls. They had safety in numbers and the best ocean-going vessels and iron-age weaponry of the time.

Ion, the young sea king or marine-general, did not pay too much attention to discipline and protocol. Firstly he jumped at the chance to sort out his landlubber comrades without seemingly paying any attention to the consequences. When he then received a direct order from his commander to return to land and hand himself over, he refused to obey. He sailed off into the sunset with the entire Frisian Fleet and a few thousand marines and sailors. The cargo alone, in today's terms, must have been worth quite a few million dollars.

Minerva Nyhellenia, on the other hand, seemed to have been the unfortunate victim of circumstances. She was saved by the marines but could not return. The Folk Mother and General Assembly would have made an example of anyone remotely involved in the uprising. She had been second in line to become head of state or Folk Mother. She had been a Burgh Matron of one of the most prestigious citadels, Walhallagara, for some time. Despite her piousness and all the love and respect she commanded, she should not have sided with one of the offending parties. Whereas Kalta had a rooster on her banner, Minerva chose a sheep dog and an owl for her emblems:

"The dog", she said, "guards his master and his flock and the night owl watches that the mice shall not devastate the fields.[148]
Later, in Athenia, Minerva gave the following reply to the pagan priests when they asked her about these symbols:

---

[148] OLB: The book of Adela's followers, Chapter 26

Once they came and asked: "If you are not a witch, what are you doing with the eggs that you are always carrying with you?"

Minerva answered: "These eggs are the symbols of Frya's councils, in which our future and that of the whole human race lies concealed; time must hatch them and we must keep watch that no harm comes to them".

The priests (replied): "Well said, but what is the purpose of the dog on your right hand?"

Hellenia replied: "Does not the shepherd have a dog to keep his flock together? What the dog is to the shepherd I am in Frya's service. I must watch over Frya's flock".

"That makes good sense", said the priests, "but tell us what is the meaning of the night owl that always sits above your head? Is that light-shunning animal perhaps a sign of your clear vision?"

"No." answered Hellenia. "He helps to remind me that there are people roaming the earth who, like him, live in churches and holes. They keep to the dark, though, not like him to rid us of mice and other plagues, but to invent tricks to steal other people's knowledge that they may get a better hold to make slaves of them, and to suck their blood like vampires do." [149]

These emblems, the dog, the owl and the basket of eggs or fruit appear on numerous artifacts from antiquity.

A note on linen and paper

The reader's attention must be drawn to the casual references to flax and paper in the Oera Linda Book. Both these inventions are at least as important as markers in the development of a civilization as iron-based tools and weaponry.

The flax from which linen is derived was not only essential for the production of garments and for writing on, but was also used for sails by means of which ships could reach distant lands. In this way commerce and the spread of civilization were made possible. Paper, on

---

[149] OLB: The book of Adela's followers, Chapter 14

the other hand, was a more economical means of recording transactions and for the dissemination of knowledge than parchment (animal skin) and flax-based stationery.

In Chapter 2, we saw that Homer recorded that the Phaeacians wore linen garments 3200 years ago. In ca 530 BC Apollonia described how her mother spun and wove her own blouse of linen and her tunic of wool. We are told, once again, that the sought-after Irish linen was brought to Ireland and Europe by the Phoenicians - the same claim that is being made for Welsh tin mining. By now, however, we know where the Phoenicians' claim to fame came from.

Today, flax is grown all over the world, but Western Europe still produces the best quality linen, notably the niche producers in Ireland, Italy, Belgium and the Netherlands; a tradition that goes back thousands of years.

It is commonly believed that papermaking is one of the four great inventions of ancient China. Paper was supposedly developed in the early 2nd century AD by the Han court eunuch, Cai Lun. The Oera Linda Book, however, recorded a civil war that broke out as a result of flax having been replaced by water-lily based paper more than 1800 years earlier in the Schelde estuary in the Netherlands.

Chapter 4

The Seeds of a New Civilization

T he Celtic Revolution of 1628/7 BC happened some
566 years after the 4.2 ka BP Event. The Event was fast fading into
obscurity and had become just another legend and myth. Overnight,
the Fryan Federation split into three separate nations, each with its
own character. North and Western Europe still had the very
conservative and highly controlled Fryan Federation. Iberia and France
with their revolutionary Celts and their new liberal Folk Mother, Kalta,
discarded many of the vestiges of the Fryan creed such as religion and
compulsory schooling. In its stead they embraced the decadent Druids
with their Golar religion and reveled in their emancipation. From
Sidon and Tyre the Phoenicians with their Golar merchants, Druid
priests and Frisian navigators made their influence felt throughout the
Mediterranean. In Attica the pious Nyhellenia was trying to establish a
new homeland for her and her followers amongst idol worshippers
and hostile priests. In Lower Egypt the Hyksos of mixed Frisian,
African and Phoenician descend were reshaping the Egyptian
civilization and upgrading the infrastructure and technology. In
Palestine Abraham had died 39 years before. Isaac's twin sons, Jacob
and Esau were already 54 years old.

The Fryan Federation with their Frisian creed was still fending
off the Magyarar from the North and East but by all accounts they
were shrinking and sinking. Every time they appeared to be making
headway, they suffered a further setback. Two hundred years after the
2193 BC catastrophe they had to face the Magyarar and lost their fleet
and a number of their armed forces as a result of the treacherous
conduct of Wodin, Tunis and Inca. Nef Tunis added insult to injury by

monopolizing the Mediterranean trade. Then, 373 years later, they lost their fleet and mariners again – this time to Ion and Minerva. In addition, Kalta expropriated all their holdings in Iberia and Britannia.

One gets the impression that the Federation was never able to adapt from a super power, which everyone respected, to a middle-sized country which had to defend its dominion. While they still tried to preserve their religion and creed and dreamed of a bygone era, their rivals, with the aid of their fellow countrymen, eroded their foundations.

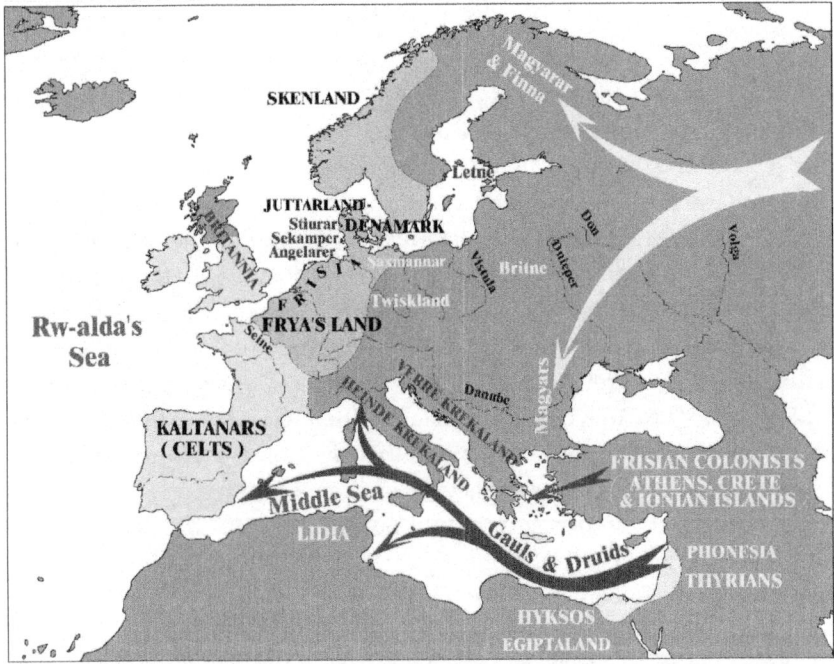

Figure 31: Frya's Land and Frisian influence ca. 1600 BC

The only accessible real estate still available on the European coast was the barren shoreline and islands of the Aegean Sea which were inhabited by superstitious Neolithic tribes of hunter-gatherers. Among the rock-strewn hills of Attica, Nyhellenia Minerva, the exiled Fryan Burgh Matron and her followers laid the unplanned foundations of a new civilization.

By all accounts her administration was quite successful. As with her own followers, she soon earned the respect and love of the locals. To the dismay of the Frisians even the Shamanistic-type pagan priests, or sorcerers, although they ridiculed her pious ideas, exploited her popularity by declaring her a deity after her death,

So great was their reverence for her, or perhaps more than likely for political reasons, that they refused the Frisians permission to elect a successor. As a deity her wisdom was now always available to them and they did not need anyone else. No successor would be able to live up to her in any case. This, at least, is what they told the Frisians.

The Virgin Goddess of Warriors, Wisdom, Poetry, Medicine, Commerce, Crafts and Music thus came into being. In Greece she became known as Athena, and later in Rome by her own name: Minerva. The name Hellenia, Helena or Helen, the bringer of light or clarity, became as Greek as Moussaka and Ouzo.

The Athenian Frisians nevertheless went ahead and elected Gert as their new Folk Mother; an act that the Hellinggar priests – the later Oracles of Homer - would not forgive or forget.

The Ionians

When Tunis and Inca parted ways at Cadiz in 2000 BC, they divided the fleet in proportion to their followers. Ion and Minerva did the same in 1628 BC when they went their separate ways.

> Then Ion, who wished to go on, went with his spear and banner, calling to the young people to know who would volunteer to join him. Minerva, who wanted to stay there, also did so.
>
> The majority stayed with Minerva but the young sailors went with Ion. Ion took Kalta's lamp and her matrons and Minerva kept her own lamp and her own matrons.[150]

---

[150] OLB: The book of Adela's followers, Chapter 28

We can understand that Kalta's maids did not want to stay with Nyhellenia. She already had her 21 maids and there were no more vacancies. Perhaps there was also an element of professional rivalry. The young navigators, on the other hand, were for the most part single and would have been conscripts doing their three-year national service in the Frisian Navy and Marines. Their fathers and mothers were thousands of kilometres away and the life of adventure offered by Ion would have been so much more exiting than building a fortress with Minerva and her *boring* followers.

After leaving Minerva in Attica, Ion did not sail too far. Just around the corner, off the west coast of Greece, he found a group of islands and set up base camp on the largest of these. It would appear that this was Kefalonia, also known as Cephallenia in ancient times. In The Iliad, written some 800 years later, Homer refers to the Ionians from Cephallenia. Could there be a link between Cephallenia and Nyhellenia?

Once Ion and his followers were established and, we may presume, chose a new Burgh Matron from Kalta's maids, they were ready for the second order of business. They were no longer under the strict code of ethics of their previous Folk Mother, nor under the jurisdiction of the pious Minerva. They were now free to take up the small matter of a missing boat with the Tyrians. The *Pirates of the Mediterranean*, also known as the *Sea People*, had arrived.

> *Between the Fere and Heinde Krekalandum (Italy and Greece) Ion found some islands to his liking. On the largest he built a burgh in the woods between the mountains. From these small islands he took revenge by robbing the Thiriar ships and lands, therefore these islands were called both Rawer Elanda (Pirate Islands) and Ionhis Elanda.*[151]

In time the Ion-his Elanda became the Ionian Islands as we know them today. It is not surprising that ancient myths have it that the Ionians were descended from the hero Ion, son of Xuthus, son of Hellen, progenitor of all the Hellenes.

---

[151] OLB: The book of Adela's followers, Chapter 28

Over the next 1 500 years, these Gypsies of the seas would spread their influence, maritime skills, weaponry and genes around the Aegean Sea. They would become the scourge of the Pharaohs of Egypt and of the kings of Tyre and, for that matter, anyone with a merchant fleet. Sometimes they fought against the Egyptians or anyone else, and sometimes with them as mercenaries. In times of hardship they would even become traders and merchants themselves. Their calling card was always the same: The Sea People were here – no forwarding address given.

One gets the impression that Ion and his band of rogues did not want to embarrass their country of origin or their families in far-away Frisia with their new occupation. They therefore simply referred to themselves as the Sea People. In fact, so effective was this shroud of mystery with which they covered themselves, that we are still mystified by them more than 3600 years later.

In 2000 BC, long before Ramesses II or even 350 years before Ion and Minerva, the Oera Linda Book already referred to Tunis and his followers, or perhaps specifically the Frisian mariners, as the Sea People:

Many Magyarar fled back with their troops, and the sea-people took ship, accompanied by a body of stalwart Finns as rowers.[152]

In order to understand the success of Ion and his legacy that served the Ionians and the Sea People for centuries, we have to bear their fleet in mind. The Ionians, or Sea People, like the Phoenicians, Tyrians, Hyksos and Frisians, had the best maritime technology and weaponry of the time. They could apply their trade with impunity. In 21st century terms we can liken them to corsairs in possession of a fleet of aircraft carriers and destroyers.

Again, for the sake of chronology, we have to leave the Ionians for a while and return to Athens.

---

[152] OLB: The book of Adela's followers, Chapter 23.

The Minoans

When Sea King Ion left Minerva Nyhellenia in Attica to build her fortress, she and her followers had to elect a new Sea King in the place of Ion. The choice fell on Minno. In his own writings we gather that Minno was with Minerva during her time in Athens. He wrote at length about her and all her good attributes. We also read that in his old age he returned to his country of birth, Frisia, where he spent his last days in peace. From this, we infer that he was one of the young adventure seeking marines who had fled with Ion and Minerva from Flyland in 1627 BC. Now he returned an older and wiser man:

> *In my youth I sometimes grumbled at the strictness of the law but later I often thanked Frya for her Tex and our forefathers for the laws that they compiled from it. Wralda or Alvader (Father-of-all / God) has given me many years and I have travelled over many lands and seas and after all I have seen I am convinced that we alone were chosen by Alvader to have laws.* [153]

We may assume that Minerva was over 40 when they left Frisia because she was a strong contender for the position of Folk Mother or Head of State of the Fryan Federation. A candidate for the position would have had to be a mature person with a good track record as a Burgh Matron. The Oera Linda Book is mute as to the time of her death but it would appear that she governed in Athens into her old age. Thus, she may have been in her seventies when she died which would have been ca. 1600 BC. This is, however, pure conjecture. We also do not know when her successor was elected. This may have been any time from shortly after her death to as long as 30 years after.

The book shows that a successor to a Folk Mother or Burgh Matron was not necessarily elected immediately. In the case of Athenia it would appear that there were bitter political rivalry and negotiations before the Frisians eventually decided to elect a new Folk Mother against the wishes of the pagan priests. This period without a Frisian

---

[153] OLB: The book of Adela's followers, Chapter 13.

governor could have been as long as 30 or 40 years. It would then explain the skirmish that broke out when the Frisians did elect Gert as their new leader. By now the locals would have forgotten Minerva as a person and the priests would have been firmly entrenched in the government of the land or, more likely, as oracles and spiritual leaders.

Minno himself does not say why or when he left Athenia for Crete but it seems to have been as a result of the political turmoil in Athenia after Minerva's death. It is evident that he left before a new Folk Mother was elected; possibly as early as 1600 BC. He would not have been willing to serve under a pagan priest.

This date coincides with the start of the Neopalatial or New Palace Period (MMIII) of Crete. Archaeologists classify this period as the apex of the Minoan civilization. Again, the Oera Linda Book's account is credible. Sea King or General Minno penned down the events thus:

> *When Nyhellenia died, we wanted to choose another mother. Some wished to go to Texland to recruit one, but the priests who were deeply entrenched among their own people, would not permit it, and accused us before the people of being unholy.*[154]

> *When I sailed away from Athenia with my people, we arrived at last at an island named by my crew Kreta, because of the wild cries that the inhabitants raised on our arrival. When they saw that we did not plan to wage war, they became quiet, so that at last I was able to exchange a boat and some iron implements for a harbour and a piece of land.*

> *After we had been settled there for a while, and they saw that we had no slaves, they were puzzled, but when I explained to them that we had laws applicable to everybody, they wished to have the same. They hardly had them, though, when the whole land was in confusion.*

> *The rulers and priests alleged that we had made their subjects rebellious and the people came to us for aid and protection. When the rulers, though, saw that they were about to loose their dominion they gave the people their freedom and came to me for a law book.*

---

[154] OLB: The book of Adela's followers, Chapter 14.

The people, however, were not accustomed to freedom, and the rulers remained in power after their own desires.[155]

Here we see Minno the philanthropist in true Frisian style. If freedom and democracy served the Frisians so well, surely everyone should grasp it? It is clear from this utterance, however, that these principles are not to be taken for granted. Unless a people grew up with a reverence for the law and the common good of society, they will not take hold. This may sound philosophical but, in the 3600 years since the Frisians landed on Crete, man has not changed. One only has to look at the many countries around the world where newly founded democracies since the Second World War have failed, or are abused by despots. The author's of the Oera Linda Book, and certainly Minno, experienced this. It is doubtful whether a 19th century Dutch author could have dreamt this up.

Minno continued:

When this storm had passed, they began to sow divisions among us. They told my people that I had called on their assistance to make myself permanent king. Once I found poison in my meat, so when a ship from the Fly sailed past[156], I quietly took my departure.

My own adventures aside, I merely want to say with this history that we must not have anything to do with Finda's people, from wherever they may be, because they are full of deceit, as much to be feared as their sweet wine with deadly poison.[157]

It would appear that by the time Minerva died the Athenian Frisians had not only re-established trade and cordial relationships with their country of origin, but there might also have been a fair amount of emigration of Frisians from Western Europe to the warmer climes of the Mediterranean - to Avaris (Egypt), Athens (Greece) and Knossos (Crete). In fact, the story of Ion and Minerva's travels were related to the Motherland ten years after they had fled from Flyland.

---

[155] OLB: The book of Adela's followers, Chapter 15.
[156] Regular sea-trade with Frisia / Frya's Land.
[157] OLB: The book of Adela's followers, Chapter 15

Three ships from the Aegean arrived in Frisia to purchase weapons and by all accounts they were well received.[158]

The Athenians wanted to fetch a successor to Minerva from Texland in Frisia. The local pagan priests in Attica, however, resisted the move. We can only assume that, by their reasoning, this would have strengthened the Frisian Folk Mother and the Fryan Federation's influence in the area. They need not have worried. As we came to know the Frisians, their religion would not have allowed a pagan people into their Federation, nor would they allow their own people back after having been exposed to a foreign influence for so long. This was the main reason why they never had policies or campaigns for expansion or conquests. In fact, when they had the opportunity to win back some of their estranged eastern states, the highly esteemed Adela advised against it. She felt, and the assembly agreed, that their previous fellow countrymen would had been too corrupted by the Magyarar influence.

> *Yesterday there were among you those who would have hoped to call the whole nation together to force the eastern states to return to their duty. In my humble opinion, though, that would have turned out wrong. Imagine first there was a very serious lung disease among the livestock, and this was still raging fiercely, would you dare to send your healthy livestock among the sick ones? Certainly not. Moreover, everyone will agree and admit that this will put the whole herd at risk. Who, then, would be so foolish as to risk their children among a people that is totally corrupted?*[159]

But, let us return to Crete. Minno does not tell us how long he stayed on Crete, but what is clear is that when he left, he did this on his own – his followers remained behind. We may assume that, true to Frisian tradition, they would have elected a Burgh Matron for this new unofficial colony. Again, this seems to be borne out by 20th century archaeological work carried out on Crete around the Palace of Knossos

---

[158] OLB: The book of Adela's followers, Chapter 28.
[159] OLB: The book of Adela's followers, Chapter 1.

and other Minoan sites. Archaeologists suggest that the old Minoans had a matriarchal system of governance.

In 1867, when the Oera Linda manuscript surfaced, the palace of Knossos and the Minoan Civilization had yet to be discovered. Knossos was unearthed early in the 20th century and the term Minoan was only coined towards the latter half of the century. Homer did refer to Minos as the founder king of Crete in his Odyssey written in ca 800 BC but in the 19th century AD this was regarded as myth.

The fact that the Greeks regarded Minos as the first king of Crete should be interesting to archaeologists. Why did they not refer to anyone from the Earlier Minoan Period as the founder? It is suggested that the 1628 BC eruption of Thera severely affected the Cretan population. Once again the Frisians arrived at just the right time. As was the case with Athens, they were able to settle on Crete without much resistance.

From the writings of Minno we can see that he was a true son of Frya in religion and creed. It is important to bear this in mind when we have another look at the Minoan civilisation. As with the Hyksos, archaeologists have noted that there is a glaring absence of idols and statues at MMIII Minoan sites. In addition, we do not find elaborate temples dedicated to the gods as we find on mainland Greece; again in accordance with the Oera Linda Book. There is no possibility that a 19th century deceiver could have dreamed up the matriarchal form of government and this aversion to idolatry. What should be abundantly clear by now is that these people were monotheists who abhorred idolatry, witchcraft and the occults. This would explain the absence of such objects. In fact, it is most likely that they may have had a church not to dissimilar to what we find in modern Christian communities – without the steeple of course, which is a remnant of Roman Catholicism.

With all due respect to modern archaeologists and the fine work they are doing, it would appear that they too often put a religious connotation to the artwork and buildings they uncover. What could be just a normal city hall or recreational facility becomes a temple. A room that does not appear to be a bedroom or a kitchen becomes a place of worship instead of a lounge, reception area or a dining room.

A painting of three affluent ladies dressed for a social event become Queens or Priestesses, while three youths jumping over a bull, which obviously is an ancient form of American rodeo or Spanish bullfighting, become some kind of bull worship where the bull is supposedly offered afterwards. A lady with a flask at a spring or trough with a boy waiting to let his lamb drink and some more ladies waiting in the queue, become The offering of the Lamb (Pitsa panels, Corinth).

Figure 32: Three Queens or Priestesses
(or perhaps just Three Belles at the Ball?)

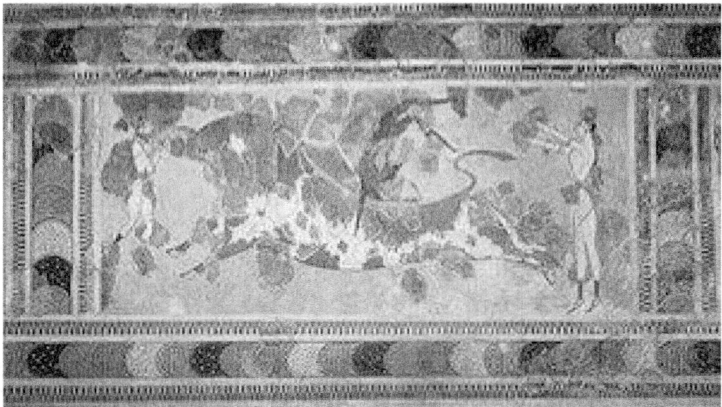

Figure 33: Bull leaping in Bull Worship
(or perhaps just secular Minoan Rodeo?)

Figure 34: Goddess
(or just an ornament for the mantelpiece?)

One may compare this with archaeologists 3000 years from now discovering a statue of a basketball player reaching for the net and declaring that it represents an offering to the gods.

From the above it is likely that most of the murals, jewellery, vases and other art work were only for decorative and aesthetic purposes. No doubt, as was the case in Athens, the influence and later assimilation into the surrounding shamanistic religions eventually gave rise to mythology and its influence on the arts around the Aegean.

As time went by, these Minoans became very wealthy merchants but, mundane as it may sound, they were no different from any modern Western society. They had the same likes and dislikes, the same creed, a similar religion and the same affinity for sport, recreation, the arts, luxuries and mementos. The ladies vied with one another at social functions, and the youth tried to impress the opposite sex. In short, apart from technology, they were identical to us as Homer described them in his Odyssey.

Another topic we should address here is the fact that the Middle Minoan civilisation is categorised as belonging to the Bronze Age. We know from the Oera Linda Book that the Frisians were in the Iron Age before 2193 BC. If one looks at the architecture of the Minoans and the later Mycenae, it is doubtful whether they could have built such buildings and the large amount of stone cutting these buildings required without the aid of iron tools. Is it not possible that the absence of iron implements could simply be ascribed to oxidation, otherwise known as ordinary rust? This was, after all, 3600 years ago. It is also evident that the Middle Minoan Period was of very short duration – perhaps as little as 50 years.

According to the Oera Linda Book, Greece and perhaps Crete as well, may have been part of the pre-2193 BC Fryan Federation. Most evidence of the early Cretan civilization may well have been wiped out by the global disaster. The little that remained, including Linear A and Linear B writings, may therefore have been part of the earlier period, or at best those of the primitive peoples the Frisians found there in 1600 BC – again under the control of princes and priests.

If one looks at the splendour and sophistication of the architecture and arts of the Middle Minoan Period, the Linear A and B clay tablets do not fit in. The Oera Linda Book mentions that Sea King Ion was at Walhallagara to load a consignment of paper when the fight between the army and the navy broke out.[160] The federation's written communications, and therefore that of middle Minoan Crete and the Hyksos would all have been on paper which would explain why we find no evidence thereof today.

We notice that when Minerva founded Athens and Minno founded Knossos, other primitive peoples already inhabited these areas. In all cases there were Priests or Princes in charge – from Scandinavia to Phoenicia and from Athens to Crete. These populations all appear to have migrated from the East after 2193 BC - probably from the Altai Mountain region as mentioned earlier.

---

[160] OLB: The book of Adela's followers, Chapter 27.

In addition to the fact that they all seemed to have been oligarchies with similarities in superstition, religion and forms of worship, there are also the references to cattle with golden horns. We read in the Oera Linda Book that the Magy in Finland and Northern Europe promised each of his subjects a cow with golden horns if they would infiltrate Frisian society[161]. In Homer's Odyssey, Ulysses made a special offering to the gods by having a heifer's horns gilded before the ceremony.

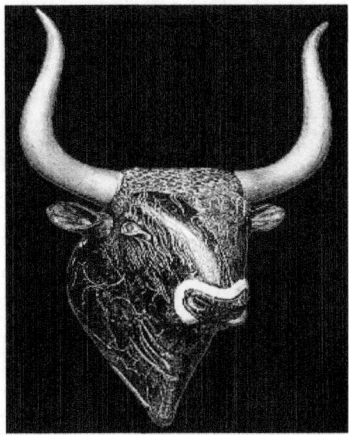

Figure 35: Late Minoan Bull's Head with golden horns.

Little Palace at Knossos
(ca. 1500 - 1450 BC)
(post-Frisian occupation)

The Iliad and Odyssey of Homer

In 1871 AD, four years after the appearance of the Oera Linda manuscript, the wealthy self-taught archaeologist, Dr Heinrich Schliemann, started excavations on a hill called Hisarlik near the Turkish town of Chanak. The site had already been identified as the likely site of Homeric Troy by the Scottish journalist Charles McLaren in 1822. Schliemann's find, the Priam Treasure, was named after King Priam who, according to Homer and Dares of Phrygia[162], was the king of Troy when the city was ransacked by the Achaeans.

---

161 OLB: The book of Adela's followers, Chapter 1.
162 History of the Fall of Troy

Archaeological work continued intermittently for the remainder of the 19th century and into the 20th century. By 1938, the work done by Wilhelm Dörpfeld (1893/4) and Carl Blegen (1932-1938) revealed that there were at least nine cities on top of one another. Only in the early 21st century was the most likely layer for Homeric Troy dated with relative certainty. Archaeologists announced that Troy VIIa was destroyed by warfare in ca 1188 BC. The announcement was made some 130 years after the Oera Linda manuscript was first examined by Dr E Verwijs at Leeuwarden in Friesland. As was the case with King Minos of Crete, Troy was regarded as a myth in the 19th century.

In The Book of Adela's Followers, the Oera Linda Book has the following entry:

In the year one thousand and five[163] after Aldland was submerged, this was inscribed on the eastern wall of Fryasburch:

After we have not seen any Krekalandar in Almanland for twelve years, there came three ships, more beautiful than any we had or had ever seen. On the largest of them was a king of the Ihonhis Islands. His name was Ulysus and the claims about his wisdom were great.

This king was told by a priestess that he would become king over all the Krekalanda, so the advice was to get a lamp that was lighted from the lamp in Texland. To obtain this, he had brought great treasures with him, above all, jewels for women, none in the world made more beautiful.

They came from Troy, a city that the Krekalandar had conquered. All these treasures he offered to the mother, but the mother did not want to know of it. At last, when he saw that he had nothing to gain, he went to Walhallagara. There was a matron in office whose name was Kat, though commonly called Kalip, because her lower lip stuck out like a masthead.

Here he tarried for years, to the annoyance of all that knew it. According to the matrons' claims, he eventually got a lamp from her; but it did him no good, because when he got to sea his ship was lost and he was taken up naked and destitute by the other ships.[164]

---

[163] 1188 BC
[164] OLB: The book of Adela's followers, Chapter 30

Here we have further prove that the Ionhis Elanda were the Ionian Islands. Homer described Ulysses as having hailed from Ithaca, one of the Ionian Islands.

It is interesting to note that the book states that they had not seen a Greek ship in Frisia for twelve years. This number of years could signify a period of preparation for the Achaean campaign against Troy, the actual siege and battles, which, according to Homer, lasted 10 years, plus some time afterwards for Ulysses to have reached Friesland. Dares mentioned that the Trojan War lasted for 10 years, 6 months and 12 days. This apparent insignificant bit of information in the Old Frisian manuscript actually serves as further vindication of the Oera Linda Book (and of Homer and Dares).

Both Homer and Dares described the combined Achaean fleet as having consisted of more than 1100 ships. Ovid mentioned a fleet of a thousand ships:

> But soon afterwards, he brought into that land a ravished wife, Helen, the cause of a disastrous war, together with a thousand ships, and all the great Pelasgian nation.[165]

If one works on a hundred combatants per ship, it would mean that the initial assault on Troy comprised more than 100 000 warriors. Dares reported that more than one and a half million men from both sides eventually perished in the war. Whatever the actual size of the conflict, it must have been substantial and the logistics would have been enormous. Every ocean-going vessel in the Aegean would have been involved. This would explain the 12-year absence of Greek merchant shipping to Frisia as reported in the Oera Linda Book.

According to Homer's Odyssey, Ulysses returned alone from his 10 years of travels after the Trojan War. His ships and their crews conveniently perished under the most heroic circumstances and he was the only surviving witness to their most extraordinary exploits. After all, he had to come up with a very good story to explain why he had been away from his beloved wife and son for 20 years.

---

[165] P. Ovidius Naso, *Metamorphoses, Book XII.*

About the only facts Ulysses' account have in common with the Oera Linda Book are that he survived naked after his ship had been wrecked and that Kalip (Calypso) stayed on an island. She was not this mythical nymph he described, but the Burgh Matron of Walhallagara on one of the seven islands in the Schelde Estuary; literally within a stone's throw from the mainland. He was definitely not held captive against his will. Homer describes him sitting dejected on the shores of his remote island prison staring longingly over the vast ocean. This must have struck a cord with Penelope, his wife, when he related his tragic story to her after his return. Talk about travelling salesmen!

Origins of the Aegean Tribes

When Ion and Minerva arrived in Attica in 1627 BC, the area was inhabited by a stone-age people who were goatherds, clothed in skins and who lived on meat, wild roots, herbs and honey. They lived along the slopes of their land's mountains, and the Frisians called them *Hellinggars*. Their greatest past-time was the ongoing fights, plundering and stealing of women and children between neighbouring tribes. To them the Frisians with their awe-inspiring fleet and superior weapons presented an opportunity to gain the upper hand over their rivals. One can realistically infer that they all vied for Frisians' friendship and support. In return, the Frisians would obtain land on which to settle and, where required, wives for their sailors and rowers for their boats.

The feuds between the local tribes, however, did not end with the arrival of the Frisians. For the next 1200 years they continued to settle their differences by violence but, instead of clubs and stones, they now had swords, axes and composite bows. In addition, piracy became a very competitive business and everyone vied for market share. In time and with the assistance of Frisian administration, technology and genes, the Aegean city states evolved – another legacy from the Fryan Federation.

In Homer's Odyssey we read how people discussed their cattle rustling and sheep and horse-stealing exploits in much the same manner as 21st century businessmen would discuss their investments on the stock exchange. The Stolen Lamb we often find on the menus in Greek restaurants acquires quite a new significance.

The following map depicts the early years, between 1627 BC and 1553 BC of the spread of the Frisian civilisation in the Aegean.

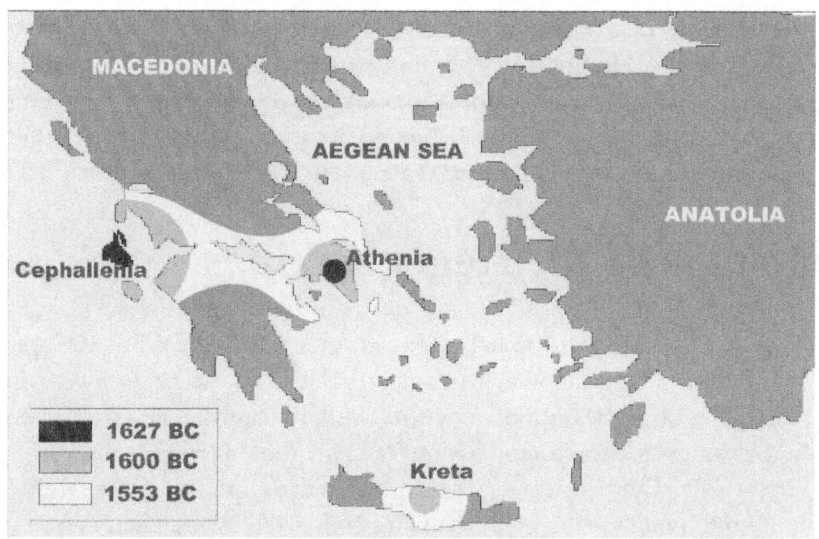

Figure 36: Frisian influence in the Aegean ca 1553 BC

The map shows a likely migration of the Frisians in the Aegean since the arrival of Minerva Nyhellenia around 1627 BC until the departure of Gert in ca. 1553 BC.

Ion, who settled on Cephallenia, started his new life's calling with a single revenge attack on the Tyrian fleet. This must have been quite profitable. What started as legitimate revenge became a career and later hereditary. The local inhabitants, who were quite familiar with pillaging and robbery, must have proven to be a welcome source of able combatants and sailors.

In the 5th century BC, some 1 200 years after the founding of Athens, Herodotus attempted to reconstruct the origins of the various peoples around the Aegean. In the intervening period we had the massive Thera eruption or eruptions, the Trojan War and numerous other wars and feuds with the accompanying founding and destruction of towns and cities. Communities and tribes were destroyed and assimilated into others and new warlords and city states came into being. Yet, despite this very volatile and fluid history, Herodotus vindicates the Oera Linda account:

> *Afterwards he (Croesus) turned his thoughts to the alliance which he had been recommended to contract, and sought to ascertain by inquiry which was the most powerful of the Grecian states. His inquiries pointed out to him two states as pre-eminent above the rest. These were the Lacedaemonians and the* Athenians, *the former of Doric, the latter of* Ionic blood. *And indeed these two nations had held from very, early times the most distinguished place in Greece, the (one) being a* Pelasgic, *the other a Hellenic people, and* the one having never quitted its original seats, *while the other had been excessively migratory; for during the reign of Deucalion, Phthiotis was the country in which the Hellenes dwelt, but under Dorus, the son of Hellen, they moved to the tract at the base of Ossa and Olympus, which is called Histiaeotis; forced to retire from that region by the Cadmeians, they settled, under the name of Macedni, in the chain of Pindus. Hence they once more removed and came to Dryopis; and from Dryopis having entered the Peloponnese in this way, they became known as Dorians.*
>
> *What the language of the Pelasgi was I cannot say with any certainty. If, however, we may form a conjecture from the tongue spoken by the Pelasgi of the present day- those, for instance, who live at Creston above the Tyrrhenians, who formerly dwelt in the district named Thessaliotis, and were neighbours of the people now called the Dorians - or those again who founded Placia and Scylace upon the Hellespont, who had previously dwelt for some time with the Athenians- or those, in short, of any other of the cities which have dropped the name but are in fact Pelasgian; if, I say, we are to form a conjecture from any of these, we must pronounce that* the Pelasgi spoke a barbarous language. *If this were really so, and the entire Pelasgic race spoke the same tongue,* the Athenians, who were certainly Pelasgi, *must have changed their language at the same time that they passed into the Hellenic body; for it is a certain fact that the people of Creston speak a language unlike any of their neighbours, and the same is true of the Placianians while the language spoken by these two people is the*

same; which shows that they both retain the idiom which they brought with them into the countries where they are now settled.

The Hellenic race has never, since its first origin, changed its speech. This at least seems evident to me. <u>It was a branch of the Pelasgic, which separated from the main body</u>, and at first was scanty in numbers and of little power; but it gradually spread and increased to a multitude of nations, chiefly by the voluntary entrance into its ranks of numerous tribes of barbarians. The Pelasgi, on the other hand, were, as I think, a barbarian race which never greatly multiplied.[166]

The Neolithic *Hellinggars*, which the Oera Linda Book described as the original inhabitants of Attica, were Herodotus' *Hellenic People* or *Hellenes*. These Hellenes, who never changed their language, are described as Lacedaemonians who were excessively migratory and of Doric blood – a distinct ethnic group. Herodotus tracks their migration from Phthiotis just north of Athens to Histiaeotis at the foot of Mount Olympus. They were later forced out of this location by the Cadmeians and moved to the Pindus Mountains to the west, where they became known as the Macedni. They moved a third and a fourth time – from the Pindus to Dryopsis and then lastly to the Peloponnese where they became known as the Dorians. From Herodotus' account we can see that there never was a Dorian Invasion. They were one of the original tribes of pre-historic Greece who moved around and finally settled in the Peloponnese. It would appear that they derived their name from their leader, Dorus, under whom they migrated to Phthiotis. Later we also find them as far afield as Crete.

---

[166] The *History* of Herodotus, Book I, p. 19.

Figure 37: Migration of Dorians
(From Herodotus' Histories)

The Athenians, on the other hand, were given the ethnic classification of Ionians or of Ionic blood by Herodotus. These were the descendants of the 1627 BC Frisian exiles who founded Athens and those who settled on the Ionian Island of Cephallenia under Ion. In time they colonised all of the Aegean – from Crete to Troy and from the Ionian Islands to Ionia, Lidia and Phrygia and across Anatolia to Persia despite having been a minority group wherever they went.

Some of Homer's Greek heroes of the Trojan-Grecian War were Ionian descendants such as the blond-haired Achilles, Ajax and Ulysses. Dares, from the Trojan point of view, also described their heroes as having had fair complexions and blond hair such as Alexander and Hector. It would appear that the Trojans were essentially of Frisian descent while the Greeks, or Achaeans, were a mixture of Frisians and the ancient tribes of Greece. There is a distinct possibility that the enmity between the Greeks and the Trojans could have had a racial connotation with the Trojans having been the more sophisticated or snobbish Frisian descendants of pure Frya's blood. It is nevertheless clear that Frisian descendants fought on both sides

The Ionian Athenians were called a Pelasgic Race with a barbarous language. One of the most credible explanations of the term Pelasgic came from Vladimir Georgiev[167] He asserted that pelasgoi came from pelasgos (sea) which would then mean that the <u>Pelasgic people are the Sea People</u> – precisely what the Oera Linda Book called them 4 000 years ago.

Contrary to modern proposals, the Pelasgians were not the original primitive inhabitants of Greece. Both Herodotus and the Oera Linda Book claim that they were the latecomers and this hypothesis proposes that they were the Frisian founders of the later advanced Greek civilisation. It is also significant to note that Ovid and other ancient scribes referred to them as the *Great Pelasgian* nation.

The following map serves to illustrate how the descendants of the Frisians could have spread their presence and influence during the next 100 years, from 1553 BC to 1450 BC. In the Peloponnese they would again rub shoulders with their old neighbours from Phthiosis, now called the Dorians.

---

[167] Vladimir Ivanov Georgiev (1908-1986) was a prominent Bulgarian linguist, philologist, and educational administrator

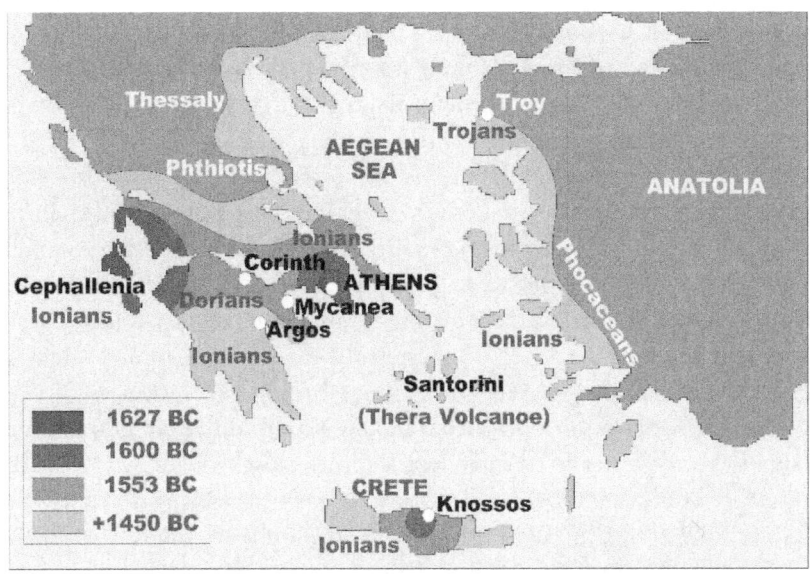

Figure 38: Frisian influence in the Aegean by 1450 BC
(after the eruption of Mount Thera on the island(s) of
Santorini.)

Achaeans, Argives and Danaans

The next topic that needs to be examined in Homer's Epics is
the relationship between the Achaeans, the Argives and the Danaans.
At a first glance it would appear as if Homer regarded these names as
synonyms, which create some confusion among readers.

Homer purportedly wrote the Iliad and Odyssey some 400
years after the Trojan War which, in turn, was concluded 439 years
after Ion, Minerva and Minnos arrived in Attica. That is almost twice
as long as from Columbus's travels to present-day America. Much can
happen in 839 years.

As stated earlier, most of the estimated 5000 Frisians who
colonised Attica and the Ionian Islands in 1627 BC were single. The
married couples remained in the citadel at Athens but the rest would
have inter-married with the locals – especially Ion and his henchmen.
The blond hair, blue eyes and fair complexion of the Frisians would

have remained a trait of these Frisian descendants for centuries to come. This is exactly how Homer described Ulysses from the Ionian Island of Ithaca with his yellow hair and fair skin, as well as other Danaans, such as Achilles and Ajax from the Peloponnese.

One must assume that the Ionian Islands soon became too small for the pirates with their young families. Some would have relocated to their in-laws on the main land and with time they would have moved further afield to Argos and Mycenae on the Peloponnese. Still later they would have inhabited Ionia off the Anatolian coast. Ionia was obviously named after the settlers from the Ionian Islands. As we have seen, the term Ionian was an ethnic classification.

Legends have it that the Danaans derived their name from Danaus who came to Argos from Lidia close to Ionia. Danaans therefore would have been a group of Ionians of Frisian descent who were followers of Danaus. Danaus appeared to have ruled in Argos in the distant past and any Ionian with his traits or complexion would automatically have been called a Danaan.

The Argives denoted a geographical identity. They were the inhabitants of Argos and surrounds. Perhaps most, but not all Argives would have been Danaans and not all Danaans would necessarily have been Argives. Some of them would have been Dorians.

The third group Homer referred to the most was the Achaeans. This would have been more of a political affiliation or a league – in other words, all those who fought together against the Trojans. This would have included not only the Danaans and Argives, but also allies from Northern Greece, Crete, the Ionian Islands, etc.

The Founding of Rome

Ancient writers and legends have it that Rome was founded by refugees from Troy after it had been ransacked by the Achaeans. The Oera Linda Book confirms this:

> *In order to make myself well understood, I must let alone for a while my account of the Scotch people, and write something about the near Krekalanders (Italians). The Krekalanda formerly belonged to us*

only, but from time immemorial, descendants of Lyda and Finda have established themselves there. Of these last there came in the end a whole troop from Troy. Troy is the name of a town that the far Krekalanders (Greeks) had taken and destroyed. When the Trojans had nestled themselves among the near Krekalanders, with time and industry they built a strong town with walls and a citadel named Rome, that is, Spacious.[168]

The Achaeans which included the Pelasgics defeated Troy. It would take almost a thousand years before the descendants of the Trojans, who became known as the Romans, got their own back.

The Barbarians

In many of the writings of the ancient Greeks, Egyptians and the Romans, references are made to *barbarians* and *barbarian-* or *barbarous languages* – be it around the Aegean Sea, Western Europe, North Africa and the Middle East. The name barbarian comes from the Greek *Barbarŏs* or *Barbaroi*. The word is said to have imitated the *bar-bar sound* which is what the language of these non-Greek speakers would have sounded like to the Greeks.

Our understanding of the word is that it denotes savages or primitive and uncivilised peoples. This is one of the reasons why there has been so much confusion throughout the centuries to make sense of the evolution of Grecian and other civilizations in antiquity. Some scholars suggest that the term barbarians two thousand years ago simply meant Non-Greeks or Foreigners. It is, however, evident that not all non-Greeks or foreigners were called Barbarians – only those that spoke the Bar-bar language.

It is proposed here that the term Barbarian was meant to denote a specific and highly developed nation or, at worst, a specific ethnic group with unique features and a unique language. Most references in the ancient texts to barbarŏs should have been interpreted as a proper noun with a capital B instead of a common collective noun.

---

[168] OLB: *The writings of Beden*, Chapter 3.

(Compare *Barbarian* as in *European* to *barbarian* as in *savage*). They were certainly not savages although many of the ancient scribes stereotyped them as such. Admittedly, certain groups on the fringes of civilization did behave like or were associated with savages.

Herodotus, in the introduction to his Histories, wrote:

> *These are the researches of Herodotus of Halicarnassus, which he publishes, in the hope of thereby preserving from decay the remembrance of what men have done, and of preventing the great and wonderful actions of the Greeks and the Barbarians from losing their due meed of glory:*[169]

Herodotus is regarded as the Father of History or the first professional historian. Modern archaeology and research vindicate him as a very credible historian. His successors in ancient Greece and into the Middle ages, however, thought that he was unreliable:

> *Thucydides criticised Herodotus in his essay "On the Malignity of Herodotus", describing Herodotus as "Philobarbaros" (barbarian-lover) for not being pro-Greek enough, which suggests that Herodotus might actually have done a reasonable job of being even-handed*[170]

As stated earlier, Herodotus speculated about the origins of the Greeks and stated that the Athenians were a Pelasgic people of Ionic blood, spoke a barbarous language and were indeed descendants of the Barbarians. He also stated categorically that the Hellenes were the original inhabitants of Greece and that the Barbarian Pelasgics were the late-comers. This is exactly what the Oera Linda Book tells us. We also noted earlier that even Ovid referred to the great Pelasgic nation.

Clearly these references to the Athenians, the Pelasgics and the Barbarians are not of savages but of a group of people whom they greatly admired and whom they saw at least as the Greeks' equals.

---

[169] The *History* of Herodotus, Book I
[170] Wikipedia on Herodotus

Josephus (90 AD), the biblical apostle Paul and others also referred to the Barbarians with respect and admiration:

> ... (58) and I suppose I have sufficiently declared that this custom of transmitting down the histories of ancient times hath been better preserved by those nations which are called Barbarians, than by the Greeks themselves.[171]

This certainly does not sound like savages. In the Bible we find the following in two of Paul's letters:

Romans 1:14
(14) I am debtor both to the Greeks, and to the Barbarians; both to the wise, and to the unwise.

1 Corinthians 14:10-11
(10) There are, it may be, so many kinds of voices in the world, and none of them is without signification.
(11) Therefore if I know not the meaning of the voice, I shall be unto him that speaketh a barbarian, and he that speaketh shall be a barbarian unto me.[172]

Dares of Phrygia who himself was a Barbarian who fought on the Trojan side during the war with the Archaeans, ascribed the following sentiments to the king of the Trojans. As early as ca 1200 BC King Priam referred to himself as a Barbarian, and seemingly proud of the fact:

> Now, Priam concluded, since the Greeks refused to do as he wished, he would send an army to make them pay for their crimes, lest they think Barbarians worthy of scorn.[173]

---

[171] Josephus: *Against Apion*, Book 1.11
[172] The Holy Bible: King James Version. 1995. Logos Research Systems, Inc.: Oak Harbor, WA
[173] Dares of Phrygia, History of the Fall of Troy

In describing some of the heroes on both sides Dares, like Herodotus, described a number of them, Achaeans and Trojans alike, as having been of fair complexion with blond or auburn hair. It would therefore appear that these two groups had a common ancestry. From the above quote it would further appear that those amongst the Greeks who were still of a fair complexion and with blond hair were no longer regarded as Barbarians; neither by themselves nor by the Trojans. They were apparently further on the road to being assimilated into the local population than the Trojans.

The Trojans, on the other hand, still seemed to have been trying to preserve their original language and perhaps even their racial exclusivity. It may well have been that one of Helen of Troy's attractions to the Trojans were her blonde hair and fair complexion. She was the ideal Trojan. It would appear that, before the fall of Troy, the civilization in Phrygia (a derivative of Frya?) and Ionia (colonised from the Ionian Islands) in Asia Minor was further advanced than that of the Greeks. The Ionian School (University) of Philosophy in Melitus, which was the most advanced institution of learning in antiquity, attested to the fact. Other famous Barbarians were the fabulously rich King Midas and King Croesus of the Lydians[174] who purportedly minted the first coins in history.

It is proposed here that the Frisians or, at least the West Europeans, were the Barbarians of old. After they colonised Lower Egypt and later Attica, the Ionian Islands and Crete, they moved on to Asia Minor where they founded the empire of Phrygia as well as Lydia, Caria and Lucia. Eventually they, as the Sea People, drove out the Hittites and migrated right into Persia. In Chapter 6 the Frisian influence on the Persian Empire is described in more detail. The reader will then understand why the Persians were also classed as Barbarians, or speakers of the Bar-bar language.

---

[174] Lydia was in Asia Minor and is not be confused by the Oera Linda Book's Lyda (Libya) in North Africa

DNA Mapping

The following section is an attempt at reconciling the Oera Linda Book with human migrations since 2193 BC and what we find in the average genetic profile of the inhabitants of Greece. It would appear that the most dominant DNA Y-haplogroups in the general populace are E3b originating from North Africa, I from Central Europe or Scandinavia, and J from the Middle East – all about 25% each. The other two haplogroups of significance are R1b from Western Europe (±12%) and R1a from Central Asia (±10%).

The only haplogroup indigenous to the Middle East would be J, which according to Herodotus, migrated from the coast of the Indian Ocean (the Erythraean or Arabian Sea) to Phoenicia.

> *According to the Persians best informed in history, the Phoenicians began to quarrel. This people, who had formerly dwelt on the shores of the Erythraean Sea, having migrated to the Mediterranean and settled in the parts which they now inhabit, began at once, they say, to adventure on long voyages, freighting their vessels with the wares of Egypt and Assyria.*[175]

The Fertile Crescent in the Middle East was particularly hard-hit by the 2193 BC catastrophe and the population was decimated. The area was repopulated by refugees who, initially at least, came mostly from Arabia. It was only later, from 2000 BC onwards, that the J haplogroup was spread around the Mediterranean by the Arabian Gola from Phoenicia.

It is proposed here that haplogroup I could be the oldest inhabitants of the Aegean which dates back to pre-2193 BC. We find them as a fairly dominant group right across Western and Central Europe, from Scandinavia to Greece. The second oldest group would be E3b from North Africa, who migrated to the Aegean after 2193 BC. A combination of these two haplogroups would then have been the predecessors of the Dorians.

---

[175] The *History* of Herodotus, Book I, p. 1

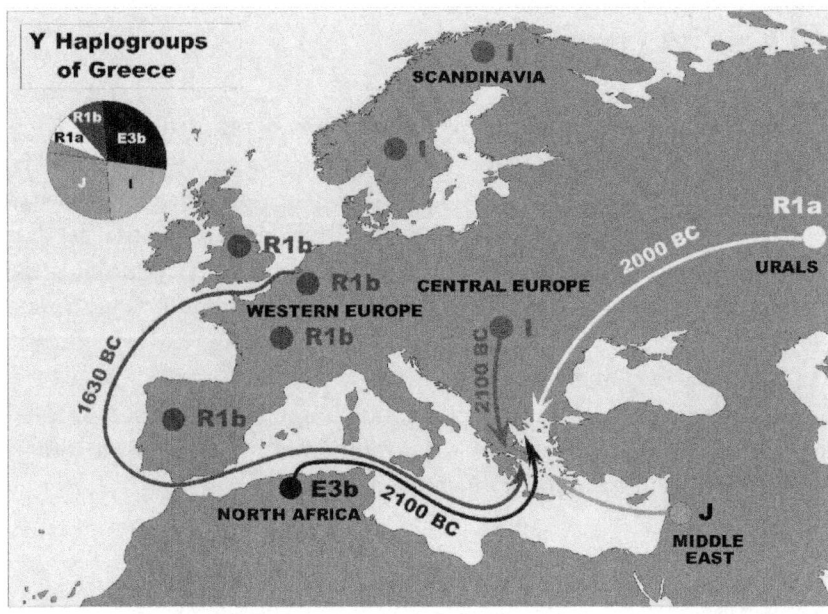

Figure 39: Suggested re-population of Greece after 2193 BC

In The Oera Linda Book we read:

> *When Atland was submerged there was also much suffering on the shores of the Middle Sea. As a result, many people from Finda's land came to our Heinde- and Fere Krekalanda and also many from Lyda's land. There were also many of our people that went to Lyda's land[176]. The result of all this was that the Heinde- and Fere Krekalanda were lost to the rule of the Mother.[177]*

When Jon and Minerva arrived in Attica in 1627 BC, some 566 years after the 2193 BC global disaster, they found the Neolithic Hellingars (E3b and I) under the leadership of the priests or princes from the Altai Region in the East (R1a).

---

[176] These were most likely the predecessors of the modern Berbers in North Africa. The name *Berber* came from the Arabic word for Barbarian. (Afrikaans: *Barbaar*)
[177] OLB: The book of Adela's followers, Chapter 24.

While we were labouring on the citadel the leaders came along and when they saw that we had no slaves, it did not please them and they let her understand it, as they thought she was a sovereign.

But Minerva asked: "How did you come by your slaves?"

They answered: "Some we have bought and others were won in battle."

Minerva said: "If nobody would buy slaves they would not steal your children and you would not have wars about it. If you wish to remain our allies, you must set your slaves free."

This the chiefs would not do and wanted to drive us away; but the bravest of their people came and helped us man our burgh, which we now made of stone.[178]

In our model, the R1b haplogroup would represent the Frisians from Western Europe that arrived in 1627 BC with Jon and Minerva. It would appear that the J haplogroup from the Middle East was essentially absent from Attica at that stage and only arrived much later when Greece became a political, financial and cultural giant on the international scene.

Thus far we have seen that the Phoenicians owed their rise to fame to the Frisians from Western Europe, as did the Hyksos Dynasty in Lower Egypt. The Greek, Trojan, Phrygian and in fact all the advanced civilizations in and around Asia Minor were founded by these West Europeans.

---

[178] OLB: The book of Adela's followers, Chapter 28.

Chapter 5

Expulsion

Cecrops I

I n ca 1553 BC, 74 years after Minerva had laid the foundations of Athens, there were essentially four groups of descendants of the Fryan Federation in the Aegean. In the citadel of Athenia and on the Island of Crete we find two groups of exclusive or conservative Frisians who tried to maintain their creed and ethnic roots. Both inside and outside the walls of Athens there would have been the descendants of those who intermarried and were assimilated by the indigenous people. Further afield, on the Ionian Islands, the Northern Peloponnese and surrounding areas, the third and fourth generations of Ion's pirates were blending with the surrounding population.

The Athenian Frisians disregarded the wishes of the local priests and elected a new Folk Mother by the name of Gert. The supporters of Gert called themselves the *Gertmanne*. It is evident, however, that not all Frisians supported this act of defiance. The priests were furious and incited the locals to arms. They had accepted Minerva as a deity and the election of a new Folk Mother was sacrilege. One may also assume that the locals resented the Athenian Frisians with their haughty attitude and segregated lifestyle; so they attacked the Frisian citadel. The fortifications were too well constructed, though, and the Frisians held out; that is, until an Egyptian priest by the name of *Sekrops* (Cecrops) arrived on the scene.

When Hellenia or Minerva died, the priests conferred as though they were with us, and that it should clearly appear so, they had Hellenia declared a goddess. They also refused to have any other mother chosen, saying that they feared there was no one among her matrons whom they could trust like Minerva, whose nickname was Nyhellenia.

But we would not recognise Minerva as a goddess, because she herself had said that no one could be as good or perfect as Wralda's spirit. Therefore, we chose Gert, Pire's daughter, as our Mother.

When the priests saw that they could not fry their herrings on our fire (have it their way), *they left Athenia, and said that we would not accept Minerva as a goddess out of envy, because she had shown the natives so much affection. Thereupon they gave the people images of her, declaring that they might ask everything of them, as long as they remained obedient.*

From all these tales the stupid people became resentful towards us and at last they attacked us. We, however, had built our stone bulwark with two horns all the way to the sea. *They could therefore not get to us. Though, what happened is that an Egyptian who was a high priest, bright of eye, clear of brain, and enlightened of mind, whose name was Sekrops, came to give them advice.*[179]

This *bulwark with two horns all the way to the sea* is known as the *Long Walls of Athens*. The Persians, amongst others, destroyed these walls in 480 BC but it seems that they were rebuilt a few times. The Spartans destroyed the walls again in 404 BC as part of a surrender deal.

---

[179] OLB: The book of Adela's followers, Chapter 29.

Figure 40: Remains of the Long Walls of Athens.
Originally built by the Frisians in ca 1600 BC

The Oera Linda Book says that they built the citadel of Athenia an hour away from the harbour. These walls, therefore, would have been some four kilometres long. Some portions still exist today. It seems likely that the small natural harbour where Ion and Minerva dropped anchor in 1627 BC could have been the present day Dutch sounding *Zea Marina* or *Zea Port* near Athens. The Oera Linda book says that the harbour was too small for all the ships.

In Greek mythology we find Cecrops I as the first mythical king of Athens. He purportedly ruled from ca 1556 BC to ca 1500 BC and taught the Athenians to read and write. According to the myths, he introduced marriage, ceremonial burial and forbade any offering to the gods. He taught the Athenians the art of navigation on the open seas and brought in new laws and the improved administration of justice. All these innovations and the timeframes are almost exactly what the Oera Linda Book claims for the Frisian colonists. How did the so-called 19th century hoaxers manage to date and fit Cecrops so seamlessly into their tale? What is even more puzzling is that the mythological Cecrops is said to have been half man and half snake or reptile. Surely the Oera Linda Book could have chosen a more realistic character – if the book had been a hoax.

Reading between the lines, it should be quite evident that Cecrops and/or his followers inherited and then claimed all the accomplishments and innovations of the previous owners of Athens, the loathed Frisians or Barbarians, for himself. This was not the first or last time this had happened in history. From this episode we can now realistically deduce that the Greek Alphabet came from Frya's People in Western Europe.

Figure 41: Cecrops I

The Oera Linda Book echoes a fringe theory which claims that Cecrops came from Egypt:

> *There was a rumour that he was kind to us because he was the offspring of a Fryan girl and an Egyptian Priest as he had blue eyes and many of our girls had been abducted and sold in Egypt.[180]*

---

[180] OLB: The Book of Adela's Followers, chapter 30

The reader will notice that the time slot of Cecrops fits in exactly with the time that the Hyksos ruled in Lower Egypt under their last Pharaoh, Assis. This was also shortly before the Biblical famine in Canaan. In Chapter 3 the argument was raised that the Hyksos were of mixed Frisian, Egyptian and African decent. This Egyptian and Fryan background of Cecrops fits in with that theory. In the Dictionary of Greek and Roman Antiquities (edited by William Smith [1870]) we read:

> *The later Greek writers describe Cecrops as having immigrated into Greece with a band of colonists from Sais in Egypt (Diod. i. 29; Scholl. Ad Arist. Plut. 773) But this account is not only rejected by some of the ancients themselves but by the ablest critics of modern times.*

In chapter 7.7 of the *Geography* by Strabo (Greek geographer, philosopher and historian, 64/63 BC – ca. 24 AD) it is claimed, however, that the name Cecrops was of Barbarian origin and in a further fragment he also claims that Cecrops I came from Egypt:

> *Moreover, the barbarian origin of some is indicated by their names — Cecrops, Codrus, Aïclus, Cothus, Drymas, and Crinacus.*

> *There were two kings of Athens named Cecrops. The first of this name, first king of Attica and Boeotia came from Egypt.*

The *Dictionary of Greek and Roman Antiquities* also tells us that: *From these traditions it appears, that Cecrops must be regarded as a hero of the Pelasgian race* (Sea Peoples) – a sentiment that is echoed by the Oera Linda Book:

> *From the other Krekalander you may have heard a great deal of bad about Sekrops, because he was not of good repute, but I dare say he was an enlightened man, highly regarded both by the locals and by us, for he was not for the oppression of people like the other priests, but he was virtuous and knew how to value the wisdom of distant nations.*

Because he realised this, he allowed us to live according to our own Segabok (Law Book). There was a rumour that he was kind to us because he was the offspring of a Fryan girl and an Egyptian priest as he had blue eyes and many of our girls had been abducted and sold in Egypt. He never confirmed this himself, though. Whatever the case, he certainly showed us more friendship than all the other priests put together.[181]

Cecrops, it would appear, was on an assignment from Egypt and he had a lot of political backing. He realised that the inhabitants of Attica would not be able to subdue the Frisians so he called for reinforcements from Tyre. The Tyrians eagerly responded. We may assume that by now they had had enough of the plundering of their ships and towns by the Ionians and could have thought that the Athenians were behind it all. Cecrops' orders may well have been to clear out the pirates in the Aegean or perhaps, as we shall see later, this may have been part of a much more sinister strategy.

When Sekrops saw that he could not breach our wall with his men, he sent messengers to Thirhis. Thereupon three hundred ships full of soldiers of the wild mountain peoples arrived unexpectedly and sailed into our harbour whilst we with all our men were fighting on the ramparts.

When they had taken the harbour, the wild soldiers wanted to plunder the town and our ships. One soldier had already ravished a girl, but Sekrops would not permit it and the Thiriar sailors, who still had Frya's blood in their veins, said: "If you do that we will burn our ships, and you shall never see your mountains again."

Sekrops, who had no inclination towards murder or destruction, sent messengers to Gert to claim the burgh, offering her free exit with all her floating and movable assets and those of her followers who felt like it. The wisest of the burghers seeing that they could not hold the burgh, advised Gert to accept at once, before Sekrops became furious and changed his mind. Three months later Gert

---

[181] OLB: The Book of Adela's Followers, chapter 30

departed with the best of Frya's children and seven times twelve ships.[182]

In Chapter 30 of the Book of Adela's Followers, Ulysses' scribe, writing some 360 years later, gave a bit more insight into the background and character of Cecrops. By then, in 1188 BC, the old harbour in Athens, which was built during Minerva's time, had been replaced. From the scribe's account it is evident that not all the Frisians left Athens in 1553 BC – only the right-wing followers of Gert; known as the Gertmanne. The more moderate Frisians remained and later played a pivotal role in the development of the Hellenistic and Greek civilisations.

From this king (Ulysses) there remained here a writer[183] *of pure Frya's blood born in the new harbour of Athenia. What follows is what he wrote for us about Athenia from which one may decide how true the Mother Hellicht had spoken when she said that Frya's morals would not prevail in Athenia:*

"From the other Krekalander you may have heard a great deal of bad about Sekrops, because he was not of good repute, but I dare say he was an enlightened man, highly regarded both by the locals and by us, for he was not for the oppression of people like the other priests, but he was virtuous and knew how to value the wisdom of distant nations.

Because he realised this, he allowed us to live according to our own Segabok (Law Book). There was a rumour that he was kind to us because he was the offspring of a Fryan girl and an Egyptian priest as he had blue eyes and many of our girls had been abducted and sold in Egypt. He never confirmed this himself, though. Whatever the case, he certainly showed us more friendship than all the other priests put together.

When he died his successors started tampering with our laws and gradually made so many disgusting changes that finally nothing remained of equality and freedom but the shadow and the name. In addition, they would not allow the decrees to be recorded in writing so

---

[182] OLB: The book of Adela's followers, Chapter 29
[183] This scribe remained in Frisia after Ulysses returned to Greece.

that the knowledge thereof was hidden from us. Formerly all cases in Athenia were pleaded in our language; afterwards it had to be in both languages and at last in the native language only.

In the first years the men of Athenia only took wives from our own race, but as the young men grew up with the native girls, they also took from them. The crossbred children that came from this were the most beautiful and cleverest in the world but they were also the most wicked. Sitting on both sides, they would not subscribe to the laws and customs except when it was in their own interest.

As long as a ray of Frya's spirit existed, all building materials were made to a common standard, and no one could build his house larger or better than that of his neighbours. When some of the bastardized townspeople got rich by our (trade) voyages and by the silver that their slaves mined in the silver countries, they went to live out on the cliffs or in the valleys. There, behind high enclosures of trees or walls, they built mansions with costly furniture, and to be in high esteem with the vile priests, they placed there likenesses of false gods and unchaste statues. Sometimes the vile priests and rulers desired the boys rather than the girls, and often led them astray from the paths of virtue by rich presents or by force.

Because wealth was held in higher regard by this spoilt and bastardized race than virtue and honour, one sometimes saw lads who decorated themselves with wide expensive robes; to the shame of their parents and the matrons, and to the ridicule of their own sex. If our simple elders came to a general assembly in Athenia to make complaints, they were jeered: "Hear, hear! There is a sea monster going to speak!"

Such is Athenia become, like a morass in a tropical country full of leeches, toads, and poisonous snakes, in which no man of decent morals can set his foot.[184]

The *splendid flowing robes* became fashion and even today we still associate the ancient Hellenic, Greek and Roman politicians and intelligentsia with this type of dress.

---

[184] OLB: The book of Adela's followers, Chapter 30

The jeering: *Hear, Hear! There is a sea-monster going to speak!* would indicate that, even in Athens, the Frisians were known as the *Sea People*. They were not only very prudish and aloof but, more than likely, conceited, haughty and arrogant. The fact that justice was dispensed to all Athenians in the Frisian language only, confirms this view:

> *Formerly all the cases in Athenia were pleaded in our language, but afterwards in both languages, and at last in the indigenous language only.*

This would explain the hostility they experienced from the rest of the populace. No doubt the essential elements of their democratic institutions and legal system were adopted by the locals but the Frisians would not get the credit for it – the pagan priests made sure of that. Even the *Bar-bar* language of the foreigners was eventually eradicated from all state institutions. The exact same process can be observed today in South Africa where Afrikaans, the former un-official language of all state departments, has been replaced since 1994. In fact, there appear to be remarkable parallels between South Africa and the ancient Greece of 3500 years ago.

It may well be that the discrimination against those moderate Frisians who did not leave with the Gertmanne became so untenable that they eventually migrated to Anatolia or Asia Minor. In these new settlements which became known as Ionia, Lidia and Phrygia they maintained their creed, Bar-bar language and civilization for another few centuries. Even after the fall of Troy some 368 years later, the civilization in Phrygia was still much more advanced than in Greece. It was only after Alexander the Great's invasion of Asia Minor that Phrygia disappeared into obscurity. The savage Alexander not only destroyed all the highly advanced Barbarian states in Asia Minor, but also the great Barbarian civilization of Persia.

During Cecrops' reign, he allowed the Frisians who remained in Athens to *live according to our own Law Book*. After his death his successors soon began to *tear up our charters*. You do not tear up clay tablets. Here, again, we have two references to paper documents, and once again we can understand why we do not find any evidence today, 3500 years later, of a Frisian presence in the Aegean.

Three months after Cecrops' ultimatum had been accepted, and only 74 years after they had founded Athenia, the Gertmanne sailed away on 84 ships. Once again they went in search of a place of their own where they could settle and practise their religion and racially segregated lifestyle unhindered. Perhaps they would not had been welcome in Frisia after having been exposed to foreign influences for such a long time or perhaps Cycrops left them no option. The latter seems probable. We read that, soon after they had left Athens, a smaller fleet of 30 ships with women and children from Tyre joined them; the merchants of the Mediterranean were determined to purge their sea routes of the Sea People. In fact, they were escorted out of town by a sea king from Tyre.

> *Three months later Gert departed with the best of Frya's children and seven times twelve ships.*
>
> *When they were one day's sailing out of the harbour, there came thirty ships from Thirhis with wives and children. They were on their way to Athenia, but when they heard how things stood there, they went with Gert. The Sea King of the Thiriar brought them all through the strait, which at that time ran into the Red Sea.*
>
> *At last, they landed at Pangap, that is, in our language Five Waters, because here five rivers flow together to the sea. Here they settled. That land they called Gertmannia.*
>
> *The King of Thirhis seeing afterwards that all his best sailors were gone, sent all his ships with his wild soldiers to catch them, dead or alive. When they arrived at the strait, though, both the sea and the earth trembled. The land was lifted up so that all the water ran out of the strait, and the mud and grime rose up like a rampart before them. This happened on account of the virtues of the Gertmanna, as every one may clearly see.*[185]

It is opportune that we stop here for a few observations:

---

[185] OLB: The book of Adela's followers, Chapter 29.

1. We see that not everyone left with Gert – only the best. One may assume that they meant those Frisians who were not prepared to be ruled by a pagan government and, equally important, those who were still of pure Fryan blood. The uncompromising stance of the conservative Frisians against integration with outsiders can be likened to what we find among Jewish communities over the centuries. In fact, the Oera Linda Book records that when a remnant of these people returned to Frisia more than 1 200 years later, they were essentially the same – even in the use of their language.

2. The Frisians sailed directly from the Mediterranean to the Red Sea through a natural strait where the Bitter Lakes and the Suez Canal are today. This sea route would have enabled the Egyptians to control any maritime traffic between the East and the Mediterranean and the Frisians would not have been able to return unnoticed. Strabo vindicates the Oera Linda Book when he wrote around the start of the Christian era some 1560 years later:

> *Strato conjectures that ... ...in ancient times Egypt was covered by the sea as far as the bogs about Pelusium, Mt. Casius, and Lake Sirbonis; at all events, even to-day, when the salt-lands in Egypt are dug up, the excavations are found to contain sand and fossil-shells, as though the country had been submerged beneath the sea and the whole region round Mt. Casius and the so-called Gerrha had once been covered with shoal water so that it connected with the Gulf of the Red Sea; and when the sea retired, these regions were left bare, except that the Lake Sirbonis remained; then the lake also broke through to the sea, and thus became a bog. In the same way, Strato adds, the beaches of the so-called Lake Moeris more nearly resemble sea-beaches than river-banks[186]*

3. The fleet seemed to have known exactly where it was going, which means that they must have had accurate maritime maps and some knowledge of their destination.

---

[186] Strabo's Geography, Book 1, Chapter 3, P187

4. The Oera Linda Book refers to a massive earthquake that closed the strait between the Mediterranean and the Red Sea. This event was so powerful that the book reported damage right up to India.

We have already seen in Chapter 3 that, in terms of Biblical chronology, the seven-year famine of the Old Testament started in 1553 BC. From the Oera Linda Book it is back-calculated that the Frisians were expelled from Athens in ca 1553 BC, and archaeologists estimate that the Middle Minoan Civilization came to an end at about this time. It is therefore reasonable to suspect that Thera erupted in 1553 BC for the second time in 75 years, the first eruption having taken place in 1628 BC. Neither the Bible nor the Oera Linda Book recorded any of the eruptions, mainly because the Frisians and the Israelites were too far away. They only felt the earthquakes. Those who witnessed or experienced the eruption were either killed or their accounts of the occurrence did not survive.

Exodus of the Hyksos

Conventional Egyptian chronology shows that at the end of the Second Intermediate Period, towards the latter part of the Seventeenth Dynasty, the Hyksos were driven out of Egypt, probably in ca 1525 BC. This would have happened 28 years after the Frisians in Athens and the Frisian descendants in Tyre had been expelled. Clearly, this was an orchestrated effort in the Eastern Mediterranean to drive out or ethnically cleanse the region of a particular group, such as the Sea People, during the mid-16th century BC. This episode strengthens the stance that the Hyksos were of Frisian, or West-European origins.

Josephus, or rather Manetho whom he quoted, described the Hyksos as a large group of people who had a standing army of 240 000 men in the garrison at Avaris. The total population could therefore have been well over a million people, but it is equally possible that a large number of their troops might have been either native Egyptians or mercenary recruits from Libya and surrounds. After they had been evicted from Egypt they went to Palestine where they supposedly founded Jerusalem. This would have been 199 years before the

Israelites arrived in the Promised Land in 1326 BC after their Biblical exodus from Egypt and their 40 years of wandering in the desert. Josephus relates the story thus:

> *(86) He says further, 'That under a king, whose name was Alisphragmuthosis, the shepherds were subdued by him, and were indeed driven out of other parts of Egypt, but were shut up in a place that contained ten thousand acres; this place was named Avaris'. (87) Manetho says, 'That the shepherds built a wall round all this place, which was a large and a strong wall, and this in order to keep all their possessions and their spoils within a place of strength, (88) but that Thummosis the son of Alisphragmuthosis made an attempt to take them by force and by siege, with four hundred and eighty thousand men to lie around them, but that, upon his despair of taking the place by that siege, they came to a composition with them, that they should leave Egypt, and go, without any harm to be done to them, wherever they would; (89) and that, after this composition was made, they went away with their whole families and effects, not fewer in number than two hundred and forty thousand, and took their journey from Egypt, through the wilderness, for Syria; (90) but that as they were in fear of the Assyrians, who had then the domination over Asia, they built a city in that country which is now called Judea, and that was large enough to contain this great number of men, and called it Jerusalem.*[187]

For lack of evidence of any other scenario, we shall accept Manetho's account that the Hyksos went to Jerusalem. However, we dispute the statement that they actually founded the city. We know that Melchizedek was already king of Salem 241 years before when Abram entered Canaan in 1766 BC. It would make sense that the Hyksos sought refuge there with the descendants of the monotheist Melchizedek who, as will be shown shortly, was either of Frisian descent or a convert to Fryan theology. Jerusalem was close to the Hyksos' distant relatives and trading partners, the Tyrians.

---

[187] Josephus: *Against Apion*, Book I, (14).

In Judges 19 in the Bible we read the chilling story of the Levite and his concubine who travelled from Bethlehem in Judah to his home in the hills of Ephraim. En route they went past Jerusalem:

Judges 19:10-11
(10) However, the man was not willing to spend that night; so he rose and departed, and came opposite Jebus (that is, Jerusalem). With him were the two saddled donkeys; his concubine was also with him. (11) They were near Jebus, and the day was far spent; and the servant said to his master, "Come, please, and let us turn aside here into this city of the Jebusites and lodge in it."
(12) But his master said to him, "We will not turn aside here into a city of foreigners, who are not of the children of Israel; we will go on to Gibeah".[188]

Here we have Salem which became Jebus (Jebus-Salem?) and later Jeru-Salem; inhabited by foreigners. This Biblical reference to foreigners seems to support Manetho's narrative.

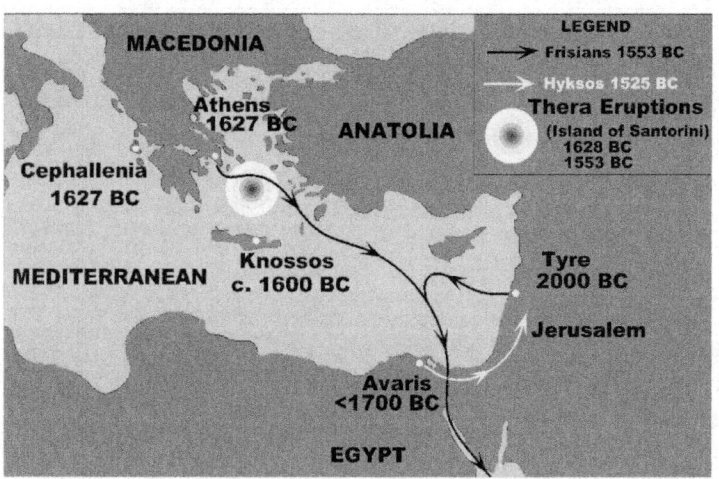

Figure 42: Expulsion of the Frisians in the 15th century BC
(from Avaris, Athens and Tyre).

---

[188] The New King James Version. 1996, c 1982. Thomas Nelson: Nashville

Manetho recorded that the Hyksos travelled over land which would mean that their fleet was either destroyed or confiscated by the Egyptians. Unlike the Frisians from Athens, they could not sail away to distant lands but had to settle relatively close to where they came from – they fled overland with all their women, children and earthly possessions. In addition, since they were a seafaring people, it is unlikely that they would have ventured too far from the sea.

It is quite possible that the Hyksos' fleet and a large part of the population were wiped out by tsunamis from the Thera eruption 28 years before. If this was the case, it would mean that the Egyptians seized the opportunity and attacked when the Hyksos were still weakened. This could also explain why they left Avaris overland and not by sea. Manetho would not have despoiled his saga of an Egyptian victory and heroism with such a triviality.

The observations of the Athenians that Cecrops was of mixed race[189] and well disposed towards the Frisians fit in with the broader picture. He may well have been of combined Hyksos and Egyptian stock and grew up under Hyksos rule in Egypt. His successful expulsion of the Athenians may have further served as a motivation for the revolt against the Hyksos in Lower Egypt a few years later.

The similarities between the eviction of the Frisians from Athens and the Hyksos from Avaris are striking, especially in light of the fact that they were reported by two very different sources – the one from ancient Egypt and the other from Western Europe. Both groups were of West-European descent and both were attacked by forces under Egyptian command during the same period. In both instances the two cities were unsuccessfully laid to siege, and in both cases the beleaguered occupants were eventually allowed safe passage from the cities they had founded.

The Egyptians may have celebrated their victories over Athens and Avaris, however, it cost them dearly over the next millennium. The Ionians in the Aegean (a.k.a. the Sea Peoples) would have increased their piracy against the Egyptian fleet to avenge the treatment of their Athenian brethren, and the banished Hyksos would

---

[189] Manetho referred to people of *ignoble birth*

have strengthened their numbers. The fact that the Egyptians did not accomplish as much, or were as prosperous as the former Hyksos rulers, says it all.

The Philistines

In an attempt to trace the West-European Frisians' impact on history, a few markers seem to be present. Whenever we come across one, and especially more than one of the following markers, it warrants special attention:

1. A maritime history - the Fryan nation was a seafaring people and maritime excellence would have been one of their great legacies.

2. Iron-age technology - here we can include weaponry and chariot warfare. We now know from the Oera Linda Book that Western Europe was in the Iron Age when the rest of man was still in either the Bronze or Stone Ages.

3. Monotheism in whatever shape or form - we have abundant evidence of how a single-belief system can evolve and even degenerate into radically different religions. A few basic principles would nevertheless have remained.

4. The absence of temples, votives, and statues.

5. An apparently underlined advanced civilization without a written history – we have already had a look at the Minoans, the Athenians, and the Hyksos. None of them seemed to have left any written record of their past mainly because, as proposed earlier, it was all done on paper and in a language the locals would not have understood. The only references we have of them today are those that were written by their adversaries on stone or clay and most likely centuries later. These accounts would also be skewed – especially where religion is concerned. Their enemies would not have known the very private details of their worship.

6. A tradition of female rulers or deities - throughout history, a woman's status in the Middle and Far East was no more than any other material possession. It was only in Western Europe where they were

regarded as equals as we find in Celtic Hill Graves and in the Oera Linda Book.

7. Minoan-type civilization and art forms - we have seen that the Western Europeans founded the Middle Minoan Civilization on Crete. Similar works of art were unearthed at Hyksos and Philistine sites.

8. Other indicators would include aspects such as a very structured administration, symmetrical city layouts, possibly the use of oven-baked brickwork in their buildings and subterranean water reticulation in their cities.

If we measure the Philistines (and possibly the Amorites) against these markers, they would appear to meet most, if not all, of these criteria. For a long time scientists have been suggesting that the Philistines were an ethnic group that was distinctly different from the rest of the Middle-Eastern nations. It would appear that they might have spoken an Indo-European language. Both the Bible and ancient Egyptian writings state that the Philistines were akin to, or hailed from Caphtor, the name for Crete in antiquity. The Greeks later called them Palestines.

There are numerous references to the Philistines and their five cities, Gaza, Ashdod, Ashkelon, Gath and Ekron in the Bible, e.g. Joshua 13: 3.

Archaeological excavations undertaken by M Dothan at Ashdod indicate that the founding of that city dates back to about 1550 BC – exactly the time when the Hyksos were expelled from Lower Egypt.

Considering the similarities in the two groups, there is a distinct possibility that the Hyksos might have been the forefathers of the Philistines. The Philistines were continually at war with the Israelites during the reign of the Judges and king David. Occasionally the Israelites were even subservient to them. It might have been that the Philistines were still carrying a grudge against the Israelites because Joseph had caused them the loss of their Hyksos reign. We read how Samson used to go a' courting the comely girls of the Philistines and how David had slain Goliath – the West-European-type giant. The Oera Linda Book has a number of references to people that were very tall – Adela was seven feet!

In its Grace Journal 8.1 (Winter 1967) 21-31, The Grace Theological Seminary published a paper on the internet written by Robert W Benton entitled *The Philistines and the Early Kingdom of Israel*. While numerous studies and dissertations were written about the Philistines, Robert Benton's essay seems to capture the essence of what we know of these mysterious people. He states:

> *Thus, a 'sea people' with a definite association with the Minoan culture settled in large numbers along the Mediterranean to build a strong alliance which would threaten the stability of the struggling Israelite nation.*[190]

There is only one point of disagreement with Robert Benton. The chronology proposed in this book suggests that the Israelites were the latecomers and that they were the aggressors who upset the stability in the region; not the Philistines.

Some other observations made by Robert Benton are the following:

> *These cities (Gaza, Ashdod, etc.) which have been well-established and occupying strategic places were then knit together by a common government. 'Their power and threat to Israel was due to a large extent to their political organisation.'*
>
> *Further evidence of the versatility of the Philistines is to be seen in their sea trade. It is clear from Egyptian records that some of the Philistine towns were engaged in a lively mercantile industry, exploiting the sea lanes between Egypt and Phoenicia.*

From what we know now, it is quite likely that these Philistines traded as far as Spain, Holland, Denmark, Norway and even Sweden – the Frisians' Skenland.

Benton also refers to their iron-age status:

---

[190] Benton, RW: *The Philistines and the Early Kingdom of Israel*. Published by the Grace Theological Seminary, Grace Journal 8.1 (Winter 1967) 21-31.

The monopoly of iron – the account of 1 Samuel indicates a distinct advantage held by the Philistines in the iron industry (13:19-22). Albright indicates the Philistines first used iron in the twelfth and eleventh centuries according to evidence found in the Tell-el-Far'ah tombs. The distinctive aspect of their control of the iron industry was their knowledge of the carbonization of the metal.

The Monotheists

Now that we have some background to the Frisians, the Tyrians, the Hyksos, the Philistines, the Athenians and the Israelites, we can have a closer look at the interaction between these groups.

Nef Tunis founded Tyre in 2000 BC and shortly afterwards started trading with the Egyptians; in ca 1998 BC. This was less than 200 years after the 2193 BC global disaster. Popular opinion (but not necessarily historical fact) ascribed all kinds of achievements to the Phoenicians. We are told that they invented Hindu-Arabic Ciphers, they started tin mining in Wales in ca 2000 BC, and they were the first ones to have brought linen to Ireland and Europe. This, of course, would all have had to depend on their ability to navigate the oceans. Herodotus (484 BC – 425 BC) tells us that:

[1.1] According to the Persians best informed in history, the Phoenicians began to quarrel. This people, who had formerly dwelt on the shores of the Erythraean Sea, having migrated to the Mediterranean and settled in the parts which they now inhabit, began at once, they say, to adventure on long voyages, freighting their vessels with the wares of Egypt and Assyria.[191]

In Chapter 1 the 2193 BC Event is proven beyond reasonable doubt. From Herodotus' account we must, therefore, deduce that the Phoenicians migrated from the south of the Arabian Desert on the Indian Ocean to the Mediterranean shortly after the 2193 BC Global Disaster; as part of the mass migrations world-wide. At what stage

---

[191] The History of Herodotus, Book 1 – CLIO, Translated by George Rawlinson, 1942

and from where would they have been able to acquire material and the expertise to venture on long sea voyages? The Oera Linda Book's explanation is the most logical: The Phoenicians only started their international trade once they went into partnership with the West Europeans with their hard oak sea going vessels.

Abram, the progenitor of the Israelites, entered Canaan in ca 1766 BC from Haran in Mesopotamia. This was 234 years after the Frisian exiles founded Tyre and after they went into partnership with the Phoenicians. By now the lucrative trade that the Frisian found Tyre and the Phoenician Sidon had built up in the Mediterranean and along Europe's Western sea board would have enticed more entrepreneurs from Western Europe to enter the market. At this early stage these West Europeans would have been the only other maritime power that could have matched the exploits of the traders from Phoenicia. By then Frisian influence and religion would also have spread throughout the Levant.

The Biblical Abram grew up in the city of Ur in Babylonia; the sacred city of the moon god Sin of the Babylonians. Sin was later equated with Nanna, the Illuminator, and the Sumerian god of the moon. This devotion to the moon continued for millennia in the Middle East and Asia Minor right up to the city of Byzantium. In fact, the crescent moon on the Turkish banners, which stemmed from Sin and Nanna, eventually became the emblem of the religion of Islam.

It is interesting to note that Abram's father, Terah, left Ur and settled in Haran, the other sanctuary of Sin. Haran was also the name of Abram's brother who died in Ur. The names of both Thera's daughters, Sarai and Milka, can be traced back to honorary names for Sin. It is evident that Terah and his kin worshipped idols and the moon god in particular. In the Old Testament of the Bible we find the following verse in Joshua 24:14:

(14) Then Joshua said to the people, " Now respect the Lord and serve him fully and sincerely. Throw away the gods that your ancestors worshipped on the other side of the Euphrates River... "[192]

---

[192] The Holy Bible : New Century Version, containing the Old and New Testaments. 1991. Word Bibles: Dallas, TX

Abram, therefore, was not initially an adherent to the later monotheistic faith that became known as Judaism. He was an idol worshipper and a pagan at the time of his calling. The first time he came into contact with the true nature of the theology of the unseen, omnipotent, omnipresent and omniscient God of the Bible was when he met Melchizedek,[193] the righteous king, in Canaan. In Genesis 14:18 to 20 we read the following:

(18) Then Melchizedek, the king of Salem[194] and a priest of God Most High, brought him bread and wine. (19) Melchizedek blessed Abram with this blessing:
"Blessed be Abram by God Most High,
Creator of heaven and earth.
(20) And blessed be God Most High,
who has helped you conquer your enemies.
Then Abram gave Melchizedek a tenth of all the goods he had recovered."[195]

The Bible makes further reference to Melchizedek in Psalm 110: 4 and again in the New Testament in Hebrews 7:17 where the Apostle Paul wrote about Jesus:

(17) And the psalmist pointed this out when he said of Christ,
'You are a priest forever in the line of Melchizedek'.[196]

This Salem of King Melchizedek was later known as Jerusalem, the Holy City. According to Genesis 14 then, Abram was clearly not the first monotheist in Canaan. It is quite possible that Melchizedek was either of Frisian descent or might have been a convert to Frisian monotheism. The Oera Linda Book makes quite a few references to Frisian missionary work or tuition given to foreigners. In Genesis 20

---

[193] Strong, J. 1996. *Concordance of the Bible : Melchizedek = "my king is Sedek"* (Righteous)
[194] Strong, J. 1996. *Concordance of the Bible: Salem = Peace.*
[195] Holy Bible : New Living Translation. 1997. Tyndale House: Wheaton, Ill.
[196] Holy Bible : New Living Translation. 1997. Tyndale House: Wheaton, Ill.

we once again read of Abram, whose name had changed to Abraham, encountering another likely monotheist, king Abimelech of Gerar.

As stated earlier, Abram arrived in Canaan some 234 years after Nef Tunis with his band of Frisian outcasts and Finnish sailors founded Tyre. As their very prosperous trade with Frya's Land increased, more Frisian entrepreneurs would have joined in. By the time that Abram arrived in Canaan, Frisian influence and religion would have had a noticeable impact on the Levant. The Oera Linda Book's concept of God, the Spirit and Father of all and the unseen, omnipotent, omnipresent and omniscient *I Am* is just too unique and too similar to Judaism to ignore. Two hundred and fifteen years later, in 1551 BC, Abraham's grandson, Jacob went to Egypt with his extended family of some 70 souls. They were given free-hold by the monotheistic Hyksos who, in turn, were evicted from Egypt only 26 years later – in ca 1525 BC.

In the book of Exodus, Chapter 2, we read about the birth and flight of Moses from Egypt. He was born of Hebrew slave parents, but grew up in the Egyptian royal court. One must therefore assume that he was not raised as a monotheist, but rather in the polytheistic pagan religion of the indigenous Egyptians. After slaying an Egyptian, Moses fled to Midian in present-day Saudi Arabia, where he met a priest by the name of Reuel (friend of God), also known as Jethro. Josephus tells us that Jethro was a Barbarian and therefore not a local; by this book's hypothesis then: a West European.

> *(263) So he* (Jethro) *made him* (Moses) *his son, and gave him one of his daughters in marriage; and appointed him to be the guardian and superintendent over his cattle; for of old all the wealth of the* barbarians[197] *was in those cattle.*[198]

Who was this non-Semitic Barbarian and how did he not only came to know God but was also a priest and even called a friend of God in the Bible? In fact, it seems quite obvious that he converted Moses to monotheism. As in the case of Melchizedek, it is suspected

---

[197] See *Barbarians* in Chapter 4.
[198] *Jewish Antiquities*: Book 2, Ch. 11.2.

that this priest may have been a convert to Frisian religion or, perhaps more than likely a descendant of the Frisians who founded Tyre more than 630 years before.

Moses married one of Jethro's daughters and spent the next 40 years under his influence and tuition. It is suggested here that the main reason for Moses' sojourn in Midian was to be converted to and trained in monotheism. The first mention in the Bible of Moses getting to know God was at the Burning Bush. The fact that God had to introduce himself as the *God of your fathers* showed that Moses did not know Him at that stage. When he returned to Egypt after 40 years he was probably the only Israelite who truly understood the concept of God as we find it in the subsequent history of the Hebrews.

During their enslavement in Egypt and under the influence of the Egyptians, the Israelites appear to have lost whatever little knowledge they had of God. The frequent references to the *God of your fathers* or the *God of our fathers* were not to indicate a longstanding religion, but rather a forgotten one.

In Exodus 3:13-15 (NKJV), Moses deemed it necessary to have some form of identification from God to relate to the Israelites:

> *(13) Then Moses said to God, " Indeed, when I come to the children of Israel and say to them, 'The God of your fathers has sent me to you,' and they say to me, 'What is His name?' what shall I say to them?" (14) And God said to Moses, "I AM WHO I AM". And He said, "thus you shall say to the children of Israel, 'I AM has sent me to you'." (15) Moreover God said to Moses, "Thus you shall say to the children of Israel: 'The Lord God of your fathers, the God of Abraham, the God of Isaac, and the God of Jacob, has sent me to you. This is My name forever, and this is my memorial to all generations.*[199]*

In the Oera Linda Book, under the writings of Apollonia, we read the following:

---

[199] The New King James Version. 1996, c 1982. Thomas Nelson: Nashville

> *These are passing things which appear by Wralda's life, and which appear through his wisdom, and not otherwise; but whereas life continues, nothing can remain stationary; therefore all created things change their locality, their form, and their thoughts. So neither the earth nor any other created object can say, I AM; but rather, I was.*[200]

By implication then, this quote from the Oera Linda Book says that it is only the unchangeable Creator who can say I AM.

This lack of a religious tradition or knowledge of God by the Israelites is displayed during their journey through the desert when they erected a golden calf to worship the minute Moses turned his back. This action was definitely not evidence of a history of pious monotheism, nor was the frequent apostatizing of their religion in their subsequent history. In fact, the Bible confirms that the Israelites did not worship God during their sojourn in Egypt.

The reader is again referred to Joshua 24: 14 -15:

> *(14) Then Joshua said to the people, "Now respect the Lord and serve him fully and sincerely. Throw away the Gods that your ancestors worshipped on the other side of the Euphrates River and in Egypt. Serve the Lord. (15) But if you don't want to serve the Lord, you must choose for yourselves today whom you will serve. You may serve the gods that your ancestors worshipped when they lived on the other side of the Euphrates River, or you may serve the gods of the Amorites who lived in this land. As for me and my family, we will serve the Lord".*[201]

A few centuries after the Hyksos had fled Avaris and settled in Palestine, the Israelites again followed them after their Biblical Exodus from the Nile Delta in Egypt. These two groups had therefore been rubbing shoulders for hundreds of years, and there are remarkable parallels in their histories. In fact, it is evident that the Israelites' eventual monotheism and even some influences on their language originated from and was shaped by Frya's People and their religion

---

[200] OLB: The writings of Adelbrost and Apollonia, Chapter 5.

[201] The Holy Bible : New Century Version, containing the Old and New Testaments. 1991. Word Bibles: Dallas, TX.

from Western Europe – hence the parallels between the Oera Linda Book's description of their religion and the Bible.

A note on Thera

The Thera volcano on Santorini has long been viewed as a major factor in the development, upheaval and migration of peoples and civilizations in and around the Aegean Sea and the Eastern Mediterranean.

Scientific evidence shows that a catastrophic eruption occurred during the mid- second millennium BC with a volcanic explosivity index (VEI)[202] of between 6 and 7. The eruption is considered to have been one of the largest in recorded history. The eruption would have had a devastating impact on the area and climate around the Mediterranean in particular, but also all over the world – whether from earthquakes, explosive force, atmospheric changes, fallout or tsunamis.

The Oera Linda Book makes no mention of Thera from the founding of Athens up to the time when the Gertmanne left. We may therefore assume that an eruption did not occur between ca 1627 BC and 1553 BC.

The eruption of Thera has been a controversial subject among archaeologists and volcanologists for a long time. Radiocarbon analyses of vegetative material found in the area were undertaken by three separate laboratories in Oxford, Vienna and Heidelberg. They all concluded, as mentioned before, that the eruption took place between 1627 and 1613 BC with a 95% probability of accuracy.

Archaeologists, on the other hand, base their findings on artifacts from their excavations and Late Bronze Age chronologies that clearly indicate that the eruption must have taken place some time later, between 1550 and 1500 BC. exodus, which would go a long way

---

[202] VEI is a measure of the size of a Volcanic Eruption. An increase of 1 on the scale represents a ten-fold increase in the size of the explosion. Mount St Helens in the USA erupted with a VEI of 5 in 1980. It is estimated that the eruption of Mount Vesuvius that destroyed Pompeii and Herculeum in 79 AD was also approximately 5.

towards explaining the ten plagues and the cloud or smoke column, which could have served as a
beacon, and could have guided the Israelites through the Sinai desert during the early part of the Exodus.

It is interesting to note that the 60 meter-high tephra layer on Santorini displays three identifiable layers which seem to represent different phases of eruption.

All three groups may be right. Perhaps there were at least three eruptions – the first being a violent Plenian-type eruption in ca 1628 BC which destroyed much of Santorini and left the caldera as we still see it today. This could have created climatic changes in Europe and further a field as seen in the undeniable tree-ring data on both sides of the Atlantic.

A second violent eruption from below the water-filled caldera would explain the seven-year drought in the Middle East from 1553 BC as predicted by Joseph in the Bible. This explosion, which might have been caused by a build-up of steam, was possibly not as violent as the first one, but still large enough to have caused localized climatic changes. This would have led to the relocation of Joseph's father, Jacob, and his extended family to Egypt in 1551 BC.

Eruptions of this nature would be similar to the eruption of Vesuvius in 79 AD which destroyed the cities of Pompeii and Herculeum. This eruption gave no prior warning or, if it did, the locals did not know how to interpret the signs or they did not have sufficient time to evacuate. Mount St Helens in the United States produced a similar eruption in 1980 but then scientists were able to alert the authorities beforehand.

The proposed 1628 BC eruption of Thera would have been the Big One. The volcano, however, remained active and produced further but less violent eruptions in 1553 BC and 1336 BC. Thera, of course, is not the only volcano in the Mediterranean. There are numerous volcanoes from Italy and Sicily right up to Turkey. While the 1628 BC and 1553 BC eruptions can be ascribed to the volcano on Santorini, the third possible eruption could have happened elsewhere.

The second eruption, in 1553 BC, which was accompanied by a massive earthquake that severely affected the Minoan civilization on Crete and elsewhere, was the one that concerns us here. In this instance the fallout would have covered the cities and houses on Crete, but apparently there was sufficient time for the populations in the surrounding areas to have evacuated. This would also explain the earthquake reported in the Oera Linda Book, which closed the *Strait of Suez* and which might still have caused catastrophic tsunamis. If this scenario is true, it would mean that Cecrops actually did the Frisians a favour by expelling them from Athens beforehand.

These massive floods would have destroyed the low-lying Avaris and its harbour. Therefore, Mother Nature and not the Egyptians destroyed all evidence of the Hyksos' civilization. In fact, it is most likely that the Egyptians would have preferred to occupy Avaris and made use of the harbour and other infrastructure after the Hyksos had left peacefully. It does not make sense that they would have destroyed everything with the view of rebuilding it afterwards, which they obviously did not do.

A third eruption in 1336 BC would fit in nicely with the Biblical exodus from Egypt. Some speculate that an eruption 700 km away could have caused three days' of darkness, while the Red Cliffs of Santorini could explain the water in Egypt that turned into blood. Tsunamis would have left large, shallow lakes of stagnant water, which could have been the cause of frogs, mosquitoes and other pestilences. A smoke column on the horizon by day and a fire column by night could have been a beacon to the Israelites to determine their direction in the featureless Sinai desert.

It would have been nice to tie all the questions and answers around the Thera volcano's eruption at the time of the Exodus into a neat little bundle and present it to the reader. Unfortunately, however, the link between Thera and the Jewish Exodus presented here remains mere speculation.

Chapter 6

The Punjab

The Voyage

According to the Oera Linda Book, the Gertmanne sailed from Athens to present-day Pakistan and up the Indus River to the Punjab where they settled. Judging by their fleet of 114 ships, they could have numbered anything from 4000 to 6000 people.

As the Gertmanne passed through the Bitter Lakes or the *Strait of Suez* into the Red Sea, an enormous earthquake closed the strait and laid the land to waste right up to India. The king of Tyre wanted his fleet to pursue the Frisians but the closure of the strait prevented them from doing so. To the Gertmanne this was divine deliverance but it also meant that all maritime ties with Europe had been cut.

The flight of the Gertmanne must have been an extraordinary endeavour. The Oera Linda Book says nothing about their journey. In fact, the next time we hear of the Gertmanne is some 1250 years later when a remnant of them returned to Western Europe. For all practical purposes, they disappeared off the face of the earth. We shall try to reconstruct their history and legacy in West and Southern Asia.

From Athens to the northern regions of the Punjab would have been a journey of close to 9000 kilometres along some of the most desolate coastlines in the world. Although they were famed for their seamanship, there were not only experienced sailors on board but also woman, children, infants and old people. They had all their worldly possessions with them with which they had to start a new life in some foreign land. One may assume that they had some livestock with them such as goats and cows to provide milk for the children. They may even have had horses and chariots on board.

In order for us to gain some understanding of the hardships the Gertmanne must have endured, we just have to turn to another epic journey some 1 230 years later which appear to have been quite exacting.

Lucius Flavius Arrianus Xenophon (ca. 86 AD – 150 AD) known in English as Arrian of Nicomedia, was a Roman historian of Greek ethnicity. He recounted the journey of Nearchus, the admiral of Alexander the Great's navy, from India to the Persian Gulf – a distance not even half of that of the Gertmanne. It would appear that Arrian might have quoted from Nearchus's biography or logbook when he described the condition of these battle-hardened sailors when they met Alexander again after having covered about two-thirds of their voyage:

> *Archias, however, had a happy thought, and said to Nearchus: 'I suspect, Nearchus, that these persons who are traversing the same road as ours through this desert country have been sent for the express purpose of finding us; as for their failure to recognize us, I do not wonder at that; we are in such a sorry plight as to be unrecognizable.*[203]

No doubt Nearchus' account of all the hardships they encountered must be taken with a pinch of salt. The old Greeks would never have spoiled a good story with facts.

From Nearchus' tales we see that the Grecian navy mostly sailed by day and spent their nights on land. Perhaps Gert and her followers did the same. They would also have had to spend prolonged periods on land to search for water or barter for food. Their livestock, such as there might have been, would have had to find grazing and they would have had to harvest food for these animals whenever the opportunity arose.

In cases of illness or inclement weather, they might have had to spend longer periods on shore than they would have liked. They would equally not have wanted to sail the Arabian Sea in the Monsoon season. When they eventually arrived at the mouth of the Indus, they

---

[203] Arrian : *Indica*, XXXIV

still had to sail more than 1 000 kilometres against the flow of the river to reach their final destination; unlike Nearchus who sailed downstream. The journey of the Gertmanne, therefore, could have taken as long as two years.

New Beginnings

The exiles from Athenia or, as they called themselves, the *Gertmanne*, arrived in the Punjab in ca 1552 to 1551 BC – only 642 years after the 2193 BC event. It is important that we keep this in mind. It would explain why they could settle in that part of the world without encountering much resistance. The region would still have had a relatively small population.

> *At last they landed at Pangap, that is, in our language Five Waters, because here five rivers flow together to the sea. Here they settled. That land they called Gertmannia.*[204]

This entry in the Oera Linda Book was the last about the Gertmanne for the next 1250 years. The next time we encounter them again in the Oera Linda Book, is under the Writings of Konered, Chapter 6, written in ca 300 BC. Konered quoted from the diary of Liudgert, an old admiral from the Punjab and from a letter Liudgert wrote to Konered's father.

According to Liudgert, the Gertmanne wanted to settle on the eastern side of the Punjab but, when they realised that the area was already occupied by a people from another foreign country, they decided to relocate to the west. They would not make the same mistake as in Athens where they tried to share their lives with pagan priests.

> *On their arrival, our forefathers also settled to the east of the Punjab, but on account of the priests, they likewise went to the west.*[205]

---

[204] OLB: The book of Adela's followers, Chapter 29.
[205] OLB: *The writings of Konered*, Chapter 6.

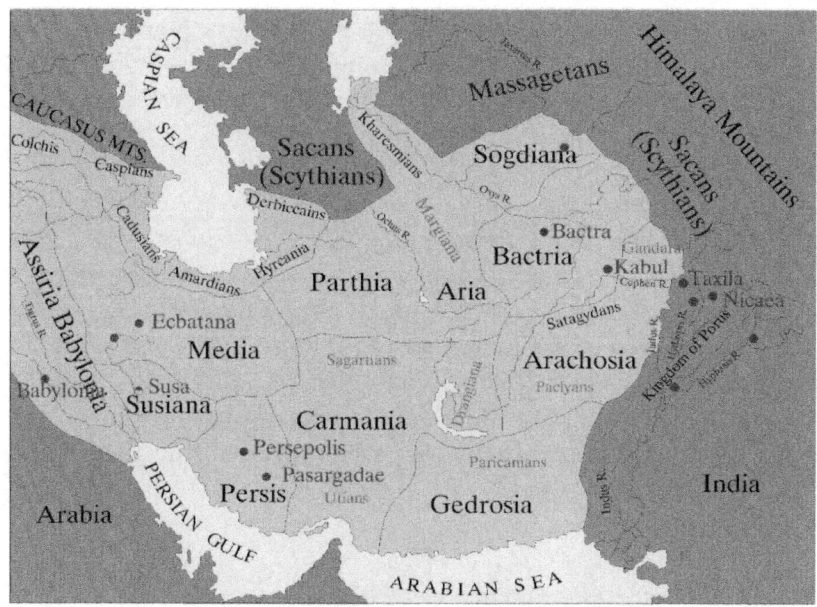

Figure 43: The Persian Empire ca. 500 BC

Their relocation to the west and their subsequent migration to the north-west would have placed them in the area of Arachosia, Gandara, Bactria and Sogdiana where Alexander the Great found them 1 224 years later. It is possible that Gandara was the original Gertmannia where the ex-Athenian Frisians settled and where Liudgert was born. After more than 1 200 years Liudgert and his clan were still sailors and they were still living in the area where their forefathers had settled.

> *On the west of the Punjab where we come from, and where I was born, the same fruits and crops grow as on the east side. Formerly there existed also the same crawling animals, but our forefathers burnt all the under wood, and so diligently hunted all the wild animals, that there are scarcely any left.*[206]

During the next millennium subsequent generations continued to migrate westwards right up to the Persian Gulf. They founded the

---

[206] OLB: *The writings of Konered*, Chapter 6.

harbour of *Ny-Gertmannia* where their fleet could take in water. This *New Gertmannia* later became the province of *Gertmania* as recorded by Herodotus in 440 BC and later *Carmania* by the time of Alexander the Great in ca 330 BC. Today it is known as the province of *Kerman* in Iran. The evolution of Kerman Province's name in Iran is very well documented and cannot be disputed. Other historical documents quoted by Wikipedia refer to Kerman as *Karmania, Kermania, Germania, Carmonia*, and *Žermanya*. Again, the Oera Linda Book's account fits in extremely well with the facts and gives us a very logical explanation.

> *When we arrived at New Gertmania[207] (New Gertmania is the port that we had made ourselves in order to take in water), we met Alexander with his army. Nearchus went ashore, and stayed three days. Then we proceeded further on. When we came to the Euphrates, Nearchus went ashore with the soldiers and a large body of people; but he soon returned, and said:*
>
> *"The king requests you, for his sake, to take a short voyage to the end of the Red Sea; after that each shall receive as much gold as he can carry."*

Herodotus wrote in his Histories:

> *125. Now the Persian nation is made up of many tribes. Those whom Cyrus assembled and persuaded to revolt from the Medes were the principal ones on which all the others are dependent. These are the Pasargadae, the Maraphians, and the Aspians, of whom the Pasargadae are the noblest. The Achaemenidae, from which spring all the Perseid kings, is one of their clans. The rest of the Persian tribes are the following:*
>
> *The Panthialaeans, the Derusiaeans, the <u>Germanians, who are engaged in husbandry</u>[208]; the Daans, the Mardians, the Dropicans, and the Sagartians, who are nomads.[209]*

---

[207] Possibly in the region of the Iranian city, Bandar Abbas in the Strait of Hormuz.
[208] Exactly what the Oera Linda Book says.
[209] Herodotus: *Histories*, book I, p. 47.

Apart from the Germanians, we find here two other tribes that seem suspiciously familiar: the Achaemenidae and the Daans. Remember the Achaeans and the Danaans from Greece?

Cyrus the Great (c.600 BC or 576 BC - 530 BC), also known as Cyrus II or Cyrus of Persia, was the first Zoroastrian Persian emperor. He was the founder of the Persian Empire under the Achaemenid dynasty.

Herodotus continues with his description of the Persians; a description that could equally fit anyone from Western Europe:

131. The customs which I know the Persians to observe are the following:

They have no images of the gods, no temples, nor altars, and consider the use of them a sign of folly. This comes, I think, from their not believing the gods to have the same nature with men, as the Greeks imagine.

133. Of all the days in the year, the one which they celebrate most is their birthday. It is customary to have the board furnished on that day with an ampler supply than common. The richer Persians cause an ox, a horse, a camel, and an ass to be baked whole and so served up to them: the poorer classes use instead the smaller kinds of cattle.

They eat little solid food but abundance of dessert, which is set on table a few dishes at a time; this it is which makes them say that "the Greeks, when they eat, leave off hungry, having nothing worth mention served up to them after the meats; whereas, if they had more put before them, they would not stop eating." They are very fond of wine, and drink it in large quantities. To vomit (belch or burp) *or obey natural calls in the presence of another is forbidden among them.*[210] *Such are their customs in these matters.*

134. When they meet each other in the streets, you may know if the persons meeting are of equal rank by the following token: if they are, instead of speaking, they kiss each other on the lips. In the case where one is a little inferior to the other, the kiss is given on the cheek; where the difference of rank is great, the inferior prostrates himself

---

[210] Yet, they were called *barbarians*?!

upon the ground. Of nations, they honour most their nearest neighbours, whom they esteem next to themselves; those who live beyond these they honour in the second degree; and so with the remainder, the further they are removed, the less the esteem in which they hold them. The reason is that they look upon themselves as very greatly superior in all respects to the rest of man, regarding others as approaching to excellence in proportion as they dwell nearer to them;

136. ...Their sons are carefully instructed from their fifth to their twentieth year, in three things alone, - to ride, to draw the bow, and to speak the truth.[211]

An interesting observation from Herodotus was that the Persians and the Medes were not merely different nations, but they were in fact from two different races. This tells us that they, or their forebears, did not originally come from the same geographical area. One of the groups came from elsewhere. He described Cyrus II (The Great) as a mule:

Cyrus was that mule. For the parents of Cyrus were of different races, and of different conditions – his mother a Median princess, daughter of King Astyages, and his father a Persian.[212]

Arrian of Nicomedia wrote the following in his *Anabasis Alexandri - The Campaigns of Alexander*:

Book IIIb

He now arrived in the land of the people formerly called Ariaspians, but afterwards named Euergetae, because they assisted Cyrus, son of Cambyses, in his invasion of Scythia. Alexander honoured these people, for the service which their ancestors had rendered to Cyrus; and when he ascertained that the men not only enjoyed a form of government unlike that of the other barbarians in that part of the world, but laid claim to justice equally with the best of the Greeks, he set them free,

---

[211] Herodotus: *Histories*, book I, p 49-52.
[212] Herodotus: *Histories*, book I, p 35.

and gave them besides as much of the adjacent country as they asked for themselves; but they did not ask for much.[213]

Book VIII, Indica:

The Nysaeans are not an Indian race; but part of those who came with Dionysus to India; possibly even of those Greeks who became past service in the wars which Dionysus waged with Indians; possibly also volunteers of the neighbouring tribes whom Dionysus settled there together with the Greeks, calling the country Nysaea from the mountain Nysa, and the city itself Nysa.[214]

In both Herodotus' and Arrian's writings we recognise the same type of people who founded Athens in Greece. When Alexander the Great arrived in the area, the descendants of the Frisians had already been in that part of the world for more than 1200 years. Except for the handful who returned to Europe with Alexander, they were fully assimilated into the local population and entrenched in the *Persian* Empire. They were still monotheists who abhorred idolatry and they still maintained the same form of government and administration. In fact, we can now understand why Cyrus (The Great) was apparently sympathetic to the monotheistic Jews' request to return to Jerusalem to rebuild their temple; the Israelites and the next of kin of the Hyksos Dynasty met again – 1000 years later!

This view is supported from the Bible in Ezra 1:2-3:

(2) Thus says the king of Persia:
All the kingdoms of the earth the Lord God of heaven has given me. And He has commanded me to build Him a house at Jerusalem which is in Judah. (3) Who is among you of all His people? May his God be with him, and let him go up to Jerusalem which is in Judah, and build the house of the Lord God of Israel (He is God), which is in Jerusalem.[215]

Here the king of the Persians states unequivocally that, in his opinion, the God of Israel is the God of the Persians. The animosity

---

[213] Arrian: *Anabasis Alexandri*, Book IIIb, 27-*The Ariaspans*.
[214] Arrian: *Anabasis Alexandri*, book VIII (*Indica*), (I).
[215] The New King James Version. 1996, c1982 . Thomas Nelson: Nashville

that exists today between Iran and Israel is quite ironic if one considers that 2500 years ago these two nations had virtually the same religion. It was also the Persians under Cyrus who, through his edict of restoration, re-established the Jewish state and had the temple rebuilt in Jerusalem.

The old religion of Persia is known as Zoroastrianism and their oldest writings are known as the *Avesta*. Historians tell us that the religion dates back to some time after the *Aryan Invasion* in ca. 1500 BC. This just happens to coincide with the arrival of the Oera Linda Book's Gertmanna in India, Pakistan and their later incursions into Persia. The Avesta, which consists of a number of books, was only compiled in its current format some one thousand years later.

The Book of Adela's Followers in the Oera Linda Book was compiled ca. 530 BC in Western Europe. At the time they still referred to themselves as the *children of Frya*. The Gertmanna in South Asia used the same title. If the Oera Linda Book is true, there may just be some references to them in the Avesta. This is what I found in the *Khorda Avesta* (Book of Common Prayer):

119. *We worship the Fravashi of the holy Frya.*
120. *We worship the Fravashi of the holy Yoishta, of the Fryana house.*[216]

In the Yasna Avesta, Chapter 36:

12. *When among the laudable descendants and posterity of the Turanian Fryana the right ariseth, through activity of piety that blesseth substance; then shall Good Thought admit them, and Mazda Ahura give them protection at the Fulfillment.*

The Avesta does mention numerous other names of *Fravashi* that is worshipped. Could anyone, though, realistically claim that these references to Frya and Fryana are just coincidences? How do the adherents to the Oera Linda Hoax Theory explain this?

---

[216] The house / family / descendants of Frya

The Fravashi could be guardian angels as some seems to think or, it could simply mean spirit, as in *We worship the spirit of the holy Frya*.

Professor Mary Boyce (1920-2006) speculated that the fravashis could be the remnants of the hero-cult of the Iranian Heroic Age (c. 1500 BCE onwards), when ancestor-worship was widespread.

The Iranians

The Gertmanne might have helped to shape the Persian Empire, but to give them all the credit would be a mistake. Admiral Liudgert tells us that as the Frisians moved west, they encountered the Iranians, whom he called the *Ira*. This tells us that the names *Ira, Iran and Iranian* are much older than the names *Persia* and *Persian which were* invented by the Greeks. This was not common knowledge in 19th century Europe although the Iranians themselves were quite aware of the fact.

> *To the west of the Pangab are the Ira, or outcasts, the Gedrostne, or runaways, and the Orietten, or forgotten. These names are given by the priests out of spite, because they fled from their customs and religion.*
>
> *On their arrival, our forefathers also settled to the east of the Punjab, but on account of the priests they likewise went to the west. In that way we came to know the Ira and other people. The Ira are not savages, but good people, who neither pray to nor tolerate images; neither will they suffer priests or churches; but as we adhere to the light of Fasta, so they always maintain fire in their houses.*[217]

The Frisians found the Ira or Iranians quite agreeable. Their religion, culture, diet and level of development were apparently not all that different from that of the West-Europeans. From the little The Oera Linda Book says about the Ira, it is quite likely that their ancestors were the Harappans, because *they likewise moved from the Punjab* to the

---

[217] OLB: *The writings of Konered,* Chapter 6.

West. To date, archaeologists have not found any temples or idols in this Indus Valley's urban civilization. The Harappan Civilization, although Bronze Age, was a highly developed people, as their city layouts and buildings attest. They buried their dead and their diet was similar to that of the Ira. No other civilisation in South Asia meets these criteria.

It is thus reasonable to speculate that the *Persian Empire* was founded and populated by descendants from both the Frisians from Western Europe and the Harappans from the Indus Valley.

The Harappan Civilization is also important in this discourse for the following reasons:

As is the case with all the other ancient civilisations, the Harappans experienced some disaster in ca 2200 BC. Here again we find evidence of the 2193 BC event.

After the disaster, their civilization was invaded by refugees under the leadership of Shaman priests from the Altai region in Central Asia. The Oera Linda Book only states that these priests came from another country but modern researchers identified them as from Sino-Mongolian descend. From DNA mapping and what we know of their religion, it is quite evident that they originated from the same area as the Magyarar and their Magy, who invaded Scandinavia in 2092 BC.

When the Shamanists invaded the Indus Valley, the Iranians moved west where the Gertmanne later met them.

> But the priests, who came from another country, traced out these people and had them burnt, so that they do not dare to declare openly their creed. In this country all the priests are fat and rich. In their churches there are all kinds of monstrous images, many of them of gold.

The Aryans

In the ancient texts of Zoroastrianism, the Avesta, and in the oldest texts of Hinduism, the Rig-Veda, we find the term *Arya*; a name by which the old Indo-Iranians were apparently identified. Historians seem to agree more or less that both Zoroastrianism, the monotheistic religion of old Persia and Hinduism, the polytheistic set of beliefs in India, came into existence in the mid-second millennium BC. The so-called Aryans arrived on the scene in ca 1500 BC during the much speculated *Aryan Invasion* and, as it happened, at exactly the same time as the Oera Linda Book's Gertmanne. To this date, however, nobody have been able to give an explanation as to where these Aryans supposedly came from; that is, apart from the Oera Linda Book. The name Aryan or Aryan race was relegated to infamy by the Nazis during the first half of the 20th century AD in their quest for a super race. Since then, all references to these Aryans have been treated with suspicion.

The inscription at the Naqsh-e Rostam necropolis, located about 12 km northwest of the ancient city of Pārsa (Persepolis) in Fars Province, Iran, gives us the following on Darius I of Persia (550–486 BCE), also known as Darius the Great:

> *I am Darius, the Great King, King of Kings, King of countries containing all kinds of men, King in this great earth far and wide, son of Hystaspes, an Achaemenian, a Persian, son of a Persian, an Aryan, having Aryan lineage.*

Darius was without a doubt very proud of his Aryan descend. The debate on who these Aryans were and whether there ever was an Aryan or Indo-Aryan invasion in South Asia has been continuing for centuries. All evidence gathered for this book points to the fact that the A-ryans were the F-ryans – the Gertmanne from Athenia who settled relatively peaceful in the Punjab.

On his website *adaniels info site hosted by Tripod*, Aharon Daniel published a dissertation entitled *Aryans and Dravidians – a controversial issue*. This concise account seems to capture the essence of the accepted theories regarding the Aryans.

> *According to general Indian legend, the Aryans arrived in north India somewhere from Iran and southern Russia at around 1500 BC. Before the Aryans, the Dravidian people resided in India. The Aryans disregarded the local cultures. They began conquering and*

taking control over regions in north India and at the same time pushed the local people southwards or towards the jungles and mountains in north India. According to this historical fact the general division of Indian society is made. North Indians are Aryans and south Indians are Dravidians. But this division isn't proper because of many reasons.

Many Indians immigrated from one part of India to other parts of India and not all local people of north India were pushed southwards by the Aryans. Some stayed and served the Aryans and others moved to live in the forests and the jungles of north India. Before the arrival of the Aryans there were also other communities in India like Sino-Mongoloids and Austroloids. There were also other foreign immigrations and invaders who arrived in India, from time to time.

There are many that completely doubt that there was ever any Aryan invasion in India. This scepticism is based on the dating of the Aryan invasion of India and the fact that Hinduism and the caste system are believed to have been established as the result of the meetings between the intruding Aryans and original residents of India, the Dravidians.

The caste system is believed to have been established by the Aryans. The <u>fair skinned Aryans</u> who occupied parts of India established the caste system, which allowed only them to be the priests (Brahman), aristocracy (Kshatria) and the businessmen (Vaisia) of the society. Below them in hierarchy were the Sudras who consisted of two communities. One community was of the locals who were subdued by the Aryans and the other was the descendants of Aryans with locals. In Hindu religious stories there are many wars between the good Aryans and the dark skinned demons and devils. The different gods also have dark skinned slaves. There are stories of demon women trying to seduce good Aryan men in deceptive ways. There were also marriages between Aryan heroes and demon women. Many believe that these incidences really occurred in which, the gods and the positive heroes were people of Aryan origin. And the demons, the devils and the dark skinned slaves were in fact the original residence of India whom the Aryans coined as monsters, devil, demons and slaves. Normally the date given to Aryan invasion is around 1500 BC.[218]

---

[218] Aharon Daniel: *India History: Aryans and Dravidians - A controversial issue.*

Aharon Daniel confirms here what the Oera Linda Book says about the foreign priests: Before the arrival of the Aryans there were also other communities in India like Sino-Mongoloids... In the model proposed in this book, these would be the Shamans from the Altai region.

It is quite interesting to note that old Admiral Liudgert did not mention this racial segregation, the caste system, when he arrived in Western Europe. He must have been wise enough to conclude that the Fryan people would not understand it.

Another web-page on the Aryans by Richard Hooker also gives a good description of our Gertmanne. In their defence we can only conclude that, once again, this is how outsiders described them. Perhaps they were not too fond of writing as Richard Hooker describes them, or perhaps their writings did not survive because, inter alia, it would have been written on paper and in a language foreign to later generations. Again, they left no paper trial, so let us look at some quotes from Hooker's page:

- *They were unquestionably a tough people, and they were fierce and war-like.*
- *Their culture was oriented around warfare, and they were very good at it. They were superior on horseback and rushed into battle in chariots.*
- *They maintained the Aryan tribal structure, with a raja* (reeve?) *ruling over the tribal group in tandem with a council.*
- *What did the Aryans do with their time? They seem to have had a well-developed musical culture, and song and dance dominated their society. They were not greatly invested in the visual arts, but their interest in lyric poetry was unmatched. They loved gambling. They did not, however, have much interest in writing even though they could have inherited a civilization and a writing system when they originally settled in India.*
- *When they arrived, the vast northern plains were almost certainly densely forested. Where now bare fields stretch to the horizon, when the Aryans arrived lush forests stretched to those very same horizons.*

Clearing the forests over the centuries was an epic project and one that is still preserved in Indian literature.[219]

Old Admiral Liudgert mentioned this bush clearing in his letter written around 300 BC, and quoted by Konered in the Oera Linda Book. This is further undeniable proof that the Oera Linda Book cannot be a 19th century hoax.

21. On the west of the Pangab where we come from, and where I was born, the same fruits and crops grow as on the east side. Formerly there existed also the same crawling animals, <u>but our forefathers burnt all the underwood</u>, and so diligently hunted all the wild animals, that there are scarcely any left.[220]

Richard Hooker's observation, *They seem to have had a well-developed musical culture, and song and dance dominated their society*, matches old king Alcinous's description of the Phaeacians to Ulysses in 1188 BC when he said: *We are extremely fond of good dinners, music, and dancing.* Today, 3500 years later, Europeans are still fond of good dinners, music, and dancing.

DNA Evidence

A report by Bijal P. Trivedi written in May 2001 entitled *Genetic evidence suggests European migrants may have influenced the origins of India's caste system*, appear to provide the ultimate proof that the Gertmanne were the Aryans. The report is reproduced here verbatim:

A new study has revealed that Indians belonging to higher castes are genetically closer to Europeans than are individuals from lower castes, whose genetic profiles are closer to those of Asians.

The study compared genetic markers—located on the Y chromosome and the mitochondrial DNA—between 265 Indian men of

---

[219] Richard Hooker: Ancient India, The Aryans.
[220] OLB: *The writings of Konered,* Chapter 6

various castes and 750 African, Asian, European and other Indian men. To broaden the study, 40 markers from chromosomes 1 to 22 were analyzed from more than 600 individuals from different castes and continents. The comparison of the markers among these groups confirmed that genetic similarities to Europeans increased as caste rank increased

The study, led by Michael Bamshad of the University of Utah, in Salt Lake City, and his colleagues, is reported to be the most comprehensive genetic analysis to date of the impact of European migrations on the structure and origin of the current Indian population. The article appears in the current issue of Genome Research

The caste system, defined in ancient Sanskrit texts, determines a person's rank in society: The Brahmin, who were traditionally priests and scholars, held the highest rank in Hindu society. Warriors and rulers made up the Kshatriya who were the next in line to the Brahmin. Merchants, traders, farmers, and artisans were the third caste called the Vysya. The Shudra were the fourth rank and consisted of labourers. Because of strict rules forbidding marriage between men and women of different castes, these four classes remained distinct for thousands of years.

Bamshad's team found that Y chromosomes from the Brahmin and Kshatriya closely resembled European Y chromosomes rather than Asian Y chromosomes. The Y chromosomes from the lower castes bore more similarities to the Asian Y chromosome. The mitochondrial DNA showed the same pattern.

The authors believe their results support the notion that Europeans who migrated into India between 3,000[221] and 8,000 years ago may have merged with or imposed their social structure on the indigenous northern Indians and placed themselves into the highest castes.

Analysis of the paternally transmitted Y chromosome among Indians in general indicated that the Y chromosome had a more European flavour. Maternally inherited mitochondrial DNA among

---

[221] The Oera Linda Book tells us this happened 3500 years ago.

Indians is more Asian than European. This suggests that the Europeans who entered India were predominantly male.[222]

This system of a racially segregated caste system introduced by (West) Europeans into India was repeated almost 3500 years later when descendents of the same Europeans introduced Apartheid into South Africa. History just keeps on repeating itself. The last word on the Aryans we shall give to Professor Norman Brown out of Pakistan and Western Asia:

> *The evidence of the Rig Veda shows that during the centuries when the Aryans were occupying the Punjab and composing the hymns of the Rig Veda, the north-west part of the subcontinent was culturally separate from the rest of India. The closest cultural relations of the Indo-Aryans at that period were with the Iranians, whose language and sacred texts are preserved in the various works known as the Avesta, in inscriptions in Old Persian, and in some other scattered documents. So great is the amount of material common to the Rig Veda Aryans and the Iranians that the books of the two peoples show common geographic names as well as deities and ideas.*[223]

As was the case in Phoenicia, Egypt, Palestine, Crete and Greece, the Frisians brought South and West Asia into the Iron Age. The Persian Empire was built on West-European technology, weaponry, expertise and administration.

It is ironic that the Nazis were searching for their super Aryan race all over the world while they were bombing the daylight out of the Norwegians and the Frisians. The true Aryans were in their backyard all along!

---

[222] Bijal P. Trivedi: Article in *Genome Research*, May 2001.
[223] Brown, N: *Pakistan and Western Asia*. Quoted by various authors but not verified here

The Magi

Throughout the Oera Linda book we read of the conflict that existed for millennia between Frya's People (the proto-Frisians) and the Magy from Finland and Sweden. We have seen how the Magy with his Magyarar and Finnar followers infiltrated Scandinavia from the East after the 2193 BC disaster; later the whole of Central and Northern Europe followed. Around the Mediterranean, we came across the Gola (Gauls) and the Treowits (Druids) and in Greece we found the pagan priests who later became the oracles of Homer and Herodotus. South and Western Asia were not left out. In India, the Oera Linda Book made mention of pagan priests to the east of the Punjab who terrorized the Ira and the Gedrostne. Aharon Daniel identified them as of Sino-Mongolian origins. It becomes evident, therefore, that these Magy, Magi, Oracles, Druids or Priests played a significant role in Eurasian history.

In his Histories, Herodotus mentioned them on numerous occasions, but called them the *Magi*, similar to the Oera Linda Book's *Magy* in Scandinavia. He does not, however, describe them merely as a separate class such as priests but, like the Oera Linda Book, identifies them as from a different race altogether and a separate tribe in their own right:

101. Thus Deioces collected the Medes into a nation, and ruled over them alone. Now these are the tribes of which they consist: the Busae, the Paretaceni, the Struchates, the Arizanti, the Budii, and the Magi[224]*,*

The Magi are a very peculiar race, different entirely from the Egyptian priests, and indeed from all other men whatsoever. The Egyptian priests make it a point of religion not to kill any live animals except those that they offer in sacrifice. The Magi, on the contrary, kill animals of all kinds with their own hands, excepting dogs and men. They even seem to take a delight in the employment, and kill, as readily

---

[224] The *Histories* of Herodotus, Book I

as they do other animals, ants and snakes, and such like flying or creeping things. However, since this has always been their custom, let them keep to it. I return to my former narrative.[225]

It is interesting to note that Herodotus describes the Magi as entirely different from the Egyptian priests whereas the Oera Linda Book described them as very similar to the Egyptians. We must remember, though, that the authors of the Oera Linda Book, unlike Herodotus, were not professional historians or academics and they were very distant from Egypt.

They were not wild people, like many of Finda's race; but, they are like the Egiptalandar, they have priests like them and in their churches they also have statues.
The priests are the only masters; they call themselves Magyarar, and their headman is known as Magy.[226]

According to Herodotus, the foreign Magis with their Eastern occultist practices were so deeply lodged into the Median Empire that the Magi Smerdis almost succeeded in taking over the Empire when Cambyses was on his Egyptian campaign. The Medians attached great importance to the opinion of the Magi:

107. Astyages, the son of Cyaxares, succeeded to the throne. He had a daughter who was named Mandane concerning whom he had a wonderful dream. He dreamt that from her such a stream of water flowed forth as not only to fill his capital, but to flood the whole of Asia. This vision he laid before such of the Magi as had the gift of interpreting dreams, who expounded its meaning to him in full, whereat he was greatly terrified.

Even the Persian Empire was later infiltrated:

---

[225] The *Histories* of Herodotus, Book I (140).
[226] OLB: The Book of Adela's Followers, chapter 23

When all is ready, one of the Magi comes forward and chants a hymn, which they say recounts the origin of the gods. It is not lawful to offer sacrifice unless there is a Magus present.[227]

We encounter the Magi on various occasions in the Bible where it was translated from the Greek *Magos* to, inter alia, *Wise Men*. In E. F. Murphy's *Handbook for spiritual warfare* he gives the following definition:

The Greek word is magos. It can be translated 'magician, sorcerer, wizard, enchanter, astrologer' or simply 'wise men' (Matt. 2:1f). F. F. Bruce explains how the term was used in the ancient world:
'The magi were originally a Median priestly caste, but in later Greek and Roman times the word was used more generally of practitioners of all sorts of magic or quackery'.[228]

The *Smith's Bible Dictionary* gives a somewhat different explanation:

The Magi took their places among "the astrologers and stargazers and monthly prognosticators." It is with such men that we have to think of Daniel and his fellow exiles as associated. The office which Daniel accepted, Dan. 5:11, was probably rab-mag—chief of the Magi. 2. The word presented itself to the Greeks as connected with a foreign system of divination, and it soon became a byword for the worst form of imposture. This is the predominant meaning of the word as it appears in the New Testament. Acts 8:9; 13:8.3. In one memorable instance, however, the word retains its better meaning. In the Gospel of St. Matthew, ch. 2:1-12, the Magi appear as "wise men"—properly Magians—who were guided by a star from "the east" to Jerusalem, where they suddenly appeared in the days of Herod the Great, inquiring for the new-born king of the Jews, whom they had come to worship. As to the country from which they came, opinions vary greatly; but their following the guidance of a star seems to point to the

---

[227] The *Histories* of Herodotus, Book I (132).
[228] Murphy, E. F. 1997, c1996. *Handbook for spiritual warfare*. Thomas Nelson: Nashville

banks of the Tigris and Euphrates, where astronomy was early cultivated by the Chaldeans. [See Star of the East.] (Why should the new star lead these wise men to look for a king of the Jews? (1) These wise men from Persia were the most like the Jews, in religion, of all nations in the world. They believed in one God, they had no idols; they worshipped light as the best symbol of God.[229]

The last sentence in the above quotation matches the Oera Linda Book's description to a tee. From the above it seems that there were essentially two types of Magi (Greek: Magos). The one was the Wise Men who studied astronomy. The other group was the priests who dabbled in the occult and in astrology. To outsiders they would have appeared to be the same. This confusion exists right up to the present.

We have seen the influence that the monotheistic Frisians had on the Persian Empire and on Judaism. In Chapter 2 we have an extract from the writings of Apollonia where she gave a description of her village or burgh. In this discussion, paragraph 1 of her description gains new significance:

My burgh lies near the north end of the Liudgarda. The tower has six sides, and is ninety feet high, flat-roofed, with a small house upon it out of which they look at the stars.[230]

The Frisians were a maritime nation. It was therefore essential that they had to study astronomy in order to navigate the oceans. This knowledge they imparted on the Persian Empire and should cast a new light on the Wise Men from the East who paid tribute to the Babe of Bethlehem. Let us now turn our attention to the cultic Magi.

The Oera Linda Book showed that the Magy and the Magyarar in Scandinavia came from the East and that they practiced Shamanism. Archaeological, genetic and linguistic evidence points to their place of origin as the Altai Mountains where Russia, China, Kazakhstan and Mongolia meet. We have seen the similarities of these Magyarars with

---

[229] Smith, W. 1997. *Smith's Bible dictionary*. Thomas Nelson: Nashville
[230] OLB: *The writings of Apollonia*, Chapter 7.

the pagan priests and oracles in Greek mythology. In Hungary their name lives on as the *Magyar*. In Phoenicia, we identified them as the *Gola* who gave rise to the Gauls and the Druids. They in turn influenced the Celts.

The pagan priests in India were of Sino-Mongolian descends and in the empires of the Medes and the Persians they were known as the cultic Magi with their perverse theology. The Greeks referred to them as Magos. In The new Strong's dictionary of Hebrew and Greek words we find the following:

> *Mag´-os; of foreign origin [7248]; a Magian, i.e. Oriental scientist; by implication a magician:* — *sorcerer, wise man.*[231]

The Land of Magog

From the above explanation we may realistically infer that the Magi in the Middle East and the Magy from Scandinavia, as well as some other shamanistic priests, originated from the Altai mountainous region in Western Mongolia. This leads us to another interesting deduction. In the Bible, in Ezekiel 38:1-3, we find the following regarding the mysterious *Gog of the Land of Magog*:

> *(1) Now the word of the Lord came to me, saying, (2) "Son of man, set your face against Gog, of the land of Magog, the prince of Rosh, Meshech, and Tubal, and prophesy against him, (3) and say, 'Thus says the Lord God: "Behold, I am against you, O Gog. The prince of Rosh, Meshech, and Tubal.*

Ezekiel 39:1-2 repeat the above but now give us a clue as to the locality of the land of the Magog:

> *And you, son of man, prophesy against Gog, and say, 'Thus says the Lord God: "Behold, I am against you, O Gog, the prince of Rosh, Meshech, and Tubal; (2) and I will turn you around and lead you on,*

---

[231] Strong, J. 1997, c1996. *The new Strong's dictionary of Hebrew and Greek words*. Thomas Nelson: Nashville.

bringing you up from the far north, and bring you against the mountains of Israel.[232]

Biblical scholars have all along accepted that the name Gog means mountain. They thus deduced that this mountain must refer to the Caucasus Mountains to the north. The land of Magog would therefore mean the land of the Scythians between the Black and Caspian Seas. J. H. Smith in *The new treasury of scripture knowledge* echoes the accepted theory:

> *Gog. i.e. mountain, in reference to the Caucasus Mountains, chief seat of the Scythian people. Rather, "Gog (the prince) of the land of Magog, the prince of Rosh, Meshech, and Tubal." By Magog is most probably meant the Scythians or Tartars, called so by the Arabian and Syrian writers, and especially the Turks, who were originally natives of Tartary (inhabiting parts of Russia and central and western Siberia); and by Rosh, the Russians, descendants of the ancient inhabitants on the river Araxes or Rosh. Josephus concurs in identifying Magog with the Scythians (Ant. i. vi. 1). But compare "Og" (Dt 3:1-13). 1 Ch +5:4. Re 20:8, 9. Magog. Jerome identifies Magog as the "Scythian nations, fierce and innumerable, who live beyond the Caucasus and the Lake Maeotis, and near the Caspian Sea, and spread out even onward to India." Ge 10:2. 1 Ch 1:5. Compare "Agag," Nu 24:7. the chief prince of. or, prince of the chief of. Rather, prince of Rosh. The meaning is that Magog is the head of the three great Scythian tribes, of which "Rosh" is the first. Gesenius identifies Rosh with Russia*[233]

Whereas the New King James version of the Bible refers to the land of Magog as being in the *far north,* other translations mention the *distant north, uttermost parts of the north* or the *recesses of the north.* These would all appear to point to a land well beyond the Caucasus Mountains. It is thus proposed here that Gog (mountain) refers to the

---

[232] The New King James Version. 1996, c 1982. Thomas Nelson: Nashville.

[233] Smith, J. H. 1992; Published in electronic form, 1996. *The new treasury of scripture knowledge,* Thomas Nelson: Nashville TN

Altai Mountains in Western Mongolia. The *land of the Magog* would then imply to be the *land of the Mongol* and the cultic Magi would be synonymous to Gog, the prince of Magog. Even the Greek *Magos* for *Magi* sounds very similar to the Greek and Hebrew *Magog*:

> 3098.   *mag-ogue´; of Hebrew origin. [4031]; Magog, a foreign nation,*[234]

Without the Oera Linda Book, it is unlikely that this reconstruction would have been possible. History has shown other invasions from that part of the world, such as that of the brutal Genghis Khan from 1206 AD onwards. The subsequent Mongol Empire extended from the Eastern shores of China right into Central Europe – arguably the largest land empire the world has ever seen.

In researching this book it became evident that the two groups of people in antiquity who had the most influence on Eurasian history were the Shamanists from Central Asia and the Frisians from Western Europe; in DNA terminology, the R1a and R1b haplogroups. The R1a group appears to have brought a permissive paganism and conquest by either deceit or military means, whereas the R1b group from Western Europe brought monotheism, technology and their fair share of conquests to the party. All other religions and civilizations were variants and compromises between these two groups.

Figure 44 shows the migration of the two groups.

---

[234] **Strong, J. 1997, c1996.** *The new Strong's dictionary of Hebrew and Greek words.* **Thomas Nelson: Nashville.**

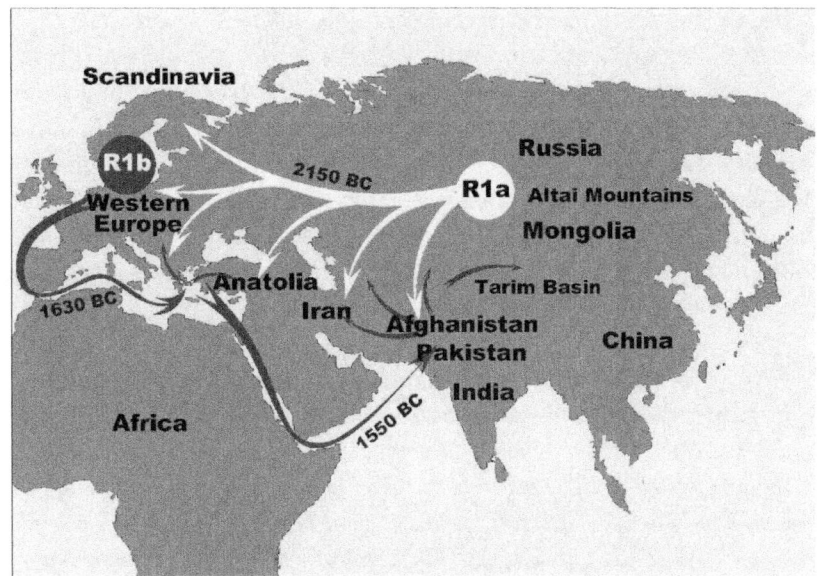

Figure 44: Migration of the R1a & R1b Haplogroups
(After 2193 BC)

King Alexander

Alexander the Great, or *King Alexander*, as the Gertmanne called him, arrived in the Punjab in ca 328 BC, more than 1 200 years after the Gertmanne. In ca 300 BC, Frethorik Oera Linda recorded the following in the Oera Linda Book:

> *Liudgert, the admiral of Wichhirte, became my comrade and afterwards my friend. Out of his diary I have taken the following history:*
>
> *After we had lived 12 times 100 and twice 12 years (1224 years) at the Five Waters (Punjab), whilst our seafarers were navigating all the seas they could find, came Alexander the King, with a powerful army from the upper regions of the river towards our villages. No one could withstand him; but we <u>sea-people</u>, who lived by*

the sea, put all our possessions on board ships and took our departure.[235]

Here we find the Frisians back at what they knew and loved best - the oceans and the discovery of distant lands. The only difference now is that their exploits passed on from the Atlantic and Mediterranean to the Arabian Sea, the Bay of Bengal, the Indian Ocean and most likely further east to Indonesia, the South China Sea, the Philippines and perhaps even Australia. It is reasonable to suspect that these Sea People drew the amazing maps from antiquity.

When Alexander heard that such a large fleet had escaped him, he became furious, and swore that he would burn all the villages if we did not come back. Wichhirte was ill in bed. When Alexander heard that, he waited until he was better. After that he came to him, speaking very kindly—but he deceived, as he had done before.

Wichhirte answered: "Oh greatest of kings, we sailors go everywhere; we have heard of your great deeds, therefore we are full of respect for your arms, and still more for your wisdom; but we who are free-born Frya's children. We may not become your slaves; and even if I would, the others would sooner die, for so it is commanded in our laws."

Alexander said: "I do not desire to take your land or make slaves of your people. I only wish to hire your services. That I will swear by both our gods, so that no one may be dissatisfied."

When Alexander had shared bread and salt with him, Wichhirte chose the wisest part. He let his son fetch the ships. When they had all returned, Alexander hired them all. By means of them, he wished to transport his people to the holy Ganges, which he had not been able to reach before. Then he chose among all his people and soldiers those who were accustomed to the sea. Wichhirte had fallen sick again, therefore I went alone with Nearchus, sent by the king. The voyage came to an end without any advantage, because the Ioniars and

---

[235] OLB: The writings of Frethorik and Wiliow, Chapter 2.

the Phœnicians were always quarrelling, so that Nearchus himself could not control them.[236]

The *Ioniar* Liudgert refers to here in 328 BC would be the descendants of Ion from the Ionian Islands of 1627 BC and the Phonisiar the descendants of Tunis from Tyre of 2000 BC.

> *In the meantime, the king had not sat still. He had let his soldiers cut down trees and make planks, with which, with the help of our carpenters, he had built ships. Now he would himself become a sea king, and sail with his whole army up the Ganges; but the soldiers who came from the mountainous countries were afraid of the sea. When they heard that they must sail, they set fire to the timber yards, and so our whole village was laid in ashes.*

> *At first we thought that this had been done by Alexander's orders, and we were all ready to cast ourselves into the sea: but Alexander was furious, and wished his own people to kill the soldiers. However, Nearchus, who was not only his chief officer, but also his friend, advised him not to do so. So he pretended to believe that it had happened by accident, and said no more about it. He wished now to return, but before going he made an inquiry as to who were really the guilty ones. As soon as he ascertained it, he had them all disarmed, and made them build a new village. His own people he kept under arms to intimidate the others to build a burgh.*

> *We were to take the women and children with us. When we have arrived at the mouth of the Euphrates, we could then either choose a place to settle there or come back. Our pay would be guaranteed to us in either case.*

> *Upon the new ships, which had been saved from the fire, he placed the Joniars and the Greeks. He himself went with the rest of his people along the coast, through the barren desert; that is, through the land that the Earth had heaved up out of the sea when she raised the strait after our forefathers had passed into the Red Sea.*

> *When we arrived at New Gertmania (New Gertmania is the port that we had made ourselves in order to take in water), we met*

---

[236] OLB: The writings of Frethorik and Wiliow, Chapter 2.

Alexander with his army. Nearchus went ashore, and stayed three days. Then we proceeded further on.[237]

The fact that the Gertmanne considered it necessary to establish a permanent port at the mouth of the Persian Gulf to take in water would indicate that this was one of their major trading routes. This port of Ny Gertmannia would have been used by vessels from Egypt, Palestine, Babylonia and the Punjab. It is quite likely that the fleet of King Solomon of Israel made use of the facilities and traded with the Gertmanne. In 1 Kings 9:26-28 and 1 Kings 10:22 we are told of Solomon's Red Sea Fleet:

1 Kings 9:26-28
(26) King Solomon also built a fleet of ships at Ezion Geber, which is near Elath on the shore of the Red Sea, in the land of Edom. (27) Then Hiram sent his servants with the fleet, seamen who knew the sea, to work with the servants of Solomon. (28) And they went to Ophir, and acquired four hundred and twenty talents of gold from there, and brought it to King Solomon.

1 Kings 10:22
(22) For the king had merchant ships at sea with the fleet of Hiram. Once every three years the merchant ships came bringing gold, silver, ivory, apes, and monkeys.

Judging from the merchandise that Solomon imported, the land of Ophir was most likely India. Let us now continue with Admiral Liudgert's diary:

When we came to the Euphrates, Nearchus went ashore with the soldiers and a large body of people; but he soon returned, and said:
"The king requests you, for his sake, to take a short voyage to the end of the Red Sea; after that each shall receive as much gold as he can carry."

---

[237] OLB: The writings of Frethorik and Wiliow, Chapter 2

When we arrived there, he showed us where the strait had formerly been. There he spent thirty-one days, always looking steadily towards the desert.

At last there arrived a great troop of people, bringing with them 200 elephants, 1000 camels, timber, ropes, and all kinds of implements necessary to drag our fleet to the Mediterranean Sea. This astounded us, and seemed most extraordinary; but Nearchus told us that his king wished to show to the other kings that he was more powerful than any of the kings of Tyre had ever been. We were only to assist, and that surely could do us no harm. We were obliged to yield, and Nearchus knew so well how to regulate everything that our ships lay in the Mediterranean Sea before three months had passed.

When Alexander heard how his project was concluded, he became so audacious that he wished to dig out the dry strait in mockery of the Earth; but Wr-alda abandoned his soul, so that he destroyed himself by wine and rashness before he could begin it.[238]

Nowhere in Arrian's accounts which he wrote from Grecian sources and perhaps even from Nearchus's own diary, do we read anything of the Gertmanne. The Greeks obviously would not have wanted to share their glory with anyone else. They did not do so in Athens, so why would they change now? Even today, large companies seldom mention the contribution of contractors in their achievements. However, one only needs to ask a few simple questions:

- How did Alexander's army manage to build 1 800 ships in the Punjab in such a short time according to Arrian's claims?
- From where did they get the wood?
- From where did they get the artisans and tools to build the ships?
- From where did they get the rigging and sails? and
- From where did they get the crews?

It should be abundantly clear that the Greeks did not tell the whole story. The Grecian account is as absurd as the claim that

---

[238] OLB: The writings of Frethorik and Wiliow, Chapter 2.

Alexander founded all those cities he called Alexandria. He did not found them, he only renamed them.

A major achievement Arrian failed to mention was Alexander's relocation of the fleet from the Red Sea overland to the Mediterranean. According to the Oera Linda Book, Nearchus was present, but perhaps his scribe was not.

It is also interesting to note that the Gertmanne were the first to state unequivocally that Alexander died from excessive drinking – another one of those little facts the Greeks choose to ignore – their great leader had a heavy hand.

The Euro-Indians

By now it should be abundantly clear to the reader that the Aryans, also known as the Gertmanne, hailed from Western Europe. The ramifications of this statement are far-reaching.

Since the 18th century AD linguists have been using the term Indo-European and later Proto-Indo-European to explain the development and migration of languages between Europe and Asia. According to the theory that is most widely accepted, these languages would have developed out of the Proto-Indo-Iranian languages of the Bronze Age Sintashta and Andronova cultures from an area in the vicinity of the Caspian Sea. The appearance of these languages from Mesopotamia to the Indian sub-continent is linked to the Indo-Aryan invasion or migration, which would have taken place in ca 1500 BC. Evidence for this migration is largely based on linguistic theories.

If the Oera Linda account is true, it would mean that there never was an Indo-Aryan or Indo-Iranian invasion, at least not by military conquest in the strictest sense, and definitely not from the North. Our whole concept of the development of our European languages would therefore be wrong. The evolutionary migration of these languages would not have been from Central to South Asia and then to Europe. In fact, it would have been precisely the opposite. It would also mean that the term Indo-European cannot be applied to the European languages, as the languages from West and Southern Asia would not have had any influence on the European languages. In addition, the Germanic language family would therefore be much older than even Greek and Latin. Instead of referring to European languages as Indo-European, one should rather refer to the South and West-Asian languages as Euro-Indian.

Under the Writings of Konered, Chapter 6 in the Oera Linda Book we find a description of the Punjab written by Liudgert, the old admiral, in a letter to Konered's father. Here are some extracts:

> *Among my father's papers I found a letter from Liudgert the Gertman. Omitting some passages which only concern my father, I proceed to relate the rest.*
>
> *Pangap, that is five waters, and where we came from, is a river of extraordinary beauty, and is called five waters, because four other streams flow through its mouth into the sea. Far away to the east is another large river, the Holy or Sacred Ganges. Between these two rivers is the land of the Hindos. Both rivers run from the high mountains to the plains. The mountains from where they spring are so high that they lie up to the heavens, and therefore these mountains are called the Himmellaia Mountains.*[239]

The name Himalaya Mountains in Asia, which the Gertmanne called the *Himellaia Mountains* is a typical European word and means the mountains that stretch or lie up up to the heavens. In German, heaven is *himmel* and in Afrikaans *Hemel*. The suffix *-laia* would be almost the same in both Afrikaans and English: *lie up (to).*

It must be pointed out that ancient Fries is the root language of English, Afrikaans and German, and obviously of Fries, Flemish and Dutch, to mention but a few. For this reason a speaker of any of these languages will recognise words in ancient Fries.

The *Grand Trunk Road* in South-west Asia was known in ancient times as *Uttarapatha*, the *Upper Path* – another example of the West- European influence.

---

[239] OLB: *The Writings of Konered*, Chapter 6.

Coming still further westward, we arrive at the Gedrostne. As regards the Gedrostne; they have been mixed with other people, and speak a variety of languages. These people are really savage murderers, who always wander about the country on horseback hunting and robbing, and hire themselves as soldiers to the surrounding princes, at whose command they destroy whatever they can reach.

Gedrostne (Afrikaans: *drosters*) is a typical Germanic-type word that means *deserters*. On Alexandrian maps, we still find the region *Gedrosia*, which today is known as *Baluchistan* in southern Iran and Pakistan.

The Tocharians

In the 1980s, archaeologists started discovering naturally mummified bodies in the Taklimakan desert in the Tarim Basin in western China. Many of these mummies had blond to red hair and their features are distinctly Caucasoid.

One mummy, known as Yingpan Man, was almost 2 metres tall and wore clothes that seemed to have come from Western Europe.

Professor Victor Mair of Pennsylvania was the project leader of a team that did genetic analysis and mapping of the mummies. He stated that the earliest mummies in the Tarim Basin were exclusively Caucasoid, or Europoid. He further commented:

The new finds are also forcing a re-examination of old Chinese books that describe historical or legendary figures of great height, with deep-set blue or green eyes, long noses, full beards, and red or blond hair. Scholars have traditionally scoffed at these accounts, but it now seems that they may be accurate.[240]

Scientists have concluded that the textiles found with these mummies are of European design and texture and similar to those found on Austrian salt miners of ca 1300 BC. Irene Good, an

---

[240] Mair, VH: *Mummies of the Tarim Basin*, Archaeology, vol. 48, no. 2, pages 28-35 (March/April 1995)

anthropologist and specialist in early Eurasian fabrics, concluded that the woven diagonal twill pattern indicated the use of a rather sophisticated loom and is the easternmost known example of this kind of weaving technique.

Figure 45: The Beauty of Loulan

One of the oldest mummies found in the Tarim Basin and one of the most famous of the Tocharian Mummies is known as the Beauty of Loulan. Could this be the face of one of our Gertmanne? Perhaps even Gert herself? The reconstruction here is an artist's impression of what she looked like when she died at age 40. (With acknowledgement to Wikipedia)

The Tarim Basin lies to the north of the Himalayas and is adjacent to Sogdiana, one of the suggested settlements of the Gertmanne.

If some of these Tarim Basin mummies are of the Gertmanne or descendants of the Gertmanne of the Oera Linda Book, it would mean that the Caucasoid, or Europoid mummies found amongst them, should not be older than, say, 3 500 years; that is from after ca 1553 BC. The key to unlocking the Tocharian A and B languages could then more than likely be found in ancient Fries.

A note on Iron Working in India

An interesting paper by Rakesh Tewari, the director of U.P. State Archaeological Department in India, appears on the webpage of *Archaeology Online* on the internet. The paper is entitled *The Origins of Iron-working in India*.

Tewari notes that the subject of ancient iron working in India and surrounds remains a much-debated research problem which is not unconnected with the equally debatable question of its association with the supposed arrival, in the second millennium BCE, of immigrants from the west, as often suggested on the basis of the Rigveda.

> *Since then there has been fresh evidence for even earlier iron-working in India. Technical studies on materials dated c. 1000 BCE at Komaranhalli (Karnataka) showed that the smiths of this site could deal with large artefacts, implying that they had already been experimenting for centuries (Agrawal et al. 1985: 228-29). Sahi (1979: 366) drew attention to the presence of iron in Chalcolithic deposits at Ahar, and suggested that 'the date of the beginning of iron smelting in India may well be placed as early as the sixteenth century BCE' and 'by about the early decade of thirteenth century BCE iron smelting was definitely known in India on a bigger scale. On the basis of four radiocarbon measurements, ranging between 3790 + 110 BP and 3570 + 100 BP, available for the Megalithic period (without iron) Sharma (1992: 64, 67) has proposed a range of 1550-1300 BCE (uncalibrated) for the subsequent iron bearing period at Gufkral (Jammu & Kashmir).*[241]

---

[241] R Tewari, *The Origins of Iron-working in India*, *Archaeology Online* webpage, U.P. State Archaeological Department in India.

Here again we find undeniable evidence in support of the Oera Linda chronicles. The appearance of iron-working in India at exactly the same time that the Iron Age Frisians arrived in the Punjab cannot be ignored.

Chapter 7

Homeward Bound

The Greek Dark Ages

Historians commonly refer to the *Greek Dark Ages*
as the period from ca 1200 BC up to ca 800 BC when Homer wrote his
Iliad and *Odyssey*. The Oera Linda Book also had its dark ages during
the same time. In Chapter 30 of the Book of Adela's Followers, we have
the notes regarding Ulysses and Athens in 1188 BC. In Chapter 31, the
narrative continues with the loss of Denmark in 591 BC and the lives of
Adela and Apollonia. Nothing seems to have been recorded in the
intervening period of almost 600 years – at least not by the Oera Linda
family.

We have seen that the Frisians wrote their laws as well as
important events and life's lessons on the walls of their citadels.
Perhaps they had nothing to report or perhaps the Fins and the Celts
kept them so busy that they could not write anything. It is also
possible, of course, that such records as there may have been did not
survive the numerous floods and wars along the west coast of Europe.
The Oera Linda Book does make mention of quite a few books such as
the *Book of Songs*, the *Book of Narratives*, the *Hellenia Book* and the *Book of
the Adelinga* which might have contained records of this period, but
which did not survive. Perhaps these dark ages might even have been
the result of a third volcanic eruption or eruptions in ca. 1200 BC as
speculated. We know that the Hekla volcano in Iceland erupted with a
massive Volcanic Explosivity Index (VEI) of 5 in ca 1159 BC. In Chapter
5 we suggested that the Thera volcano on Santorini may also have

erupted during the same time. Temperatures plummeted and the resultant growth depression in trees around the North Atlantic lasted for more than a decade. It would therefore seem reasonable to suspect that some major natural disaster or disasters in the Northern Hemisphere caused the Greek Dark Ages.

After the writings of Apollonia, the Oera Linda book is again silent for a further 220 years. It resumes with the writings of Frethorik.

The 305 BC Event

Frethorik Oera Linda recorded a second (or third?) natural disaster which devastated the Netherlands, Friesland, Denmark and Norway in 305 BC. Here is his account:

> *The Magy prided himself on his cunning, but the Earth made him know that she would not tolerate any Magy or idol on the holy bosom that had borne Frya. As a wild horse tosses his mane after he has thrown his rider, so Irtha shook her forests and her mountains. Rivers spread over the fields; the sea raged; mountains spouted fire to the clouds and what they vomited forth, the clouds flung upon the earth. At the beginning of the Arnemaand* (harvest month) *the earth bowed towards the north, and sank down lower and lower. In the Wolfamaand* (Wolf Month, winter month) *the low lands of Fryasland were buried under the sea. The woods in which the images were were torn up and scattered by the wind.*
>
> *The following year the frost came in the Herdemaand* (Louwmaand, January), *and covered Fryasland under a sheet of ice. In Sellemaand* (Sprokkelmaand, February) *there were storm winds from the north, driving mountains of ice and stones. When the spring-tides came the earth raised herself up, the ice melted; with the ebb the forests with the images drifted out to sea. In the Winne-, or Minnamaand* (Bloeimaand, May), *every one who dared went home. I came with a matron[242] to the citadel Liudgarda. How sad it looked there. The forests of the Lindawrda were almost all gone. Where Liudgarda*

---

[242] Wiliow, his later wife.

used to be was sea. The waves swept over the ring dyke. Ice had destroyed the tower, and the houses lay heaped over each other. On the slope of the dyke, I found a stone on which the writer had inscribed his name. That was my marker.

The same thing that happened to our burgh happened to the others. In the high lying lands, they had been destroyed by the earth, in the low-lying lands by water. Only Fryasburgh on Texland was not damaged, but all the land to the north was under the sea, and has never resurfaced. On the banks of the Flymeer[243], as we were told, thirty salt swamps were found where the forests and the ground had been swept away. At Westflyland there were fifty. The canal, which had run across the land from Alderga, was filled up with sand and destroyed. The seafaring people and other sailors who were at home had saved themselves with their wives and children on their ships. The black people at Lydasburgh and Alkmarum had done the same. As the blacks were driven south, they saved many girls, and as no one came to claim them, they took them for their wives.

The people who returned all went to live within the ring dyke of the burgh, as outside there was nothing but mud and marsh. The old houses were all smashed together. People bought cattle and sheep in the upper lands and in the great houses where formerly the maidens lived, cloth and felt were made for a livelihood. This happened 1888 years after the submersion of Atland. (305 BC)[244]

Here we have record of another huge disaster that struck the west coast of Europe almost 2 000 years after the 2193 BC event. This was not just another flood. Frethorik described earthquakes, tsunamis, rogue icebergs, volcanic activity and extremely strong winds. In addition, temperatures dropped because Fryasland was concealed under a sheet of ice.

Strabo (64 BC–24 AD), a Roman historian, referred in his *Geography* (7.2.1) to legends of a devastating flood that had struck the Cimbri:

---

[243] Flyland is the area around the Ijsselmeer (Flymar in the OLB) and means *Marshland, Swampland or Moorland.*

[244] OLB: The writings of Frethorik and Wiliow, Chapter 1.

II. As for the Cimbri, some things that are told about them are incorrect and others are extremely improbable. For instance, one could not accept such a reason for their having become a wandering and piratical folk as this – that while they were dwelling on a Peninsula they were driven out of their habitations by a great flood-tide.[245]

Even two thousand years ago the historian Strabo did not believe their story. This peninsula was most likely Jutland in Denmark from where the Cimbri came. Under the *Writings of Konered* in the Oera Linda Book, Konered describes how the Danes who survived the disaster turned to piracy – the start of the Vikings:

Afterwards many of the Denemarkers returned from the higher lands, but they settled more to the south; and when the mariners returned who had not been lost, they all went together to Zeeland. By this arrangement, the Jutlanders retained the land to which Wralda had conducted them.

The Zeeland sailors, who were not satisfied to live on fish alone, and who hated the Gauls, took to robbing the Phœnician ships.[246]

In casting doubt on the plausibility of their legend, Strabo unwittingly confirmed the Cimbri and the Oera Linda Book's story that they turned to piracy after their country had been devastated by floods. The Phonisar, or Phoenicians here, refer to the Carthaginians from Carthage in North Africa; the city that was founded by Nef Tunis from Tyre, or his Phoenician descendants, after 2000 BC.

The people who live on the south side[247] *of the Mediterranean Sea come for the most part from Phœnicia. The Phœnicians (Carthaginians) are a bastard race of the blood of Frya, Finda, and Lyda. The Lyda people were there as slaves, but by the unchastity of the women, these black people have degenerated the other people and dyed them brown. These people and the Romans are constantly struggling*[248]

---

[245] Strabo (64 BC–24 AD), *Geography* (7.2.1).
[246] OLB: *The writings of Konered*, Chapter 2
[247] Carthage, North Africa
[248] Punic Wars

for the supremacy over the Mediterranean Sea. The Romans, moreover, live at enmity with the Phœnicians; and their priests, who wish to assume the sole government of the world, cannot bear the sight of the Gauls.[249]

We know that the Romans fought their Punic Wars (264 BC to 146 BC) against the Phoenicians or Poenicus of Carthage. Strabo continues:

And the assertion that an excessive flood-tide once occurred looks like a fabrication, for when the ocean is affected in this way it is subject to increases and diminutions, but these are regulated and periodical. And the man who said that the Cimbri took up arms against the flood-tides was not right, either; nor yet the statement that the Celti, as a training in the virtue of fearlessness, meekly abide the destruction of their homes by the tides and then rebuild them, and that they suffer a greater loss of life as the result of water than of war, as Ephorus says.

Strabo clearly thought that the Cimbri was a Celtic People. It would appear, for that matter, that everybody north of the Alps and the Rhine was regarded as Celts. This understandable misconception continues to this day. The Celts, Germans and Frisians, amongst others, shared a common language, culture and heritage. To outsiders (and archaeologists) they would all appear to be the same. It is only the Oera Linda Book that provides us with the finer nuances of their differences. The mentioning of taking up arms against the flood tides by the Cimbri could only be a reference to dikes, ramparts and terpen mounds. How else does one fight against floods?

---

[249] OLB: *The Writings of Beden,* Chapter 3.

Figure 46: Typical raised mound or terp.
These terpen mounds are man-made to protect villagers from floods. The above picture of *de Hallig Hooge*, Germany, was taken in August 2005 by Sandra Buhmann. (From Wikimedia Commons)

Current thinking has it that the numerous terps or terpen mounds found in Friesland and surrounds were first constructed from between 800 BC to 500 BC. In The Book of Adela's Followers, however, we find record of terpen mounds more than 4000 years ago:

This stands written on the walls of Fryasburgh in Texland. It also stands in Stavia and in Medeasblik:
Obedient children! When they came to themselves again, they made this high mound and built this burgh on it, on the walls they wrote the Tex, and that every one should be able to find it they called the land about it Texland. Therefore it shall remain as long as the earth shall be the earth.[250]

In the 6th century BC Apollonia again made mention of a terp:

"Where did your house stand?" Trast asked.
"On the bank of the Rhine", the man answered.
"Did it not stand on a knoll or a terp?" Trast asked.

---

[250] OLB: *The Book Of Adela's Followers,* Chapter 2.

"No", said the man, "My house stood alone on the bank. I built it alone, but I could not make a terp alone."[251]

The reader will appreciate that terpen mounds are invaluable from an archaeological viewpoint. They are and contain some of the physical evidence of this lost civilization. Unfortunately many of these terps have been excavated and used for fertiliser over the last two centuries. Another remark from Strabo which should be of interest to us:

(They)...meekly abide the destruction of their homes by the tides and then rebuild them, and that they suffer a greater loss of life as the result of water than of war...

Professor S. van Baars, Assistant Professor of Soil Mechanics at the Delft University of Technology, quotes a list of 337 recorded events that resulted in 1735 dike failures in the Netherlands between 1134 and 2006. This equates to a flood event on average every two and a half years. From a very cursory glance at historical data, it appears that disastrous floods had occurred between two to four times every century with hundreds of thousands of lives lost and hundreds of villages and towns obliterated. It seems that every generation experienced at least one catastrophic flood. From the Oera Linda Book, Strabo and Professor van Baars it is evident that the Frisians' battle with the North Sea has been going on for thousands of years.

---

[251] OLB: The Writings of Adelbrost and Apollonia, Chapter 6

Table 4: Some prominent flood disasters on Europe's North Sea Coast over the last 12 centuries.

DATE	EVENT	DEATHS
26 December 838		2437
28 September 1014		Thousands
16 February 1064	St. Juliana Flood	Thousands
1170	1st All Saints Flood	Unknown
1196	St. Nicholas Flood	Unknown
1219	St. Marcellus Flood	36 000
14 December 1287	St. Lucias Flood	50 000 to 80 000
5 February 1288	St. Agatha Flood	Thousands
23 November 1334		Thousands
January 1362	Grote Mandrenke	25 000 to 100 000
19 November 1404	1st St. Elizabeth's Flood	2 000
18 November 1421	2nd St. Elizabeth's Flood	10 000 to 100 000
18 November 1424	3rd St. Elizabeth's Flood	Unknown
1477	Damianus Flood	Thousands
1530	St. Felix's Flood	100 000
1532		Thousands
1 November 1570	All Saints Flood	20 000+
12 October 1634	Burchardi Flood	15 000
9 December 1703		Thousands
25 December 1717	Christmas Flood	14 000
5 February 1825		800
1953		1835
1995		200 000 evacuated

By looking at this table and a number of books written on the subject, we can now understand why almost no record remained of the Old Frisian civilization. It is indeed a miracle that the Oera Linda Book survived. Apart from these floods, Professor van Baars tell us that at least 10 serious plagues ravaged the country between the 14th and 17th centuries AD. Each time the resultant death toll was anything from 15% to 30 % of the total population. In addition, several periods of famine occurred which killed up to 16% of the remainder. Lastly there were numerous devastating wars such as the Frankish Wars, the 100 year civil war, the 80 year war with the Spaniards and the World Wars of the 20th century. Keeping and preserving historical records amongst so much death and destruction are astonishing feats in themselves. The following paintings were done by eyewitnesses to some of the disasters:

Figure 47: All Saints Flood, 11 November 1570
(Allerheiligenvloed by Hans Moser)

Figure 48: Burchardi Flood, 11 & 12 October 1634

Let us now return to the 305 BC disaster.

The Manhattan Tsunami

The following extracts were taken from an article published in The New York Times on 29 December 2008:

> *But several geologists have collected evidence indicating that something very big and unusual occurred in waters near the New York area around 300 B.C., give or take a century. And Dallas Abbott, a research scientist at Columbia University's Lamont-Doherty Earth Observatory, is asserting that a meteorite, landing somewhere in the Atlantic, generated the tsunami.*
>
> *At a meeting of the American Geophysical Union in San Francisco earlier this month, Dr Abbott reported finding minute carbon spheres and smaller-than-dust diamonds in sediment layers,*

which she said were the distinctive calling cards of a meteorite's impact.

"I think it's pretty convincing," Dr. Abbott said. "We always find the impact ejecta in the tsunami layer, never outside."

A few years ago, the geologist Steven Goodbred, then at the State University of New York at Stony Brook, was not looking for tsunamis or meteorites when he first examined sediment cores taken along the South Shore of Long Island. Dr Goodbred was interested in the history of oysters in that area. But in the very first core, he saw a strange layer several inches thick containing fist-size gravel.

"We started joking immediately, 'It's a tsunami,' " recalled Dr Goodbred, now a professor at Vanderbilt University in Nashville.

Subsequent cores, taken in Great South Bay, also contained that layer, deposited about 2 300 years ago. When Dr Goodbred presented his findings at a conference a couple of years ago, he failed to convince other scientists. They said the layer was more likely caused by a big storm, not a tsunami.

Then Dr Goodbred met other scientists who had found similar sediment layers nearby. Cecilia McHugh, a professor at Queens College, had seen a sediment layer a foot and a half thick at Sandy Hook in New Jersey. That, too, was laid down about 2 300 years ago. And Frank Nitsche, another research scientist at Lamont-Doherty, had discovered a layer of wood debris in sediment cores from the upstate reaches of the Hudson River."

"Then Dr Abbott joined the project and found possible evidence of a meteorite".[252]

An AD 2008 scientific report that exactly matches the Oera Linda Book's description, geographical area and time span cannot be a coincidence and cannot be ignored. This was clearly the cause of Strabo's Cimbrian Flood. The report stated that this 300 BC tsunami was not as bad as the AD 2004 tsunami that killed 180 000 people in South-east Asia. Judging from Frethorik Oera Linda's account, it was much worse. The impact seems to have been so severe that it caused

---

[252] *The New York Times*, 29 December 2008.

tectonic plate movements, hurricanes, volcanic activity and fracturing of the ice and icebergs in the Arctic. Again the Oera Linda Book is proven correct, and for that matter, also the Manhattan Tsunami.

The last paragraph of the article must be recorded here:

> *But unless researchers find a crater in the ocean floor, an Indian legend telling of a day of fire and water or many more thick sediment deposits, convincing other scientists of what they believe happened 2 300 years ago will continue to be an uphill battle.*

The Oera Linda Book is not an Indian legend but a written and dated eyewitness report. Hopefully the battle will not be so uphill now.

Caught up in War

When Alexander the Great died in 323 BC his empire was plunged into a power struggle. The Gertmanne and their families who had escorted him from India back to the Mediterranean now found themselves stranded with nowhere to go. Nearchus offered to have them resettled on the Phoenician coast but they declined. They would rather go in search of their old country of which they had heard of in their legends; a place called Fryasland. They would accompany Nearchus to Athenia and from there they would continue their search.

> *After his death his empire was divided among his commanders. They were each to have preserved a share for his sons, but that was not their intention. Each wished to keep his own share, and to get more. Then war arose, and we could not turn back.*
>
> *Nearchus wished us to settle on the coast of Phœnicia, but that no one would do. We said we would rather risk returning to Fryasland. Then he brought us to the new port of Athens, where all the true children of Frya had formerly gone. We went soldiers with our provisions and weapons. Among the many rulers, Nearchus had a friend named Antigonus. These two had only one object in view, as they told us — to follow the royal race, and to restore the old freedom of*

all the Greek lands. Antigonus had, among many others, one son named Demetrius, afterwards called the "State Winner."[253]

The Antigonus we read of here would have been Antigonus I Monophthalmus (Antigonus the One-eyed, 382 BC - 301 BC). He was a Macedonian nobleman, general and satrap under Alexander the Great. Demetrius, his son, would later become known as Demetrius I Poliorcetes (The Besieger), king of Macedon (294–288 BC). The Oera Linda Book refers to *The Besieger* as the *State Winner*. Once again the Oera Linda Book's description and dating fit seamlessly into the known history.

The Gertmanne found themselves in the middle of a war and an opportunity to make some money. Perhaps most of the rewards they had received from Alexander had already been spent in the *boutiques* of Athens. The return to Fryasland would have had to wait for a while. If the Oera Linda dates are correct, they only arrived in Fryasland 20 years after Alexander died.

Both Demetrius and his father had already suffered comprehensive military defeats against Ptolemy at the Battle of Gaza (312 BC) and against Seleucus I Nicator in the Babylonian War (311 BC - 309 BC). Antigonus lost almost two thirds of his empire; Seleucus now had all the eastern satrapies. The Antigonid Dynasty was in deep trouble. In his Lives of the Noble Greeks and Romans, commonly called *Parallel Lives* or *Plutarch's Lives*, Plutarch (c. AD 46 – 120) wrote in the Life of Demetrius:

1. Meantime his father called him to take the conduct of the war against Ptolemaeus

4. The approaching battle aroused the attention not only of the parties concerned, but of all other princes; for besides the uncertainty of the event, so much depended upon it that the conqueror would not be master of Cyprus and Syria alone, but superior to all his rivals in power.[254]

---

[253] OLB: The writings of Frethorik and Wiliow, Chapter 2.
[254] Plutarch: *Life of Demetrius*, Chapter 15.

The 76 year old Antigonus realized that he was about to loose everything and he ordered Dimitrius to take Cyprus. This would be their last chance. Fortunately for Dimitrius, admiral Nearchus had a few friends who were only too willing to offer their services to the highest bidder. Under the leadership of an Athenian Sea King by the name of Friso, the Gertmanne set sail for Salamis in Cyprus.

Once he attacked the town of Salamis. After he had been fighting there for some time, he had to engage the fleet of Ptolemy. Ptolemy was the name of the ruler who reigned over Egypt. Demetrius won the battle; not by his own soldiers, but because we helped him. We had done this out of friendship for Nearchus, because we knew that he was of bastard birth by his white skin, blue eyes, and fair hair.[255]

The naval Battle of Salamis in 306 BC was not a mere victory for Demetrius over Ptolemy I of Egypt. With the assistance of Friso and the Gertmanne, Egypt's naval power was totally destroyed and Cyprus captured. Plutarch described the defeat that Ptolemy and his brother Menelaus suffered at Salamis:

1. Ptolemaeus advanced with 150 ships, and he had ordered Menelaus, with 60 more, to come out of the harbour of Salamis, in the heat of the battle, and put the enemy in disorder by falling on his rear.

2 Against these 60 ships, Demetrius appointed a guard of 10, for that number was sufficient to block up the mouth of the harbour. His land forces he ranged on the adjoining promontories, and then bore down upon his adversary with 180 ships.

3 This he did with so much impetuosity, that Ptolemaeus could not stand the shock, but was defeated, and fled with 8 ships only, which were all that he saved. For 70 were taken with their crews, and the rest were sunk in the engagement.

4 His numerous train, his servants, friends, wives, arms, money, and machines, that were stationed near the fleet in transports, all fell into the hands of Demetrius, and he carried them to his camp.[256]

---

[255] OLB: The writings of Frethorik and Wiliow, Chapter 2.
[256] Plutarch: *Life of Demetrius*, Chapter 16.

After the Battle of Salamis, Demetrius unsuccessfully had siege laid to the Island of Rhodes (305 – 304 BC). Once again the Gertmanne was involved by transporting troops and supplies to the front. History tells us that private contractors were employed during this operation which bears out the Frisian version. When they eventually returned to Athens, they found that Demetrius had defiled both Friso's daughter and son in his absence.

This episode rings true to the character of Demetrius as we get to know him from other sources. His excesses and permissive lifestyle filled even the liberal Athenians with revulsion. The following account from Plutarch confirms the Oera Linda Book's description of Demetrius:

> 2 *Some things we choose to pass over out of regard to the character of the city of Athens: but the virtue and chastity of Democles ought not to be left under the veil of silence.*
>
> 3 *Democles was very young; and his beauty was no secret to Demetrius. Indeed, his surname unhappily declared it, for he was called Democles the Handsome.*
>
> 4 *Demetrius, through his emissaries, left nothing unattempted to gain him by great offers or to intimidate him by threats; but neither could prevail. He left the wrestling ring and all public exercises, and made use only of a private bath. Demetrius watched his opportunity, and surprised him there alone.*
>
> 5 *The boy seeing nobody near to assist him, and the impossibility of resisting with any effect, took off the cover of the caldron, and jumped into the boiling water. It is true, he came to an unworthy end, but his sentiments were worthy of his country and of his personal merit.*[257]

The embittered Friso had his two children commit suicide to save their souls and decided to return to Fryasland with the Gertmanne. He would show them the way. The other Athenians of Frisian descends were not particularly willing to relocate to Western Europe. In order to assist them in making up their minds, Friso duly

---

[257] Plutarch: *Life of Demetrius*, Chapter 24

set fire to their neighbourhood and storehouses. They lost everything and now had no other option but to join the exodus.

Now Friso wished to go with all his people to Frya's land, where he had been formerly, but most of them would not go. So Friso set fire to the village and all the royal storehouses; then no one could remain there, and all were glad to be out of it. We left everything behind us except wives and children, but we had an ample stock of provisions and weapons.[258]

As they left Athens, Friso had one last parting shot to vent his anger and hatred for Demetrius. He sailed into the old harbour and set fire to a number of Greek vessels. The Greeks regrouped and gave chase with their Phoenician fleet. Six days later they caught the Frisians on the open seas. To make matters worse the wind turned and the Frisians could not get away. They were struck with panic but Friso, the experienced naval commander, was delighted. He would turn adversity into opportunity. The headwind slowed down his fleet but the very same wind would carry his burning arrows further than those of the pursuing Phoenicians.

When we were at a cable and a half distance[259] from them the Phœnicians began to shoot, but Friso did not reply until the first arrow fell six fathoms[260] from his ship. Then he fired, and the rest followed. It was like a shower of fire; and as our arrows went with the wind, they all remained alight and even reached the third line. Everybody shouted and cheered, but the screams of our opponents were so loud that it pierced our hearts.

When Friso thought that it was sufficient he called us off, and we sped away; but after two days' slow sailing another fleet of thirty ships came in sight and gained upon us. Friso cleared for action again, but the others sent forward a small rowing boat with messengers who asked permission to sail with us, as they were Joniars. They had been forced by Demetrius to go to the old harbour; there they had heard of

---

[258] OLB: The writings of Frethorik and Wiliow, Chapter 2.
[259] 330 meters
[260] 12 meters

the battle, and girding on their stout swords, had followed us. Friso,
who had sailed a good deal with the Joniars, said "Yes", but Wichirte,
our king, said "No".

"The Joniars", he said, "are idol worshippers. I myself have
heard them call upon them."

"That comes from their intercourse with the real Greeks",
Friso said. "I have often done it myself, and yet I am as pious a Frya's
man as the finest of you".

Friso was the man to take us to Fryasland; therefore, the
Joniars went with us. It seems that this was pleasing to Wralda, for
before three months were past we coasted along Britain, and three days
later we could shout "Ho'n seen!" (What a Blessing!)[261]

The Homecoming

In 1627 BC Ion and Minerva fled from Walhallagara in
Fryasland to Athens and the Ionian Islands. Their descendants
dropped anchor outside the harbour of Stavia 1324 years later. Their
emotional and exuberant shouts of *Ho'n sêen!* (What a blessing!),
reverberated across the water. The myths and legends the old people
had spoken about were lying in front of them. They had returned to
their *Holy Land.*

Since that fateful day, more than 13 centuries before, when
their ancestors left Western Europe behind them, civilizations, empires
and dynasties came and went. The Hyksos, the Minoans and the
Hittites disappeared into the mists of time. The Assyrians, the
Babylonians, the Medes and Persians rose to world dominance and
disappeared again into obscurity. Even the empire of Alexander was
gone and soon the Romans would take their place on the world stage.
This time, however, the Frisians would not be left out of the fray.

In Fryasland the locals did not share in the euphoria of the
strangers from the other side of the world. They were still reeling from
the devastation of two years before and mourning the deaths of their
loved ones. Under the mud and rubble they would still find bodies to

---

[261] OLB: The writings of Frethorik and Wiliow, Chapter 2.

be buried. Their houses were destroyed, their livestock decimated and their lands denuded by earthquakes, hurricanes and tsunamis. Saltwater lakes and marshes covered the landscape. From Denmark to the Scheldt homeless and starving refugees moved into the desolate villages. As if the humanitarian crisis was not enough, they still had to fend off the Magyarar to the North-East, the Twisklanders from the East and the Celts from the South. The last thing they needed was more mouths to feed. This was the scene that greeted Friso as he stepped off his ship.

The west coast of Europe was so devastated that it is no wonder that the pious Norwegians and some of the Frisians joined the Danes in becoming pirates. As was the case with Ion more than a millennium before, piracy became a trade and a legacy that would continue for almost a thousand years. The age of the Vikings and Germans was dawning. The Phoenicians and the Carthaginians, together with the Gauls and the Celts, would pay for the rebuilding of Western Europe.

Repopulation of Fryasland

Frethorik tells us that after the 305 BC disaster, troops of poor *Saxmannar* (Saxons) from Lower Saxony (Neder-Sachsen) sought refuge around Stavia and Alderga, that is, on the eastern and southern sides of the Ijsselmeer (Flymar). They came searching for valuables in the marshes left by the floods. The Frisians put a stop to their scavenging but did allow them to settle in the desolate villages of Westflyland, the current province of Noord-Holland.

When the disaster struck, Noord-Holland was destroyed. The Oera Linda Book mentioned that surviving black crew members (Africans) who served as rowers on the ships saved some girls and later took them as wives. They settled south of Alkmaar towards Leiden. Two years later Friso and his Athenian followers with their liberal ideas, perverted religion and spoilt language arrived and settled around Stavia and Medeasblik. Wichhirte and his fellow Gertmanne from India moved to Emden or *Emude*,[262] in East Frisia in present day Germany. According to the writings of Frethorik, they had preserved their culture and language despite having been isolated from Fryasland for more than 1 300 years. After they had settled in Emude, they retained the name of *Gertmanne* which, in time, the Romans called the *Germani*. Emden is still known as the centre of East Frisia. They had come the full circle – From Frisia to Athens, then to India, Persia and back to Frisia via Athens. As in India and Persia, they called their new home Gertmannia.

---

[262] *Emude* means *Ems' mouth* or the mouth of the Ems River.

Figure 49: Repopulation of Fryasland after 305 BC.

The Ionians or *Joniar* were the descendents of Ion who settled on the Ionian Islands after the 1628 BC Celtic revolution. They joined up with Friso and the Gertmanne after Friso's defeat of the Phoenician Fleet and settled around Alderga, which would seem to have been in the present-day provinces of Flevoland and Utrecht. A smaller group of Ionians settled in Zeeland near the current town of Middelburg. Frethorik described the Ionians as idolaters, of a mixed race and very superstitious. As it turned out, this is exactly the area where stone votives and idols of Nyhellenia, also known as Minerva of Athens were discovered during the late 20th century AD - 2300 years later and 100 years after the Oera Linda Book was discovered. A coincidence? I think not.

Figure 50: Present-day and Historical Frisia
(The map shows the provinces of Fryslân (Friesland) and Noord Holland with some ancient towns depicted in capital letters.)

From this brief account in the Oera Linda Book, we glean that the very fibre of the Frisians from the Scheldt to the Ijsselmeer was irrevocably changed within the course of less than three years. Even Denmark was repopulated by Fins from the eastern side of the Baltic Sea. In the centuries that followed, the Romans, the Franks and many others, such as the Spaniards, continued the process of dismantling the Frisian creed.

The only area where the Frisians of pure Frya's blood would remain was the area around present-day Leeuwarden, Groningen and some isolated pockets towards Denmark and in Norway. Even that changed over the next 2 300 years, and the last place in Europe that retained the name Fryasland, is the small province of Fryslân – called Friesland by the Dutch.

In certain respects the 2193 BC event was not as damaging to the Frisian culture and civilization as the 305 BC disaster. Whilst the former was world-wide with innumerable loss of life and physical destruction, the survivors could still regroup and had presented a united front against external threats. In the latter case, the decay came from within. The 305 BC disaster and the indirect legacy of Alexander the Great through Antigonus and Dimitrius delivered a mortal blow to the Fryan Federation.

Friso

Unlike some myths and the view of certain commentators, Friso, the first legendary king of the Frisians did not come from India like Sea King Wichhirte and Admiral Liudgert. He was a battle-hardened Athenian. The Oera Linda Book tells us that he had been to Frisia before, and that is why he could take the Gertmanne home. He had served in the Alexandrian navy, *grew up in the wars*, was conversant in the Gaulish language and had sailed a good deal with the Joniar. In fact, by his own admission, he had even dabbled in the pagan religion of the Athenians on occasion.

With his military background and leadership skills, Friso soon rose to prominence amidst the chaos around him in Frisia. Konered tells us that Friso was elected Count of the districts around Staveren. He restructured the defences and trained the Frisians in modern warfare. He regarded their matriarchal system and Folk Mother as folly and obsolete. In fact, he blamed the decline of the Fryan Federation on their naïve and pious system of government. He would reverse the process.

Friso, who was already powerful by his troops, was chosen as count of the districts around Staveren. He laughed at our mode of defending our land and our sea battles; therefore he established a school where the boys might learn to fight in the Greek manner.[263]

The older folks did not trust him and it would appear as if they always regarded him as a foreigner – he was not brought up in their ways. The younger generation, however, supported Friso, and thus Europe's first two party democracy came into being – the conservative Mother's Sons and the progressive or liberal Father's Sons. Friso steamrollered the Mother's Sons and for all practical purposes became the first hereditary albeit uncrowned king of the Frisians.

Martinus Hamconius in his 17th century chronicle *Frisia seu de viris rebusque illustribus* list Friso as the first king of the Frisians from ca 304 BC to 264 BC – the same time as the Oera Linda Book. During his reign of close on 40 years, he established a militaristic style hereditary monarchy. According to the Oera Linda Book, though, he was never crowned as king. He was succeeded by his son Adel I Atharik.[264] In terms of archaeological notation, Friso lived during the Mid La Tène period.

Friso understood the politics of the day. After the death (or separation in Athens) of his first wife, he married the daughter of Wilfrethe, the previous count of Staveren. His eldest son and successor, Adel I Atharik, married Ifkia, the daughter of Bertholda, the ruler of Suobaland in Saxanamark (Saxony). Witto, his second son married Siuchthirte, the daughter of Wilhem, the count of Juttarland, whilst his one daughter, Wemod, married Kauch, the son of Gertmanner king Wichhirte. The other daughter married the Fries, Hachgana Oera Linda, the brother of Konered who was count of Liudwerd (Leeuwarden). His two brothers-in-law from his first wife married the daughters of chiefs from the interior. It is no wonder the elder femmes used to say:

---

[263] OLB: *The writings of Konered*, Chapter 2.
[264] Atha-rik means Friend-rich, to have many friends. See also Athenia or Athens, the City of Friends.

Friso does like the spiders. At night he spreads his webs in all directions, and in the day he catches all his unsuspecting friends in them. Friso says he cannot suffer any priests or foreign rulers, but we say that he cannot suffer anybody but himself; therefore, he will not allow the burgh of Stavia to be rebuilt; therefore, he will not have the mother again. To-day Friso is your counselor, to-morrow he will be your king, in order to have full power over you. [265]

Friso and his successors systematically dismantled the Frisian matriarchal system. The Folk Mothers continued to at least the fourth generation after Friso. Prontlik, who was burned out of Fryasburch during the reign of Black Adel, appears to have been the last Folk Mother. Since Friso they were Heads of State only in name. Contrary to popular belief, it is suspected that none of Friso's descendants up to Black Adel were ever officially crowned as kings. Although they may have played the part, this was rather done through notoriety and coercion. Democracy and the Folk Mothers were still in place. In The Writings of Beden, we read the following about Black Adel, the fourth king after Friso:

When his father died he succeeded, and then he wished to retain his office as well, as the kings of the East used to do. The rich would not suffer this, so all the people rose up, and the rich were glad to get out of the assembly with whole skins. [266]

Until Friso and the Gertmanne's arrival, the Frisians were constantly fighting the Magyarar, the Fins and amongst themselves. These new immigrants, however, brought some stability to Fryasland:

Frethorik, my husband, lived to the age of 63. In 108 years, he is the first of his nation who died a peaceful death; all the others died by violence, because they all fought with their own people and with foreigners for justice and duty [267]

---

[265] OLB: *The Writings of Konered*, Chapter 3.
[266] OLB: *The Writings of Beden*, Chapter 3.
[267] OLB: *The Writings of Frethorik and Wiliow*, Chapter 4.

Through his alliances with the neighbouring states and tribes, Friso revitalised the Frisian economy. He restored the shipbuilding and armament industries, re-built the towns and defences in Denmark and established peace between the Jutlanders, the Seelanders of Denmark and the Norwegians. He made sure, however, that the burghs nearer to the Folk Mother were not rebuilt thus further reducing her influence. The conservative Mother's Sons objected but nobody paid attention.

To the Danes he supplied ships and they, together with the Frisians and the Norwegians, took to piracy against the Gauls, the Celts and the Phoenicians. The spoils from their raids further enhanced the Frisian economy and cemented Friso's political power base. For the next almost one thousand years, the Viking longboats from Scandinavia struck fear into all who saw their sails appearing on the horizon.

This Viking scourge effectively isolated the areas around the North Sea, and more specifically North Western Europe from about 300 BC onwards. This would explain why we have almost no record of their history from Roman or even Biblical sources. Nobody dared enter into their domain.

The Germans

The Gertmanne from India were a most extraordinary group of people. En route from India to Fryasland they, under the leadership of Friso, completely destroyed Egypt's naval power at the Battle of Salamis, captured Cyprus, gutted the Grecian fleet and defeated the Phoenicians decisively in a sea battle. Any other people would have written numerous books, biographies and tales of heroism. The Gertmanne, however, just mentioned it in passing. To them it was all in a day's work.

After they had arrived in Flyland, they settled around Emden and again called their new home Gertmannia. The name of Folk Mother Gert, whose election in ca 1556 BC caused the Frisian expulsion from Athens and the flight to India and Iran, was finally immortalised in Europe. The Oera Linda Book is the only source that explains the connection between Germania in ancient Iran and Gertmannia

(Germany) in Europe. The description is so unpretentious that it is just not possible to view the account with any suspicion. If the book had been a deception, the authors would have wanted to make sure that the reader did not miss this crucial point. Tacitus, a Roman Senator and historian (ca 56 AD – ca 117 AD) confirmed the Oera Linda Book's modest account. He wrote in his Germania some 350 years later:

> The Germans, I am apt to believe, derive their original from no other people; and are nowise mixed with different nations arriving amongst them: since anciently those who went in search of new buildings, travelled not by land, but were carried in fleets; and into that mighty ocean so boundless, and, as I may call it, so repugnant and forbidding, ships from our world rarely enter.
>
> For the rest, they affirm <u>Germany to be a recent word</u>, lately bestowed: for that those who first passed the Rhine and expulsed the Gauls, and are now named Tungrians, were then called Germans: and thus by degrees <u>the name of a tribe prevailed</u>, not that of the nation; so that by an appellation at first occasioned by terror and conquest, they afterwards chose to be distinguished, and assuming a name lately invented were universally called Germans.
>
> Hence amongst such a mighty multitude of men, the same make and form is found in all, eyes stern and blue, yellow hair, huge bodies, but vigorous only in the first onset.[268]

The motley group that arrived with Friso from the Aegean did not only introduce idolatry, superstition and modern warfare into the Frisian society, but also a male dominated system of government. The Gertmanne soon became the leading tribe in Western Europe. After more than a millennium of free roaming and conquest, they were no longer accustomed to the patronage of a Folk Mother. Although they still claimed to be pious, their experience taught them that strength lied in numbers. They would allow all comers into their fold regardless of colour, creed or religion. The first and only order of business would be

---

[268] Tacitus, Gaius Cornelius: *The Germania*. Translated by Thomas Gordon.

to reclaim their inheritance from the Gauls and the Celts. This would be done by military commanders and not by missionaries.

It is worthwhile to note here one of the many peculiarities that the Gertmanne brought with them from India and Persia. Remember that the Oera Linda Book described the common bonds between some Iranian tribes and the Germans. Tacitus described the Germans' habit of making important decisions whilst under the influence of alcohol:

> *To continue drinking night and day without intermission is a reproach to no man. Frequent then are their broils, as usual amongst men intoxicated with liquor; and such broils rarely terminate in angry words, but for the most part in maimings and slaughter.*
>
> *Moreover in these their feasts, they generally deliberate about reconciling parties at enmity, about forming affinities, choosing of Princes, and finally about peace and war. For they judge, that at no season is the soul more open to thoughts that are artless and upright, or more fired with such as are great and bold. This people, of themselves nowise subtile or politic, from the freedom of the place and occasion acquire still more frankness to disclose the most secret motions and purposes of their hearts. When therefore the minds of all have been once laid open and declared, on the day following the several sentiments are revised and canvassed;[269]*

Herodotus of Halicarnassus, some 500 years before Tacitus, described the Persian's exact same approach to making important decisions.

> *It is also their general practice to deliberate upon affairs of weight when they are drunk; and then on the morrow, when they are sober, the decision to which they came the night before is put before them by the master of the house in which it was made; and if it is then approved of, they act on it; if not, they set it aside. Sometimes, however, they are sober at their first deliberation, but in this case they always reconsider the matter under the influence of wine.[270]*

---

[269] Tacitus, Gaius Cornelius: *The Germania*. Translated by Thomas Gordon.
[270] Herodotus: *Histories*, book I, p 50

There are a large number of other similarities between Herodotus' description of the Persians and Tacitus' description of the Germans , such as gambling, feasting and singing. We shall only look at one more here but the reader is encouraged to compare these two historians with one another and indeed also with the Oera Linda Book.

In the earlier chapters of this book, we have seen that the Persians, as with the Hyksos, the Minoans and others, did not have idols. Herodotus' remark is repeated here:

131. The customs which I know the Persians to observe are the following: they have no images of the gods, no temples or altars, and consider the use of them a sign of folly.

Almost 600 years later, Tacitus made the same observation regarding the Germans:

For the rest, from the grandeur and majesty of beings celestial, they judge it altogether unsuitable to hold the Gods enclosed within walls, or to represent them under any human likeness.

Although Friso was not one of the Gertmanne, he had an eventful association with them. He could even trace his and their ancestry to the same *Sea People* that founded Athens. He had fought and won a number of naval battles with the help of these descendants of the Greek and Persian Empires and with their assistance and vigour he would re-unify the Fryan Federation. His successors would continue the process.

The Mother's Sons, or *The true children of Frya* as they regarded themselves, would never have allowed any people but those of pure Frya's blood and religion into their fold. To Friso all that mattered was the number of hands that could hold swords and spears. Through the spoils from piracy, rebuilding the military and maritime industries and securing alliances by marrying his family off to influential tribes, he would re-unify Fryasland. By the time he died most of Western Europe belonged to a somewhat loose coalition that became known as the Gertmanne, Germani or Germans. Amongst their number would later be such diverse groups as the Franks, the Saxons, the Lithuanians

(Hlith-hawar i.e. face hitters or strikers), the Tartars (Tartarar i.e. to tar on, to provoke) and the Teutones (Thioth's Sons – i.e., Sons of the People). The list goes on.

Adel Atharik, the amenable son of Friso, and his wife Ifkia, continued the process of unification through diplomacy, education and integration. The Oera Linda book describes their diplomatic tours and mixed schooling policies. Those schools where their integration policies were successfully implemented were recorded with great ceremony in, what they called, *The Book of Friendship* and afterwards a festival was held[271]. More than two thousand years ago they campaigned for (racial) tolerance – similar to the twentieth century policy in America which became known as *bussing*. During the 19th century racism or racial prejudice in Europe was not on or anywhere near the agenda. If the Oera Linda Book was a 19th century hoax, it is highly unlikely that anyone could have dreamed up a non-existing social issue such as integration.

The Missing Chapters

After Adel Atharik, the chronology of the Oera Linda Book becomes quite blurred as a result of some chapters that are missing before and after Adel IV Asega Askar, also known as Asinga Ascon or Black Adel.

In this last portion of the book, reference is made to what we may assume to be the Punic and Gallic Wars and Julius Caesar's excursion into Britain in 55 BC.

> *These people and the Romans are constantly struggling for the supremacy over the Middle Sea[272]. The Romans, moreover, live at enmity with the Phœnicians; and their priests, who wish to assume the sole government of the world, cannot bear the sight of the Gauls.*
>
> *First, they took Marseilles from the Phœnicians —then all the countries lying to the south, the west, and the north[273], as well as the*

---

[271] OLB: *The Writings of Konered*, Chapter 6.
[272] Punic Wars
[273] Gallic Wars

southern part of Britain[274]—and they have always driven away the Phœnician priests, that is, the Gauls, of whom thousands have sought refuge in North Britain.[275]

From this we may deduce that the author could not have been Beden; he would have had to be over 200 years old. This unknown author started his writing with Black Adel, but, as with Beden, the remainder of his work is missing.

The following figure is an attempt to understand the transition from the pious Frisian culture to the war mongering and nomadic Teutones, Cimbri, Ambrones and Germans as we came to know them from Roman historians.

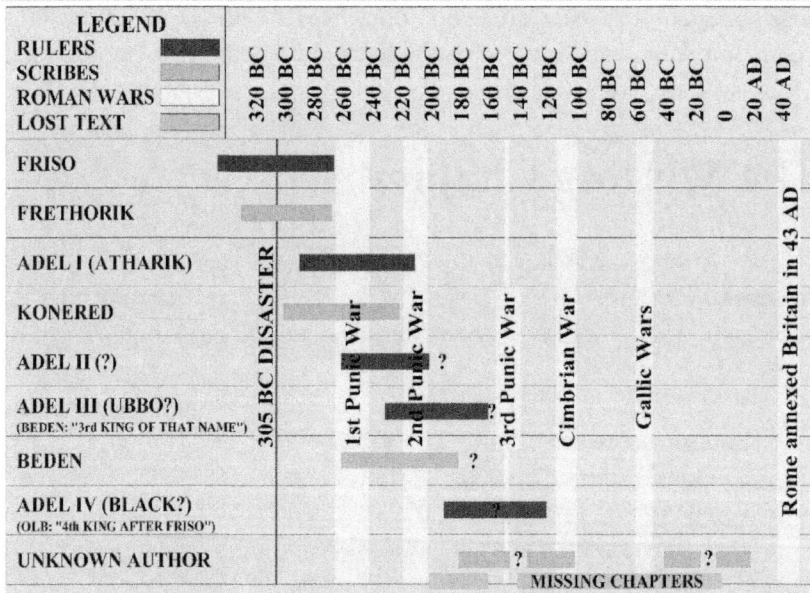

Figure 51: A suggested chronology from Friso to Black Adel

---

[274] This may refer to Caesar's incursion of 55 BC or perhaps even Rome's occupation of Britain in 43 AD

[275] OLB: The Writings of Beden, Chapter 3.

In order to give the reader an idea of the period in question, well documented Roman campaigns from other sources are shown. The Punic wars between the Romans and Carthaginians are merely shown to put this Frisian history in context and not to hint at any direct involvement by the West Europeans. The Cimbrian and Gallic Wars on the other hand, must have had a dramatic impact on Frisian history. We can only assume that these were described in the missing chapters between and after the writings of Beden and the history of Black Adel.

Up to Beden, the reader may be quite comfortable that the chronology is accurate to within about twenty years.

The four generations of the Oera Linda family from Frethorik's father to Beden were all counts or judges in succession at Liudwerd (Leeuwarden). The last three, Frethorik, Konered and Beden contributed to the Oera Linda Book.

It is apparent that Konered died before Adel I Atharik. The narrative was continued by Beden but all that remains of his writings is one paragraph. This nevertheless tells us that his uncle Konered was the brother of his father, Hachgana. He also tells us that Adel III (Ubbo?) was king during his time and that he was the third king by that name.

Nowhere in the Oera Linda Book do we read that Friso was ever called Adel. From this we may then assume that there was a second Adel between Atharik and Ubbo(?). We know nothing of Adels II and III. The story is picked up again with Adel Assega or Black Adel, the fourth king after Friso.

From the narrative we see that Black Adel was mobilising for war but it would appear from our diagram above that he would have been too early for the Cimbrian campaigns. He abolished schooling for boys and instead started training them in warfare.

If we wish to remain free, it behoves our young men to leave reading and writing alone for a time; and instead of playing games of swinging and wrestling, they must learn to play with sword and spear. When we are completely prepared, and the boys are big enough to carry helmet and shield and to use their weapons, then, with your help, I will attack the enemy. The Gauls may then record the defeat of their helpers[276] *and soldiers upon our fields with the blood that flows from their wounds. When we have once expelled the enemy, then we must follow it up till there are no more Gauls, Slaves, or Tartars to be driven out of Frya's inheritance.*[277]

To the conservative Frisians, the school system would have been one of the pillars of their society that placed them above the surrounding ruffians. They objected but they were too weak to put a stop to it. In time this policy of Black Adel lead to the Cimbrian wars during which more than 100 000 men, women and children were killed. It is also from this action that we get our impressions, via Roman historians, of the savage, primitive and warlike inhabitants of West and Northwest Europe in antiquity. The infamous Black Adel left an equally infamous legacy.

In order to make myself well understood, I must let alone for a while my account of the Scotch people, and write something about the near Krekalanders (Romans). The Krekalanda formerly belonged to us only, but from time immemorial descendants of Lyda and Finda have established themselves there. Of these last there came in the end a whole troop from Troy. Troy is the name of a town that the far Krekalanders (Greeks) had taken and destroyed. When the Trojans had nestled themselves among the near Krekalanders, with time and industry they built a strong town with walls and citadels named Rome, that is, Spacious.

When this was done, the people by craft and force made themselves masters of the whole land.[278]

Although the above quote appears in the Oera Linda Book under The Writings of Beden it is evident that this entry, together with the history of Black Adel, was written more than a century later by some unknown author.

---

[276] This may be a reference to the Romans
[277] OLB: The Writings of Beden, Chapter 3.
[278] OLB: *The Writings of Beden*, Chapter 3.

The chronology and events after the writings of Beden becomes quite vague and indeed, as some modern commentator observed, a jumbled mess. This last portion of the Oera Linda Book is not of much value to date events and personages. What is infinitely more important is that it illustrates the degenerative process by which a relatively advanced civilization regressed into barbarism. It started by abolishing schools and literacy. Two thousand years later, in 1821, Heinrich Heine[279] in his play *Almansor* used the now well known phrase:

Dort, wo man Bücher verbrennt, verbrennt man am Ende auch Menschen.
(Loosely translated: There where men burn books, they will end up burning people.)

Even the Oera Linda Book remarked on the importance of literacy. Apollonia wrote:
I had been to the Saxanamarka, at the burgh Mannagardaforde (Munster). *There I saw more poverty than I could discover wealth here. She explained: When a young man courts a young girl at the Saxanamarka, the girls ask:*
"Can you keep your house free from the banished Twisklanders? Have you ever killed any of them? How many cattle have you already caught, and how many bear and wolf skins have you brought to market?"
And from this it comes that the Saxons have left the cultivation of the soil to the women, that not one in a hundred can read or write; from this it comes, too, that no one has a motto on his shield, but only a misshapen form of some animal that he has killed; and lastly, from this comes also that they are very warlike, but sometimes as stupid as the beasts that they catch, and as poor as the Twisklanders with whom they go to war.
The earth and the sea were made for Frya's people. All our rivers run into the sea. The Lyda's people and the Findas people will

---

[279] Christian Johann Heinrich Heine (1797 –1856): Journalist, essayist, literary critic, and one of the most significant German Romantic poets.

exterminate each other, and we must people the empty countries. In movement and sailing is our prosperity. If you wish the highlanders to share our riches and wisdom, I will give you a piece of advice. Let the girls, when they are asked to marry, before they say yes, ask their lovers: What parts of the world have you travelled in? What can you tell your children about distant lands and distant people? If they do this, then the young warriors will come to us; they will become wiser and richer, and we shall have no occasion to deal with those nasty people.[280]

The young warriors did not return. Instead they marched on to do battle with the *nasty people* and became nasty themselves. Their first victories, although spectacular, were short-lived. They decimated whole legions of Romans but in the end, the Heinde Krekalander were victorious. The Father's Sons went in search of glory and found death. They signed away the title deeds to their inheritance with their blood; and yet, a small ember of the Fryan Federation remained glowing.

Tacitus described a tribe towards the north-west coast of Europe which would appear to be in the region of Leeuwarden, Groningen and Emden. These people were the Mother's Sons, the ones who clung to Frya's creed:

Hitherto, I have been describing Germany towards the west. To the northward, it winds away with an immense compass. And first of all occurs the nation of the Chaucians: who though they begin immediately at the confines of the Frisians, and occupy part of the shore, extend so far as to border upon all the several people whom I have already recounted; till at last, by a Circuit, they reach quite to the boundaries of the Chatti.[281] A region so vast, the Chaucians do not only possess but fill; a people of all the Germans the most noble, such as would rather maintain their grandeur by justice than violence. They live in repose, retired from broils abroad, void of avidity to possess more, free from a spirit of domineering over others. They provoke no wars, they ravage no countries, they pursue no plunder. Of their bravery and power, the

---

[280] OLB: *The Writings of Adelbrost and Apollonia*, Chapter 7.
[281] Celts

chief evidence arises from hence, that, without wronging or oppressing others, they are come to be superior to all. Yet they are all ready to arm, and if an exigency require, armies are presently raised, powerful and abounding as they are in men and horses; and even when they are quiet and their weapons laid aside, their credit and name continue equally high.[282]

What is most significant from this portion of the book, is that the Cimbrian and Teuton invasions of the Roman empire was not the result of a gradual evolutionary or haphazard migration south, but the result of a deliberate and premeditated attempt to reclaim what they regarded as their rightful inheritance. The Oera Linda Book makes it very clear that they did not believe they had a legitimate claim to the Italian Peninsula and that is why they did not attack Rome when they had the opportunity to do so. After the Battle of Arausio in 105 BC they had Rome on her knees having destroyed the largest army the Romans had ever sent into battle. Yet, they let Rome of the hook and turned west towards France (Gaul).

---

[282] Tacitus, Gaius Cornelius: *The Germania.* Translated by Thomas Gordon.

Conclusion

This book set out to prove that an advanced civilization existed in Europe during a period which scientists call the *Subboreal Phase of the Holocene, pre-history* and *early antiquity*. I have shown that we actually have documentary and other proof of a people that led man out of the Stone and Bronze Ages into the Iron Age. They introduced the concepts of monotheism, democracy, and free enterprise and left us with our modern alphabet, numerals and much more.

Once we accept the credibility of *The Oera Linda Book*, a whole new perspective on the history of man is gained. These fair-skinned, blond *giants* from Western Europe, who have been regarded as *gods* from Scandinavia to India, appear in numerous writings, legends and folklore from antiquity. Their physical stature, religion, maritime technology, architecture, government system, weaponry and warfare filled the primitive peoples from the Baltic to the Punjab with so much awe that they were deified wherever they went. They became the *gods* in Greek and Roman mythology. Homer referred to them as *akin to the gods* and we find them in the Rig-Veda, the Avesta, possibly amongst the Tarim Basin mummies and in ancient Chinese writings. Even the Bible makes mention of them. In Genesis 6 verse 4 (NKJV) we find the following:

(4) There were giants on the earth in those days, and also afterward, when the sons of God came in to the daughters of men and they bore children to them. Those were the mighty men who were of old, men of renown.

The Israelites, after their exodus from Egypt, sent spies into Palestine to do a recognisance of their intended destination. There they found the descendants of Nef Tunis. We read in the Bible in Numbers 13 verse 33:

(33) And there we saw the giants, the sons of Anak, which come of the giants: and we were in our own sight as grasshoppers, and so we were in their sight.

It is interesting to note that the inhabitants of the Netherlands are, on average, still the tallest people in the world with an average length of 1,85m (6 ft 1 in).

The 2193 BC event was literally and figuratively speaking a watershed in world history and particularly in the history of the children of Frya. Before the disaster, their position in Western and Central Europe went unchallenged, but the flood of refugees after the disaster, and at a time when they themselves were weakened, changed all that. Their dominion, culture and civilization were now under siege. The conservative elements were desperately trying to adhere to their creed and religion, but as their exiled brethren moved further afield, they exploited their own strengths. Their creed was delivered a further mortal blow after the 305 BC event when they allowed foreign influences into their fold. They broke every one of their commandments such as:

- *You shall not exploit the other races,*
- *You shall not have slaves, and*
- *You shall not participate in idolatry.*

No doubt some of them relished the fact that they were regarded as gods by the rest of humanity. In the process they turned completely on their own religion and ignored their prescribed codes of conduct. Even in Fryasland they turned away from only worshipping Wr-alda to also worshipping their Earth Mother Frya and other idols under the influence of the Magyarar, the Gauls and the Celts. The resulting dismembering of their religion and creed hastened their demise.

From the book of Genesis in the Bible we see that this behaviour did not start after the 2193 BC event, or *the Deluge*, but long before that.

As they spread their technology and civilization, they tried to preserve their own privileged position and genetic purity but this was done at the expense of other races. In the caste system in India, which exists to this day, we see the dramatic outcome of an egoistic racial segregation when left unopposed. It is more than likely that when they started the process of segregation it could have been seen as a means of also protecting the indigenous peoples from exploitation but, as time went by, these noble intentions became blurred and eventually disappeared.

Three thousand years later the same experiment was repeated by descendants of the same Fryan Federation. Again the intention was purportedly to protect each group from domination and exploitation by the other. In this case it became known as *Apartheid* (Separateness).

From Wikipedia on the internet it was gleaned that a course at a very prominent university in the Netherlands states:

> *One of the Characteristics of Frisian historiography and literature from the Middle-Ages up to the nineteenth and twentieth century is the existence of a comprehensive corpus of fantastic, apocryphal and mystified historic works, which deal with the origins and identity of the Frisians. Well known examples are medieval myths of origin like the Gesta Frisiorum or the Tractatus Alvini, sixteenth-century humanistic scholary books by e.g. Suffridus Petrus, Ocko van Scarl en Martinus Hamconius and nineteenth-century* <u>forgeries</u> *like the Tescklaow and the* <u>infamous</u> *Oera Linda Book.*

When one sees a term like *a comprehensive corpus of works*, one should take note. The landscape of history is riddled with so-called *hoaxes* and *forgeries* but when a certain myth doggedly persists, there must be something behind it. In most cases these *hoaxes* and *forgeries*

are labelled as such mainly because they do not fit in with our understanding of history or into our own frames of reference. In many cases they were originally distorted for selfish political aims. A fallacy, if proclaimed loud enough and long enough, will become fact. This can, of course, be argued both ways.

From the analyses done by the author on ancient historical works and the evidence of modern scientific research, most of the facts in *The Oera Linda Book* have been verified as correct. This book does not only reflect the history of the Frisians or the Dutch, nor even that of Europe only, but is a chronicle of world history and as such belongs in the domain of historians around the globe.

Certain mythical aspects such as the earth mothers of the black, yellow and white races, as well as the comments on a person called *Jesus, Buddha* and *Krishna* were deliberately left out. It is felt that these will not contribute to a critical evaluation of the book as an account of pre-historical Europe.

The *Jesus of Kashmir* mentioned in the Oera Linda Book cannot be confused with *Jesus of Nazareth*. The historical Jesus of the Bible is too well documented in both Biblical and non-Biblical sources to doubt that he lived during the early part of the first century. According to the Oera Linda Book the *Jesus of Kashmir* lived in ca 593 BC and that he was also known as Buddha and Krishna. We do know, however, that Buddha and Krishna were not contemporaries of Jesus Christ. There are still Indian and Pakistani legends, and purportedly even a grave in Kashmir, of a person of note by the name of *Jesus* who dwelled there in ancient times. Some persons seem to confuse these two – perhaps even with malicious intent. It must also be born in mind that the name was not uncommon in ancient times. The Bible makes mention of several other persons by the name of *Jesus.* It is equally possible that the tale of Jesus of Kashmir was inserted in the Oera Linda Book much later as counter propaganda or disinformation against early Christian missionary work.

The origins and influence of the *Sea People* around the ancient Mediterranean were only mentioned briefly. They were no doubt of West-European descent, and their connections with Anatolia, Troy, the ancient university of Ionia, the Kingdom of Lydia, which minted the first coins, Kings Croesus and Midas and the Hittites, to mention but a few, will keep scholars busy for years. Even ancient *Phrygia* is most likely a derivative of *Frya*. This will be left to future researchers, who may also find that the Samaritans mentioned in the Bible were actually the Hittites from Hattusa in Anatolia who were seriously harassed and eventually subdued by the Sea People. From archaeological evidence it would appear that the Hittites just packed their bags at some stage and vanished. It is suspected that the Assyrians resettled the Hittites in Palestine after they had exiled the ten tribes of Israel. The Bible tells us that the ten tribes never returned.

2 Kings 17:6, 24,27

(6) In the ninth year of Hoshea, the king of Assyria took Samaria and carried Israel away to Assyria, and placed them in Halah and by the Habor, the River of Gozan, and in the cities of the Medes.

(24) Then the king of Assyria brought people from Babylon, Cuthah, Ava, Hamath, and from Sepharvaim, and placed them in the cities of Samaria instead of the children of Israel; and they took possession of Samaria and dwelt in its cities.

(27) Then the king of Assyria commanded, saying, 'Send there one of the priests whom you brought from there; let him go and dwell there, and let him teach them the rituals of the God of the land.

From this history we can now better understand Jesus' words to the Samaritan women at the well in John 4: 22.

(21) Jesus said to her, "Woman, believe Me, the hour is coming when you will neither on this mountain, nor in Jerusalem, worship the Father (22) You worship what you do not know; we know what we worship, for salvation is of the Jews.

The more or less 600 000 inhabitants of Frylân with Ljouwert (Leeuwarden) as their provincial capitol are, un-officially at least, the only descendants of the greatest civilization in antiquity. Their legacy is incalculable. Even English, the modern-day world language of trade, commerce and diplomacy, is a legacy of the Fryan Federation. Some 500 years ago old English and old Frisian were still remarkably similar, and in antiquity they were one language – *the language of Wr-alda*. The following well-known phrase illustrates the point:

English: *Bread, butter and green cheese are good English and good Friese.*

Frisian: *Brea, bûter en griene tsiis is goed Inelsk en goed Frysk.*

In concluding this book, I am convinced beyond any doubt that the Oera Linda Book is an authentic and highly credible historical document. Over the past 140 years numerous researchers have examined the book. For every person that believed in its authenticity, another have tried unsuccessfully to prove it a hoax. It is therefore to be expected that this research will also be received with its fair share of scepticism. No doubt many will defend their turf and hard-earned reputations, but once the dust has settled reason will prevail.

There is so much more to discover from this ancient manuscript, called the *Oera Linda Book*.

Appendix 1

Frisland

> *If a new discovery is totally outside of contemporary science, it will usually be disparaged by scientists. If it later is proved to be genuine, the scoffing scientists silently accept it, hope that nobody notices their earlier sneering, and they might even claim that their disparagement never happened. History shows many instances of this process. Yet apparently the lessons of history have no impact on the behaviour of these 'suppressors of dissent.'*
>
> **William "Bill" J. Beaty**

In our investigation into the authenticity of the Oera Linda Book we have seen that it is an all too common knee-jerk reaction to ridicule anything that challenges our paradigms. As with the original verdict on *The Curse of Akkad* that had to be reconsidered in the light of further discoveries and studies, both the *Admonitions of Ipuwer* and the *Oera Linda Book* now also demand that we reconsider their status as so-called *hoaxes* or *fallacies*. Any logical and objective analysis of the facts presented leaves us with no alternative. By letting the evidence guide us and setting our prejudices aside, it should be abundantly clear to the reader that the Oera Linda Book is an authentic document.

We started our investigation by looking for and finding overwhelming evidence that the Oera Linda Book's claim that their world was destroyed in 2193 BC is true. In fact, the turmoil and trauma of the event was so severe that it heralded the birth of a new world order and the start of a new calendar. The date of 2193 BC became their year zero. Everything before was gone, forgotten or very soon relegated to legend and myth. This date separated the Old World of Aldland from the New World. Throughout the book we find references to the destruction or submergence of *Aldland* or *Atland* and yet, the book does not tell us *where* this *Old Land* was located. It is as though none of the survivors of the event had ever been to Aldland themselves or wanted to talk about it. We shall thus have to apply our analytical skills to see if there are any answers to the questions:

1. *Where was the Frisian's old Altland or Atland?*
and,
2. *If it had existed, what happened to it?*

In Chapters 23 and 24 of the *Book of Adela's Followers* the Oera Linda manuscript gives some clues as to where Aldland may have been located or, rather, where it was not located. We read how Sea King Tinus and Admiral Inka had sailed through the Baltic Sea and then through the North Sea along the coasts of Denmark and the Netherlands to Cadiz in Spain in ca 2000 BC; 193 years after the 2193 BC event. At Cadiz the two brothers parted ways. Tinus sailed east and entered the Mediterranean through the Strait of Gibraltar. Inka, however, seemingly turned west in search of some remnant of Aldland. He did not follow his brother through the Strait. From the description it is quite clear that Aldland was not in the Baltic, the North Sea or the Mediterranean. It seems obvious that Aldland must have been a considerable distance from Europe otherwise they would have known whether anything had survived the disaster of 193 years before. They would not have had to go in search of it.

The Book of Adela's Followers, Chapter 24:
When Tunis wished to return home with his ships, he first went towards Dennemarka (Denmark) *but he was not allowed to land*

there, for so the Mother had ordered. He was also not allowed to land at Flyland (Marshlands, Netherlands) *or anywhere else. In this way he would have perished with all his people from want and hardship, so he landed at night to steal and sailed on by day. Thus sailing along the coast they came at last to the colony of Kadik* (Cadiz, Spain).

Tunis wanted to sail through the straits of the Middle Sea (Strait of Gibraltar) *to enter the service of the rich king of Egiptalandum* (Egypt) *as he had done before, but Inka said he had had enough of all those Finda's people* (Easterners). *Inka thought that perchance some high-lying part of Atland might have remained as an island, where he and his people might live in peace.*

As the two cousins could not agree, Tunis planted a red flag on the beach, and Inka a blue one. Then every one could choose whom he wanted to follow, and amazingly, most of the Finna and Magyarar walked over to Inka, who had refused to serve the kings of Finda's people. When they had counted the people and divided the ships accordingly, the fleets separated.

Nef Tunis sailed along the coast through the gateway of the Middle Sea (Mediterranean).

Here we see that Inka wanted to avoid Finda's people (Easterners) by going west in search of Atland / Aldland. In chapters 7 & 23, however, we are told that Aldland was Finda's People's motherland in the east. This paradox may indicate that Frya's people and Finda's people each had their own Aldland or Atland.

Chapter 7:

In earlier times most of Finda's people lived together in their motherland, namely Aldland, which now lies under the sea. They were thus far away and therefore we had no need for wars. When they were driven away and came hither to plunder, national defence, commanders, kings and war followed. From this came ordinances and from the ordinances came laws.

Chapter 23:

One hundred and one years after Aldland sank, a people came out of the East (overland).

and,

These people do not even have a name but we call them Finna

The above descriptions are the sum total of the Oera Linda Book's clues as to where Aldland may have been. From these descriptions, it is impossible to guess at its locality had it not been for another seemingly unrelated document which historians also declared a hoax. The following evidence should be indisputable and yet, historians and scientists, particularly geologists, find it almost impossible to believe for no other reason than it does not seem to be in accordance with present day geological models and theories. The underlying facts are actually quite simple and rational if only we would make allowance for some critical thinking and logical deductions. Historians rejected the document 250 years ago as a fraud. The now centuries old verdict still stands despite the fact that present day knowledge and technology is worlds apart from that of the 17th and 18th centuries.

This, of course, will not be the first time that academics reject any dissenting views. J Harlen Bretz (1882 – 1981) best known for his research that led to the acceptance of the *Missoula Floods*, against the prevailing view of *uniformitarianism*, took 40 years to be vindicated. The German geophysicist Alfred Wegener's 1912 theory on continental drift was ridiculed for some 40 years before it became the standard albeit somewhat altered model under the title of *Plate Tectonics*. The American physicist Robert H. Goddard who is today known as the founding father of solid fuel rockets was scorned in the 1920's press for his theories. The New York Times published an apology to Goddard some 49 years later and 24 years after his death. The list goes on and on.

The Italian *Hoax*

In 1558 Nicolo Zeno published a book in Venice. He alleged that his forefathers, Nicolo and Antonio Zeno undertook an exploration voyage in the North Atlantic some 175 years earlier; during the latter part of the fourteenth century. He based his findings on a map and a series of letters written around AD 1380 which he claimed to have discovered in an old storeroom at his family home. According to the younger Zeno, the brothers Nicolo and Antonio became shipwrecked on an island called Frisland somewhere between Scotland and Iceland.

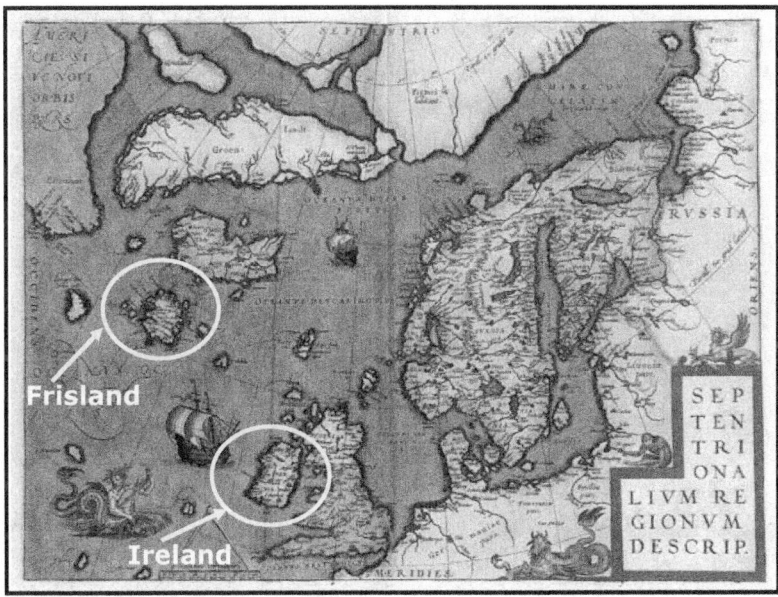

Figure 52: Zeno Map published by Nicolo Zeno in 1558
(200 years before the marine chronometer was invented)

The Zeno brothers remained on Frisland in the service of a prince called Zichmni for the next fourteen years. Nicolo Zeno died on the island and Antonio returned to Italy. From Zeno's map it would seem that Frisland was approximately the size of Ireland (84 000 km^2).

After the publication of his book, Frisland on Nicolo Zeno's map was shown on all subsequent maps for more than 200 years by renowned cartographers such as Ruscelli (1561), Lafreri (1590), the Flemish born Gerardus Mercator (1595) and Vincenzo Coronelli (1650-1718). On these maps, the island of Frisland is variously called Frislant, Frisland, Frislanda or Frislandia. In our discussion we shall refer to Frisland.

Leaving the Zeno book narrative aside, we shall only look at the Zeno Map purportedly drawn by the elder Zeno Brothers in c. A.D. 1380. Some very prominent academics such as Professors Charles Hapgood and William Hobbs, professor Taylor of London University, Captain Arlington H. Mallery and many other 20th century scholars came to the conclusion that the Zeno Map was extraordinarily accurate and far exceeding 14th century skills. The consensus was that the map could not have been drawn in the 14th century and was, in fact of much greater antiquity:

> *The suggestion of a vast antiquity behind this map is conveyed by a feature to which Captain Mallery first drew attention. He pointed out that the Zeno map shows Greenland with no ice cap. The interior is filled with mountains. Rivers are shown entering the sea, in some cases at the points where at present great mountain glaciers are moving down through the mountains to the coast. He called attention to a flat area stretching across Greenland, interrupted by some mountains halfway across, and stated that seismic expeditions in recent years found that the under-ice topography agreed with the Zeno map.*

Opponents to the theories of the abovementioned scholars cannot find credible arguments to disprove them – the next best tactic, therefore, is to ignore their work.

The marine chronometer, a very accurate and robust watch necessary to determine points of longitude whilst sailing on a ship, was only perfected by John Harrison, carpenter and clockmaker, in 1759. Before his invention, longitude could not be established during ocean voyages. The academic fraternity of the 18th century was very reluctant to acknowledge Harrison's great achievement and he never received the official recognition for his invention during his lifetime. The scientists of his time could not bring themselves so far as to bestow this honour on an amateur. He did receive the monetary compensation, though, after King George III intervened. Professor Hapgood, on the latitudes and longitudes of the Zeno map established without the aid of a maritime chronometer four centuries earlier, had the following to say:

In the second place, a polar type of projection applied empirically to the map shows that the latitudes and longitudes of many places scattered all over the map are amazingly correct. It is unbelievable that anyone in the 14th century could have found accurate latitudes for all these places, to say nothing of accurate longitudes.

The Zeno Map of the North Atlantic was by far the most accurate map in the 14th century. On the map of Greenland, Iceland, Norway, Sweden, Finland, Denmark, North-Western Europe and the British Isles there are no less than 32 points of very accurate coordinates. Despite its amazing accuracy, however, the map shows some smaller unknown islands such as Estland, Podalida, Icaria and Estotiland. Perhaps some of these were real islands that existed then and are known today by different names such as the Shetlands, the Orkney-, and the Faroe Islands. A number of the smaller islands and a large, peculiarly shaped island by the name of Frisland with towns, cities and the size of Ireland, however, were never found. By the 18th century, historians had concluded that the map and the so-called voyage were part of a *hoax* fabricated by Zeno to prove that his ancestors discovered North America before Christopher Columbus, another Italian. The Zeno brothers were said to have been in Greece and in Venice at the time they were supposed to have been in the North Atlantic. In fact, Nicolo Zeno senior purportedly wrote his last will and testament in 1400 AD; six years after he was supposed to have died in Frisland. It was thus assumed that the so-called expedition never took place. Frisland on the Zeno map was declared a phantom island that never existed and, together with a number of smaller islands, was taken off the maps.

How is it possible that the Zeno Map, the most accurate map of its time, also contained the most blatant mistakes in the form of phantom islands?

One may forgive the fabrication of a few small islands. The invention of Frisland, a phantom island the size of Ireland, on the other hand, is inexcusable. Early long distance navigators of the open seas would have needed places to take in fresh water, supplies and to effect repairs. To them, setting course for a land that did not exist could have meant certain death. It is unlikely that responsible cartographers such as those mentioned would knowingly have invented a fable for personal gain when sailors could have died as a result thereof. Let us then have a closer look at Frisland on Zeno's map and compare this with the Oera Linda chronicles and their references to Atland.

We have seen in chapter 24 of the Oera Linda Book that the previously inhabited Aldland seems to have been somewhere West of Europe. We have also seen that when Cousin Inka set sail for Aldland 193 years after it had disappeared, he did not know whether any part had survived the 2193 BC disaster. This would suggest that this Old Land must have been a considerable distance from Europe; perhaps somewhere in the Atlantic Ocean (The Atland Ocean?). Now we find an ancient map of a large inhabited Island near the Faroese in the North Atlantic which seems to have disappeared below the waves.

Another perplexing aspect of this phantom island is its name: Frisland. It is highly unlikely that anybody in 14th century Venice would have known of the Frisians of the Oera Linda Book or the Book itself. Yet, the Italian map and all other replicas of the Zeno map gave this mysterious island a name that is amazingly compatable with the Oera Linda chronicles. Are we to believe this is once again just another coincidence?

Figure 53: Frislant on Mercator's map of the arctic (1595)

It is noticeable that the geographic names on the different versions of the *Zeno Map* all agree. Along the west coast we see two large bays named the Northern Gulf (*Golfo Norda*) and the Southern Gulf (*Sudoro Golfo*) separated by a peninsula with Cape Deria and the town of Banar. It would appear that the main harbour of the Northern Gulf was the port of Bondendea whilst Sanestol served the Southern Gulf. On the South coast, there is a small peninsula at Anefes with a group of islands with the name Monaco next to it. Some maps also put the name Porlanda or Port Orlanda next to Monaco. Perhaps the one referred to the islands and the other to a town or port on the islands. In the southeast corner, we find the town of Sorand next to a small bay to the east of the town. As we move northwards along the east coast, we find another bay with the town of Godmee on its northern shore. Further on there are the towns of Doffias, Frisland and Rouea. The last feature to be highlighted is the island of Thini off the coast of the Piglu peninsula.

Lafreri's map of 1590 shows the same towns as the others but here we also see two mountain ranges trending north-west to south east around the middle of the island.

Figure 54: Lafreri's map of Frisland (1590)

Lastly, we come to Ruscelli's map of the North Atlantic which was published some 3 years after Zeno's map. We recognize Greenland, Iceland, Norway, Sweden, Denmark and Northern Scotland. However, in the area where we would more or less expect to find the Faroe Islands, Ruscelli also placed the phantom island of Frisland.

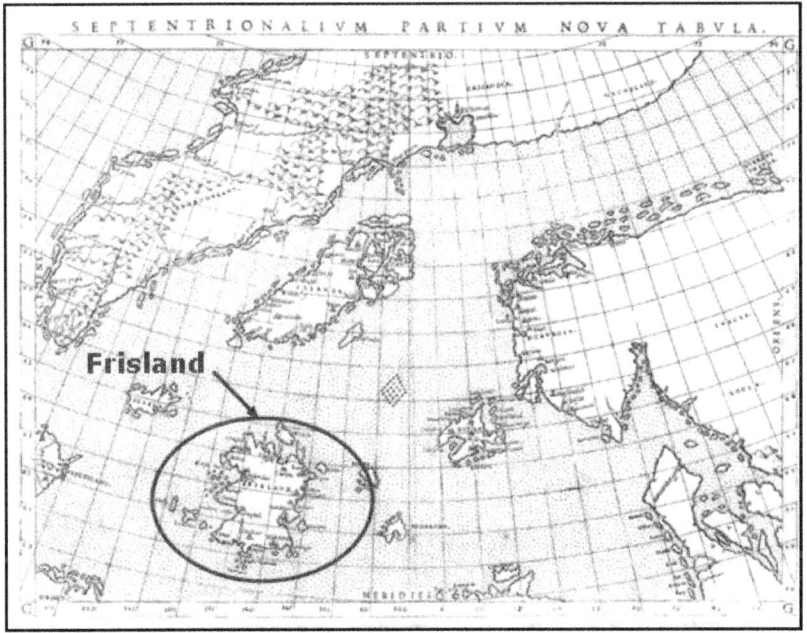

Figure 55: The *Zeno Map* by Ruscelli, Venice, 1561

It is noticeable that Ruscelli's Map shows Frisland but not the Faroe Islands. We find this on many of the old maps. Other maps show the Faroe Islands (Usually called "Fare" or "Farei") but not Frisland. Mercator shows both, but as insets on his larger map. From his representation, however, their geographic position relative to one another is not evident.

The Faroe Islands

The early history of the Faroe Islands is quite nebulous. According to legend, St. Brendan, an Irish Monk, was the first person to have discovered the Faroe Islands in the 6th century AD. He purportedly visited the Islands on two or three occasions around AD 512 to AD 530. In the late 7th century to early 8th century monks from Ireland used the Faroese (and Iceland) as a hermitage. The community, being celibate, eventually died out. Pollen analyses show that oats were grown in the Faroese around AD 650. Around AD 825, Dicuil wrote a book in which he seemingly refers to the Faroe Islands. He stated that when one sails from the Northern shores of Scotland under full sail and with a fair wind for two days and two nights, one reaches some islands with an abundance of birds and sheep on them.

Around AD 1000, the inhabitants of the Faroe Islands were converted to Christianity and in 1035 the Islands became part of the Kingdom of Norway. This heralded the end of the Viking Age of the Faroese. The first record of the Islands that we find on a map is *Farei* on the Hereford map of AD 1280. This map is, however, typical of the dark ages and it bears no resemblance to any actual geography. The *Carta Marina* (1539) by Olaus Magnus is the earliest detailed map of the Nordic countries and clearly shows the Faroe Islands (called *Fare*) but, no Frisland.

Despite the vague early history of the Faroe Islands, it is fair to say that people had been aware of the Faroe Islands, as we know them today, since the early 6th century AD – in other words, for at least 1500 years. Zeno claimed that his ancestors roamed all over the North Atlantic in the late 14th century. Why does the Zeno map, then, not show the Faroe Islands? This leaves four possible answers – either (1) the map of Frisland and/or (2) the elder Zeno brothers' travels were indeed fabrications, (3) Zeno's map is older than 1500 years and actually pre-dates the Faroe Islands or (4) The map had nothing to do with the letters discovered by the younger Zeno. It may well be that the younger Zeno just assumed that the map he found with his great-grandfather's letters was the one refered to in the letters whereas the older Zeno may have known that the map was wrong and just kept it as some unexplained mystery which had no bearing on his travels. There may be any number of explanations but the truth is we may never know the history of the Zeno Map. The fact that we cannot explain the origins of the Zeno map, though, does not mean that the map is a fraud. Modern Science and technology may just allow us to determine whether the map is authentic or not.

Frisland bathymetry

The following satellite image of the sea floor around the Faroe Islands gives us some idea as to the uniqueness of the underwater topography in this part of the North Atlantic.

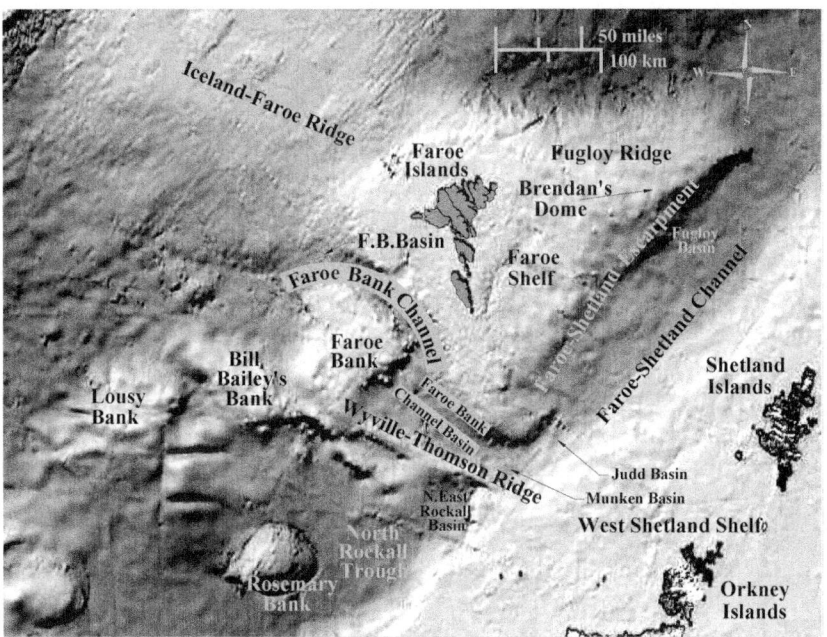

Figure 56: Satellite image of the N.E. Atlantic sea floor

From the shores of the Faroe Islands, the Faroe shelf gradually slopes down to a depth of 300 metres some 120 kilometres east of the Islands at the edge of the Faroe-Shetland Escarpment. At the escarpment the sea floor then suddenly plunges in excess of 1000 metres to the bottom of the Faroe Shetland Channel. The Faroe Bank Channel and Channel Basin south and south west of the Islands are in places more than 700 metres below the Faroe Shelf and the top of the Faroe Bank. Bill Bailey's bank ranges in depth from 200 metres to more than 1200 metres. At the edges of the Lousy and Rosemary Banks the sea floor is more than 1500 metres below sea level. The reader will agree that this specific landscape is unique to this part of the North Atlantic and cannot occur anywhere else on earth.

The above image only became possible by the advent of satellite imagery over the last 20 years or so. In the 14th century the only features known to the ancient mariners were the Faroe Islands and the distant Shetland and Orkney Islands. All that was visible in-between was the vast expanse of the Atlantic Ocean. There was absolutely no way to visualize the seafloor in the region.

The following figure is an enlargement of Frisland on Ruscelli's 1561 map.

Figure 57: Frisland on Ruscelli's map, 1561

Let us now superimpose the above outline of Ruscelli's Frisland on the satellite image of the N.E. Atlantic sea floor around the Faroe Islands.

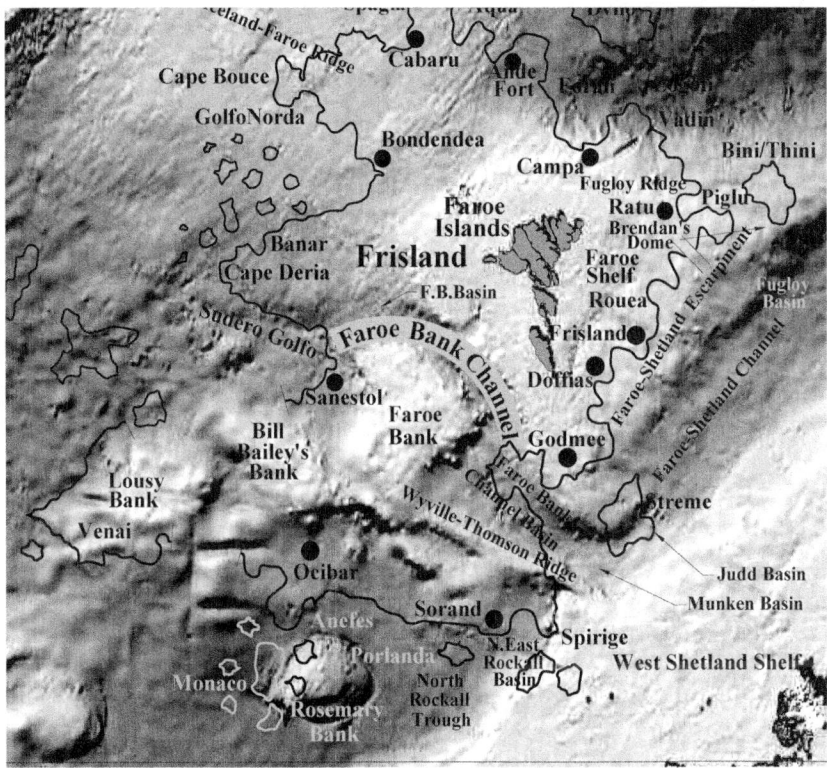

Figure 58: Ruscelli's Frisland superimposed on a satellite image of the N.E. Atlantic

Note the resemblance between the Lousy Bank and the outline of the Zeno's Map detached *Venai* peninsula, the Rosemary Bank and the *Monaco* cluster of Islands, the Faroe Bank Channel linking the *Sudoro Golfo* on the west and the Bay of *Godmee* on the east - the list goes on. From the above figure it should already become clear to the reader that the outline of Frisland mirroring the satellite image cannot be a quirk.

For the sake of clarity the next figure shows Frisland superimposed on a bathymetric map with 100 metre contour intervals.

On this second map, modern day geographical names are shown in black whereas the names on Ruscelli's map are shown in grey.

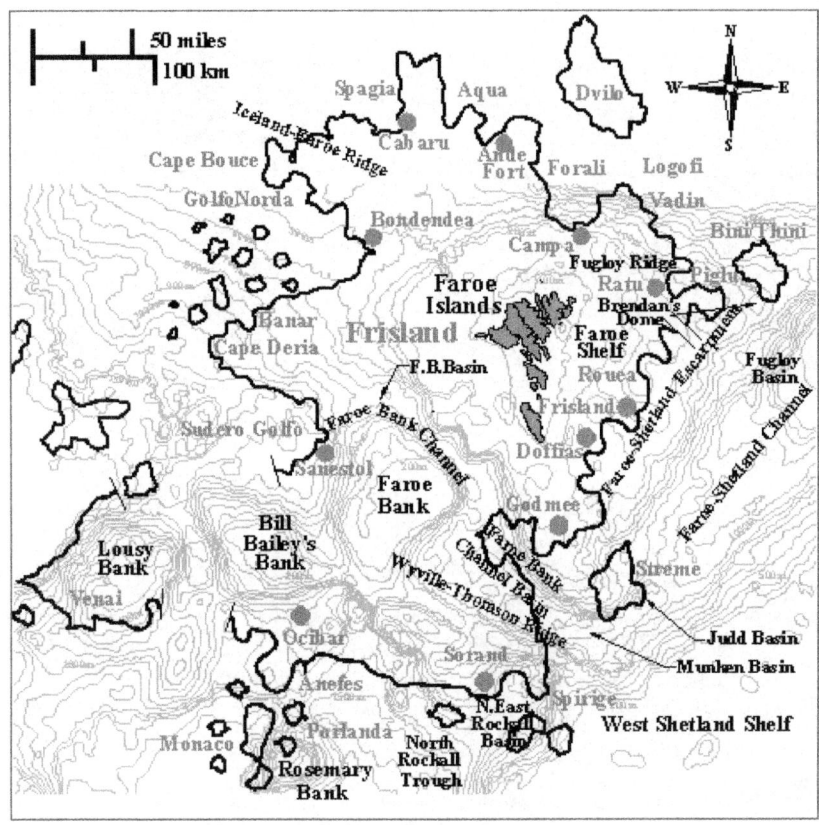

Figure 59: Ruscelli's Frisland superimposed on a bathymetric map of the N.E. Atlantic

In order to emphasize the resemblance between Ruscelli's map and the underwater topography the following key map shows 9 out of many irrefutable points of conformity. The reader is encouraged to compare this key map with the previous satellite image and bathymetric map. The map represents an area of some 420 000 square kilometers – all ocean except for the 1400 km² (0.33%) Faroe Islands. From this map Frisland is estimated to have been between 80 000 km² to 95 000 km². On Zeno's map we saw that Frisland was comparable in size to the 84 000 km² Ireland. Again, this resemblance cannot be a coincidence.

The other point to be highlighted on the key map is some projected fault zones and vertical displacements between the different blocks as Frisland apparently broke up during subsidence.

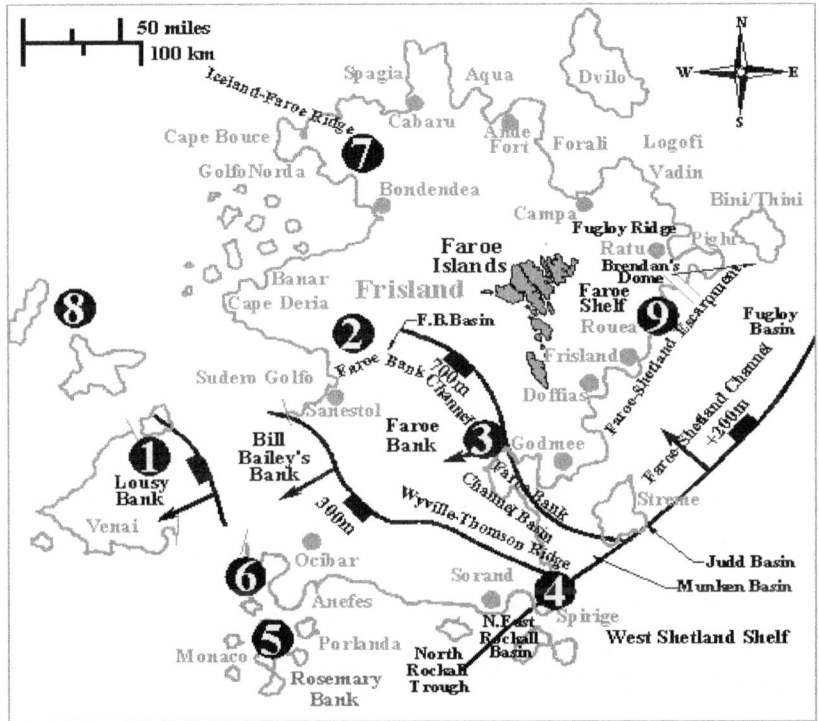

Figure 60: Points of conformity between Ruscelli's Frisland and the bathymetry of the N.E. Atlantic

A detailed study shows many more undeniable points of agreement but the 9 points shown above and described below should suffice to demonstrate that the Zeno Map represents the ancient sea floor around the Faroe Islands and that the map is an authentic document.

- The outline of the Venai peninsula (1) unmistakably matches the contours and satellite image of the present Lousy Bank to depths in excess of 1000 metres.

- The Sudero Golfo on the west side of Frisland (2) and the Bay of Godmee (3) on the East coast of Frisland fit exactly in with the modern Faroe Bank channel and Faroe Bank Channel Basin.
- The small bay east of the town of Sorand (4) matches the North-East Rockall Basin both in terms of locality and size.
- The Port Orlanda / Monaco cluster of Islands (5) on the Zeno Map tie in exactly with the 200 metre deep Rosemary Bank.
- The southern coast of Frisland at Anefes and Ocibar (6) exactly matches the 1200 metre depth contour in the area (also see figure 58).
- The Frisland coastline from Bondendea to Cape Bouce (7) at the Northern Gulf (Golfo Norda) exactly matches the underwater topography
- The small islands west of the southern Gulf (8) fits in with the underwater topography.
- The East Coast of Frisland lies parallel to and coincides with the Faroe Shetland Escarpment (9) which plunges from about 300 metres to a depth in excess of 1500 metres at the Fugloy Basin.

Geologists have identified the Faroe-Shetland escarpment on the edge of the 6.5 km thick Faroe Shelf Basalts as an **Eocene shoreline** – in almost the exact same location where the Zeno map shows Frisland's eastern shoreline. According to the Zeno map, the top of the escarpment existed as a shoreline until a few thousand years ago (and did not cease to exist during the Eocene 36 to 58 million years ago). If the Zeno Map is a figment of someone's imagination, how did he or they manage to make such an accurate guess? This discovery would have been impossible before the late 20th century and is one of the most convincing features proving that the Frisland map is authentic.

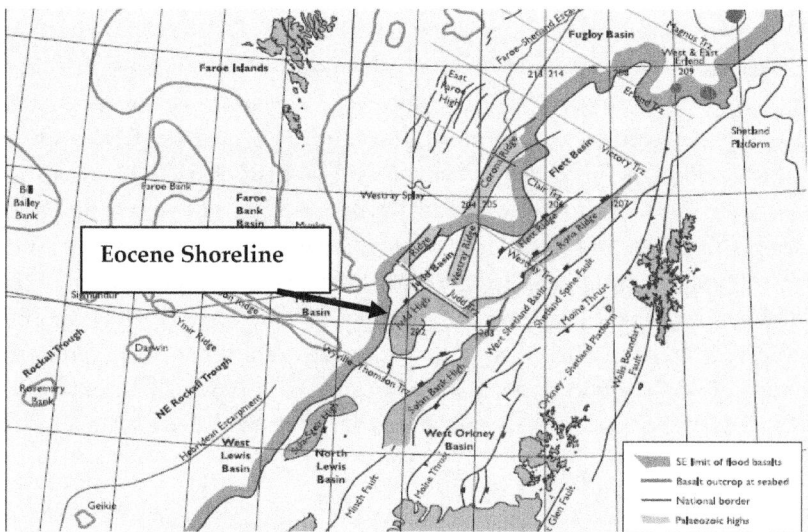

Figure 61: Eocene Coastline of the Faroe Shelf
(With acknowledgement to Aage Bach Sorenson)

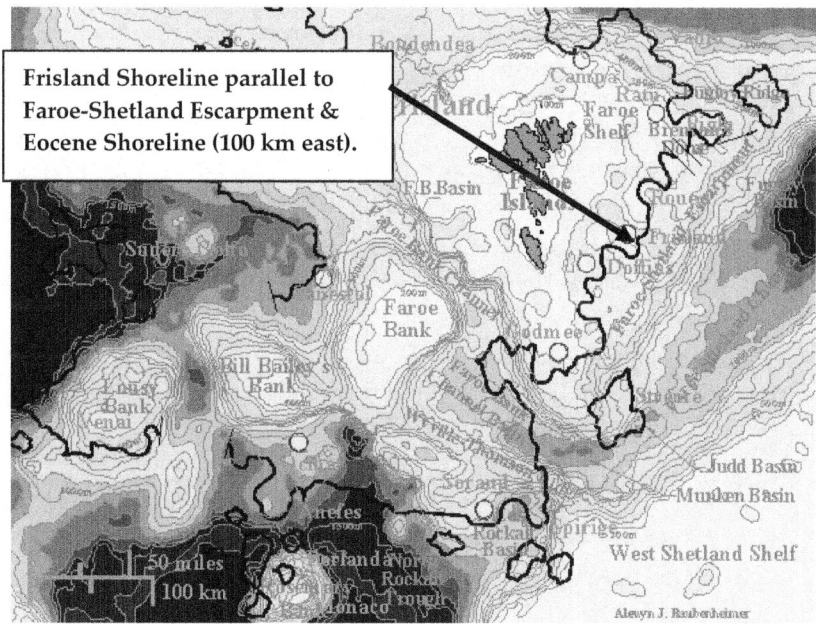

Figure 62: Eocene & Frisland Coastlines along Escarpment

The similarities between the bathymetry of the N.E. Atlantic and Frisland on the Zeno map suggest only one conclusion – Frisland was a real land that disappeared below the waves in recent geological times. If we are then to assume that a landmass of more than 80 000 square kilometers broke up and subsided by as much as 1600 metres in places, we have to take a closer look at the geology of the region. How stable is the area and are there any evidence of other massive ground movements, subsidences or landslides? Fortunately for this investigation, the N.E. Atlantic is of great economic interest to the oil, gas and fishery industries. As a consequence, geologists, seismologists, marine biologists and a host of other scientists have done extensive exploration and research in the area and have produced a wealth of scientific data and reports.

Submarine Landslides

A very pertinent aspect to this investigation is the number of sub-marine landslides that have been discovered in the North-East Atlantic Ocean north of the Faroe Islands. The individual landslides have been dated from over 200 000 years to about 4000 years ago. Two of the younger landslides on the Norwegian Margin are the *Storegga-* and the *Trænadjupet* slides. According to Haflidi Haflidason et al in *The Storegga Slide: architecture, geometry and slide development* (2004), the Storegga Slide and the Trænadjupet Slide to the North are the youngest on the Norwegian margin and dates to 7250 ^{14}C and about 4000 ^{14}C years ago respectively. It is of note that the approximated date of the 4000 year old Trænadjupet Slide comes very close to the Oera Linda Book's date of 4193 BC for the destruction of Aldland and also the likely date for the submergence of Frisland.

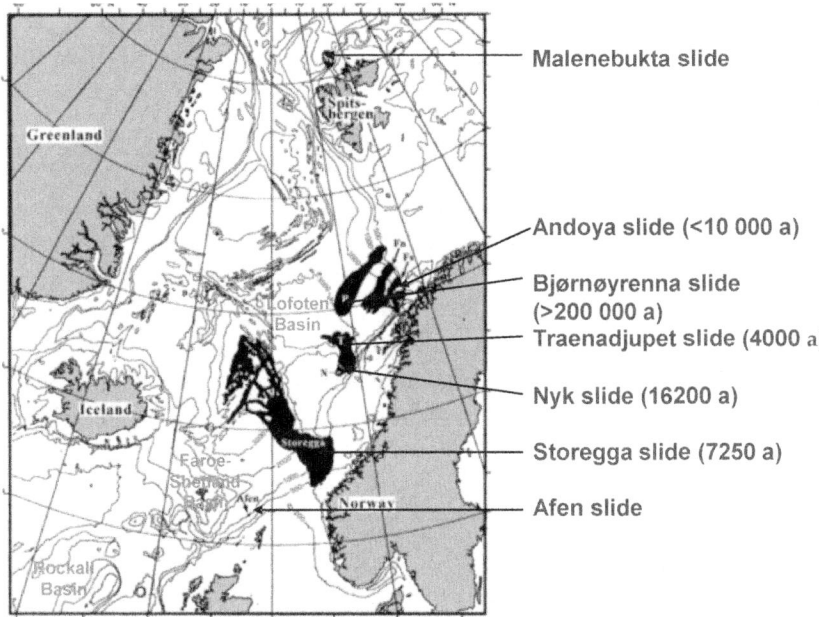

Figure 63: Submarine Landslides on the Norwegian Margin
(With acknowledgement to Haflidi Haflidason et al in *The Storegga
Slide: architecture, geometry and slide development* [2004])

The Storegga Slide is considered to be one of the largest, if not the largest, exposed submarine slide in the world and affected an area of some 95 000 km². This is greater than Ireland or the proposed subsided Frisland. It was not a single slide, though, but rather a series of slides. The Slide received special attention because of the Ormen Lange gas field; the second largest gas field in Norway which was discovered in 1997. Before the commercial development of the gas field concerns were raised regarding the stability of the Storegga Slide.

Although speculation abound, the cause of the Storrega Slide has not yet been determined. One theory is that the slide was the result of gas hydrate dissociation at the end of the last ice age. The proponents of this theory find support for their hypothesis in the increased levels of Methane gas found in Greenland ice cores for the same period. In short, my understanding of the theory is that, as the ice melted and the weight on the continental shelf reduced, the Norwegian Continental Shelf experienced isostatic rebound or uplift. This liberated the pressurized gas hydrates which then *fluidized* the sea floor resulting in this massive slide.

A new slide is unlikely to occur until after the end of the next Ice Age (Petter Bryn et al in *Explaining the Storegga Slide*, 2005). Based on this assumption and the observation that *there is no more slide material in the area*, they concluded that a present day large scale regional failure is highly unlikely. The Ormen Lange Gas Field was declared safe for development and officially became operational in 2007. This theory, of course, does not explain the Trænadjupet Slide which occurred some 3000 years later, nor some of the other slides when there was no Ice Age to influence events.

Let us now move closer to our area of interest. The Faroe Islands and the Faroe Shelf consist of Continental Flood Basalts up to 6.5 km thick which extend to the Faroe-Shetland Escarpment on the west side of the Faroe-Shetland Channel or Trough. We have already seen that Geologists have identified the Eastern edge of these basalts as an ancient shoreline – exactly what the Zeno map tells us. As noted earlier, satellite images of the region clearly shows that the Faroe Shelf and the Rockall Plateau to the south broke away from the Eurasian Continental Shelf. In addition, large mudslides have now also been discovered along this escarpment and to the north of the Fugloy Ridge as stated by Tove Nielsen and Antoon Kuijpers in their report: *Geohazard studies offshore the Faroe Islands: slope instability, bottom currents and sub-seabed sediment mobilization (2004).* The discovery of the approximately 4000 year old Trænadjupet Slide together with the Oera Linda Book and the the Zeno map which are very likely of similar age, help us to put the Frisland Slide in context.

The satellite image following from the Norwegian Geotechnical Institute shows the Storrega and Trænadjupet Slides and has been adapted here to also show the slide which caused Frisland to disappear into the North Atlantic.

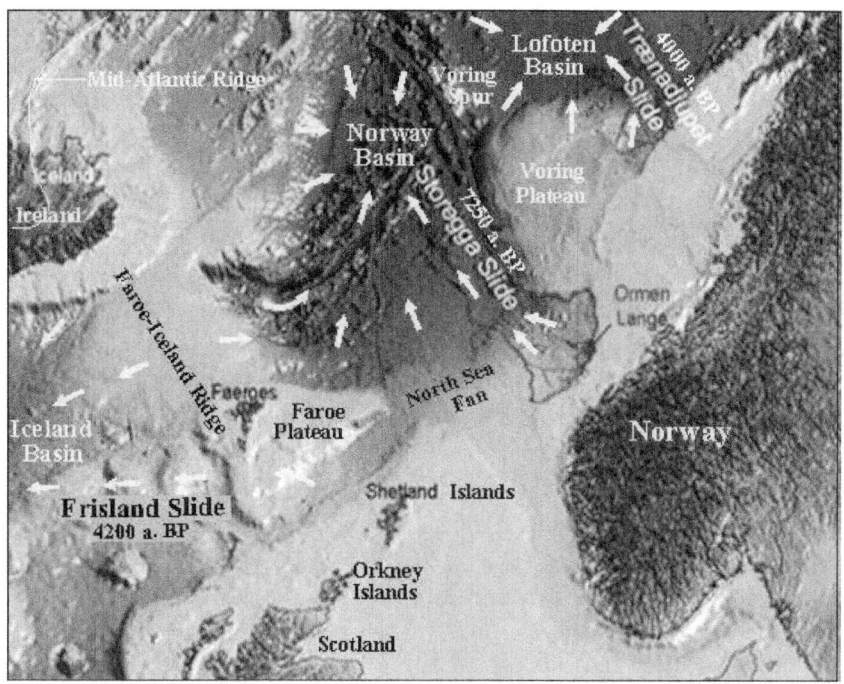

Figure 64: Sub-marine landslides in the N.E. Atlantic
(Adapted from a figure of and with acknowledgement to the
Norwegian Geotechnical Institute)

From the above satellite image it can be seen that the
Trænadjupet slide moved towards the Lofoten Basin, the Storegga
slide towards the Norway Basin and the Frisland slide subsided and
moved in the direction of the Iceland basin.

From all the above evidence it should be clear to the reader
that the Zeno Map meets all the conditions to fit exactly into this area –
not only in terms of the physical dimensions and outlines, but also in
terms of the timing, the geological precedents and the structural
geology of the area. No hoaxer or deceiver could have created such an
accurate *phantom island*.

Darwin Mounds

During 1998 the Southampton Oceanography Centre did an environmental survey to the north and west of Scotland. Using a deep tow, side scan sonar system TOBI (Towed Ocean Bottom Instrument), the research vessel RRS Charles Darwin discovered some unique coral reefs (Lophelia pertusa) at a depth of about 1000 metres. These coral reefs subsequently became known as *Darwin Mounds* after the RRS Charles Darwin. The roughly circular reefs were scattered over an area of about 100 square kilometres just south of the Wyville-Thomson underwater ridge and on the western edge of the deep North-East Rockall Basin.

The discovery of the field was made in an area that lies about equidistant from Scotland and the Faroe Islands near the territorial boundary between them. The following two figures show the location of these coral structures adjacent to the North-East Rockall Basin.

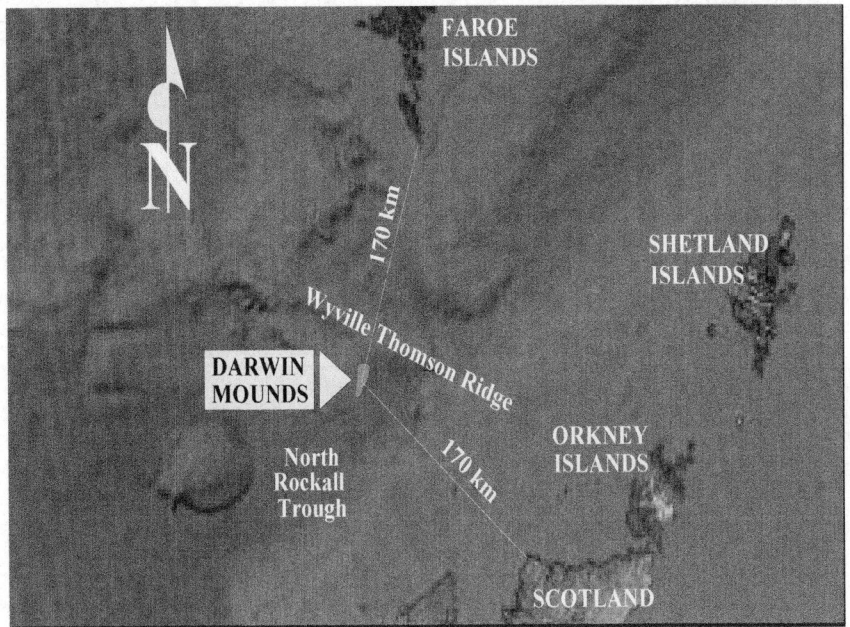

Figure 65: Location of Darwin Mounds in the North Atlantic

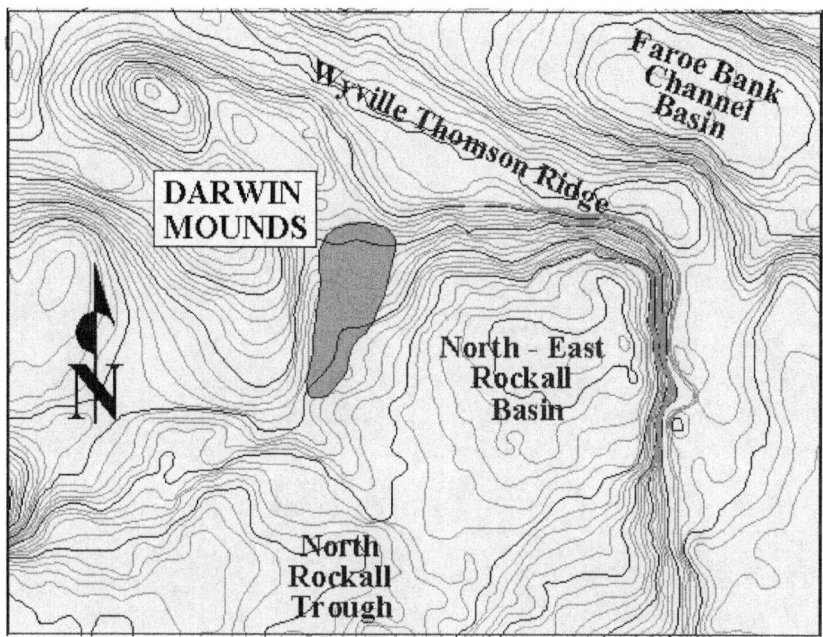

Figure 66: Darwin Mound Field next to the N-E Rockall Basin
The field consists of hundreds of roughly circular mounds up to 75 metres in diameter and 5 metres above the surrounding sandy sea floor.

Geologists have speculated that the Darwin Mounds may have formed on what they call *sand volcanoes*, which in turn may have been caused by the slumping of the adjacent basin. According to this theory, the volcanoes were formed when the slumping process caused the fluidised sands to be dewatered – at 1000 meters below sea level? Surely, these volcanoes should have been levelled again by water motion or sea currents. What caused them to remain intact and stable enough for so long that corals could grow thereon?

Sonar images of the Darwin mounds show one of their unique features, namely their so-called *tails* which apparently distinguish them from other Lophelia Reefs. These tails extend for several hundred metres from the mounds and lie parallel to the deep ocean currents. The tails may have been formed by corals breaking off and then washed downstream from the mounds. The important fact is that the tails indicate that these corals are growing in strong ocean currents and not in calm waters.

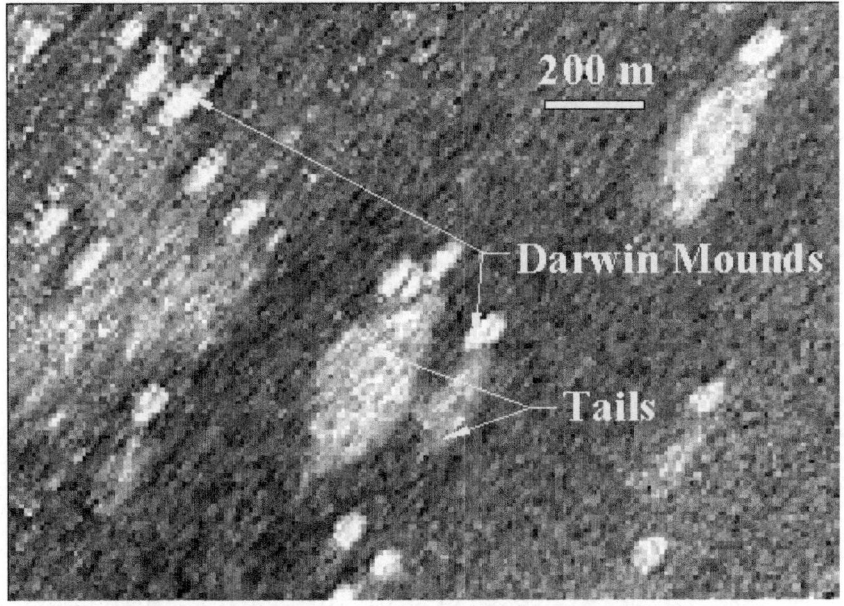

Figure 67: Sonar images of Darwin Mounds
(With acknowledgement to the Southampton Oceanography Centre)

The next photograph shows what would appear to be a coral mound that formed on loose sand. This in itself would be highly irregular. Corals are very slow growing and underwater currents would prevent any corals from establishing themselves on such a dynamic base. They need a solid and stable foundation. This poses the question whether these corals could possibly have started on solid and nutrition rich foundations. Through time these foundations mighy have become covered with sand but the corals, once having been established, continued to grow despite sand building up around them.

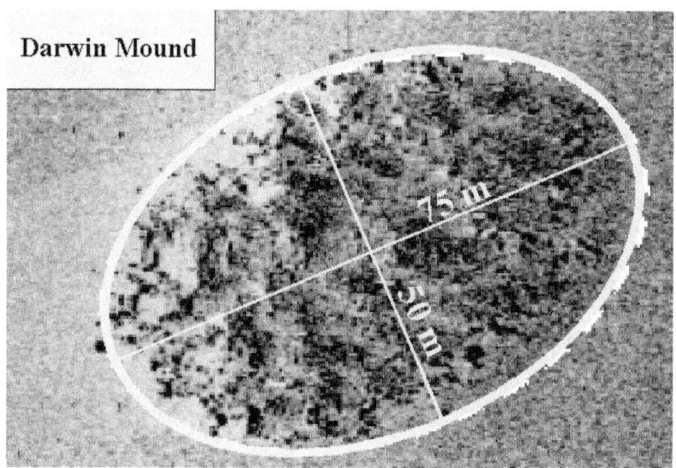

Figure 68: Enlarged Sonar image of Darwin Mounds
(With acknowledgement to the Southampton Oceanography Centre)

If we are now to superimpose the Darwin Mounds and the surrounding bathemetry on the map of Frisland, a very interesting picture emerges.

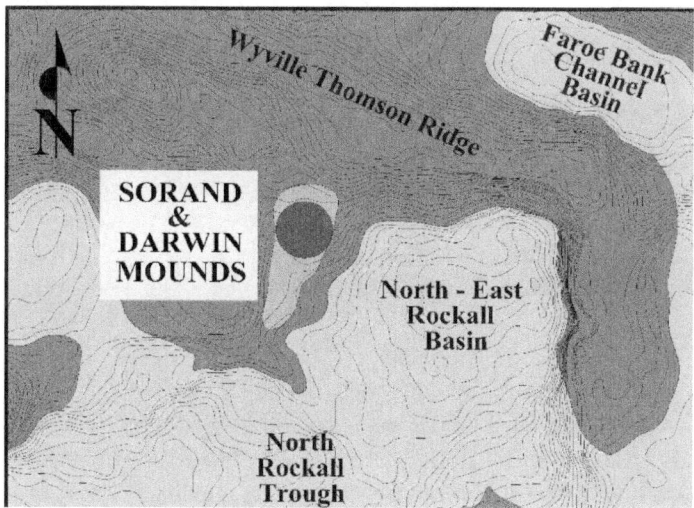

Figure 69: Darwin Mounds superimposed on Frisland

It is noticeable that the Darwin Mounds discovered by the RRS Charles Darwin near the N.E. Rockall basin lie on the flattest ground in the area – exactly where we would expect the town of Sorand, as indicated on the map of Frisland, would have been. I would like to suggest that these corals may actually have taken hold on the remains of Sorand. This figure is an attempt to superimpose Frisland on the present contours in the area.

If these Darwin Mounds are growing on the remains of Sorand, what about Frisland's other towns? Numerous cold water corals have been mapped around the Faroe-Shetland Basin

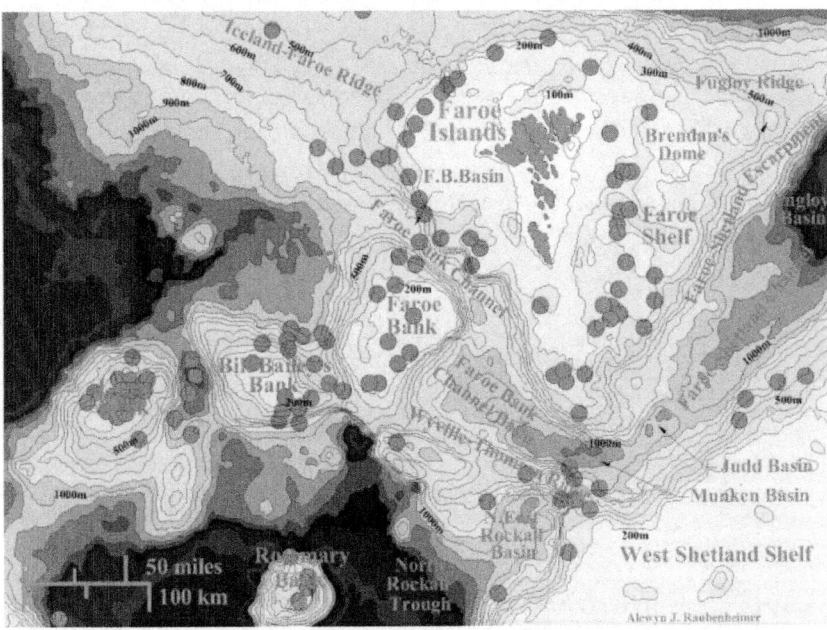

Figure 70: Coral Reefs (Lophella perusa) of the Faroe-Shetland Basin.

Numerous cold water corals have been mapped around the Faroe-Shetland Basin. On the east side of the Faroe shelf the corals occur mostly at depths down to 300 metres towards the escarpment but they have also been found down to 700 meters on the west side. Towards the South and South-West, however, the corals even exist down to 1000 meters.

Another unique feature of these corals is that they apparently grow in both the north flowing warmer waters of the North Atlantic Drift, i.e. the northern extension of the Gulf Stream at depths of 200 to 500 metres, as well as at depths in excess of 1000 meters and devoid of any light in the very cold North Atlantic Deep Water returning from the arctic.

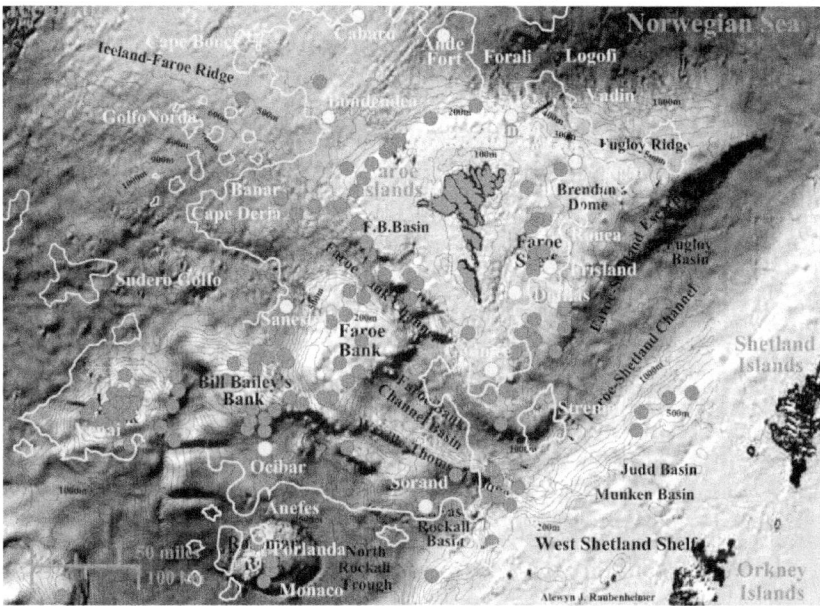

Figure 71: Frisland & the **Coral** Reefs of the Faroe-Shetland Basin.

If we now superimpose Frisland on this coral map, we see that almost all the corals are found in the areas circumscribed by the outlines of Frisland and the surrounding smaller islands and especially along Frisland's old shoreline. Of particular significance is the occurrence of these corals in the vicinity of the towns of Sorand, Godmee, Doffias, Frisland, Rouea, Ratu and Campa.

It is noticeable that the occurrence of these corals are not depth or temperature related, but rather seem to follow the outlines of Frisland as it broke up and subsided towards the south-west. The correlation is just too significant to ignore. Perhaps more in-depth investgations into the basis of these corals could yield very interesting results.

A last possible clue to the mystery may be the Island of Streme. The contour map and satellite image do not show any remains of the Island. Perhaps it was completely destroyed as it plunged into the Faroe-Shetland Trough or Channel. There may, however, be another explanation.

Perhaps the Faroe Shelf sheared off between Frisland and Streme. The present day Shetland Islands may have been Streme. Their outlines do seem similar. Whilst this possibility was not investigated to any extend, it is known that man made structures or dwellings some 5000 years old do exist on the Shetland Islands. Whether Streme is the Shetlands or not, the archaeology of the Shetlands could, nevertheless, give us valuable insights into the submerged Frisland.

The following figure shows Frisland today – AD 2014.

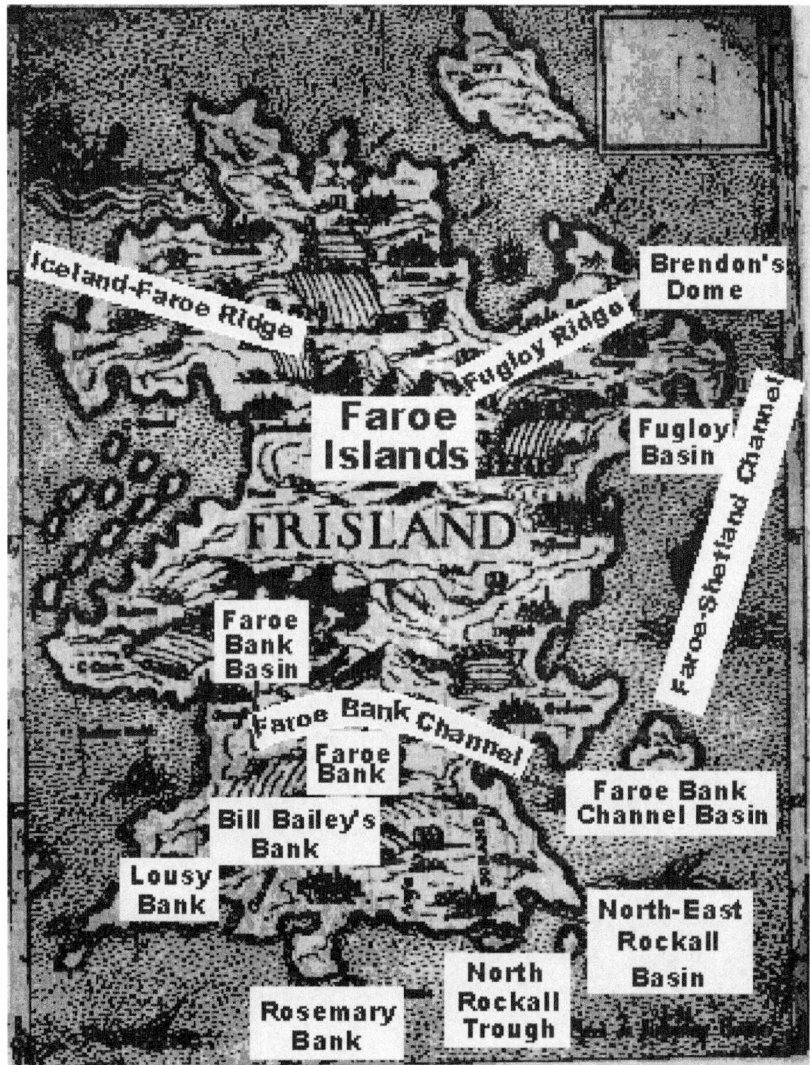

Figure 72: Lafreri's map of Frisland (A.D. 2014)

Appendix 2

The Oera Linda Book

Translated into English by William Sandbach, 1896

Please note:

The table of contents and the titles to the chapters are not part of the original manuscript and translations. They have been inserted in this appendix for ease of reference.

Some editing was done where it was felt that Sandbach's translation does not reflect the original Frisian meaning.

CONTENTS

The Letters

1256 AD

Okke my Son,

You must protect these books with body and soul. They contain the history of all our people, as well as of our forefathers. Last year I saved them from the flood with you and your mother; but they got wet, and began to perish. In order not to lose them, I copied them on imported paper. Should you inherit them, you must also copy them. Your children must do so too, so that they may never be lost.

Written at Liuwert After Atland sank, it is the three thousand four hundred and forty-ninth year; that is by Christian calculation, the twelve hundred and fifty sixth year.

Hidde, surnamed oera Linda. — Watch.

803 AD

Beloved Heirs,

For the sake of our dear forefathers, and for the sake of our dear freedom, I beg you a thousand times. Oh beloved, never let the eye of a monk glance over these writings. They speak sweet words but they secretly tamper with everything that relates to us Frisians.

To gain rich endowments they conspire with puppet kings. These know that we are their greatest enemies because we speak to their people of liberty, rights, and the duties of rulers. Therefore they seek to destroy all that we derive from our forefathers, and all that is left of our old customs.

Oh Beloved, I have been in their courts. If Wralda wills it and do not strengthen us, they will altogether exterminate us.

Written at Liudwerd. (In the) Eight hundredth and third year by the Christian concept.

Liko, surnamed ovira Linda.

The Book of Adela's Followers

Chapter 1 – The 559 BC Commission

Thirty years after the day the Folk Mother was murdered by the Chief Magi, was a dreadful time. All the states that lie on the other side of the Weser had been cut off from us and came under the control of the Magi, and it was feared his rule would come over the whole land. To withstand this disaster a general assembly was called of all those men who were in good standing with the matrons (famna). After more than three days, however, the meeting was in disarray and no further than when they had started. At last Adela asked to be heard, and said:

You all know that I was Burgh Matron (burchfam) for three years. You also know that I was elected to be Mother and also that I did not want to become Mother because I wished to marry Apol. What you do not know, however, is that I have watched everything that has happened as if I had been really Folk Mother. I have been travelling about to see what was happening. In this way many things became clear to me that others do not know.

You said yesterday that our kinsmen on the other side of the Weser were timid and cowardly. I may tell you, though, that the Magi has not won anything by his weapons, but only by cunning and, moreover, by the greed of the dukes and their nobles.

Frya has said we must not allow amongst us any but free people; but what have they done? They imitated our enemies and instead of executing their prisoners or letting them go free, they have despised Frya's advice and have made slaves of them. Because they have done so, Frya could no longer protect them: they took freedom away from others and that is certainly why they lost theirs. This you yourself know, but I will tell you how they came to sink so low.

The Finn women had children. These grew up with our Fryan children. Sometimes they played and gambolled together in the fields, or else they were together by the hearth. There they heard with delight the wicket tales of the Finns because they were bad and new. So they became alienated despite the efforts of their parents.

When the children grew up, and saw that the children of the Finns were not allowed to handle weapons, and only worked, they came to despise work and became arrogant.

The leading men and their sturdy sons crawled to the unchaste Finnish girls; and their own daughters, led astray by this vile example, allowed themselves to be charmed by the handsome Finnish lads to the ridicule of their degenerated parents. When the Magi got sniff of this he took the most attractive of his Finns and Magyarar and promised them cows with golden horns to let them be taken in (employed) by our people in order to spread his doctrines. His people did even more. Children disappeared, were taken away to Uppsala, and after they had been brought up in his filthy doctrines, were sent back.

When these pretended labourers had mastered our language, they got the dukes and elite on board and convinced them that they should become subject to the Magi - then their sons would succeed them without having to be elected.

Those who by their good deeds had received a piece of land in front of their house, they promised from their side they would also receive a piece behind; those who had a piece before and behind, would be allocated a complete circuit; and those who had a complete circuit, a whole freehold. Where the elders were staunch Fryans, they turned their attention to their degenerate sons.

Yesterday there were among you those who would have hoped to call the whole nation together to force the eastern states to return to their duty. In my humble opinion, though, that would have turned out wrong. Imagine first there was a very serious lung disease among the livestock, and this was still raging fiercely, would you dare to send your healthy livestock among the sick ones? Certainly not. Moreover, everyone will agree and admit that this will put the whole herd at risk. Who, then, would be so foolish as to risk their children among a people that is totally corrupted?

If I may give you advice I would say to you to choose a new Folk Mother before anything else. I know that you are in a difficulty about it, because out of the thirteen Burgh Matrons that we still have, eight are competing for the dignity; but I would pay no attention to that.

Tuntia, the Burgh Matron of Medeasblik, is not a candidate, yet, she is full of wisdom and clarity, and quite as committed to our people and her duty as all the rest together.

I would further advise you that you should go to all the burghs, and write down all the laws of Frya's Tex, and all the histories, yes all that is to be found on the walls, in order that it may not be lost or destroyed with the burghs.

It stands written: The Folk Mother and every Burgh Matron shall have, apart from helpers and messengers, twenty-one matrons (assistants) and seven apprentice matrons. If I might add more, I would write that all the respectable girls in the burghs should be taught; for I say in faith and time will prove it that if you want to remain true Frya's children never to be conquered by lust nor weapons, you must take care that your daughters grow up to become true Fryan wives.

The children must be taught how great our nation had been, what great men our forefathers were, how great we still are, if we compare ourselves to others.

They must be told of the heroes, of their gallant deeds and distant sea voyages. All these stories must be told by the hearth and in the field, wherever it may be, both the joy and the sorrow. If men are to become steadfast in the brain and the heart, then all teaching about this must stream from your wives and your daughters.

Adela's advice was followed.

These are the names of the Grevetmen (Counts) under whose auspices this book is composed:

Apol, Adela's husband; three times he was sea-king; now he is Count over Astfliland and over the Linda areas. The burghs Liudgarda, Lindahem, and Stavia are under his hat (jurisdiction).

The Saxman Storo, Sytia's husband; Count over the high moorlands and forests. Nine times he was chosen as Duke, that is commander. The burghs Buda and Mannagardaforda are under his jurisdiction.

Abelo, Jaltia's husband; count over the Southern Flylands (marshlands). Four times he was commander. The burghs Aken, Liudburgh, and Katsburgh are under his jurisdiction.

Enoch, Dywcke's husband; count over West Flyland and Texland. Nine times he was chosen as sea-king. Waraburgh, Medeasblik, Forana, and Fryasburgh are under his jurisdiction.

Foppe, Dunro's husband; count over the Seven Islands. Five times he was sea-king. The burgh Walhallagara is under his jurisdiction.

Chapter 2 – The Earth Mothers

This stands written on the walls of Fryasburgh in Texland. It also stands in Stavia and in Medeasblik:

It was Frya's day, and it was seven times seven years since Fasta was appointed as Folk Mother by Frya's desire. The burgh of Medeasblik was ready, and a Burgh Matron was chosen. Fasta would light the new lamp and this was done in the presence of all the people, when Frya called from her watch-star so that every one could hear it:

Fasta, take your stylus and write the things which I may not speak.

Fasta did as she was told. Thus we, Frya's children, discovered our earliest history. This is our earliest history:

Wralda, who alone is good and eternal, made the beginning, then came time. Time wrought all things, also the earth. The earth bore grass, herbs and trees, all beautiful animals and all bad animals. All that is good and beautiful she brought forth by day, and all that is wicket and bad she brought forth by night.

After the twelfth Yule festival she (earth) gave birth to three maidens:—

Lyda out of glowing,

Finda out of hot, and

Frya out of warm dust.

When the last came, Wr-alda breathed his spirit upon her in order that men should be bound to him. When she was full grown she took pleasure and delight in the visions of Wralda.

Hatred entered them. They each bore twelve sons and twelve daughters; every Yule-time two. From this came all mankind.

Lyda

Lyda was black, with curly hair like those of the lambs: her eyes shone like stars; yes, her glares surpassed those of birds of prey.

Sharp Lyda. She could hear a snake slither and a fish in the water would not escape her sense of smell.

Agile Lyda. She could bend a strong tree, yet when she ran no flower-stem would break under her feet.

Violent Lyda. Her voice was loud and when she screamed in anger everything fled.

Wonderful Lyda. Of laws she knew nothing; her actions were governed by her passions. To help the weak she would kill the strong, and when she had done it she would weep by their bodies.

Poor Lyda. She turned grey by her foolish behaviour, and at last she died heart-broken by the wickedness of her children.

Foolish children. They accused each other of their mother's death. They howled and fought like wolves, and while they did this the birds devoured the corpse. Who can withhold tears from this?

Finda

Finda was yellow, and her hair was like the mane of a horse. She could not bend a tree, but where Lyda killed one lion she killed ten.

Seductive Finda. Her voice was sweet and no bird could sing like her. Her eyes allured and enticed, but whoever looked upon them became her slave.

Unreasonable Finda. She wrote thousands of laws, but she never followed up on (enforced) one. She despised the frankness of the good, but to flatterers she would almost give her own self.

That was her downfall. Her head was too full; her heart too vain. She loved nobody but herself, and she wanted that all should love her.

False Finda. Honey-sweet were her words, but those who trusted them found sorrow at hand.

Selfish Finda. She wished to rule everybody, and her sons were like her. They made their sisters serve them, and they slew each other for the leadership.

Treacherous Finda. One wrong word would irritate her, and the cruellest deeds did not affect her. If she saw a lizard swallow a spider, she shuddered; but if she saw her children kill a Fryan, her bosom swelled with pleasure.

Unfortunate Finda. She died in the bloom of her life, and it is unknown how she had fallen.

Hypocritical children. Her corpse was buried under a costly stone, pompous inscriptions were written on it, and loud lamentations were heard at it, but in private not a tear was shed.

Despicable people. The laws that Finda left were written on golden pages, but for the good for which they were made they were not of any use. The good laws were abolished, and selfishness instituted bad ones in their place.

O Finda! Then the earth was full of blood, and your children were mowed down like grass. Yes Finda! Those were the fruits of your vanity. Look down from your watch-star and weep.

Frya

Frya was white like the snow at sunrise, and the blue of her eyes vied with **the** rainbow.

Beautiful Frya. Like the rays of the sun, the locks of her hair shone, which were as fine as spiders' webs.

Clever Frya. When she opened her lips the birds ceased to sing and no leaves moved.

Powerful Frya. At the glance of her eye the lion lay down at her feet and the adder withheld his poison.

Pure Frya. Her food was honey, and her beverage was dew gathered in the cups of flowers.

Sensible Frya. The first she taught her children was self-control, the second was the love of virtue and when they were grown she taught them the value of liberty; for she said:

> *Without liberty all other virtues serve to make you slaves, your origins to eternal disgrace.*

Generous Frya. She never allowed metal to be dug from the earth for personal gain, but when she did, it was for the benefit of all.

Most happy Frya. Like the stars around the earth, her children clustered around her.

Wise Frya. When she had brought up her children to the seventh generation, she called them all to Flyland, and there gave them her Tex, saying,

Let this be your guide, then it will never go ill with you.

Exalted Frya. When she had thus spoken the earth shook like Wralda's sea. The ground of Flyland sank beneath her feet, the sky became black and green from tears, and when they looked for their mother she had already risen to her watch star; then at length thunder spoke from the clouds, and lightning wrote in the sky, *Watch!*

Far-seeing Frya. The land from which she had risen was now a stream, and except her Tex, all was destroyed that came from her hand.

Obedient children! When they came to themselves again, they made this high mound and built this burgh on it, on the walls they wrote the Tex, and that every one should be able to find it they called the land about it Texland. Therefore it shall remain as long as the earth shall be the earth.

Chapter 3 – Frya's Tex

Hail to the Children of Frya! In the end they shall see me again. Though him only can I recognise as free who is neither a slave to another nor to his own passions. Here is my advice:

When in dire distress, and when sound advice and good deeds avail to nothing, then call on the spirit of Wralda; but do not appeal to him before you have tried all other means. I tell you with reason and time will prove its truth that those who give way to discouragement sink under their burdens.

Wralda's spirit may only be thanked with bended knees, yes thrice fold; for what you have received from him, for what you enjoy, and for the hope he gives you in times of distress.

You have seen how quickly I provide assistance. Do the same to your neighbour. Do not wait until someone begs you; the afflicted would curse you, my matrons would erase your name from the book, and I would have to denounce you as a stranger.

Let not your neighbour express his thanks to you on bended knees; that is for Wralda's spirit only. Envy would assail you, Wisdom would ridicule you, and my matrons would accuse you of sacrilege.

Four things are given for your enjoyment, namely air, water, land, and fire. Wralda, though, is the sole possessor of them. Therefore I advise you, you should choose upright men who will fairly divide the labour and the fruits, so that no-one shall be exempt from work or from the duty of defence.

Should anyone be found amongst you who sell his freedom, he is not of your nation; he is a bastard with bastardized blood. I advise you to drive him and his mother out of the land. Tell this to your children in the morning, at noon and in the evening, until they dream of it at night.

Should any man rob another of his freedom, even his debtor, you must lead him away on a leash like a slave. I advise you, though, burn his body and that of his mother in an open place and bury their ashes fifty feet below the ground, so that no grass shall grow on them because such grass would kill your cattle.

Never meddle with the people of Lyda nor of Finda. Wralda would help them so that any violence that goes out from you would return on your own heads.

Should it happen that they want advice or something else from you, you should help them. If they come to rob you, though, then fall upon them like a raging fire.

Should any of them desire one of your daughters as a wife, and she is willing, explain to her foolishness; but if she still wants to follow her suitor, let her go in peace.

If your son wishes for a daughter of theirs, you must do the same as with your daughter; but neither the one nor the other may ever return, for they would introduce foreign morals and customs, and if these were accepted by you, I could no longer watch over you.

Upon my servant Fasta I have placed my hopes. Therefore you must accept her as your Honorary Mother. If you follow my advice, she will hereafter remain my servant as well as all pious matrons who succeed her. Then shall the lamp which I have lighted for you never be extinguished. Its light shall always illuminate your intellect, and you shall always remain as free from foreign domination as the sweet river-water from the salt water of the boundless sea.

Chapter 4 – Ordinances and Laws

This has Fasta spoken:

All ordinances which have existed a century, that is, a hundred years by the rotation of the carrier and its Yule, may by the advice of the Mother and by common consent be inscribed on the burgh walls; and when inscribed thus they are laws, and it is our duty to respect them all.

Should need or force impose any regulations on us in conflict with our laws and customs, we must observe these, but should they weaken, we must always return to the old. That is Frya's will, and must be that of all her children.

Chapter 5 – Frya's Day

Fasta said:

Anything that any man wants to do, whatever it may be, on the day appointed for Frya's honour, shall eternally fail, for time has now proven that she was right; and it is become a law that people without crises or constraints should do nothing else on Frya's day other than having a joyful feast.

Chapter 6 – Laws for the Governance of Burghs

These are the laws applicable to Burghs.

When a burgh is built, its lamp must be lighted at the original lamp in Texland. That, though, may not be done by anyone other than the Mother.

2.　Every Mother shall choose her own matrons. The same shall apply to the Burgh Matrons of other burghs.

3. The Mother at Texland may choose her own successor, but should she die before having done so, one must be elected at a general assembly of the whole nation.

4. The Mother at Texland may have twenty-one matrons and seven assistants, so that there may always be seven to watch over the lamp day and night. To the matrons on the other burghs serving as mothers, the same number.

5. Should a matron wishes to marry, she must inform the mother, and immediately return to the community before she contaminates the air with her passionate breath.

6. To the Mother and every Burgh Matron there will be allocated twenty-one burghers; seven elder wise men, seven elder soldiers and seven elder mariners.

7. Of these, three of every seven shall return to their homes every year and they may not be replaced by their own descendants up to the fourth generation.

8. Each may have three hundred young burgh defenders.

9. For this service they shall study Frya's Tex and the laws; from the wise men they must learn wisdom, from the elder commanders the skill of warfare, and from the sea-kings the skill required for sea voyages.

10. Of these defenders one hundred will return home every year, though, should some have been disabled, they may remain at the burgh for life.

11. At the election of the defenders no-one of distinction in the burgh will have a voice, neither the magistrates nor other leaders, but only the common folk.

12. The Mother at Texland shall be given three times seven gallant messengers, and three times twelve fast horses. In the other burghs each Burgh Matron shall have three messengers with seven horses.

13. In addition, every Burgh Matron shall have fifty farm hands approved by the people. For this only those that are not able and strong enough for defence or sea voyages may be considered.

14. Every burgh must manage itself and provide in its needs from its own area and from the share it receives from the market.

15. If anyone is chosen to any office on the burgh and he refuses, he may not become a burgher and therefore not have a vote. If he is already a burgher, he shall loose the honour.

16. Should anyone seek advice from the Mother, or from any Burgh Matron, he must announce himself to the scribe who will take him to the Burgh Master. Lastly he must go to a physician to see whether he harbours any ill intent. If he is approved, he will lay aside his weapons and seven guards will accompany him to the Mother.

17. If the case concerns only one state, there must not be less than three delegates. If it is for the whole of Fryasland, there must be an additional twenty-one delegates. This is to ensure that no mischief arises nor any fraud is committed.

18. In all matters the Mother must take care and ensure that her children, that is, Frya's people, must remain as peaceful as possible. This is the greatest of her duties and all of us are to support her in this.

19. If she is called upon in any legal case to give a verdict between a Count and the community and she is uncertain about the case, she must pronounce in favour of the community so that there may be peace and because it is better that one man should be disadvantaged than many.

20. If any one comes to the Mother for advice, and she has advice, she should give it immediately. If she does not have advice immediately, she may let him wait for seven days. If she is then still unable to advise him, he must go away and he must not complain, for no advice is better than bad advice.

21. If a Mother has given bad advice out of ill will, she should be killed or driven out of the land, deprived of everything.

22. Should her burghers be accomplices, they are to be treated in a similar manner.

23. If her guilt is doubtful or only suspected, it must be considered and debated, if necessary, for twenty one weeks. Should half the votes find her guilty, people will deem her not guilty. If two-thirds are against her, she must wait a whole year. If the votes are then the same, she must be considered guilty, but may not be put to death.

24. Should there be some who believe she is innocent and wish to follow her they may do so with all their movable property and live

stock and nobody should despise them, for the majority can also stray like the minority.

Chapter 7 - General Laws

1. All Frya's children are born equal. Therefore they must have equal rights on land and elsewhere, that is water, and in all that Wralda has given.

2. Every man may court the wife of his choice and every girl may pledge herself to him she loves.

3. If a man has taken a wife, he must be given a house and yard. If there is none, it must be built for him.

4. If he has gone to some other town for a wife and he wants to stay there, they must give him a house and a yard there and the enjoyment of the commons.

5. Every man must be given a backyard to his house. No-one shall have a front yard, much less right around. Only if he has done a deed for the common benefit may this be given to him. His youngest son may inherit this. After him the town must take it back again.

6. Every town shall have a common as required, and the keeper shall ensure that everyone cultivates and take care of his own portion so that those coming afterwards will not suffer any loss.

7. Every town may have a market-place for buying and selling or for bartering. All other land shall remain farmland and forests. The trees therein shall not be felled by anyone without common consent nor without the knowledge of the forester, for the forests are for common use. Therefore no person is master of them.

8. Market fees may not be more than one-twelfth of the transaction, both for residents and outsiders. Also, the market portion may not be sold in preference to the other goods.

9. All market receipts must be divided annually into a hundred parts three days before the Yule Day.

10. The Count and his marshals shall take twenty parts of this; the keeper of the market ten parts, and his assistants five parts; the Folk Mother one part, the midwife four parts, the town ten parts; the poor, that is those that cannot or may not work, fifty parts.

11. Those coming to market may not practice usury. Should any do so, it will be the Matrons' duty to disclose them throughout the land so that they may never be elected to any office because they have greedy hearts. For self enrichment they will betray everybody; the people, the Mother, their family and lastly their own selves.

12. If any anybody is so wicket as to knowingly sell sick animals or other goods as though in good condition, the market keeper must expel him and the matrons must name him throughout the land.

In earlier times most of Finda's people lived together in their motherland, namely Aldland, which now lies under the sea. They were thus far away and therefore we had no need for wars. When they were driven away and came hither to plunder, national defence, commanders, kings and war followed. From this came ordinances and from the ordinances came laws.

Here follow the laws which were thus established:

Chapter 8 – Military Conscription

1. Every Fryan must ward off assailants and enemies with all such weapons as he may be issued with or find and is able to use.

2. When a boy is twelve years old, he must miss every seventh day of his tuition (school) to become skilled with weapons.

3. When he is skilled, he is issued with weapons and passed out as a warrior.

4. After three years as a warrior, he becomes a burgher and may then partake in the election of his headman (officer).

5. After seven years as a voter, he may partake in the election of a commander or king and may be elected himself.

6. Every year he must be re-elected.

7. Except for the king, all officials may be re-elected who conducts themselves correctly and in accordance with Frya's directives.

8. No king may remain king for longer than three years lest he becomes entrenched.

9. After having rested for seven years, he may be elected again.

10. Should the king be slain by the enemy, his next of kin may also compete for the honour.

11. If his term of office has expired or he dies during his service he may not be succeeded by his next of kin nearer than the fourth generation.

12. Those that fight with weapons in their hands cannot think clearly and remain wise; therefore it follows that no king must bear arms in battle. His wisdom must be his weapon, and the love of his warriors must be his shield.

Chapter 9 – Folk Mothers and Kings

These are the rights of Mothers and Kings.

1. If war breaks out, the Mother sends her messengers to the King; the King sends messengers to the Counts to defend the country.

2. The Counts call all the citizens together and decide how many men shall be sent.

3. All the resolutions must immediately be sent to the Mother by messengers and witnesses.

4. The Mother lets all resolutions be gathered and gives an average number, that is, the middle number of all resolutions together, which the people as well as the King should be satisfied with for the time being.

5. If the armed forces are on campaign, the King only have to consult with his headmen (officers), though there must always be three burghers without voice (observers) from the Mother sitting in front. These burghers must send daily messengers to the Mother so that she would know if anything is done contrary to the counsels of Frya.

6. If the king wishes to do anything which his council opposes, he may not persist in it.

7. If an enemy appears unexpectedly, then the king's orders must be obeyed.

8. If the king is not present, the next in command must be obeyed, and so on in succession according to rank.

9. If there is no headman present, one must be chosen.

10. If there is no time to choose, any one may come forward who strongly feels himself capable.

11. If a king has defeated a formidable enemy, his descendents may place his name behind their own. The king may, if he so wishes,

choose an open piece of ground for a house and ground; the ground shall be enclosed, and may be so large that there shall be seven hundred steps to the boundary in all directions from the house.

12. His youngest son may inherit this, and that son's youngest son after him; then it shall return to the community.

Chapter 10 – Casualties and Prisoners of War

Here are the rights to protection for all Fryans:

1. Whenever laws are made or new rules established, it must be for the common good, but never to the advantage of individual persons, or to individual families nor to individual states or anything that is singular.

2. Whenever in time of war either houses or ships are destroyed, in whatever manner, either by the enemy or by the general consent of the people, all the people together will help to repair the losses, so that no one may neglect the common cause for the sake of his own interest.

3. When war has come to an end and there are some so maimed that they can no longer work, the whole community must take care of them and at festivals they shall sit in the front so that the youth will honour them.

4. If there are widows and orphans, they must also be supported and the sons may inscribe their fathers' names on their shields to the honour of their families.

5. If any who have been taken prisoner by the enemy should return, they must be taken far away from the camp because they may have been released on treacherous promises. Thus they will not be able to keep their promises and yet retain their honour.

6. If we take prisoners, they must be taken deep into the country and taught our free customs.

7. If they are afterwards set free, it must be done with kindness by the matrons, in order that we may gain comrades and friends, instead of haters and enemies.

Chapter 11 – Crimes against Neighbouring States

From Minno's writings

Should there be any man so wicked as to commit robbery, murder, arson, rape or any other wicked crime upon our neighbours and our neighbours want revenge, it is fitting that the offender be killed in the presence of the offended so that no war break out whereby the innocent would suffer for the guilty.

If the aggrieved are willing to spare his life and accept compensation in stead of revenge, they may do so. Should the offender be a king or a count or anyone who is responsible to watch over the morals of the nation, we must compensate for the crime but he must receive his punishment. Further, if he bears an honorary name of his forefathers on his shield, his family may no longer do so. This is so that that relatives will watch over the morals of one another.

Chapter 12 - Navigators

Laws for navigators; Navigator is the honorary name for seafarers.

1. All Frya's sons have equal rights, and therefore every stalwart youth may apply to the Olderman to become a seafarer, who may not refuse him as long as there is any vacancy.

2. Navigators may elect their own masters.

3. The merchants must be chosen and appointed by the community to whom the merchandise belongs and the navigators have no voice in their election.

4. If during a voyage it is found that the king is bad or incompetent, another may be put in his place, and on return home the king himself may lodge his complaint with the Olderman.

5. If the fleet returns with profits, the navigators may have one-third thereof divided as follows: The king (Admiral) twelve portions, the rear admiral seven, the boatswains each two portions, the captains three, and the rest of the crew each one part; the youngest apprentices each one-third of a portion, the middle apprentices half a portion each, and the eldest two-thirds of a portion each.

6. If any have been disabled, the community must take care of them for life and they must be seated in front at public festivals, at private festivals, yes at all festivals.

7. If any die on a voyage, their nearest relatives must inherit their portion.

8. Should there be widows and orphans as a result, the community must provide for them; if they fell in battle, the sons may bear the names of their fathers on their shields.

9. If an apprentice is killed, his inheritance shall be a whole portion.

10. If he was betrothed, his bride may ask for seven portions in order to dedicate a monument to him, but for this honour she must then remain a widow for the rest of her life.

11. If a community equips a fleet, the organisers must provide the best provisions for the voyage and for the wives and children.

12. If a navigator is worn out and poor and has no house or ground, it must be given to him. If he does not want a house or ground, his friends may take him in and the community must bear the cost unless his friends decline to be compensated.

Chapter 13 – Minno's Writings

Important matters from Minno's writings -

Minno was an old sea-king, seer and philosopher. He gave laws to the Kretar (Cretans). He was born on the Lindawrda, and after all his wanderings he had the good fortune to die at Lindahem.

Should our neighbours have a piece of land or water that we desire, it is proper that we should offer to buy it. If they do not want to sell it, they must be allowed to keep it. This is according to Frya's Tex and it would be wrong to go against that.

Should the neighbours quarrel and nag over any matter other than land and they request us to pronounce a verdict, one should consider withholding such advice, though should one not be able to stay out of the matter, it must be done honestly and fairly.

If someone comes and says, "I am at war, now you must help me"; or another comes and says, "My son is under age and incompetent, and I am old, so I wish to appoint you as guardian over him and over my property until he is of age", one should refuse in order that we may not come into disputes over matters which are in conflict with our free customs.

Should a foreign merchant come to the open markets at Wyringen or at Almanland and he cheats, he must immediately be fined, and it must be made known by the matrons over the whole country. If he comes back, nobody must buy from him and he must return as he came. Thus, should merchants be chosen to go to market or to sail with a fleet, only those who are well known and in good standing with the matrons should be chosen. If it happens, nevertheless, that there is a bad man amongst them who wants to defraud others, he must be opposed. If he has already done so, it must be corrected and the criminal banished from the land so that our name will be held in honour everywhere.

If we find ourselves in a foreign market, be it near or far, and it happens that that nation wants to harm or rob us, we should immediately fall on them; for although we desire to do everything for the sake of peace, our neighbours should never underestimate us or think we are afraid.

In my youth I sometimes grumbled at the strictness of the law but later I often thanked Frya for her Tex and our forefathers for the laws that they compiled from it. Wralda or Alvader (Father-of-all / God) has given me many years and I have travelled over many lands and seas and after all I have seen, I am convinced that we alone were chosen by Alvader to have laws.

Lyda's people cannot make laws nor obey them; they are too stupid and uncivilized. Many of Finda's offspring are clever enough, but they are greedy, haughty, false, immoral and bloodthirsty. The toad blows himself up, but he can only crawl. The frog cries "Work, work;" but he do nothing else but hop and make himself ridiculous. The raven cries "Spare, spare;" but he steals and devours everything that he gets into his beak.

Finda's people are just like these. They have a lot to say about good laws; every one wishes to make regulations to prevent the wrong, but in themselves nobody wants to be bound by these. He who is the most cunning and therefore the strongest, crows king over the others who must be subject to him until another comes to drive him off his perch.

The word "Eva" is too sacred for common use, therefore men have learned to say "Evin." "Eva" means that knowledge which is implanted in the breast of every man in order that he may know what is right and wrong, and by which he is able to judge his own deeds and those of others; that is to say, if he has been well and not badly brought up.

There is also another meaning attached thereto. "Eva" also means tranquil, smooth like water that has not been disturbed by a strong wind or something else. If the water is disturbed, it becomes troubled, uneven but it always tends to become calm again. That is its nature, just as the inclination towards justice and freedom that exists in Frya's children.

This tendency we have through the spirit of Wralda, our father, which speaks strongly in Frya's children and, therefore, will eternally be with us.

Eva is also a symbol for Wralda's spirit, who remains eternally just and undisturbed even though the body may suffer. Eternal and unalterable are the signs of wisdom and righteousness, which must be sought by all pious people, and must be possessed by all judges.

If men want to make regulations and rules that will remain good and fair, they must be equal for everybody. The judges must pronounce their decisions according to these laws.

If any offence is committed for which there is no law, a general assembly of the people shall be called; the judgement shall be passed in accordance with the inspiration of Wralda's spirit so as to be fair and just. By doing this, our judgment will never be wrong.

If instead of doing right, men commit wrong, there will arise quarrels and division among people and states. Thence arise civil wars, and everything is thrown into chaos and destroyed. O foolishness! While you are harming each other, the vicious Finda's people with their false priests come and attack your ports, ravish your daughters, corrupt your morals, and finally throw the bonds of slavery over every freeman's neck.

Chapter 14 – Minno and Nyhellenia

From Minno's writings -

When Nyhellenia, whose real name was Minerva, was well established, and the Krekalanders (Greeks) loved her as well as our own people did, some rulers and priests came to her burgh and asked Minerva where her heritage (wealth) lay. Nyhellenia answered:

"I carry my heritage in my bosom. What I have inherited is the love for wisdom, justice and liberty. Should I lose this, I shall be like the least of your slaves. Now I can freely give advice, but then I shall have to sell it."

The gentlemen went away laughing, saying "Your obedient servants, wise Hellenia".

With that, though, they missed their goal because the people that loved her and followed her took up this name as a name of honour. When they saw that their shot had missed they began slandering her saying that she had bewitched the people, but our people and the good Krekalander knew all along that it was slander.

Once they came and asked: "If you are not a witch, what are you doing with the eggs that you are always carrying with you?"

Minerva answered: "These eggs are the symbols of Frya's councils, in which our future and that of the whole human race lies concealed; time must hatch them and we must keep watch that no harm comes to them".

The priests (replied): "Well said, but what is the purpose of the dog on your right hand?"

Hellenia replied: "Does not the shepherd have a dog to keep his flock together? What the dog is to the shepherd I am in Frya's service. I must watch over Frya's flock".

"That makes good sense", said the priests, "but tell us what is the meaning of the night owl that always sits above your head? Is that light-shunning animal perhaps a sign of your clear vision?"

"No." answered Hellenia. "He helps to remind me that there are people roaming the earth who, like him, live in churches and holes. They keep to the dark, though, not like him to rid us of mice and other plagues, but to invent tricks to steal other people's knowledge that they may get a better hold to make slaves of them, and to suck their blood like vampires do."

Once they came with a band of people. A plague had come over the land and they said: "We are all making offerings to the gods that they may take away the plague. Will you not help to still their anger, or have you yourself brought the plague over the land with your sorcery?"

"No," said Minerva, "I do not know any gods that do evil; therefore I cannot ask them whether they are willing to become better. I only know one god, that is Wralda's spirit; and as he is good, he does no evil."

"Where, then, does the evil come from?" asked the priests.

"All the evil comes from you and from the stupidity of the people who let themselves be deceived by you."

"If, then, your god is so exceedingly good, why does he not turn away the evil?" asked the priests.

Hellenia answered: "Frya has brought us to the path and the carrier, that is Time, must do the rest. For all calamities there is counsel and remedy to be found, but Wr-alda wills that we should seek it ourselves, in order that we may become strong and wise. If we will not do that, he leaves us to our own devices, in order that we may experience the results of wise or foolish conduct."

Then a ruler said: "I should think it is best to submit".

"Very possibly," answered Hellenia, "for then men would be like tame sheep, and you and the priests would not only want to take care of them, but also shear them and lead them to the shambles. This is not what our god wants, he desires that we should help one another, but he also wants everybody to become free and wise. That is also our desire, and therefore our people choose their leaders, counts, councillors, chiefs, and masters from the wisest of the good men, in order that every man shall do his best to become wise and good. Thus doing, we learn ourselves and teach the people that being wise and acting wisely alone lead to fulfilment".

"That seems like passing judgment", said the priests, "but if you now imply that the plague is caused by our stupidity, then Nyhellenia will perhaps be so good as to lend us a little of that new light of which she is so proud of."

"Yes," said Hellenia, "but ravens and other birds only fall on vile carrion, whereas the plague not only loves vile carrion but also bad customs and passions. If you wish the plague to depart from you and not return, you must do away with your bad passions and become pure from within and without."

"We would like to believe that the advice is good," said the priests, "but tell us, how shall we get all the people under our rule thereto?"

Then Hellenia stood up from her chair and said: "The sparrows follow the sower, and the people their good rulers, therefore you should begin by rendering yourselves pure, so that you may look within and without, and not be ashamed in your own mind. But, instead of cleansing the people, you have invented foul festivals, in which they have (become) drunk for so long that at last they wallow like swine in the mire to atone for your evil passions."

The people began to mock and to jeer, so that she did not dare to continue. Now everyone would think that they would have called everywhere on the people to drive us all out of the land.

(But) no, instead of defaming her, they went everywhere, also to Heinde Krekaland (Italy) right up to the Alps, proclaiming that it had pleased the highest god to send his wise daughter Minerva, surnamed Nyhellenia, amongst the people from over the sea on a cloud to give people good counsel, and that all who listened to her should become rich and happy, and in the end masters of all the kingdoms of the earth. They erected statues of her on their altars to beguile the stupid people. They attributed all kinds of advice to her that she had never given, and told of miracles that she had never performed.

By cunning they made themselves masters of our laws and customs and by fallacies they wished to explain everything and expand thereon.

They appointed matrons under their own authority, who were ostensibly under the authority of Fasta, our first Honorary Mother, to watch over the sacred lamp. That lamp, however, they lit themselves and instead of imbuing the priestesses with wisdom, and then sending them amongst the people to nurse the sick and educate the young, they made them stupid and ignorant, and never allowed them to come out.

They were also employed as advisers, but they only pretended that the advice came from their mouths; they were nothing more than the mouth pieces through which the priests announced their desires.

When Nyhellenia died, we wanted to choose another mother. Some wished to go to Texland to recruit one, but the priests who were deeply entrenched among their own people, would not permit it, and accused us before the people of being unholy.

Chapter 15 – Minno on Crete

From the writings of Minno -

When I sailed away from Athenia with my people, we arrived at last at an island named by my crew Kreta, because of the wild cries that the inhabitants raised on our arrival. When they saw that we did not plan to wage war, they became quiet, so that at last I was able to exchange a boat and some iron implements for a harbour and a piece of land.

After we had been settled there for a while, and they saw that we had no slaves, they were puzzled, but when I explained to them that we had laws applicable to everybody, they wished to have the same. They hardly had them, though, when the whole land was in confusion.

The rulers and priests alleged that we had made their subjects rebellious and the people came to us for aid and protection. When the rulers, though, saw that they were about to loose their dominion they gave the people their freedom and came to me for a law book.

The people, however, were not accustomed to freedom, and the rulers remained in power after their own desires. When this storm had passed, they began to sow divisions among us. They told my people that I had called on their assistance to make myself permanent king. Once I found poison in my meat, so when a ship from the Fly sailed past, I quietly took my departure.

My own adventures aside, I merely want to say with this history that we must not have anything to do with Finda's people, from wherever they may be, because they are full of deceit, as much to be feared as their sweet wine with deadly poison.

The end of Minno's writings.

Chapter 16 – Three Principles

Here are three principles on which these laws are founded -

1. Every man knows there are basic needs, but if these are denied, no one knows how a man will react to preserve his life.

2. All adults have a desire to sire children, and if it is withheld no one knows what evil may come of it.

3. Every one knows that he wants to live free and undisturbed, and that others wish the same.

Chapter 17 – Married at 25

To ensure this, these laws and regulations were made.

The people of Finda also have rules and regulations, but these are not made according to what is just, but only for the benefit of priests and princes and as a result their states are always full of disputes and murder.

1. If someone should be in need and he is unable to help himself, the matrons must bring this to the attention of the count because a proud Fryan would never do so himself.

2. If he is poor because he is unwilling to work, he must be driven out of the land because the cowardly and lazy are a nuisance and burden, therefore they must be got rid of.

3. Every young man ought to seek a bride and when he is twenty five he should have a wife.

4. If he is twenty five and still does not have spouse, he must be thrown out of his home. The younger men must avoid him. If he then still does not take a wife he must be considered dead until he leaves the country and not become an annoyance here.

5. If he is impotent, he must openly declare it so that no one has anything to fear or be suspicious of him. He may then come and go as he likes.

6. If he commits any carnal act afterwards, he must flee. If he does not flee he will be subjected to the vengeance of those concerned and no one may help him.

7. Should someone have anything which another desires so much that he steals it, he must restore it threefold. If he steals again he must be send to the tin mines. If the aggrieved wishes to let him go free he may do so, but if he does it a third time nobody shall give him his freedom.

Chapter 18 –Bodily Harm

These rules are made for angry people:

1. If in a moment of anger or out of spite, another's limb is broken, eye taken out, or tooth or whatever, the offender must pay whatever the injured demands. If he cannot do so, the same must be done to him in public as he did to the other. If he is not prepared to suffer this, he may appeal to the Burgh Matron to be sent to work in the iron- or tin mines until he has made amends for his crime under common law.

2. If anybody is found so evil as to slay a Fryan, he must pay with his own life. Should the Burgh Matron be able to help him to the tin mines for life before his life is taken, she may do so.

3. If the accused can prove with appropriate witnesses that it was an accident, then he will be free, but should it happen again he will have to go to the tin mines to prevent improper vengeance and feuds.

Chapter 19 – Traitors and Neighbours

These are the rules concerning bastards -

1. If someone out of spite sets fire to another's house, he is no Fryan; he is a bastard with bastard blood. If he is caught in the act, he must be thrown into the fire. He may flee but he will nowhere be safe from the avenging hand.

2. No true Fryan shall slander nor gloat over the misfortunes of his neighbour. If he is harmful to himself but no threat to others, he

must be his own judge. Should he become so bad as to be a menace, it must be brought before the count. If anyone, however, makes some or other accusation behind his back instead of going to the count, he is a bastard. He must be tied to the pillory in the market-place so that the young folk may spit on him. After this he must be led over the border but not to the tin mines because even there a backbiter is to be feared.

3. If there is anyone so wicked that he betrays us to the enemy, reveals the paths and passages to our places of refuge, or sneak into them by night, he can only be from Finda's blood. He must be burned. The sailors must take his mother and siblings to a distant island and there scatter his ashes so that no poisonous herbs may sprout from them. The matrons must curse his name in all the states, until no child gets his name and the elders may denounce him.

War was over, but famine came in its place. Now there were three men who each stole a sack of wheat from different owners. They were all caught, though. Now the first owner went forth and brought his thief to court. The matrons said in all respects he acted according to law.

The other took the wheat away from his thief and let him go in peace. The matrons said he had done well.

The third owner went to the thief's house. When he saw how great the need was there, he went back and returned with a wagon full of supplies with which he drove the need from the house. Frya's matrons honoured him and wrote his deed in the eternal book while all his transgressions were erased. This was reported to the Honorary Mother and she announced it through the whole land.

Chapter 20 – The Yule

What is written hereunder is inscribed on the walls of Araburch

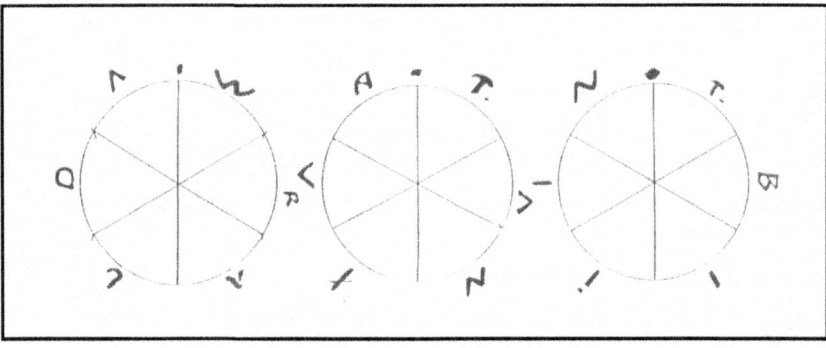

What   appear above are the signs of the Yule. It is the first symbol of Wralda, also of the start or beginning from which time came, that is, the carrier which must for ever go around with the Yule.

From this Frya formed the set hand which she used for her Tex.When Fasta was Honorary Mother, she made running or continuous script from it. The Witking, that is Sea King, Godfreiath the Old made separate numbers for both set and running script. It is therefore not too much that we have an annual festival to celebrate it. We must eternally bring thanks to Wr-alda that he let his spirit flow so strongly over our forefathers.

In her time Finda also invented a script but it was so pompous and full of flourishes and curls that her descendants soon lost the meaning of it. Afterwards they learned our writing, namely the Finns, the Thyrians and the Krekalander. But, they did not understand fully that it was taken from the Yule and that it always had to be written round like the sun. They also wanted their script to be illegible to other nations because they always had secrets. In doing this, they went quite astray, to the extend that the children could barely read and understand the writings of their elders; whilst our most ancient writings can be read as though it was written yesterday.

Here is the set script, under that the running script, followed by the numbers for both:

Chapter 21 – Boundaries

This stands inscribed upon all burghs -

Before the bad time came our country was the most beautiful in the world (in Wralda?). The sun rose higher and there was seldom frost. On the trees and shrubs grew fruit and things which are now lost. In the fields we not only had barley, oats, and rye, but wheat which shone like gold, and which could be baked in the sun's rays. The years were not counted, for one was as happy as the other.

On one side we were bounded by Wralda's Sea, on which no nation but us might or could sail; on the other side we were hedged in by the broad Twiskland, through which the Finda's people dared not come on account of the thick forests and the wild beasts.

At the morning boundary (East) we went over the extremity of the Aster Sea, at the evening (West) to the Middle Sea (Mediterranean). Also, apart from the small, there were twelve large freshwater rivers given us by Wralda to help keep our land moist, and to show our seafaring men the way to his sea. The banks of these rivers were at times all occupied by our people, as well as the fields along the Rene from one end to the other. Opposite Denamarka and Jutterland we had colonies with a Burgh Matron. Thence we obtained copper and iron, as well as tar, pitch, and some other necessities.

Opposite us we had Britannia, formerly Westland, with her tin mines. Britannia was the land of the exiles who, with the help of their Burgh Matron, was sent there to spare their lives. In order that they may never come back, though, they were first tattooed with a B on their foreheads, the banished with red paint and the other criminals with blue paint.

Over and above these our sailors and merchants had many warehouses in Heinde Krekalanda (Italy) and in Lydia. In Lydia there are black people. As our country was so spacious and big, we had many different names.

Those who lived to the east of Denamarka were called Juttar, because often they did nothing else than take out (Juta) amber. Those who lived on the islands were known as Letne, because they mostly lived a lonely life.

Chapter 22 – The 2193 BC Disaster

How the Bad Time came -

The whole summer the sun hid behind the clouds, as if it did not want to sea the earth. The wind rested in its place causing smoke and mist to hang like sails above the houses and marshes. The air was dreary and dull, and in the hearts of people there were neither joy nor happiness. In the midst of this stillness the earth began to tremble as if she was dying. The mountains split open to spew out fire and ash, others sank into her bowels, and where there were fields, mountains rose up. Aldland, called Atland by the sailors, sank down and the wild waves went so high over mountain and dale that everything was submerged. Many people were buried in the earth and many who had escaped the fire perished in the water. Not only in Finda's Land did the mountains spew fire but also in Twiskland. Forests were burned one after the other, and when the wind came from there our land was covered with ash. Rivers changed their course, and at their mouths new islands were formed of sand and floating animals.

Three years earth suffered, but when it improved the forests could be seen. Many countries were submerged, others had risen out of the sea and in Twiskland half of the forests were destroyed. Bands of Finda's people came and settled in the empty spaces. Our dispersed people were exterminated or became their hirelings. Then watchfulness was doubly impressed upon us, and time taught us that unity is our best fortress.

Chapter 23 – Wodin and the Magyarar

This is inscribed on the Waraburch by the Aldegamuda –

The Waraburch is not a matron's burgh, but the place where all imported and foreign articles brought by the sailors are stored. It lies three hours, that is one half period, south from Medeasblik.

This is the Preface.

Mountains, bow your heads; clouds and streams weep. Yes, Skenland blushes. Slave nations trample on your cloak. O, Frya!

This is the history.

One hundred and one years after Aldland sank, a people came out of the East. That people was driven out by another nation. Beyond our Twiskland they fell into dispute, divided into two groups, and each went its own way.

Of the one group no account came to us, but the other group went to the back of our Skenland. Skenland was sparsely populated and the back the least of all. Therefore they were able to conquer it without contest, and as they did no other harm, we did not wish to make war.

Now that we have learned to know them, we want to write about their customs, and after that how matters went between us. They were not wild people, like many of Finda's race; but, they are like the Egiptalandar, they have priests like them and in their churches they also have statues.

The priests are the only masters; they call themselves Magyarar, and their headman is known as Magi. He is high priest and king in one. The rest of the people are of no account, and under their rule. These people do not even have a name but we call them Finna because although their festivals are all melancholic and bloody, they are so formal that we are inferior to them in that respect. They are not to be envied, though, because they are slaves to their priests, and much more to their creeds. They believe that evil spirits are everywhere and enter into people and animals, but of Wralda's spirit they know nothing. They have stone weapons, the Magyarar of copper. The Magyarar claims that they can exorcise and recall evil spirits. The people are always in dreadful fear and there is never any joy to be seen on their faces.

When they were well settled, the Magyarar sought our friendship, they praised our language and customs, our cattle and iron weapons, which they wanted to barter for their gold and silver ornaments, and they always kept their people within their own boundaries, but that lulled our watchfulness.

Eighty years later, it was again the Yule festival, they unexpectedly overran our lands like snow driven by a storm wind. Those who could not flee were killed. Fria was called upon, but the

Skenlandar had neglected her advice. Then all forces joined, and three hours from Godashisburch they were withstood, but war continued.

Kat or Katerinne was the name of the matron who was Burgh Matron of Godaburch. Kat was proud and haughty, and would neither seek counsel nor assistance from the mother. When the burghers realised this, they themselves sent messengers to Texland to the Mother there.

Minna—this was the Mother's name—called up all the sailors and all the other young men from Ast Flyland (East Fly land) and from the Dennemarkum (Denmark). From this campaign the history of Wodin sprang, which is inscribed on the burghs and is here copied.

On the Aldergamude there lived an old sea-king. Sterik was his name, and the fame of his deeds was great. This old fellow had three nephews. Wodin, the eldest, lived at Lumkamakia, near the Eemude, in Ast Flyland, with his parents. He had been a commander once before. Tunis and Inka were naval warriors, and were just then with their father on the Aldergamude.

When the young warriors had assembled together, they chose Wodin to be their leader or king. The naval force chose Tunis for their sea-king and Inka for their rear-admiral. The navy then sailed to the Denemarka, where they took on board Wodin and his valiant host.

The wind was fair and so they shortly arrived in Skenland. When their northern brothers joined them, Wodin divided his powerful army into three bodies. Frya was their war-cry, and they drove back the Finns and Magyarar as if they were children.

When the Magy heard how his men were all being slain, he sent a delegation with truncheon and crown. They said to Wodin:

"O greatest of kings, we are guilty, but all that we have done was done from necessity. You think that we took on your brothers willingly, but we were driven out by our enemies, who are still at our heels.

"We have often asked your Burgh Matron for help, but she took no notice of us. The Magi says that if we kill half our numbers in fighting with each other, then the wild shepherds will come and kill us all. The Magy possesses great riches, but he has seen that Frya is greater than all our spirits together. He will lay down his head in her lap.

"You are the greatest military king on the earth; your people are of iron. Become our king, and we shall willingly become your slaves. What glory it would be for you if you could drive back the savages! Our trumpets would resound with it, and our praises would precede you everywhere."

Wodin was strong, fierce, and warlike, but he was not clear sighted, therefore he was caught in their snares and crowned by the Magi. Many sailors and soldiers who did not approve of this arrangement left quietly, taking Kat with them. But Kat, who did not wish to appear before either the mother or the general assembly, jumped overboard. Then a storm came and drove the ships upon the banks of the Dennemarkum, without the loss of a single man. Afterwards this strait was known as the Katsgat.

When Wodin was crowned, he attacked the savages. They were all horsemen and like a hailstorm they charged down on Wodin's troops, but like a whirlwind they were turned back, and did not dare to appear again.

When Wodin returned, the Magi gave him his daughter to wife. Thereupon he was smoked with herbs, but they were magic herbs because he gradually became so audacious that he disavowed and ridiculed the spirits of Frya and Wralda whilst bending his free head before the false monstrous statues. His reign lasted seven years, and then he disappeared. The Magi said that he was taken up by their gods and that he reigned from there over them, but our people laughed at what they said.

When Wodin had been gone for some time, disputes arose. We wished to choose another king, but the Magi would not allow it. He claimed that it was his right given him by his idols. Over and above this dispute there was one between the Magyarar and Finna, who would honour neither Frya nor Wodin; but the Magi did just as he pleased, because his daughter had a son by Wodin, and he would have it that this son was of high descent.

While all were squabbling and arguing, he crowned the boy as king, and set up himself as guardian and counsellor. Those who cared more for themselves than for justice let him work his own way, but the good men took their departure. Many Magyarar fled back with their troops, and the sea-people took ship, accompanied by a body of stalwart Finns as rowers.

Now the history of cousin (Nef) Tunis and his cousin (Nef) Inka comes in the right place.

Chapter 24 – Tunis and Inka

All this is inscribed not only on the Waraburch, but also on the burgh Stavia, which lies behind the port of Stavre -

When Tunis wished to return home with his ships, he first went towards Dennemarka but he was not allowed to land there, for so the Mother had ordered. He was also not allowed to land at Flyland or anywhere else. In this way he would have perished with all his people from want and hardship, so he landed at night to steal and sailed on by day.

Thus sailing along the coast they came at last to the colony of Kadik, so called because the harbour was formed by a stone quay (stone dyke). Here they bought all kinds of supplies but Tutia the Burgh Matron would not allow them to settle there. When they were ready, they began to quarrel.

Tunis wanted to sail through the straits of the Middle Sea to enter the service of (sail for) the rich king of Egiptalandum as he had done before, but Inka said he had had enough of all those Finda's people. Inka thought that perchance some high-lying part of Atland might have remained as an island, where he and his people might live in peace.

As the two cousins could not agree, Tunis planted a red flag on the beach, and Inka a blue one. Then every one could choose whom he wanted to follow, and amazingly, most of the Finna and Magyarar walked over to Inka, who had refused to serve the kings of Finda's people. When they had counted the people and divided the ships accordingly, the fleets separated. We heard of Nef Tunis afterwards, but nothing ever of Inka.

Nef Tunis sailed along the coast through the gateway of the Middle Sea. When Atland was submerged there was also much suffering on the shores of the Middle Sea. As a result many people from Finda's land came to our Heinde- and Fere Krekalanda and also many from Lyda's land. There were also many of our people that went to Lyda's land. The result of all this was that the Heinde- and Fere Krekalanda were lost to the rule of the Mother. Tunis had counted on this. He therefore wished to choose a good harbour from which he might go and sail for the rich rulers but, as his fleet and his people looked so dilapidated, the Kadhemer (land people) thought they were pirates, and everywhere drove them away.

At last they came to the Phonisius coast, one hundred and ninety-three years after Atland was submerged. Near the coast he found an island with two deep bays, so that there appeared to be three islands. On the middle one they established their hideout, and afterwards built a rampart around it.

When they wanted to give it a name, they were in disagreement; some wanted to call it Fryasburch or Neftunia, but the Magyarar and the Finna begged that it be called Thyrhisburch. Thyr was the name of one of their idols and it was on his day of commemoration that they landed there. In return they would for ever recognise Tunis as their king. Tunis let himself be persuaded and the others did not want to go to war about it.

When they were well established, they set some old seamen and Magyarar ashore and onwards to the burgh Sidon, but at first the coastal people did not want to know anything about them.

"You are only foreign drifters" they said, "whom we do not respect".

When we wanted to sell them some of our iron weapons, however, it at last went well. They also greatly desired our amber and their inquiries about it had no end. But Tunis, who was far-sighted, pretended that he had no more iron weapons or amber. Then merchants came and begged him to let them have twenty vessels, which they would freight with the finest goods, and they would provide as many people to row as he would require. Twelve ships were then laden with wine, honey and tanned leather, and in addition saddles and bridles mounted in gold, such as had never been seen before.

With all this treasure Tunis sailed into the Flymar. The count from West Flyland was so impressed with all these goods that he arranged that Tunis be allowed to have a warehouse at the mouth of the Flymar. Later the site was known as Almanaland and the market at Wyrringa where they bartered, the Toletmark.

The Mother advised that they should sell anything except iron weapons but nobody paid attention to her. As the Tyriar now had a free hand, they came to transport our goods near and far to the detriment of our own sailors. It was subsequently decided at a general assembly to allow only seven Thyriar ships per year and no more.

Chapter 25 – The Golar and Missellia

What the consequence of this was -

In the northernmost corner of the Middle Sea there lies an island at the coast. They now came and asked to buy it. A general council meeting was called. The mother's advice was sought, but she would rather see them far away. She reasoned that there was no harm in it, but when we saw afterwards what a mistake we had made, we called the island Missellia.

Hereafter it will be seen what reason we had for this. The Gola, as the missionary priests from Sidon were called, had noticed that the land there was sparsely populated and far from the Mother. In order to make themselves look good, they had themselves called in our language "truth devotees" (trowe widena); but they had better have been called "truth avoiders" (trowe wendena) or in short, "Triuwenden," as our seafaring people afterwards called them.

When they were well settled their merchants exchanged their beautiful copper weapons and all sorts of ornaments for our iron weapons and hides of wild animals, which were plentiful in our southern countries. The Gola, however, celebrated all kinds of vile monstrous festivals, which the coastal peoples promoted with their wanton girls and the sweetness of their potent wine.

If anyone of our nation had committed such a bad offence that his life was in danger, the Gola connived and sent him to Phonisia, that is, Palm land. When he was settled there, he had to write to his family and friends that the country was so good and the people so happy that no one could imagine it.

In Britannia there were plenty of men, but few wives. When the Gola realised this, they abducted girls from everywhere and gave them to the Britne for nothing. All these girls, though, were their servants; the children stolen from Wralda and given to false gods.

Chapter 26 – Kalta and Minerva

Now we want to write about the war of the Burgh Matrons, Kalta and Minerva, and how we thereby lost all our southern lands and Britannia to the Gola.

Near the southern mouth of the Ren and the Skelda there are seven islands, named after Frya's seven watch maidens of the week.

In the middle of one island is the burgh of Walhallagara. On the walls there the following history is inscribed. Above it stands: "Read, learn, and watch."

Five hundred and sixty-three years after Atland was submerged a wise Burgh Matron presided here. Minerva was her name. The sailors nicknamed her Nyhellenia. This name was well chosen, for the counsels she gave were new and clear above all the other.

Over the Skelda at Flyburch, Syrhed presided. This matron was full of tricks, her face was beautiful, and her tongue was shrewd; but the advice that she gave was always in mysterious words. Therefore the sailors called her Kalta, and the landsmen thought it was an honorary name.

In the last will of the deceased Mother, Rosamuda was named first, Minerva second, and Syrhed third in line as successors. Minerva did not mind that, but Syrhed was offended. Like a foreign empress, she wanted to be honoured, feared, and served, but Minerva only desired to be loved. Eventually all sailors came to pay their respects to her, even from the Denamarka and from the Flymar. This wounded Syrhed because she wanted to excel Minerva.

In order to give an impression of her great vigilance, she placed a rooster on her banner. Then Minerva went and put a sheppard's dog and a night owl on her banner.

"The dog", she said, "guards his master and his flock and the night owl watches that the mice shall not devastate the fields. The rooster has no friendship for anyone and through his immorality and pride he is all too often the murderer of his next of kin."

When Kalta saw that her scheme had failed, she went from bad to worst. She secretly sent for the Magyara to teach her sorcery. When she had had enough of this she threw herself into the arms of the Golum, though, all her malpractices could not make her better.

When she saw that the sailors avoided her more and more, she wanted to win them back by fear. When the moon was full and the sea stormy, she would walk in the wild surf, calling to the sailors that they would all perish if they did not worship her. Then she blinded their eyes, so that they mistook land for water and water for land causing many a ship to be lost with man and mouse.

At the first war festival, when all her landsmen were armed, she had casks of beer poured. In the beer she placed magic potion. When they were all drunk she mounted her war-horse, leaning her head upon her spear. Sunrise could not be more beautiful.

When she saw that all eyes were fixed on her, she opened her lips and said:

"Sons and daughters of Frya, you know that we have recently suffered much loss and misery because the sailors no longer came to buy our paper, but you do not know how this came about. I have long kept it in, but I can no longer do so. Listen, then, friends, that you may know where to bite.

"On the other side of the Skelda, where ships come from all the seas, they make paper from water lily leaves (pompa bledar) these days, thereby saving flax and outdo us. Now, as the making of paper was always our principal industry, the mother willed that people should learn it from us, but Minerva has bewitched all the people, yes bewitched, my friends, like all our cattle that died lately.

"I must come out with it. I want to tell you if I were not Burgh Matron, I would know what to do. I would have burned the witch in her nest".

When she had uttered the last word she sped away to her burgh; but the drunken people were so excited that they did not watch over their sanity. In their mad fervour they rushed over the Sandfal, and as night fell they burst into the burgh. Kalta, though, again missed her goal, for Minerva and her maidens, as well as her lamp were all saved by the gallant sailors.

Chapter 27 – The Celts

Herewith the history of Jon -

Ion, Jôn, Jhon, Jan all means "Given", though, it depends on the pronunciation of the sailors who, from habit, shortens everything so as to be called out far and load.

Ion, that is, "Given", was a sea-king, born at Alderga, who sailed from the Flymar with a fleet of 127 ships fitted out for a long sea voyage, and laden with amber, tin, copper, iron, cloth, linen, felt, soft felt from otters, beaver and rabbit fur.

He would also have taken paper from here, but when Ion came and saw how Kalta had destroyed our famous burgh, he became so upset that he went off with all his people to Flyburch, and out of revenge set fire to it, but his rear admiral and some of his people saved the lamp and the maidens. They could not, however, catch Syrhed (Kalta).

She climbed up on the furthest battlement; everyone thought she would be killed in the flames, but what happened? While all her people stood transfixed with horror, she appeared upon her steed more beautiful than ever, calling to them, "To Kalta my people!" Then the other Skelde people streamed towards her.

When the sailors saw this, they shouted, "We are for Minerva!" Then a war broke out in which thousands fell.

At the time Rosamond, that is Rosamude, was the Mother. She had done all in her power to preserve peace, though, when things became bad she made short work of it. She immediately sent messengers throughout all the districts to declare a state of emergency, and the security forces gathered from all over.

The fighting landsmen were all caught, but Ion took refuge with his men on board his fleet, taking with him both the lamps, as well as Minerva and the matrons of both burghs. Helprik the chief had him banished, but while all the security forces were still on the other side of the Skelda, Ion sailed back to the Flymar, and then straight to our islands. His men and many of our people took women and children on board, and as Ion saw that he and his men would be punished like criminals, he secretly departed.

He did the right thing, because all our islanders and all the other Skelda people who had been fighting were taken to Britannia. This step was a mistake, for now came the beginning of the end.

Kalta, who, people said, could go as easily on water as on land, went to the mainland and on to Missellia. Then came the Gola with their ships out of the Middle Sea sailing to Kadik and all along our coasts falling on and over Britannia, but they could not get a good foothold there, because the authorities were strong and the exiles were still Fryans.

Now Kalta came and said: "You were born free, and for small offences you have been made outcasts, not for your own improvement, but to mine tin by your hands. If you wish to be free again and live under my council and care, come out then, you will be given weapons and I will watch over you."

Like lightning it went through the land and before the Carrier's Yule had made one revolution, she was mistress over all of them and the Thyriar from our southern states up to the Seiene. Because Kalta was distrustful she had a burgh built in the northern mountainous area and called it Kaltasburch. It still exists but it is now known as Kerenak.

From this burgh she ruled like a real Mother, not for, but over her followers who forthwith called themselves Kaltana. The Gola, however, gradually came to rule over all of Brittania. This came about because, firstly, they no longer had any burghs; secondly, because they had no Burgh Matrons; and thirdly, because they had no real lamps. As a result of all this the people could not learn; they became stupid and foolish, and eventually robbed of all their weapons by the Gola until at last they were led about like a bull by his nose.

Chapter 28 – Ion, Minerva and Athens

Ten years after Ion went away, three ships arrived here in the Flymar; the people cried "What a blessing!"

From their accounts the mother had this written:

When Ion had reached the Middle Sea, the reports of the Gola had preceded him, so that he was not safe anywhere on the coast of Heinde Krekaland. He therefore crossed over with his fleet to Lidia, that is, Lida's Land. There the black people wanted to catch them and eat them. At last they came to Thirhis, but Minerva said, "Keep clear, for here the air has long been contaminated by the priests."

The king was descended from Tunis, as we later heard, but the priests wished to have a king of long descent according to their ideas, so they deified Tunis to the resentment of his followers.

Once they had Thir behind them, the Thiriar came and hijacked one of the ships at the rear but, as the ship was too far behind, they could not get it back again but Ion swore to take revenge.

When night came, Ion set course for the Fere Krekalandum. At last they came to a land that seemed very barren, but they found a harbour mouth there.

"Here", said Minerva, "we may perhaps not have to have any fear of rulers or priests, as they all love rich pickings."

When they entered the harbour, though, there was not room for all the ships, and yet most were too cowardly to go any further. Then Ion, who wished to go on, went with his spear and banner, calling to the young people to know who would volunteer to join him. Minerva, who wanted to stay there, also did so.

The majority stayed with Minerva but the young sailors went with Ion. Ion took Kalta's lamp and her matrons and Minerva kept her own lamp and her own matrons. Between the Fere and Heinde Krekalandum Ion found some islands to his liking; on the largest he built a burgh in the woods between the mountains. From these small islands he took revenge by robbing the Thiriar ships and lands, therefore these islands were called both Rawer Elanda and Ionhis Elanda.

When Minerva had examined the country which the inhabitants called Attika, she saw that the people were all goatherds, and that they lived on meat, herbs, wild roots and honey. They were clothed in skins, and they had their shelters on the slopes (hellinga) of the mountains, wherefore we called them Hellinggars.

At first they ran away, but when they saw that we were not after their possessions, they came back and showed great friendship. Minerva asked if we might settle there peacefully. This was agreed to on condition that we should help them fight against their neighbours who always came to abduct their children and steal their possessions.

We then built a burgh at an hour's distance from the harbour. On Minerva's advice it was called Athenia, "because", she said, "those who come after us should know that we did not come here out of greed or by violence, but were received like friends."

While we were labouring on the citadel the leaders came along and when they saw that we had no slaves, it did not please them and they let her understand it, as they thought she was a sovereign.

But Minerva asked: "How did you come by your slaves?"

They answered: "Some we have bought and others were won in battle."

Minerva said: "If nobody would buy slaves they would not steal your children and you would not have wars about it. If you wish to remain our allies, you must set your slaves free."

This the chiefs would not do and wanted to drive us away; but the bravest of their people came and helped us man our burgh, which we now made of stone.

This is the history of Jon and Minerva.

When they had related all this, they respectfully asked for iron burgh-weapons "because" they said, "our adversaries are powerful, but if we have effective weapons we shall withstand them".

When this had been agreed to, the people asked if Frya's customs would flourish in Athenia and in the other Krekalanda.

The Mother answered: "If the Fere Krekalanda are of Frya's heritage, they will flourish; if they are not thereof, there will be a long campaign over it, because then the carrier shall have to go around for five thousand years with the Yule before those Finda's people will be ripe for freedom."

Chapter 29 – Sekrops and the Gertmanne

This is about the Gertmannar –When Hellenia or Minerva died, the priests conferred as though they were with us, and that it should clearly appear so, they had Hellenia declared a goddess. They also refused to have any other mother chosen, saying that they feared there was no one among her matrons whom they could trust like Minerva, whose nickname was Nyhellenia.

But we would not recognise Minerva as a goddess, because she herself had said that no one could be as good or perfect as Wralda's spirit. Therefore we chose Gert, Pire's daughter, as our Mother.

When the priests saw that they could not fry their herrings on our fire (have it their way), they left Athenia, and said that we would not accept Minerva as a goddess out of envy, because she had shown the natives so much affection. Thereupon they gave the people images of her, declaring that they might ask everything of them, as long as they remained obedient.

From all these tales the stupid people became resentful towards us and at last they attacked us. We, however, had built our stone bulwark with two horns all the way to the sea. They could therefore not get to us. Though, what happened is that an Egyptian who was a high priest, bright of eye, clear of brain, and enlightened of mind, whose name was Sekrops, came to give them advice.

When Sekrops saw that he could not breach our wall with his men, he sent messengers to Thirhis. Thereupon three hundred ships full of soldiers of the wild mountain peoples arrived unexpectedly and sailed into our harbour whilst we with all our men were fighting on the ramparts.

When they had taken the harbour, the wild soldiers wanted to plunder the town and our ships. One soldier had already ravished a girl, but Sekrops would not permit it and the Thiriar sailors, who still had Frias blood in their veins, said: "If you do that we will burn our ships, and you shall never see your mountains again."

Sekrops, who had no inclination towards murder or destruction, sent messengers to Gert to claim the burgh, offering her free exit with all her floating and movable assets and those of her followers who felt like it. The wisest of the burghers seeing that they could not hold the burgh, advised Gert to accept at once, before Sekrops became furious and changed his mind. Three months later Gert departed with the best of Frya's children and seven times twelve ships.

When they were one day's sailing out of the harbour, there came thirty ships from Thirhis with wives and children. They were on their way to Athenia, but when they heard how things stood there, they went with Gert. The Sea King (Wet King) of the Thiriar brought them all through the strait which at that time ran into the Red Sea.

At last they landed at Pangap, that is, in our language Five Waters, because here five rivers flow together to the sea. Here they settled. That land they called Gertmannia.

The King of Thirhis seeing afterwards that all his best sailors were gone, sent all his ships with his wild soldiers to catch them, dead or alive. When they arrived at the strait, though, both the sea and the earth trembled. The land was lifted up so that all the water ran out of the strait, and the mud and grime rose up like a rampart before them. This happened on account of the virtues of the Gertmanna, as every one may clearly see.

Chapter 30 – Ulysus, Troy and Sekrops

In the year one thousand and five after Aldland was submerged, this was inscribed on the eastern wall of Fryasburch:

After we have not seen any Krekalandar in Almanland for twelve years, there came three ships, more beautiful than any we had or had ever seen. On the largest of them was a king of the Ihonhis Islands. His name was Ulysus and the claims about his wisdom were great.

This king was told by a priestess that he would become king over all the Krekalanda, so the advice was to get a lamp that was lighted from the lamp in Texland. To obtain this, he had brought great treasures with him, above all, jewels for women, none in the world made more beautiful.

They came from Troy, a city that the Krekalandar had conquered. All these treasures he offered to the mother, but the mother did not want to know of it. At last, when he saw that he had nothing to gain, he went to Walhallagara. There was a matron in office whose name was Kat, though commonly called Kalip, because her lower lip stuck out like a mast-head.

Here he tarried for years, to the annoyance of all that knew it. According to the matrons' claims, he eventually got a lamp from her; but it did him no good, because when he got to sea his ship was lost and he was taken up naked and destitute by the other ships.

From this king there remained here a writer of pure Frya's blood born in the new harbour of Athenia. What follows is what he wrote for us about Athenia from which one may decide how true the Mother Hellicht had spoken when she said that Frya's morals would not prevail in Athenia:

"From the other Krekalander you may have heard a great deal of bad about Sekrops, because he was not of good repute, but I dare say he was an enlightened man, highly regarded both by the locals and by us, for he was not for the oppression of people like the other priests, but he was virtuous and knew how to value the wisdom of distant nations.

Because he realised this, he allowed us to live according to our own Segabok (Law Book). There was a rumour that he was kind to us because he was the offspring of a Fryan girl and an Egyptian priest as he had blue eyes and many of our girls had been abducted and sold in Egypt. He never confirmed this himself, though. Whatever the case, he certainly showed us more friendship than all the other priests put together.

When he died his successors started tampering with our laws and gradually made so many disgusting changes that at long last nothing remained of equality and freedom but the shadow and the name. In addition, they would not allow the decrees to be recorded in writing so that the knowledge thereof was hidden from us. Formerly all cases in Athenia were pleaded in our language; afterwards it had to be in both languages and at last in the native language only.

In the first years the men of Athenia only took wives from our own race, but as the young men grew up with the native girls, they also took from them. The cross-bred children that came from this were the most beautiful and cleverest in the world but they were also the most wicked. Sitting on both sides, they would not subscribe to the laws and customs except when it was in their own interest.

As long as a ray of Frya's spirit existed, all building materials were made to a common standard, and no one could build his house larger or better than that of his neighbours. When some of the bastardized townspeople got rich by our (trade) voyages and by the silver that their slaves mined in the silver countries, they went to live out on the cliffs or in the valleys. There, behind high enclosures of trees or walls, they built mansions with costly furniture, and to be in high esteem with the vile priests, they placed there likenesses of false gods and unchaste statues. Sometimes the vile priests and rulers desired the boys rather than the girls, and often led them astray from the paths of virtue by rich presents or by force.

Because wealth was held in higher regard by this spoilt and bastardized race than virtue and honour, one sometimes saw lads who decorated themselves with wide expensive robes; to the shame of their parents and the matrons, and to the ridicule of their own sex. If our simple elders came to a general assembly in Athenia to make complaints, they were jeered: "Hear, hear! There is a sea monster going to speak!"

Such is Athenia become, like a morass in a tropical country full of leeches, toads, and poisonous snakes, in which no man of decent morals can set his foot.

Chapter 31 – Murder of Frana

How our Denamarka was lost to us 1602 years after Aldland was submerged.

Through Wodin's foolishness and irresponsibility, Magy had become master of Skenland's eastern part. Over the mountains and over the sea they dared not come. The Mother would not prevent it. She spoke, saying, "I see nothing to be feared in their weapons, but in taking the Skenlander back again, because they are so bastardized and spoilt. The general assembly was of the same opinion. Therefore they let him be.

A good hundred years ago the Denemarkar began trading with them; they gave their iron weapons in exchange for gold ornaments, as well as for copper and iron-ore. The mother sent messengers to advise them that they should stop this trade.

There was fear, she said, for their morals and if they lost their morals, they would also lose their freedom. But the Denemarkar had no ears, they never understood that they could lose their morals and therefore they paid no attention to her. At last it happened that they did not have any weapons and supplies, but this disaster was their punishment. Their bodies were adorned with glitter and pretence but their coffers, cupboards and sheds were empty.

Just one hundred years after the day the first ship with provisions sailed from the coast, poverty and want leaked through the windows, hunger spread her wings and came down on the land, dissension marched proudly across the street and into the houses, charity found no place, and unity departed. The child asked its mom for food; she had no food to give, only jewels. The wives went to their husbands, these went to the counts; the counts themselves had nothing to give, or hid it away.

Now they had to sell the jewels but while the sailors were away with them, the frost came and laid a plank over the sea and the straits. When the frost had made the bridge, vigilance crossed over, left the land and treachery came in its place. Instead of guarding the shores, they harnessed their horses to their sledges and drove off to Skenland.

The Skenlander, who hungered after the land of their forefathers, came to the Denemarkum. One bright night they all came. Now they said that they had a right to the land of their forefathers and while they were fighting about it, the Finna came to the defenceless villages and ran away with the children. As a result and because they had no good weapons, they lost the battle and with it their freedom, because the Magy became master. This came about because they did not read Frya's Tex, and had neglected her teachings

There are some who think that they were betrayed by the counts and that the maidens had all along been aware of it, but if any one wanted to speak about it, his mouth was shut by golden chains. We may not pass judgement over it, but we want to call on you: Do not lean too much on the wisdom and virtues of your rulers nor of your matrons because if you want to prevail, every one must guard over their own passions and over the common good.

Two years later the Magy himself came with a fleet of light karve boats to abduct the Mother from Texland and the lamp. This wicked deed he plotted one winter night in stormy weather while the wind howled and the hail rattled against the windows. The watchman, thinking that he had heard something, lighted his torch. As soon as the light from the tower fell upon the enclosure, he saw that many armed men had got over the ring wall. Now he rang the bell, but it was too late. Before they were ready, there were already two thousand in arms battering the gate. The ensuing struggle was short because the guard had not kept a good watch and they all perished.

While everybody was fiercely fighting, a vile Finn slipped into the bedroom of the mother and wanted to violate her. She fought him off so that he fell backwards against the wall. When he got up, be ran his sword through her abdomen saying: "If you will not have me, you shall have my sword".

Behind him came a sailor from Denemarka, took his sword and struck the Fin's head. There came from it a stream of black blood and a wreath of blue flame.

The Magy had the Mother nursed on his ship. When she was well enough to speak clearly, the Magy told her that she must sail with him, but that she would keep her lamp and her matrons, and she would hold a station higher than she had ever known before. Moreover, he said that he would ask her, in the presence of all his headmen, whether he would become master of all the lands and people of Frya; that she must declare and confirm this, or he would let her suffer an agonizing death.

Then, when he had gathered all his chiefs around her bed, he asked in a loud voice:

"Frana, since you are a clairvoyant, you must tell me at once whether I shall become master over all the lands and people of Frya?"

Frana made as though she took no notice of him. At long last she opened her lips and said:

"My eyes are dim, but the other light dawns upon my soul. Yes, I see it. Hear, Irtha, and rejoice with me.

"At the time Aldland sank, the first spoke of the Yule stood at the top. Then it went down, and our freedom with it. When two spokes, or two thousand years, shall have passed, the sons shall arise who have been bred of the fornication of the rulers and priests with the people, and shall witness against their fathers.

"They shall all succumb to murder, but what they have proclaimed shall endure and become fruitful in the bosoms of bold men, like good seed which is laid in your lap. The spoke shall descend for a further thousand years, and sink deeper in darkness and in the blood shed over you by the wickedness of the rulers and priests. After that, the dawn shall begin to glow.

"Seeing this, the false rulers and priests will all together strive and wrestle against freedom, but freedom, love and unity will take the people under their protection, and will rise with the Yule out of the vile pool. Justice, which at first only glimmered, shall then become a flame. The blood of the wicked shall flow over your body, but you must never take it for yourself. At last the poisonous animals shall feed thereon and die of it. All the disgraceful histories that were contrived in praise of the rulers and priests shall be offered to the flame. Thenceforth your children shall live in peace."

When she had finished speaking she sank down. The Magy, who had not understood her, shouted:

"I have asked you if I should become master of all the lands and people of Frya, and now you have been speaking to another!"

Frana raised herself up, stared at him, and said: "Before seven days have passed your soul shall haunt the tombs with the night-birds, and your body shall lie at the bottom of the sea."

"Very well", said the Magy, with unbridled rage, "Tell them I am coming!"

Then he said to his henchmen: "Throw this bitch overboard!"

This was the end of the last of the Mothers. We shall never call for revenge. Time will provide that; but a thousand times a thousand we will call with Frya, "Watch! Watch! Watch!"

Chapter 32 – The Magy Killed

How it fared afterwards with the Magy -

After the mother was murdered, he had the lamp and the matrons brought to his ship, together with all the loot he chose. Then he went up the Flymar because he wanted to abduct the matron of Medeasblik or of Stavora and make her Mother. There, however, they were on guard.The sailors from Stavora and from the Alderga would have wanted Jon's assistance but the great fleet was out on a distant voyage; so they proceeded in their small fleet to Medeasblik, and hid themselves behind the foliage of the trees. The Magy approached Medeasblik in broad daylight; though, his men ran towards the burgh unconcerned.

When all the people from the boats had landed, our sailors came forth out of the creek and shot their arrows with turpentine balls onto their fleet. They were so straight that many of their ships were soon on fire. Those guarding the ships also shot at us but they did not hit anything.

When at last a burning ship drifted towards the ship of the Magy, he ordered the helmsman to veer away, but this helmsman was the Denemarker who had felled the Fin; instead he said:

"You sent our Honorary Mother to the bottom of the sea to say you were coming. In the bustle you may have forgotten; now I will take care that you keep your word."

The Magy tried to push him off, but this helmsman, a true Fryas and as strong as an ox, clutched his head with both hands and pitched him overboard into the surging billows. Then he hoisted up his brown shield to the top, and sailed straight to our fleet. Thus the matrons came unhurt to us; but the lamp was extinguished, and no one knew how that came about.

When those on the undamaged ships heard that their Magy was drowned, they sailed away, because their crews were mostly Denemarkar. When the fleet was far enough off, our sailors turned and shot their burning arrows at the Finns. When the Finns saw that, and found that they had been betrayed, they fell into confusion, and lost all discipline and order. At that moment the defenders stormed out of the burgh. Those who did not flee were killed, and those who fled found their death in the marshes of the Krylinger wood.

Chapter 33 – Postscript

When the sailors were hiding in the creek, there was a jester from Stavoren among them, who said: "Medea may well laugh should we rescue her from her burgh".

From this the matrons named the creek "Medea Mêilakkia".

The events that happened after this everybody can remember. The matrons ought to relate it in their own way, and have it well described. We consider our task completed. Hail!

The end of the book.

The Writings of Adelbrost and Appolonia

Chapter 1 – The Death of Adelbrost

My name is Adelbrost, the son of Apol and of Adela. I was elected by my people as Count over the Linda Oorden (Districts). Therefore I will continue this book in the same way as my mother has suggested.

After the Magy was slain and Fryasburch was restored, a mother had to be chosen. During her life the Mother had not named her successor. Her will was missing and nowhere to be found. Seven months later a general assembly was called and specifically at Grenega by reason that it was on the boundary of Saxanamarka. My mother was chosen, but she would not be Mother.

She had saved my father's life, as a result of which they had fallen in love and wanted to get married. Many people wanted my mother to change her decision, but my mother said:

"An Honorary Mother ought to be as pure in her conscience as she appears outwardly and care equally for all her children.

"Now, as I love Apol more than anything else in the world, I cannot be such a mother."

Thus spoke and reasoned Adela, but all the other matrons wished to be Mother. Each state was in favour of its own matron and nobody would yield. Therefore none was chosen, and the realm became disordered. From what follows you may understand this.

Liudgert, the king who had recently passed away, had been chosen in the lifetime of the mother, seemingly with the love and confidence of all the states. It was his turn to live at the great court of Dokhem and during the Mother's lifetime great honour was bestowed on him there, because it was always full of messengers and knights from near and far; more than had ever been seen there before.

But now he was lonely and forsaken, because every one was afraid that he would make himself master above the law, and would become like the slave kings. Every ruler imagined that he did enough if he looked after his own state, and no one would cooperate with the others.

With the Burgh Matrons it was even worse. Everyone relied on her own wisdom, and whenever the Counts did anything without her, she would create distrust between them and their people. If a case concerned several states, and (only) one matron had been consulted, the rest all complained that she had spoken only in the interest of her own state.

Through all this misconduct they created division between the states and broke the bond of unity so that the people of one state became resentful towards the people of another state or at least saw them as strangers. The result was that the Gola or Trowida won all our lands up to the Skelda and the Magy up to the Wrsara. How this happened my mother has explained, otherwise this book would not have been written; although I have lost all hope that it would be of any use.

I do not write this under the delusion that I shall thereby win back the land or preserve it; that is in my opinion impossible. I write only for the future generations, that they may all know in what way we were lost, and that all men may learn from this that every crime bears its punishment.

Apollonia

People call me Apollonia.

Thirty two days after mother's death my brother Adelbrost was found murdered on the wharf, his skull split and his limbs torn asunder. My father, who lay ill, died of fright (shock). Then Apol, my younger brother, sailed from here to the west side of Skenland. There he built a burgh named Lindasburch, in order there to avenge our wrong.

Wr-alda accorded him many years for that. He had five sons, All of them brought fear to Magy and fame to my brother. After the death of my mother and brother, the most pious of the land joined together and made a covenant, called the Adelband. In order to protect us, they brought me and Adelhirt, my youngest brother, to the burgh—me to the matrons, and my brother to the warriors. When I was thirty years old I was chosen as Burgh Matron, and when my brother was fifty he was chosen as Count.

From mother's side my brother was the sixth, but from father's side the third. By right, therefore, his descendants could not put "overa Linda" after their names, but they all wished to do it in honour of my mother. In addition to this, there was given to us also a copy of "The Book of Adela's   Followers." That gave me the most pleasure, because it came into the world by my mother's wisdom.

In the burgh I have found other writings which are not in the book as well as praises to my mother, all of which I will write down later.

The Writings of Brunno

These are the writings left by Brunno, who were the scribe of this burgh:

After the followers of Adela had made copies, each in his own domain, of what was inscribed upon the walls of the burghs, they decided to choose a mother. For this a general assembly was called at this place. In accordance with Adela's first recommendation, Tuntia was proposed. That would have been accepted, though, my Burgh Matron asked to speak: she had always assumed that she would become Mother, because she sat at the burgh from which most Mothers had been chosen. When she was given her turn to speak, she opened her false lips and said:

"You all seem to place great value on Adela's advice, but that shall not shut my mouth nor silence me. Who is Adela, and where does it come from that you praise her so highly? Like me, she used to be a Burgh Matron here. Is she, then, wiser or better than I and all the others; or is she more conversant with our laws and customs? If that had been the case, she should have become mother when she was chosen; but instead, she preferred matrimony with all its joys and privileges instead of watching all alone over herself and her people.

"She is certainly very clear-sighted, but my eyes are far from dim. I have seen that she loves her husband dearly, good, that is lovely; but I also see that Tuntia is Apol's niece. Further I do not want to say anything."

The leaders understood very well where she sought lee (way), but among the people there arose disputes, and as most of the people came from here, they would not give the honour to Tuntia. The debates were ended, knives were drawn from their sheaths, and no Mother was chosen.

Shortly afterwards one of our delegates killed his comrade. Until then he was an upright man, therefore my Burgh Matron had permission to help him over the border. In stead, though, of helping him to Twiskland, she fled with him herself over the Wrsara and then to the Magy. The Magy who wanted to please his Fryas sons, appointed her as Mother of Godaburch in Skenland, but she wanted more. She told him that if he could get rid of Adela, he could become master over all of Frya's land. She was an enemy of Adela, she said, because, as a result of her trickery, she did not become Mother. If he would promise her Texland, her messenger would serve as a guide for his soldiers. All this was confessed by her messenger.

Chapter 2 – The Death of Adela

The other writing –

Fifteen months after the last general assembly, it was Friendship or Harvest Month (festival). Everybody was joyful and happy in their merriment and no one had any cares other than seeking entertainment; but Wr-alda wanted to show us that watchfulness should never be relaxed. In the midst of the festivities the fog came and covered our places in darkness. Despite these conditions, watchfulness did not return. The coastguard deserted their fires, and at the entrances no one was to be seen.When the fog lifted, the sun broke through the clouds onto the earth. Everyone came out again, rejoicing and jubilant; the young folks went about singing to their bagpipes, filling the air with their beautiful voices.

While every one was basking in joy, however, treachery had landed with horses and riders. As usual, darkness had favoured the wicked, and they had slipped in through the paths of the Linda Woods.

Before Adela's door twelve girls led twelve lambs, and twelve boys led twelve calves. A young Saxman rode a wild bull which he had caught himself and tamed. They were decorated with all kinds of flowers, and the girls' dresses were fringed with gold from the Rhine. When Adela came out of her house, a shower of flowers fell on her head; they all cheered loudly, and the fifes of the boys were heard above all.

Poor Adela! Poor people! How short a time will joy linger here?

When the procession was out of sight, a troop of Magyara horsemen charged straight up to Adela's house. Her father and her husband were sitting on the porch bench. The door was open, and within stood Adelbrost, her son. When he saw the danger to his parents, he grabbed his bow from the wall and shot the front bandit, who staggered and fell onto the grass. The second and third met a similar fate.

In the meantime his elders had seized their weapons, and slowly moved towards Jon's house. They would soon have been surrounded, but Adela came. At the burgh she had learned to use all weapons. She was seven feet tall and her sword was as long. Three times she swung it over her head, and each time a rider fell. Reinforcements came around the corner of the lane. The bandits were felled and captured; but too late - an arrow had penetrated her bosom. Treacherous Magy! The arrow head was poisoned and she died of it.

Chapter 3 – Tribute to Adela

The elegy of the burgh matron -Yes, distant-living friend, thousands already came, and more are on their way. They wish to hear Adela's wisdom. Truly, she was an empress, for she had always been the leader. O Sorrow, what good can you do? Her blouse is linen, her tunic wool; these she spun and wove herself. How could she add to her beauty? Not with pearls, for her teeth were whiter; not with gold, for her tresses were more brilliant; not with precious stones, for her eyes, though soft as those of a lamb, were so lustrous that you could scarcely look into them. But why do I talk of beauty? Frya was certainly not more beautiful. Yes friends, Frya had seven beauties of which each of her daughters inherited but one, or at most three. But even if she had been ugly, she would still have been dear to us. Was she fearless (warlike)? Listen friend. Adela was the only child of our Count. She stood seven feet tall. Her wisdom exceeded her stature, and her courage was equal to both together.

Look there. There was once a peat bog fire. Three children got upon yonder gravestone. The wind blew furiously. Everybody shouted and the mother was frantic. Then Adela came: "What are you standing around for", she cried. "Try to help them, and Wralda will give you strength".

She ran to the Krylwood and got some elder branches to make a bridge, then the others also helped, and the children were saved.

Every year the children bring flowers to the place.

There once came three Fonisiar sailors, who wanted to ill-treat the children, but Adela, having heard their screams, came and beat the scoundrels senseless, and then, to prove to them what miserable wretches they were, she tied them all three to a spindle. The foreign lords came to collect their people, and when they saw how ridiculously they had been treated they were very angry, until they were told what had happened. What did they then do? They bowed before Adela, and kissed the hem of her tunic.

Come, distant-living friend. The birds of the forest fled before the numerous visitors. Come friend, you must hear her wisdom. By the gravestone of which mention is made in her tribute, mom's body is buried. Upon the stone they had written the following words:

"Do not pass in haste, for here lies Adela"

The formulary (doctrine) which is inscribed on the outside wall of the burgh tower has not been included in "The Book of Adela's Followers". Why it has been left out I do not know. This book, though, is my own; therefore I would like to include it for the benefit of my relatives.

Chapter 4 – Doctrine from the tower (A)

Hail to all the well-intentioned children of Frya! Through them the earth shall be blessed. Learn and announce to the nations.

Wralda is the ancient of ancients or the most ancient, for he created all things. Wr-alda is all in all, for he is eternal and everlasting. Wr-alda is omnipresent but invisible, and therefore his being is called a spirit. All that we can see of him are the created beings who came through his life and go back again, because from Wralda all things proceed and return to him. From Wralda comes the beginning and the end; all things are glorified through him. Wr-alda is the only almighty being, because from him all other power is borrowed and returns to him. From him come all crafts and all crafts return to him. Therefore he alone is the creator, and nothing was created outside him.

Wralda established eternal principles that are law in all creation and there are no good laws or they must be established therein. But although everything is in Wralda, the wickedness of men is not from him. Wickedness comes from laziness, carelessness, and stupidity; therefore they may well be injurious to men, but never to Wralda. Wralda is wisdom, and the laws that he has made are the books from which we learn, nor is any wisdom to be found or gathered, but in them. Men may see a great deal, but Wralda sees everything. Men may learn many things, but Wralda knows everything. Men may unlock many things, but to Wralda everything is open. Mankind are male and female, but Wralda created both. Mankind love and hate, but Wralda alone is just. Therefore Wralda alone is good, and there is no good without him. In the progress of time all creation alters and changes, but goodness alone is unalterable; and since Wralda is good, he cannot change. As he endures, he alone exists; everything else is show.

Chapter 5 - Doctrine from the tower (B)

Among Finda's people there are false teachers who, by their over-inventiveness, have become so wicked that they make themselves believe, and their adherents declare, that they are the best part of

Wralda, that their spirit is the best part of Wralda's spirit, and that Wralda can only think by the help of their brains.

That every creature is a part of Wralda's eternal being, they have stolen from us; but their false reasoning and vigorous pompousness have led them astray. If their spirit was Wralda's spirit, then Wralda would be very stupid, instead of being sensible and wise; for their spirit ever slaves to create beautiful statues which they then worship.

Finda's people are a wicked people, for although the deceivers make themselves believe that they are gods, they have created false gods for the ignorant, and proclaim everywhere that these idols created the world and all therein; greedy idols, full of envy and anger, who desire to be honoured and served by the people, seeking their blood and offers and demanding their treasures; but these presumptuous and false men, who let themselves be called god-servants and priests, receive and collect everything in the name of these gods, who do not exist, for their own benefit. They practise all this with a liberal conscience as they regard themselves as gods who are not accountable to anybody. If someone discovers their fraud and exposes them, they are taken by their henchmen and burned for their blasphemy at solemn ceremonies in honour of their false gods; but in truth only to protect themselves.

In order that our children may be armed against these idolatrous doctrines, so the matrons must teach them from the outside the following:

Wralda was before all things, and after all things he will still be. Wralda is also eternal and everlasting, therefore nothing is outside of him. From Wralda's being, time and all things were born, and his being takes away time and every other thing. These things must be made clear and manifest in every way, so that they may be told to and understood by others.

When we have mastered thus much, then we say further: In regards to our extent, we are a part of Wr-alda's everlasting being, like the extent of all creation; but as regards our form, our qualities, our spirit, and all our thoughts, these do not belong to that Being. These are passing things which appear by Wr-alda's life, and which appear through his wisdom, and not otherwise; but whereas life continues, nothing can remain stationary; therefore all created things change their locality, their form, and their thoughts. So neither the earth nor any other created object can say, I am; but rather, I was. So no man can say, I think; but rather, I thought. The boy is greater and different from when he was a baby; he has different desires, inclinations, and thoughts. The man and father are and think differently from the boy; the old man just the same. Everybody knows that. Besides, everybody knows and must acknowledge that he is changing, that he changes every moment, even while he says, I am, and that his thoughts changes even while he says, I think.

Instead, then, of disgracefully imitating the wicked Findas and practicing occultism by saying, I am, or I am the best part of Wr-alda, and yes, through us alone he can think, we proclaim everywhere where it is necessary: We, Frya's children, exist through Wr-alda's life - in the beginning insignificant and naked, but always advancing towards perfection without ever attaining the excellence of Wr-alda himself. Our spirit is not Wr-alda's spirit; it is merely a reflection of it. When Wr-alda created us in his wisdom, he lend us brains, senses, memory, and many other good qualities. By this means we are able to contemplate his laws; by this we can learn and reason, solely for our own good. Had Wr-alda not given us our senses, we would have known nothing of these, and would have been more ignorant than a piece of sea-weed driven forth by the ebb and tide.

Chapter 6 – A Lesson

This is written on parchment; speech and answer to other matrons as an example

An unsociable, miserly man came to complain to Trast, who was the matron of Stavia. He said a thunderstorm had destroyed his house. He had prayed to Wr-alda, but Wr-alda had given him no help.

"Are you a true Frisian?" Trast asked.

"From father and forefathers", replied the man.

Then she said, "I will sow something in your conscience, in confidence that it will take root, grow, and bear fruit."

She continued: "When Frya was born, our mother stood naked and exposed, unprotected from the rays of the sun. She could ask no one, and there was no one who could give her any help. Then Wr-alda wrought in her conscience discretion and love, anxiety and fright. She looked round her, and her inclination chose the best. She sought shelter under the protective lime-trees, but the rain came and she got wet. She had seen how the water ran down the sloping leaves; so she made a roof with sloping sides supported on sticks, but the storm wind blew the rain in from under it.

"Now she saw that the tree trunk gave protection. She then built a wall of sods, first on one side, and then all round. The storm wind came stronger than before and blew away the roof. She, however, did not complaint to Wralda or about Wralda. She made a roof of rushes, and put stones upon it. Having found how hard it is to toil alone, she showed her children how and why she had done it. They acted and thought as she did. In this way we came onto houses and porches, a street and lime-trees to protect us from the rays of the sun.

"At last she built a citadel, and all the rest.

"If your house was not strong enough, then you must try and build a better one."

"My house was strong enough", he said, "but the flood and the wind destroyed it."

"Where did your house stand?" Trast asked.

"On the bank of the Rhine", the man answered.

"Did it not stand on a knoll or a terp?" Trast asked.

"No", said the man, "My house stood alone on the bank. I built it alone, but I could not make a terp alone."

"I am aware of it", Trast answered. "The maidens told me. All your life you have had a dislike towards your neighbours, fearing that you might have to give or do something for them; but one cannot get on in the world in that way, for Wr-alda, who is kind, turns away from the niggardly. Fâsta has advised us, and it is engraved in stone over all our doors: Lest you become selfish, protect your neighbours, teach your neighbours, help your neighbours, and they will do the same to you. If this advice is not good enough for you, I can give you no better".

The man blushed for shame, and slunk away.

Chapter 7 – Apollonia's Burgh

Now I would like to write myself; first about my burgh, and then about what I have been able to see.

My burgh lies near the north end of the Liudgarda. The tower has six sides. It is three times thirty feet high; flat on top, with a small house upon it from where they study the stars. On either side of the tower is a house three hundred feet long, three times seven feet wide and as high, apart from the roof which is round. All this is built of hard-baked bricks, and on the outside there is nothing else. Around the burgh is a ring dyke, with a moat three times seven feet deep and three times twelve feet wide. If one looks down from the tower, he sees the shape of the Yule.

On the ground among the southern houses all kinds of herbs from near and far grow, of which the maidens must study the qualities. Between the northern houses there are only fields. The three houses on the north are full of corn and other necessities; the two houses on the south are for the maidens for school and to live. The most southern house is the Burgh Matron's house. In the tower hangs the lamp. The walls of the tower are inlaid with costly stones. On the south wall the Tex is inscribed. On the right side of this are the ordinances, and on the other side the laws; the other matters are found upon the three other sides. Against the dyke, near the house of the burgh matron, stand the oven and the mill, worked by four oxen.

Outside our burgh wall is the place where the Burgtheeren (officers?) and the soldiers live. The ring dyke around is an hour long—not a seaman's hour, but an hour of the sun, of which two times twelve go to a day. Inside the dyke is a level five feet below the top. On it are three hundred crossbows covered with wood and leather.

Besides the houses of the inhabitants, there are along the inside of the dyke three times twelve refuge-houses for the people who live in the district. The field serves for a paddock and for a meadow. On the south side of the outer ring dyke is the Liudgarde, enclosed by the great Linda Forrest. Its shape is three-cornered, with the widest part outside, so that the sun may shine in it, for there are a great number of foreign trees and flowers brought by the seafarers.

All the other citadels are the same shape as ours, only not so large; but the largest of all is that of Texland. The tower of Fryasburgh is so high that it rends the sky, and all the rest is in proportion to the tower.

In our citadel this is the arrangement: Seven young maidens attend to the lamp; each watch is three hours. In the rest of their time they do housework, learn, and sleep. When they have watched for seven years, they are free; then they may go among the people, to look after their morals and to give advice. When they have been three years maidens, they may sometimes accompany the older ones.

The writer must teach the girls to read, to write, and to reckon. The elders, or "Greva," must teach them justice and duty, morals, botany, and medicine, history, traditions, and singing, besides all that may be necessary for them to give advice. The burgh matron must teach them how to set to work when they go among the people. Before a burgh matron can take office, she must travel through the country a whole year. Three grey-headed Burgtheeren and three old matrons must go with her. This was the way that I did. My journey was along the Rhine—on this side up, and on the other side down. The higher I went, the poorer the people seemed to me.

Everywhere about the Rhine the people dug holes, and the sand that was got out was poured with water over fleeces to get the gold, but the girls did not wear golden crowns of it. Formerly there were more, but since we lost Skenland they have gone to the mountains. There they dig iron ore and make iron. Above the Rhine among the mountains I have seen Marsata. The Marsata are people who live on the lakes. Their houses are built upon piles for protection from the wild beasts and wicked people.

There are wolves, bears, and horrible black lions; there are the Swetsar (Swiss) bordering on the Heinde Krekalandar (Italy), the followers of Kalta (Celts) and the wild Twiskar; all greedy for robbery and booty. The Marsata make a living by fishing and hunting. The skins are sewn together by the women, and prepared with birch bark. The small skins are as soft as woman's felt. The burgh matron at Fryasburgh told us that they were good, simple people; but if I had not heard her speak of them first, I should have thought that they were not

Frya's people, they looked so wild and uncivilized. Their wool and herbs are bought by the Rhine people, and exported by the sailors

Along the Rhine it was just the same as at Lydasburgh (Leiden). There was a great lake. On this lake there were also people living upon piles. But they were not Frya's people; they were black and brown men who had been employed as rowers to bring home the men who had been making foreign voyages, and they had to stay there till the fleet went back.

At last we came to Alderga. At the head of the south harbour lies the Waraburgh, a stone house in which all kinds of shells, horns, weapons and clothes are kept which were brought by the sea-people from distant lands.

A quarter of an hour's distance from there is the Alderga, a great river surrounded by sheds, houses and gardens, all richly decorated. In the river lay a great fleet ready, with banners of all colours.

On Frya's day the shields were hung on board. Some shone like the sun. The shields of the sea-king and the admiral were bordered with gold. From the river a canal was dug going past the burgh Forana (Vroonen), with a narrow outlet to the sea. This was the egress of the fleet; the Fly was the ingress. On both sides of the river are beautiful houses painted in bright colours. The gardens are all surrounded by green hedges. I saw there women wearing felt tunics, as if it were writing felt.

Just as at Staveren, the girls wore golden crowns on their heads, and rings on their arms and ankles. To the south of Forana lies Alkmarum. Alkmarum is a lake or river in which there is an island. On this island the black and brown people must remain, the same as at Lydasburgh. The burgh matron of Forana told me that the burgtheeren go every day to teach them what real freedom is, and how it behoves men to live in order to obtain the blessing of Wr-alda's spirit. If there was any one who was willing to listen and could comprehend, he was kept there until he was fully taught. That was done in order to instruct the distant people, and to make friends everywhere.

I had been to the Saxanamarka, at the burgh Mannagardaforde (Munster). There I saw more poverty than I could discover wealth here. She explained: When a young man courts a young girl at the Saxanamarka, the girls ask:

"Can you keep your house free from the banished Twisklanders? Have you ever killed any of them? How many cattle have you already caught, and how many bear and wolf skins have you brought to market?"

And from this it comes that the Saxons have left the cultivation of the soil to the women, that not one in a hundred can read or write; from this it comes, too, that no one has a motto on his shield, but only a misshapen form of some animal that he has killed; and lastly, from this comes also that they are very warlike, but sometimes as stupid as the beasts that they catch, and as poor as the Twisklanders with whom they go to war.

The earth and the sea were made for Frya's people. All our rivers run into the sea. The Lyda's people and the Findas people will exterminate each other, and we must people the empty countries. In movement and sailing is our prosperity. If you wish the highlanders to share our riches and wisdom, I will give you a piece of advice. Let the girls, when they are asked to marry, before they say yes, ask their lovers: What parts of the world have you travelled in? What can you tell your children about distant lands and distant people? If they do this, then the young warriors will come to us; they will become wiser and richer, and we shall have no occasion to deal with those nasty people. The youngest of the maids who   were with me came from the Saxanamarka. When we came back she asked leave to go home. Afterwards she became burgh matron there, and that is the reason why these days so many of our sailors are Saxons.

END OF APOLLONIA'S BOOK

The Writings of Frethorik and Wiliow

Chapter 1 – The 305 BC Disaster

My name is Frethorik, surnamed oera Linda, which means over the Linda. In Liudwardia I was chosen as Asga. Liudwardia is a new village within the ring dyke of the burgh Liudgarda, of which the name has fallen into disrepute. In my time much has happened. I had written a good deal about it, but afterwards much more was related to me. I will write an account of both one and the other after this book, to the honour of the good people and to the disgrace of the bad. In my youth I heard complaints on all sides. The bad time was coming; the bad time did come—Frya had forsaken us. She withheld from us all her guardian maidens, because monstrous idolatrous images had been found within our landmarks. I burnt with curiosity to see those images. In our neighbourhood a little old woman tottered in and out of the houses, always calling out about the bad times. I came to her; she stroked my chin; then I became bold, and asked her if she would show me the bad times and the images.

She laughed good-naturedly, and took me to the burgh. An old man asked me if I could read and write.

"No", I said.

"Then you must first go and learn", he replied, "otherwise you will not understand it".

I went daily to the writer and learnt. Eight years afterwards I heard that our burg matron had been unchaste, and that some of the burgtheeren had committed treason with the Magy, and many people sided with them. Everywhere disputes arose. There were children rebelling against their parents; good people were secretly murdered. The little old woman who had brought everything to light was found dead in a ditch. My father, who was a judge, would have her avenged. He was murdered in the night in his house. Three years later the Magy was master without any resistance.

The Saxmen had remained pious and brave. All the good people fled to them. My mother died of it. Now I did like the others. The Magy prided himself on his cunning, but the Earth made him know that she would not tolerate any Magy or idol on the holy bosom that had borne Frya. As a wild horse tosses his mane after he has thrown his rider, so Irtha shook her forests and her mountains. Rivers spread over the fields; the sea raged; mountains spouted fire to the clouds, and what they vomited forth the clouds flung upon the earth. At the beginning of the Arnemaand (harvest month) the earth bowed towards the north, and sank down lower and lower. In the Wolfamaand (Wolf Month, winter month) the low lands of Fryasland were buried under the sea. The woods in which the images were, were torn up and scattered by the wind.

The following year the frost came in the Herdemaand (Louwmaand, January), and covered Fryasland under a sheet of ice. In Sellemaand (Sprokkelmaand, February) there were storm winds from the north, driving mountains of ice and stones. When the spring-tides came the earth raised herself up, the ice melted; with the ebb the forests with the images drifted out to sea. In the Winne-, or Minnamaand (Bloeimaand, May), every one who dared went home. I came with a matron to the citadel Liudgarda. How sad it looked there. The forests of the Lindawrda were almost all gone. Where Liudgarda used to be was sea. The waves swept over   the ring dyke. Ice had destroyed the tower, and the houses lay heaped over each other. On the slope of the dyke I found a stone on which the writer had inscribed his name. That was my marker.

The same thing that happened to our burgh, happened to the others. In the high lying lands they had been destroyed by the earth, in the low lying lands by water. Only Fryasburgh on Texland was not damaged, but all the land to the north was under the sea, and has never resurfaced. On the banks of the Flymeer, as we were told, thirty salt swamps were found where the forests and the ground had been swept away. At Westflyland there were fifty. The canal which had run across the land from Alderga was filled up with sand and destroyed. The seafaring people and other sailors who were at home had saved themselves with their wives and children on their ships. The black people at Lydasburgh and Alkmarum had done the same. As the blacks were driven south they saved many girls, and as no one came to claim them, they took them for their wives.

The people who returned all went to live within the ring dyke of the burgh, as outside there was nothing but mud and marsh. The old houses were all smashed together. People bought cattle and sheep in the upper lands, and in the great houses where formerly the maidens lived, cloth and felt were made for a livelihood. This happened 1888 years after the submersion of Atland. (305 BC)

For 282 years we had not had an Eeremoeder, and now, when everything seemed lost, they chose one. The lot fell upon Gosa, surnamed Makonta. She was burgh matron at Fryasburgh in Texland. She had a clear head and sound judgement, quite good, and as her burgh was the only one that had been spared, every one saw in that her calling. Ten years later the navigators came from Forana and Lydasburgh. They wanted to drive the black men, with their wives and children, out of the country. They wished to obtain the opinion of the mother upon the subject.

Gosa asked them: "Can you take any of them back to their countries? If so, then make haste, or they will find no relatives alive."

"No", they said.

Goss replied: "They have tasted your salt and eaten your bread; they have placed their bodies and lives under your protection. You must examine your own hearts. But I will give you one piece of advice. Keep them until you are able to take them back to their homes, but keep them outside your burghs. Watch over their morals, and educate them as if they were Frya's sons. Their women are the strongest here. Their blood will disappear like smoke, till at last nothing but Frya's blood will remain in their descendants".

So they remained here.

Now, I should wish that my descendants should observe in how far Gosa spoke the truth. When our country began to recover, there came troops of poor Saxon men and women to the neighbourhoods of Stavere and Alderga, to search for gold and other treasures in the swampy lands. But the sea-people would not permit it, so they went and settled in the empty villages in West Flyland in order to preserve their lives.

Chapter 2 – Return of the Gertmanne

Now I will relate how the Gertmanne and many followers of Hellenia came back.

Two years after Gosa had become the mother (303 B.C.) a fleet arrived at the Flymeer. The people shouted "Ho-n-sêen" (What a blessing). They sailed to Stavere, where they shouted again. Their flags were hoisted, and at night they shot lighted arrows into the air. At daylight some of them rowed into the harbour in a boat, shouting again, "Ho-n-sêen." When they landed a young fellow jumped upon the rampart. In his hand he held a shield on which bread and salt were laid. After him came a grey-headed man, who said:

"We come from the distant Greek land to preserve our customs. Now we wish you to be so kind as to give us sufficient land to be able to live."

He told a long story, which I will hereafter relate more fully. The count did not know what to do. They sent messengers all round, also to me. I went, and said now that we have a mother it behoves us to ask her advice. I went with them myself. The mother, who already knew it all, said:

"Let them come, they will help us to keep our lands, but do not let them remain in one place, that they may not become too powerful over us."

We did as she said, which was quite to their liking. Friso remained with his people at Stavere, which they made again into a port as well as they could.

Wichhirte went with his people eastwards to the Emude. Some of the Johniar (descendants of Jon) who was of the opinion that they sprang from the Alderga people, went there. A small number, who thought that their forefathers had come from the seven islands, went there and settled within the ring dyke of the burgh of Walhallagara. Liudgert, the admiral of Wichhirte, became my comrade, and afterwards my friend. Out of his diary I have taken the following history:

Alexander the Great

After we had lived 12 times 100 and twice 12 years (1224 years) at the Five Waters (Punjab), whilst our sea farers were navigating all the seas they could find, came Alexander the King, with a powerful army from the upper regions of the river towards our villages. No one could withstand him; but we sea-people, who lived by the sea, put all our possessions on board ships and took our departure. When Alexander heard that such a large fleet had escaped him, he became furious, and swore that he would burn all the villages if we did not come back. Wichhirte was ill in bed. When Alexander heard that, he waited until he was better. After that he came to him, speaking very kindly—but he deceived, as he had done before.

Wichhirte answered: "Oh greatest of kings, we sailors go everywhere; we have heard of your great deeds, therefore we are full of respect for your arms, and still more for your wisdom; but we who are free-born Frya's children, we may not become your slaves; and even if I would, the others would sooner die, for so it is commanded in our laws."

Alexander said: "I do not desire to take your land or make slaves of your people. I only wish to hire your services. That I will swear by both our gods, so that no one may be dissatisfied."

When Alexander had shared bread and salt with him, Wichhirte chose the wisest part. He let his son fetch the ships. When they had all returned, Alexander hired them all. By means of them he wished to transport his people to the holy Ganges, which he had not been able to reach before. Then he chose among all his people and soldiers those who were accustomed to the sea. Wichhirte had fallen sick again, therefore I went alone with Nearchus, sent by the king. The voyage came to an end without any advantage, because the Joniars and the Phœnicians were always quarrelling, so that Nearchus himself could not control them.

In the meantime, the king had not sat still. He had let his soldiers cut down trees and make planks, with which, with the help of our carpenters, he had built ships. Now he would himself become a sea-king, and sail with his whole army up the Ganges; but the soldiers who came from the mountainous countries were afraid of the sea.

When they heard that they must sail, they set fire to the timber yards, and so our whole village was laid in ashes.

At first we thought that this had been done by Alexander's orders, and we were all ready to cast ourselves into the sea: but Alexander was furious, and wished his own people to kill the soldiers. However, Nearchus, who was not only his chief officer, but also his friend, advised him not to do so. So he pretended to believe that it had happened by accident, and said no more about it. He wished now to return, but before going he made an inquiry as to who were really the guilty ones. As soon as he ascertained it, he had them all disarmed, and made them build a new village. His own people he kept under arms to intimidate the others to build a burgh.

We were to take the women and children with us. When we have arrived at the mouth of the Euphrates, we could then either choose a place to settle there or come back. Our pay would be guaranteed to us in either case.

Upon the new ships which had been saved from the fire he placed the Joniars and the Greeks. He himself went with the rest of his people along the coast, through the barren desert; that is, through the land that the Earth had heaved up out of the sea when she raised the strait after our forefathers had passed into the Red Sea.

When we arrived at New Gertmania (New Gertmania is the port that we had made ourselves in order to take in water), we met Alexander with his army. Nearchus went ashore, and stayed three days. Then we proceeded further on. When we came to the Euphrates, Nearchus went ashore with the soldiers and a large body of people; but he soon returned, and said:

"The king requests you, for his sake, to take a short voyage to the end of the Red Sea; after that each shall receive as much gold as he can carry."

When we arrived there, he showed us where the strait had formerly been. There he spent thirty-one days, always looking steadily towards the desert.

At last there arrived a great troop of people, bringing with them 200 elephants, 1000 camels, timber, ropes, and all kinds of implements necessary to drag our fleet to the Mediterranean Sea. This astounded us, and seemed most extraordinary; but Nearchus told us that his king wished to show to the other kings that he was more powerful than any of the kings of Tyre had ever been. We were only to assist, and that surely could do us no harm. We were obliged to yield, and Nearchus knew so well how to regulate everything that our ships lay in the Mediterranean Sea before three months had passed.

When Alexander heard how his project was concluded, he became so audacious that he wished to dig out the dry strait in mockery of the Earth; but Wr-alda abandoned his soul, so that he destroyed himself by wine and rashness before he could begin it. After his death his empire was divided among his commanders. They were each to have preserved a share for his sons, but that was not their intention. Each wished to keep his own share, and to get more. Then war arose, and we could not turn back.

Nearchus wished us to settle on the coast of Phœnicia, but that no one would do. We said we would rather risk returning to Fryasland. Then he brought us to the new port of Athens, where all the true children of Frya had formerly gone. We went, soldiers with our provisions and weapons. Among the many rulers Nearchus had a friend named Antigonus. These two had only one object in view, as they told us—to follow the royal race, and to restore the old freedom of all the Greek lands. Antigonus had, among many others, one son named Demetrius, afterwards called the "State Winner."

Once he attacked the town of Salamis. After he had been fighting there for some time, he had to engage the fleet of Ptolemy. Ptolemy was the name of the ruler who reigned over Egypt. Demetrius won the battle, not by his own soldiers, but because we helped him. We had done this out of friendship for Nearchus, because we knew that he was of bastard birth by his white skin, blue eyes, and fair hair. Later Demetrius attacked Rhodes, and we transported thither his soldiers and provisions. When we made our last voyage to Rhodes, the war was over.

Demetrius had sailed to Athens. When our king realised this, he led us back. When we came into the harbour, the whole town was in mourning. Friso, who was king of the fleet, had a son and a daughter at home so remarkably fair as if they had just come out of Fryasland, and more beautiful than any one could picture. The fame of this went all over Greece, and came to the ears of Demetrius. Demetrius was vile and immoral, and thought he could do as he pleased. He had the daughter openly abducted.

The mother did not dare await the return of her joy (the sailors' wives call their husbands "joy" or "zoethart" (sweetheart). The men call their wives troost (comfort) and fro or frow, that is, vreugde (delight) and frolic; that is the same as vreugde. As she dared not wait for her husband's return, she went with her son to Demetrius, and implored him to send back her daughter; but when Demetrius saw the son he had him taken to his palace, and did to him as he had done to his sister. He sent a bag of gold to the mother, which she flung into the sea. When she came home she was out of her mind, and ran about the streets calling out:

"Have you seen my children? Woe is me! Let me find a place to hide in, for my husband will kill me because I have lost his children."

When Demetrius heard that Friso had come home, he sent messengers to him to say that he had taken his children to raise them to high rank, and to reward him for his services. But Friso was proud and passionate, and sent a messenger with a letter to his children, in which he recommended them to accept the will of Demetrius, as he wished to promote their happiness; but the messenger had another letter with poison, which he ordered them to take:

"Because", he said, "your bodies have been defiled against your will. That you are not to blame for; but if your souls are not pure, you will never come into Walhalla. Your spirits will haunt the earth in darkness. Like the bats and owls, you will hide yourselves in the daytime in boles, and in the night will come and shriek and cry about our graves, while Frya must turn her head away from you."

The children did as their father had commanded. Demetrius had their bodies thrown into the sea, and it was said that they had fled. Now Friso wished to go with all his people to Frya's land, where he had been formerly, but most of them would not go. So Friso set fire to the village and all the royal storehouses; then no one could remain there, and all were glad to be out of it. We left everything behind us except wives and children, but we had an ample stock of provisions and weapons. Friso was not yet satisfied. When we came to the old harbour, he went off with his stout soldiers and threw fire into all the ships that he could reach with his arrows.

Six days later we saw the war-fleet of Demetrius bearing down on us. Friso ordered us to keep back the small ships in a broad line, and to put the large ships with the women and children in front. Further, he ordered us to take the crossbows that were in the fore part and fix them on the sterns of the ships:

"Because", he said, "we must fight a retreating battle. No man is to pursue a single enemy — that is my order."

While we were busy with this, the wind (turned and) came from ahead, to the great alarm of the cowards and the women, because we had no slaves except those who had voluntarily followed us. We could, therefore, not escape the enemy by rowing. But Wr-alda knew well why he did this; and Friso, who understood it, immediately had the fire-arrows placed on the crossbows. At the same time he gave the order that no one should shoot before he did, and that we should all aim at the centre ship. If we succeeded in this, he said, the others would all go to its assistance, and then everybody might shoot as he best was able. When we were at a cable and a half distance from them the Phœnicians began to shoot, but Friso did not reply until the first arrow fell six fathoms from his ship. Then he fired, and the rest followed. It was like a shower of fire; and as our arrows went with the wind, they all remained alight and even reached the third line. Everybody shouted and cheered, but the screams of our opponents were so loud that it pierced our hearts.

When Friso thought that it was sufficient he called us off, and we sped away; but after two days' slow sailing another fleet of thirty ships came in sight and gained upon us. Friso cleared for action again, but the others sent forward a small rowing-boat with messengers, who asked permission to sail with us, as they were Joniars. They had been forced by Demetrius to go to the old harbour; there they had heard of the battle, and girding on their stout swords, had followed us. Friso, who had sailed a good deal with the Joniars, said "Yes", but Wichirte, our king, said "No".

"The Joniars", he said, "are idol worshippers. I myself have heard them call upon them."

"That comes from their intercourse with the real Greeks", Friso said. "I have often done it myself, and yet I am as pious a Frya's man as the finest of you".

Friso was the man to take us to Fryasland; therefore, the Joniars went with us. It seems that this was pleasing to Wralda, for before three months were past we coasted along Britain, and three days later we could shout "Ho'n seen!"

Chapter 3 – Driving out the Fins

This writing has been given to me about Nortland (Norway) or Skenland (Scandinavia):

When our land was submerged I was in Skenland. This is how it was there.

There were great lakes which rose from the earth like bubbles, then burst asunder, and from the rents flowed stuff like red-hot iron. The tops of mountains fell and destroyed whole forests and villages. I myself saw one mountain torn from another and fall straight down. When I went to see the place afterwards there was a lake there. When the earth had settled a duke of Lindasburgh came with his people and a matron who cried everywhere:

"The Magy is guilty of all the misery that we have suffered!"

They continued on their march, and their number increased. The Malty fled and his corpse was found; he had killed himself. Then the Finns were driven to one place where they might live. There were some of mixed blood who was allowed to stay, but most of them went with the Finns. The duke was chosen as king. The churches which had remained were destroyed.

Since then the good Northmen often come to Texland for the advice of the mother; still we cannot consider them real Fryans. In Denmark it has certainly happened as with us. The sailors, who call themselves famous sea-warriors, boarded their ships and later went back again.

Chapter 4: Frethorik's closing remarks

Hail! Whenever the Carrier has completed a period, (In time) posterity shall understand that the faults and misdeeds the refugees have brought with them were typical of their forefathers; therefore I will remain vigilant, and will describe as much of their manners as I have seen. The Gertmannen I can readily pass by. I have not had much to do with them, but as far as I have seen they have mostly retained their language and customs. I cannot say that of the others. Those who descend from the Greeks speak a bad language, and have not much to boast of in their manners. Many have brown eyes and hair. They are envious and impudent, and cowardly from superstition. When they speak, they put the words first that ought to come last. For "old" they say "at"; for "salt", "sat"; and for "man", "ma"—too many to mention. They also use peculiar and abbreviated names, which have no meaning. The Joniars speak better, but they drop the H, and put it where it ought not to be. When they make a statue of a dead person they believe that the spirit of the departed enters into it; therefore they have hidden their statues of Frya, Fasta, Medea, Thiania, Hellenia, and many others.

When a child is born, all the relatives come together and pray to Frya to send her servants to bless the child. When they have prayed, they must neither move nor speak. If the child begins to cry, and continues for some time, it is a bad sign, and they suspect that the mother has committed adultery. I have seen very bad things come from this. If the child sleeps, it is a good sign—Frya's servants have come. If it laughs in its sleep, the servants have promised it happiness. Moreover, they believe in bad spirits, witches, sorcerers, dwarfs, and elves, as if they descended from the Finns.

Herewith I will finish, and I think I have written more than any of my forefathers.

Frethorik.

Wiliow

Frethorik, my husband, lived to the age of 63. In 108 years he is the first of his nation who died a peaceful death; all the others died by violence, because they all fought with their own people and with foreigners for justice and duty.

My name is Wiljo. I am the maiden who came home with him from Saxsenmarken. In the course of conversation it came out that we were both of Adela's nation—then we fell in love became man and wife.

He left me with five children, two sons and three daughters. Konered was my eldest son, Hachgana my second. My eldest daughter is called Adela, my second Frulik, and the youngest Nocht. When I went to Saxsenmarken I saved three books—the book of songs, the book of tales, and the Helenia book.

I write this in order that people may not think they were by Apollonia. I have had a good deal of annoyance about this, and therefore now wish to have the honour of it. I also did more. When Gosa Makonta died, whose goodness and clear-sightedness have become a proverb, I went alone to Texland to copy the writings that she had left; and when the last will of Frana was found, and the writings left by Adela or Hellenia, I did that again. These are the writings of Hellenia. I have put them first because they are the oldest.

Chapter 5– Jesus of Kasamyr

(The Writings of Dela Hellenia)

Hail to all true Fryans.

In the olden times, the Slavonic race knew nothing of liberty. They were brought under the yoke like oxen. They were driven into the bowels of the earth to dig metals, and out of the hard mountains they had to build houses as dwelling-places for rulers and priests. Of all that they did, nothing came to themselves; everything had to enrich and empower the priests and the rulers, and to satisfy them. By this labour they grew gray and old before their time, and died without any enjoyment; although the earth produces abundantly for the good of all her children. But our runaways and exiles came through Twiskland to their boundaries, and our sailors came to their harbours. From them they heard of liberty, of justice, and laws, without which men cannot exist. This was all absorbed by the poor wretches like dew into arid soil.

When they fully understood this, the most courageous among them began to clank their chains, which grieved the rulers. The rulers are proud and warlike; there is therefore some virtue in their hearts. They debated together and shared some of their prosperity; but the cowardly hypocritical priests could not suffer this. Among their false gods they had also invented wicked cruel monsters. Pestilence broke out in the country; and they said that the gods were angry with the domineering of the wicked. Then the boldest of the people were strangled in their chains. The earth drank their blood; with this blood it fed the fruit and corn, and all those who ate thereof became wise.

Sixteen times a hundred years after Atland was submerged, something happened which nobody had contemplated. In the heart of Findasland, upon a mountain, lies a plain called Kasamyr, that is, "rare." There a child was born whose mother was the daughter of a king, and whose father was a high-priest. In order to hide the shame they were obliged to renounce their own blood. Therefore he was taken out of the town to poor people. As the boy grew up, nothing was concealed from him, so he did all in his power to acquire wisdom. His intellect was so great that he understood everything that he saw or heard. The people regarded him with respect, and the priests were afraid of his questions.

When he became of age he went to his parents. They had to listen to some hard language; and to get rid of him they gave him an abundance of jewels, but they dared not openly acknowledge him as their own blood. Overcome with sorrow at the false shame of his parents, he wandered about. While travelling he met a Fryan sailor who was serving as a slave, and who taught him our manners and customs. He bought the freedom of the slave, and they remained friends until death.

Wherever he went he taught the people not to tolerate the rich or priests, and that they must guard against false shame which always harms love. The earth, he said, bestowed her treasures to the extend her skin is scratched; so all are obliged to dig, and plough, and sow if they wish to reap, but no one is obliged to do anything for another unless it be out of common consent or goodwill. He taught that men should not seek in her bowels for gold, or silver, or precious stones to which they cling and which destroy love. To adorn your wives and daughters, he said, give them sufficient pure water.

No man is able to make everybody equally rich and happy, but it is the duty of all men to make each other as rich and as happy as possible. Men should not despise any knowledge; but justice is the greatest knowledge that time can teach, because she wards off offence and promotes love.

His first name was Jesus, but the priests, who hated him, called him Fo, that is, false; the people called him Krisen, that is, shepherd; and his Fryan friend called him Buda because he had a treasure of wisdom in his head, and in his heart a treasure of love.

At last he had to flee from the wrath of the priests, but wherever he went his teaching preceded him, whilst his enemies followed him like his shadow. When Jesus had thus travelled for twelve years he died; but his friends preserved his teaching, and spread it wherever they found listeners. What do you think the priests did then? That I must tell you, and you must give your best attention to it. Moreover, you must guard against their acts and tricks with all the strength that Wralda has given you. While the doctrine of Jesus was thus spreading over the earth, the false priests went to the land of his birth to make his death known.

They said they were his friends, and they pretended to show great sorrow by tearing their clothes and shaving their heads. They went to live in caves in the mountains, but in them they had hid all their treasures, and there they made images of Jesus. They gave these statues to simple people, and at last they said that Jesus was a god, that he had declared this himself to them, and that all those who followed his doctrine should enter his kingdom hereafter, where all was joy and happiness. Because they knew that he was opposed to the rich, they announced everywhere that poverty, suffering, and humility were the door by which to enter into his kingdom, and that those who had suffered the most on earth should enjoy the greatest happiness there.

Although they knew that Jesus had taught that men should regulate and control their passions, they taught that men should stifle their passions, and that the perfection of humanity consisted in being as unfeeling as the cold stones. In order to make the people believe that they did as they preached, they pretended poverty; and that they had overcome all sensual feelings, they took no wives. But if any young girl had made a false step, it was quickly forgiven; the weak, they said, were to be assisted, and to save their souls men must give largely to the church.

Acting in this way, they had wives and children without households, and were rich without working; but the people grew poorer and more miserable than they had ever been before. This doctrine, which requires the priests to possess no further knowledge than to speak deceitfully, and to pretend to be pious while acting unjustly, spreads from east to west, and will come to our land also.

But when the priests think that they have entirely extinguished the light of Frya and Jesus, then shall all classes of men rise up who have quietly preserved the truth among themselves, and have hidden it from the priests. They shall be of princely blood, of priestly blood, of Slavonic blood, and of Frya's blood. They will make their lamps and light visible, so that all men shall see the truth; they shall cry woe to the acts of the priests and the rulers. The rulers who love the truth and justice shall separate themselves from the priests; blood shall flow, but from it the people will gather new strength.

Finda's folk shall contribute their industry to the common good, Lyda's folk their strength, and we our wisdom. Then the false priests shall be swept from the earth. Wralda's spirit shall be invoked everywhere and always; the laws that Wralda instilled into our consciences in the beginning shall alone be listened to. There shall be neither masters, nor rulers, nor bosses, except those chosen by the general voice. Then Frya shall rejoice, and the earth will only bestow her gifts on those who work. All this shall begin 4000 years after the submersion of Atland, and 1000 years later there shall exist no longer either priest or oppression.

Dela, surnamed Hellenia, watch!

Frana's Last Will

Thus runs Frana's last will:

All noble Fryans, Hail!

In the name of Wralda, of Frya, and of Freedom, I greet you; and pray you if I die before I have named a successor, then I recommend to you Tuntia, who is burgh matron in the burgh of Medeasblik; until now she is the best.

Gosa's Prophecy

This Gosa has left behind her:

Hail to all men!

I have named no Eeremoeder, because I know none, and because it is better for you to have no mother than to have one you cannot trust. One bad time is passed by, but there is still another coming. Irtha has not given it birth, and Wralda has not decreed it. It comes from the East, out of the bosom of the priests. It will breed so much mischief that Irtha will not be able to drink the blood of her slain children. It will spread darkness over the minds of men like storm-clouds over the sunlight. Everywhere craft and deception shall vie with freedom and justice. Freedom and justice shall be overcome, and we with them. But this gain will produce its own loss.

Our descendants shall teach their people and their slaves the meaning of three words; they are universal love, freedom, and justice. At first they shall shine, then struggle with darkness, until every man's head and heart has become bright and clear. Then shall oppression be driven from the earth, like the thunder-clouds by the storm-wind, and all deceit will cease to have any more power.

Gosa.

The Writings of Konered

Chapter 1

My forebears have written this book in succession. I want to do the same above all because there are no longer any burghs in my state where events are recorded as in the past.

My name is Konered. My father's name was Frethorik; my mother's name was Wiljow. After my father's death I was chosen as his successor. When I was fifty years old I was elected as count. My father has written how the Lindaoorden and Liudgaarden were destroyed. Lindahem is still lost, the Lindaoorden partially, and the north Lindgaarden is still ravished by the salt sea. The foaming breakers wash the ring dyke of the burgh.

As my father has mentioned, the people, being deprived of their harbour, went and built houses inside the ring dyke of the burgh; therefore that portion is now called Liudwerd. The sea-people say Liuwrd, but that is bad pronunciation.

In my youth there was a portion of land lying outside the rampart, all mud and marsh; but Frya's people are diligent and hard working and they do not lose heart when they have a good object in view. By digging ditches, and making dams of the earth that came out of the ditches, we have recovered a good space of land outside the ring dyke, which has the form of a hoof three poles eastward, three southwards, and three westwards. At present we are engaged in ramming piles into the ground to make a harbour to protect our ring dyke.

When the work is finished we shall attract mariners. In my youth it looked very queer, but now there stands a row of houses. Leaks and deficiencies produced by poverty have been remedied by industry. From this men may learn that Wr-alda, our universal father, protects all his creatures, if they preserve their courage and help each other.

Chapter 2 – Friso

Now I will write about Friso.

Friso, who was already powerful by his troops, was chosen as count of the districts around Staveren. He laughed at our mode of defending our land and our sea battles; therefore he established a school where the boys might learn to fight in the Greek manner, but I believe that he did it to attach the young people to himself. I sent my brother there ten years ago, because I thought, now that we have no mother, it behoves me to be doubly watchful, in order that he may not become our master.

Gosa has given us no successor; I will not pass judgement about that, but there are still old suspicious people who think that she and Friso had an agreement. When Gosa died, the people from all around wished to choose another mother; but Friso, who was busy establishing an empire for himself, did not desire any advice or messenger from Texland. When the messengers of the Landsaten came to him, he said that Gosa had been far-seeing and wiser than all the counts together, and yet she had been unable to see any light or way out of this affair; therefore she had not had the courage to choose a successor, and to choose a doubtful one she thought would be very bad; therefore she wrote in her last will:

"It is better for you to have no mother than to have one on whom you cannot rely."

Friso had seen a great deal. He had been brought up in the wars, and he had just learned and gathered as much of the tricks and cunning ways of the Gauls and the rulers as he required to lead the other counts wherever he wished. See here how he went to work about that.

Friso had taken another wife here, a daughter of Wilfrethe, who in his lifetime had been chief count of Staveren. By her he had two sons and two daughters. By his wish Kornelia, his youngest daughter, was married to my brother. Kornelia is not good Frisian; her name ought to be written Korn-helia. Wemod, his eldest daughter, he married to Kauch. Kauch, who went to his school, is the son of Wichhirte, the king of the Gertmanna. But Kauch is likewise not good Frisian, and ought to be Kap. They have brought more bad language than good manners with them.

Now I must return to my story.

After the great flood of which my father wrote, many Jutlanders and Letlanders came out of the Baltic, or bad sea. They were driven down the Kattegat in their boats by the ice as far as the coast of Denmark, and there they remained. There was nobody to be seen; so they took possession of the land, and named it after themselves, Jutland. Afterwards many of the Denemarkers returned from the higher lands, but they settled more to the south; and when the mariners returned who had not been lost, they all went together to Zeeland. By this arrangement the Jutlanders retained the land to which Wralda had conducted them.

The Zeeland sailors, who were not satisfied to live on fish alone, and who hated the Gauls, took to robbing the Phœnician ships. In the south-west point of Scandinavia there lies Lindasburcht, called Lindasnôse, founded by our Apol, as is written in the book. All the people who live on the coast, and in the surrounding districts had remained true Frisians; but by their desire for vengeance upon the Gauls and the followers of Kalta (Celts), they joined the Zeelanders. But that connection did not hold together, because the Zeelanders had adopted many evil manners and customs of the wicked Magyars, in derision of Frya's people.

Afterwards, everybody went stealing on his own account; but when it suited them they held together. At last the Zeelanders began to be in want of good ships. Their shipbuilders had perished, and their forests as well as their land had been washed out to sea. Now three ships arrived unexpectedly, which anchored off the ring dyke of our burgh. As a result of the devastation of our land, they had lost themselves, and had sailed past the mouth of the Fly. The merchant who was with them wished to buy new ships from us, and for that purpose had brought all kinds of valuables, which they had stolen from the Celtic country and from Phœnician ships. As we had no ships, I gave them good horses and four armed couriers to Friso; because at

Staveren, along the Alderga, the best ships of war were built of hard oak which never rots.

While these sea farers were with me, some of the Jutmen sailed to Texland, and then they went to Friso. The Zeelanders had stolen many of their strongest boys to row on their benches, and many of their finest daughters to have children by. The sturdy Jutlanders could not prevent it, as they did not have proper weapons. When they had related all their misfortunes, and a good deal of discussion had taken place, Friso asked them at last if they had no good harbours in their country.

"Oh, yes", they answered, "the best; one created by Wralda. It is like your beer jug there, the neck is narrow, though a thousand large boats may lie in the belly; but we have no burgh and no defences to keep out the pirate ships."

"Then you should make them", said Friso.

"That is very good advice", said the Jutlanders, "but we have no artisans and no building tools; we are all fishermen and trawlers. The others have drowned or fled to the higher lands."

While they were arguing in this way, my messengers arrived at his court with the Zeeland gentlemen. Here you must observe how Friso understood deceiving everybody, to the satisfaction of both parties, and to the accomplishment of his own ends.

To the Zeelanders he promised that they should have yearly fifty ships of a fixed size for a fixed price, fitted with iron chains and crossbows, and fall rigging as is necessary and useful for men-of-war, but that they should leave in peace the Jutlanders and all the people of Frya's race. But he wished to do more; he wanted to invite all our sailors to go along to fight and plunder.

When the Zeelanders had gone, he loaded forty old ships with defences, wood, bricks, carpenters, masons and smiths to build burghs. Witto, that is White, his son, he sent along to oversee.

I have never been informed of what transpired; but this much is clear to me, that on each side of the harbour a strong burgh had been built, and garrisoned by people brought by Friso out of Saksenmarken. Witto courted Siuchthirte and married her. Wilhem, her father, was chief Alderman of the Jutmen—that is, chief Grevetman or Count. Wilhem died shortly afterwards, and Witto was chosen in his place.

Chapter 3 - What Friso did further

Of his first wife he still had two brothers-in-law, who were very daring. Hetto—that is, heat—the youngest, he sent as messenger to Kattaburgt, which lies far in the Saxsenmarken. Friso gave him to take seven horses, besides his own, laden with precious things stolen by the sea rovers. With each horse there were two young sea rovers and two young horsemen, clad in rich garments, and with money in their purses. In the same way as he sent Hetto to Kattaburgt, he sent Bruno that is, brown—the other brother-in-law, to Mannagarda oord. Mannagarda oord was written Mannagarda ford in the earlier part of this book, but that is wrong

All the riches that they took with them were given away, according to circumstances, to rulers, ladies, and chosen young girls. When his young men went to a tavern to dance with the young people there, they ordered baskets of spice, gingerbread, and tons of the best beer. After these messengers he let his young people constantly go over to the Saxsenmarken, always with money in their purses and presents to give away, and they spent money carefree in the taverns. When the Saxsen youths looked with envy at this   they smiled, and said:

"If you dare go and fight the common enemy you would be able to give much richer presents to your brides, and live much more princely."

Both the brothers-in-law of Friso had married daughters of the most famous rulers, and afterwards the Saxsen youths and girls came in whole troops to the Flymeer.

The burgh matrons and old maidens who still remembered their greatness, did not approve of Friso's actions, and therefore they said no good of him; but Friso, more cunning than they, let them chatter, but the younger maidens he led to his side with golden fingers. They said everywhere:

"For a long time we have had no mother, but that comes from our being come of age. At present it suits us best to have a king to win back our lands that we have lost through the imprudence of our mothers."

"Further", they said, "Every child of Frya has been given the freedom to let his voice be heard in the choosing of a leader; and if it comes to the choosing of a king, I also want to have my say. From what we can see, Wr-alda has chosen Friso for it, for he has brought him here in a wonderful way. Friso knows the tricks of the Gauls, whose language he speaks; he can therefore watch against their craftiness. Then there is something else to keep the eye upon. What count could be chosen as king without the others being jealous of him?"

All such nonsense the young maidens talked; but the old maidens, though few in number, tapped their advice out of another cask. They always spoke to every one, saying:

"Friso does like the spiders. At night he spreads his webs in all directions, and in the day he catches all his unsuspecting friends in them. Friso says he cannot suffer any priests or foreign princes, but we say that he cannot suffer anybody but himself; therefore he will not allow the burgh of Stavia to be rebuilt; therefore he will not have the mother again. To-day Friso is your counsellor, to-morrow he will be your king, in order to have full power over you."

Among the people there were now two parties. The old and the poor wished to have the mother again, but the young and the warlike wished for a father and a king. The first called themselves mother's sons, the others father's sons, but the mother's sons did not count for much, because there were many ships to build; there was prosperity for ship builders, smiths, sail makers, rope makers and other tradesmen. Moreover, the mariners brought all kinds of treasures. Of these the wives received enough, the matrons enough, the girls enough as well as all their relatives, associates and friends.

When Friso had been at Staveren nearly forty years, he died. By his efforts, many of the states had been joined together again, but that we were the better for it, I cannot agree with.

Of all the counts that preceded him there was none as renowned as Friso; for, as I said before, the young maidens spoke in his praise, while the old maidens did all in their power to make him hateful to everybody. Although the old women could not prevent his meddling, they made so much fuss that he died without becoming king.

Chapter 4 – Adel Atharik

Now I will write about his son Adel

Friso, who had learned our history from the book of the Adelingen, had done everything in his power to win their friendship. His eldest son, whom he had by his wife Swethirte, he named Adel; and although he strove with all his might to prevent the building or restoring any burghs, he sent Adel to the burgh of Texland in order to make himself better acquainted with our laws, language, and customs. When Adel was twenty years old Friso brought him into his own school, and when he had fully educated him he sent him to travel through all the states. Adel was an amiable young man, and in his travels he made many friends, so the people called him Atharik—that is, rich in friends—which was very useful to him afterwards, for when his father died he took his place without a question of any other count being chosen.

While Adel was studying at Texland there was a lovely maiden at the burgh. She came from Saxenmarken, from the state of Suobaland; therefore she was called Suobene at Texland, although her name was Ifkja. Adel fell in love with her, and she with him, but his father wished him to wait a little. Adel did as he wished; but as soon as his father had died, he sent messengers to Bertholda, her father, to ask her in marriage. Bertholda was a ruler of unblemished morals. He had sent his daughter to Texland in the hope that she might be chosen burgh matron in her country, but when he learned of their mutual affection he bestowed his blessing upon them.

Ifkja was a fine Frisian. As far as I have come to know her, she always toiled and worked to bring Frya's children back under the same laws and under one alliance. To win the people over to her, she travelled with her husband or her father through all Saxenmarken, and also to Gertmannia—as the Gertmanne had named the country which they had obtained by the efforts of Gosa. Thence they went to Denmark and from Denmark by sea to Texland. From Texland they went to Westflyland, and so along the cost to Walhallagara; thence they followed the Zuiderryn (the Waal), till, with great apprehension, they arrived beyond the Rhine at the Marsaten of whom our Apollonia has written.

After they had stayed there a while, they returned to the lowlands. As they descended towards the lowlands, and had reached the region of the old burgh of Aken, four of their servants were suddenly murdered and stripped naked. They had loitered a little behind. My brother, who was always on the alert, had forbidden them to do so, but they did not listen. The murderers that had committed this crime were Twisklanders, who had audaciously crossed the Rhine to murder and to steal. The Twisklanders are banished and fugitive children of Frya, but their wives they have stolen from the Tartars. The Tartars are a brown tribe of Finda's people, who are thus named because they provoke all nations to war. They are all horsemen and robbers. This is what makes the Twisklanders so bloodthirsty. The Twisklanders who had done the wicked deed called themselves Frijen or Franken. There were among them, my brother said, red, brown, and white men. The red and brown made their hair white with limewater— but as their faces remained brown, they were only the more ugly.

In the same way as Apollonia, they visited Lydasburgh and the Alderga. Afterwards they made a tour of all the neighbourhood of Stavera. They behaved with so much amiability, that everywhere the people wished them to stay.

Three months later, Adel sent messengers to all the friends that he had made, requesting them to send to him their "wise men" in the month of May.

(Missing Text. It would appear that Hidde Oera Linda skipped a page when he transcribed the Book in 1256 AD)

...his wife, he said, who had been matron at Texland, had received a copy of it. In Texland many writings are still found which are not copied in the book of the Adelinga. One of these writings had been placed by Gosa with her last will, which was to be opened by the oldest maiden, Albethe, as soon as Friso was dead.

Chapter 5 – Gosa's Advice

When Wr-alda gave children to the mothers of mankind, he gave one language to every tongue and on all lips. This gift Wr-alda had bestowed upon men in order that by its means they might make known to each other what must be avoided and what must be followed to find salvation, and to hold salvation for all eternity. Wr-alda is wise and good, and all-foreseeing. As he knew that happiness and holiness would flee from the earth when wickedness could overcome virtue, he has attached to the language an equitable property. This property consists in this that men can neither lie nor use deceitful words without stammering or blushing, by which means the innately bad are easily recognised.

Because our language thus opens the way to happiness and salvation, and thus helps to guard against evil inclinations, it is rightly named the language of the gods, and all those by whom it is held in honour derive honour from it. But what has happened? As soon as among our half brothers and sisters deceivers arose, who gave themselves out as servants of the good, it soon became otherwise. The deceitful priests and the malignant rulers, who always connive together, wished to live according to their own inclinations, without regard to laws and decent conduct. In their wickedness they went so far as to invent other languages, so that they might speak secretly in anybody's presence of their wicked and unworthy affairs without betraying themselves by stammering, and without showing a blush upon their countenances.

But what has that produced? Just as easily as the seed of good herbs which has been sown by good men in daylight, germinates under the ground, so time brings to light the evil seed which has been sown by wicked men in secret and in darkness. The wanton girls and effeminate youths who fornicated with the immoral priests and rulers, taught the new language to their companions, and thus spread it among the people till God's language was clean forgotten. Would you know what came of all this? Now that stammering and blushing no longer betrayed their evil doings, virtue passed away, wisdom and liberty followed; unity was lost, and quarrelling took its place; love flew away, immorality and envy sat around their tables; and where previously justice reigned, now it is the sword.

All are slaves—the subjects of their masters - envy, evil passions and covetousness. If they had only invented one language things might possibly have still gone on well; but they invented as many languages as there are states, so that one people can no more understand another people than a cow a dog, or a wolf a sheep. The mariners can bear witness to this. From all this it results that all the slave people look upon each other as strangers; and that as a punishment of their inconsiderateness and presumption, they must quarrel and fight until they are all destroyed.

Chapter 6 – Konered's Advice

Here is my advice.

If you wish that you alone should inherit the earth, you must never allow any language but God's language to pass your lips, and take care that your own language remains free from outlandish sounds. If you wish that some of Lyda's children and some of Finda's children remain, you must do the same.

The language of the East Schoonlanders has been perverted by the vile Magyars, and the language of the followers of Kaltana has been spoiled by the dirty Gauls. Now, we have been weak enough to admit among us the returned followers of Hellenia, but I am afraid that they will reward our weakness by corrupting our pure language.

Many things have happened to us, but among all the citadels that have been disturbed and destroyed in the bad time, Irtha has preserved Fryasburgh uninjured; and I may remark that Frya's or God's language has always remained here untainted. Here in Texland, therefore, schools should be established; and from all the states that have kept to the old customs the young people should be sent here, and afterwards those whose education is complete can help those who remain at home. If foreigners come to buy iron wares from you, and want to talk and bargain, they must come back to God's language.

If they learn God's language, then the words, "to be free" and "to have justice," will come to them, and glimmer and glow in their brains until it becomes a flame, and that flame will consume all bad rulers and hypocritical and dirty priests.

The local and foreign messengers were well informed about the writing, but no schools came from it. Then Adel established schools himself and after him other rulers did the same. Every year Adel and

Ifkja went to inspect the schools. If they found a friendly feeling existing between the locals and foreigners, they were very pleased.

If there were any who had sworn mutual friendship, they assembled the people, and with great ceremony let them inscribe their names in a book which was called the Book of Friendship, and afterwards a festival was held. All these customs were kept up in order to bring together the separate branches of Frya's race; but the matrons who were jealous of Adel and Ifkja said that they did it for no other reason than to make a name for themselves, and to bring all the other states under their subjection.

Among my father's papers I found a letter from Liudgert the Gertman. Omitting some passages which only concern my father, I proceed to relate the rest.

Liudgert the Gertman's letter

Pangap, that is five waters, and where we came from, is a river of extraordinary beauty, and is called five waters, because four other streams flow through its mouth into the sea. Far away to the east is another large river, the Holy or Sacred Ganges. Between these two rivers is the land of the Hindos. Both rivers run from the high mountains to the plains. The mountains from where they spring are so high that they lie up to the heavens, and therefore these mountains are called the Himmellaia Mountains. Among the Hindos and others out of these countries there are people who silently meet with one another. They believe that they are pure children of Finda, and that Finda was born in the Himmellaia Mountains, from where she went to the lowlands or plains with her children.

Some of them believe that she, with her children, floated down on the foam of the Gongga, and that that is the reason why the river is called the Sacred Gongga. But the priests, who came from another country, traced out these people and had them burnt, so that they do not dare to declare openly their creed. In this country all the priests are fat and rich. In their churches there are all kinds of monstrous images, many of them of gold.

To the west of the Pangab are the Ira, or Wranga, the Gedrostne, or runaways, and the Orietten, or forgotten. These names are given by the priests out of spite, because they fled from their customs and religion.

On their arrival our forefathers also settled to the east of the Punjab, but on account of the priests they likewise went to the west. In that way we came to know the Ira and other people. The Ira are not savages, but good people, who neither pray to nor tolerate images; neither will they suffer priests or churches; but as we adhere to the light of Fasta, so they always maintain fire in their houses.

Coming still further westward, we arrive at the Gedrostne. As regards the Gedrostne; they have been mixed with other people, and speak a variety of languages. These people are really savage murderers, who always wander about the country on horseback hunting and robbing, and hire themselves as soldiers to the surrounding princes, at whose command they destroy whatever they can reach.

The country between the Punjab and the Ganges is as flat as Friesland near the sea, and consists of forests and fields, fertile in every part, but this does not prevent the people from dying thousands upon thousands of hunger. The famines, however, must not be attributed to Wr-alda or Irtha, but to the princes and priests.

The Hindos are timid and submissive before their princes, like hinds before wolves. Therefore the Ira and others have called them Hindos, which means hinds. But their timidity is frightfully abused. If strangers come to purchase corn, everything is turned into money, and this is not prevented by the priests, because they, being more crafty and rapacious than all the princes put together, know very well that all the money will come into their pockets.

Besides what the people suffer from their princes, they also suffer a great deal from poisonous and wild beasts. There are great elephants that sometimes go about in whole herds and trample cornfields aid whole villages.

There are great spotted and black cats which are called tigers. They are as big as large calves, and they devour both men and beasts. Besides many other creeping animals there are snakes from the size of a worm to the size of a tree. The largest can swallow a cow, but the smallest are the most deadly. They conceal themselves among the fruits and flowers, and surprise the people who come to gather them. Any one who is bitten by them is sure to die, as Irtha has given no antidote to their poison, because the people have so given themselves up to idolatry. There are, besides, all sorts of lizards, tortoises, and crocodiles. All these reptiles, like the snakes, vary from the size of a worm to the trunk of a tree; according to their size and fierceness, they have names which I cannot recollect, but the largest lizards are called alligators, because they eat as greedily the putrid cattle that float down the stream as they do living animals that they seize.

On the west of the Punjab where we come from, and where I was born, the same fruits and crops grow as on the east side. Formerly there existed also the same crawling animals, but our forefathers burnt all the under wood, and so diligently hunted all the wild animals, that there are scarcely any left.

To the far west of the Punjab there is rich clay land as well as barren heaths, which seem endless, occasionally varied lovely spots on which the eye rests enchanted. Among the fruits there are many that I have not found here. Among the various kinds of corn some is as yellow as gold. There are also golden apples, of which some are as sweet as honey and others as sour as vinegar. In our country there are nuts as large as a child's head. They contain cheese and milk. When they are old oil is made from them. Of the husks ropes are made, and of the shells cups and other household utensils are made.

I have seen bramble and holly berries in the woods here. In our country there are berry trees like your lime-trees, the berries of which are much sweeter than and three times as big as your gooseberries. When the days are at the longest, and the sun is at its zenith, it is right overhead. If you sail very far to the south and look to the east at midday, the sun shines on your left side as it does in other countries on the right side. With this I will finish. It will be easy for you, by means of what I have written, to distinguish between false accounts and true descriptions.

Your Liudgert.

The Writings of Beden

Chapter 1 – Lost Chapter

My name is Beden, son of Hachgana. My uncle, not having married, left no children. I was elected in his place. Adel, the third king of that name, approved of the choice, provided I should acknowledge him as master. In addition to the entire inheritance of my uncle, he gave me some land which joined my inheritance, on condition that I would settle people there who his people would never…

(There would appear to be some twenty or more pages missing here in the original manuscript)

…therefore I will allow it a place here.

Chapter 2 – Rika's Letter

Letter of Rika the elder-matron, read at Staveren at the yule-feast -

My greeting to all of you whose forefathers came here with Friso.

According to what you say, you are not guilty of idolatry. I will not speak about that now, but I would rather address a failing which is hardly any better. You know, or you do not know, how many titles Wr-alda has. You all do know, however, that he is named universal provider, because that everything comes and proceeds from him for the sustenance of his creatures. It is true that Irtha is named sometimes the feeder of all, because she brings forth all the fruits and grains on which men and beasts are fed; but she would not bear any fruit or grain unless Wr-alda gave her the power.

Women who nourish their children at their breasts are called nurses, but if Wr-alda did not give them milk, the children would not benefit; so that, in fact, Wr-alda is really the nourisher. That Irtha should be called the universal nourisher, and that a mother should be called a feeder, one can understand, figuratively speaking; but that a father should be called a feeder, because he is a father, goes against all reason. Now I know whence all this folly comes. Listen to me. It comes from our enemies; and if this is followed, you will become slaves, to the sorrow of Frya and to the punishment of your pride. I will tell you what happened to the slave people; that you may learn from it.

The foreign kings, who follow their own will, place Wr-alda below the crown. From envy that Wr-alda is called the universal father, they wish also to be called fathers of the people. Now, everybody knows that kings do not regulate the productiveness of the earth; and that they have their   sustenance by means of the people, but still they will persist in their arrogance. In order to attain their object they were not satisfied from the beginning with free gifts, but imposed a tax upon the people. With the tax thus raised they hired foreign soldiers, whom they retained about their courts. Afterwards they took as many wives as they pleased, and the smaller princes and gentry did the same.

When, in consequence, quarrels and disputes arose in the households, and complaints were made about it, they said every man is the feeder of his household; therefore he shall be master and judge over it. Thus arose arbitrariness, and as the men ruled over their households the kings would do over their people. When the kings had accomplished that, they should be called fathers of the people, they had statues of themselves made, and erected in the churches beside the statues of the idols, and those who would not bow down to them were either killed or put in chains. Your forefathers and the Twisklanders had intercourse with the kings, and learned these follies from them. But it is not only that some of your men have been guilty of stealing titles, I have also much to complain over your wives.

If there are men among you who wish to put themselves on a level with Wr-alda, there are also women who wish to consider themselves equals of Frya. Because they have borne children, they call themselves mothers; but they forget that Frya bore children without having intercourse with a man. Yes, they not only have desired to rob Frya and the Eeremoeders of their honourable title (with whom they cannot be equal), but they do the same with the honourable titles of their neighbours. There are women who allow themselves to be called ladies, although they know that that only belongs to the wives of rulers. They also let their daughters be called matrons, although they know that no young girls are so called unless they belong to a citadel.

You all think that you are the better for this name-stealing, but you forget that jealousy clings to it, and that every wrong sows the seed of its own rod. If you do not alter your course,   in time it will grow so strong that you cannot see what will be the end. Your descendants will be flogged by it, and will not know whence the stripes come. But although you do not build citadels for the matrons and leave them to their fate, there will still remain some who will come out of woods and caves, and will prove to your descendants that you have by your disorderliness been the cause of it. Then you will be damned. Your ghosts will rise frightened out of their graves. They will call upon Wr-alda, Frya, and her maidens, but they shall receive no succour before the Yule shall enter upon a new circuit, and that will only be three thousand years after this century.

The end of Rika's letter.

Chapter 3 – Black Adel

...therefore I will first write about black Adel. Black Adel was the fourth king after Friso. In his youth he studied first at Texland, and then at Staveren, and afterwards travelled through all the states. When he was twenty-four years old his father had him elected Asega-Asker. As soon as be became Asker he always took the part of the poor. The rich, he said, do enough of wrong by means of their wealth, therefore we ought to take care that the poor look up to us. By arguments of this kind he became the friend of the poor and the terror of the rich. It was carried so far that his father looked up to him. When his father died he succeeded, and then he wished to retain his office as well, as the kings of the East used to do. The rich would not suffer this, so all the people rose up, and the rich were glad to get out of the assembly with whole skins.

From that time there was no more talk of equality before the law. He oppressed the rich and flattered the poor, by whose assistance he succeeded in all his wishes. King Askar, as he was always called, was seven feet high, and his strength was as remarkable as his height. He had a clear intellect, so that he understood all that was talked about, but in his actions he did not display much wisdom. He had a handsome countenance and a smooth tongue, but his soul was blacker than his hair. When he had been king for a year, he obliged all the young men in the state to come once a year to the camp to have a sham fight. At first he had some trouble with it, but at last it became such a habit that old and young came from all sides to ask if they might take part in it.

When he had brought it to this point, he established military schools. The rich complained that their children no longer learned to read and write. Askar paid no attention to it; but shortly afterwards, when a sham fight was held, he mounted a throne and spoke aloud:

"The rich have come to complain to me that their boys do not learn to read and write. I answered nothing; but I will now declare my opinion, and let the general assembly decide."

While they all regarded him with curiosity, he said further:

"According to my idea, we ought to leave reading and writing at present to the matrons and the old wise people.

"I do not wish to speak ill of our forefathers; I will only say that in the times so vaunted by some, the burgh matrons introduced disputes into our country, which the mothers were unable, either first or last, to put an end to. Worse still, while they talked and chattered about useless customs the Gauls came and seized all our beautiful southern country. Even at this very time our degenerate brothers and their soldiers have already come over the Scheldt. It therefore remains for us to choose whether we will carry a yoke or a sword.

"If we wish to remain free, it behoves our young men to leave reading and writing alone for a time; and instead of playing games of swinging and wrestling, they must learn to play with sword and spear. When we are completely prepared, and the boys are big enough to carry helmet and shield and to use their weapons, then, with your help, I will attack the enemy. The Gauls may then record the defeat of their helpers and soldiers upon our fields with the blood that flows from their wounds. When we have once expelled the enemy, then we must follow it up till there are no more Gauls, Slaves, or Tartars to be driven out of Frya's inheritance."

"That is right", the majority shouted, and the rich did not dare to open their mouths. He must certainly have thought over this address and had it written out, for on the evening of the same day there were copies in at least twenty different hands, and they all sounded the same. Afterwards he ordered the ship people to make double prows, upon which steel crossbows could be fixed. Those who were slack in doing this were fined, and if they swore that they had no means, the rich men of the village were obliged to pay. Now we shall see what resulted from all this bustle.

In the north part of Britain which is full of high mountains, there exists a Scotch people; the most of them spring from Frya's blood. Some of them are descended from the followers of Kaltana, and, for the rest, from Britons and fugitives who gradually, in the course of time, took refuge there from the tin mines. Those who come from the tin mines have wives, either altogether foreign or of foreign descent. They are all under the dominion of the Gauls. Their arms are wooden bows and arrows pointed with stag's-horn or flint. Their houses are of turf and straw, and some of them live in caves in the mountains. Sheep that they have stolen form their only wealth. Some of the descendants of Kaltana's followers still have iron weapons, which they have inherited from their forefathers.

In order to make myself well understood, I must let alone for a while my account of the Scotch people, and write something about the near Krekalanders (Italians). The Krekalanda formerly belonged to us only, but from time immemorial descendants of Lyda and Finda have established themselves there. Of these last there came in the end a whole troop from Troy. Troy is the name of a town that the far Krekalanders (Greeks) had taken and destroyed. When the Trojans had nestled themselves among the near Krekalanders, with time and industry they built a strong town with walls and citadels named Rome, that is, Spacious.

When this was done, the people by craft and force made themselves masters of the whole. land. The people who live on the south side of the Mediterranean Sea, come for the most   part from Phœnicia. The Phœnicians (Carthaginians) are a bastard race of the blood of Frya, Finda, and Lyda. The Lyda people were there as slaves, but by the unchastity of the women these black people have degenerated the other people and dyed them brown. These people and the Romans are constantly struggling for the supremacy over the Mediterranean Sea. The Romans, moreover, live at enmity with the Phœnicians; and their priests, who wish to assume the sole government of the world, cannot bear the sight of the Gauls.

First they took Marseilles from the Phœnicians —then all the countries lying to the south, the west, and the north, as well as the southern part of Britain—and they have always driven away the Phœnician priest, that is the Gauls, of whom   thousands have sought refuge in North Britain. A short time ago the chief of the Gauls was established in the citadel, which is called Kerenac (Karnac), that is the corner, whence he issued his commands to the Gauls. All their gold was likewise collected there. Keeren Herne (chosen corner), or Kerenak, is a stone citadel which did belong to Kalta.

Therefore the matrons of the descendants of Kaltana's followers wished to have the citadel again. Thus, by the enmity of the matrons and the Gaul's, hatred and quarrelling spread ever the mountain country with fire and sword. Our sea people often came there to get wool, which they paid for   with prepared hides and linen. Askar had often gone with them, and had secretly made friendship with the matrons and some rulers, and bound himself to drive the Gauls out of Kerenac. When he came back there again he gave iron helmets and steel bows to the rulers and the fighting men. War had come with him, and soon blood was streaming down the slopes of the mountains.

When Askar thought a favourable opportunity occurred, he went with forty ships and took Kerenac and the chief of the Gauls, with all his gold. The people with whom he fought against the soldiers of the Gauls, he had enticed out of the Saxenmarken by promises of much booty and plunder. Thus nothing was left to the Gauls. After that he took two islands for stations for his ships, from which he used later to sally forth and plunder all the Phœnician ships and towns that he could reach. When he returned he brought nearly six hundred of the finest youths of the Scotch mountain folk with him. He said that they had been given him as hostages, that he might be sure that the parents would remain faithful to him; but this was untrue. He kept them as a bodyguard at his court, where they had daily lessons in riding and in the use of all kinds of arms.

The Denamarkars, who considered themselves proud sea-warriors above all the other sea-people, no sooner heard of the glorious deeds of Askar, than they became jealous of him to such a degree, that they would bring war over the sea and over his lands. See here, then, how he was able to avoid a war. Among the ruins of the destroyed burgh of Stavia there was still established a clever burgh matron, with a few maidens. Her name was Reintja, and she was famed for her wisdom. This matron offered her assistance to Askar, on condition that he should afterwards rebuild the burgh of Stavia. When he had bound himself to do this, Reintja went with three maidens to Hals.

She travelled by night, and by day she made speeches in all the markets and in all the assemblies. Wr-alda, she said,   had told her by his thunder that all Frya's people must become friends, united as brothers and sisters; otherwise Finda's people would come and sweep them off the face of the earth. After the thunder Frya's seven watch-maidens appeared to her in a dream seven nights in succession. They had said disaster hovers over Frya's land with yoke and chains; therefore all the people who have sprung from Frya's blood must do away with their surnames, and only call themselves Frya's children, or Frya's people. They must all rise up and drive Finda's people out of Frya's inheritance.

If they would not do that, they will have slave-chains around their necks, and the foreign chiefs will ill-treat their children and flog them until the blood streams into their graves. Then shall the spirits of their forefathers appear to them, and reproach their cowardice and thoughtlessness.

The stupid people who, by the acts of the Magyars, were already so much accustomed to folly, believed all that she said, and the mothers clasped their children to their bosoms. When Reintja had convinced the king of Holstein and the others to unite, she sent messengers to Askar, and went herself along the Baltic Sea.

From there she went to the Hlithhawar (Lithauers), so called because they always strike at their enemy's face. The Hlithhawar are fugitives and banished people of our own race, who wander about in the Twisklanden. Their wives have been mostly stolen from the Tartars. The Tartars are a branch of Finda's race, and are thus named by the Twisklanders because they never will be at peace, but always provoke people to fight. She proceeded on beyond the Saxsenmarken, crossing through the other Twisklands, always repeating the same thing. After two years had passed, she came home along the Rhine. Among the Twisklanders she gave herself out for a mother, and said that they might return as free and true people; but then they must go over the Rhine and drive the Gauls out of Frya's southern lands.

If they did that, then her King Askar would go over the Scheldt and win back the land. Among the Twisklanders many bad customs of the Tartars and Magyars have crept in, but likewise many of our laws have remained. Therefore they   still have matrons, who teach the children and advise the old. In the beginning they were opposed to Reintja, but at last she was followed, obeyed, and praised by them where it was useful or necessary. As soon as Askar heard from Reintja's messengers how the Jutlanders were disposed, he immediately, on his side, sent messengers to the King of   Hals. The ship in which the messengers went was laden with women's ornaments, and took also a golden shield on which Askar's portrait was artistically portrayed.

These messengers were to ask the King's daughter, Frethogunsta, in marriage for Askar. Frethogunsta came a year after that to Staveren. Among her followers was a Magy, for the Jutlanders had been long ago corrupted. Soon after Askar had married Frethogunsta, a church was built at Staveren. In the church were placed monstrous images,   bedecked with gold-woven dresses. It is also said that Askar, by night, and at unseasonable times, kneeled to them with Frethogunsta; but one thing is certain, the burgh of Stavia was never rebuilt. Reintja was already back, and went angrily to Prontlik the mother, at Texland, to complain. Prontlik sent out messengers in all directions, who proclaimed that Askar is gone over to Idolatry.

Askar took no notice of this, but a fleet unexpectedly arrived from Hals. In the night the maidens were driven out of the burgh, and in the morning there was nothing to be seen   of the burgh but a glowing heap of rubbish. Prontlik and Reintja came to me for shelter.

When I reflected upon it, I thought that it might prove bad for my state. Therefore, we hit upon a plan which might serve us all.

This is the way we went to work. In the middle of the Krijlwood, to the east of Liudwerd, lies our place of refuge, which can only be reached by a concealed path. A long time ago I had established a garrison of young men who all hated Askar, and kept away all other people. Now it has come to   such a pitch among us, that many women, and even men, talked about ghosts, white women, and gnomes, just like the Denamarkars.

Askar had made use of all these follies to his own advantage, and now we wished to do the same. One dark night I brought the matrons to the citadel, and afterwards they went with their serving-maids (dressed like) ghosts in white along the maze, so that nobody dare go there any more.

When Askar thought he had his hands free, he allowed the Magyars to travel through his states under all kinds of names, and, except in Grenega and in my state, they were not turned away anywhere. After that Askar had become so connected with the Jutlanders and the Denmarkers, they all went pirating together; but it produced no good to them. They brought all sorts of foreign treasures home, and just for that reason the young men would learn no trades, nor work in the fields; so at last he was obliged to take slaves; but that was altogether contrary to Wralda's wish and to Frya's counsel.

As a result the punishment was sure to follow. See how the punishment came. They had all together taken a whole fleet that came out of the Mediterranean Sea. This fleet was laden with purple cloths and other valuables that came from Phœnicia. The weak crew of the fleet were put ashore south of the Seine, but the strong people were kept to serve as slaves. The handsomest were retained ashore, and the ugly and black were kept on board ship as rowers. In the Fly the plunder was divided, but, without their knowing it, they divided the punishment too. Of those who were placed in the foreign ships six died of colic. It was thought that the food and drink were poisoned, so it was all thrown overboard. The colic remained all the same and wherever the slaves or the goods went, there it came too. The Saxsenmen took it over to their markets The Jutlanders brought it to Skenland and along the coasts of the Baltic Sea, and with Askar's mariners it was taken to Britain. We and the people of Grenega did not allow either the people or the goods to come over our boundaries, and therefore we remained free from it.

How many people were carried off by this plague I cannot tell; but Prontlik, who heard it afterwards from the maidens, told me that Askar had helped out of his states a thousand times more free-men than he had brought dirty slaves in. When the pest had ceased, the Twisklanders who had become free, came to the Rhine, but Askar would not associate himself with the leaders of that vile degenerate race. He would not suffer them to call themselves Frya's children, as Reintja had offered them, but he forgot that he himself had black hair.

Among the Twisklanders there were two tribes who did not call themselves Twisklanders. One came from the far south-east, and called themselves Allemannen. They had given themselves this name when they had no women among them, and were wandering as exiles in the forests. Later on they stole women from the slave people like the Lithauers, but they kept their name. The other tribe that wandered about in the neighbourhood, called themselves Franks, not because they were free, but the name of their first king was Frank, who, by the help of the degenerate maidens, had had himself made hereditary king over his people.

The people nearest to him called themselves Thioth-his sons, that is, sons of the people. They had remained free, because they never would acknowledge any king, or ruler, or master except those chosen by general consent in a general assembly. Askar had already learned from Reintja that the Twisklander leaders were almost always at war with each other. He proposed to them that they should choose a duke from his people, because, as he said, he was afraid that they would quarrel among themselves for the supremacy. He said also that his leaders could speak with the Gauls. This, he said, was also the opinion of the mother.

Then the leaders of the Twisklanders came together, and after twenty-one days they chose Alrik as duke. Alrik was Askar's nephew. He gave him two hundred Scotch and one hundred of the greatest Saksmannen to go with him as a bodyguard. The leaders were to send twenty-one of their sons as hostages for their fidelity. Thus far all had gone according to his wishes; but when they were to go over the Rhine, the king of the Franks would not be under Alrik's command. Thereupon all was confusion. Askar, who thought that all was going well, landed with his ships on the other side of the Scheldt; but there they were already aware of his coming, and were on their guard.

He had to flee as quickly as he had come, and was himself taken prisoner. The Gauls did not know whom they had taken, so he was afterwards exchanged for a noble Gaul whom Askar's people had taken with them.

While all this was going on, the Magyars went about audaciously over the lands of our neighbours. Near Egmuda, where formerly the burgh Forana had stood, they built a church larger and richer than that which Askar had built at Staveren. They said afterwards that Askar had lost the battle against the Gauls, because the people did not believe that Wodin could help them, and therefore they would not pray to him. They went about stealing young children, whom they kept and brought up in the mysteries of their abominable doctrines. Were there people who

(Here the manuscript ends abruptly.)

Bibliography

- Aage Bach Sorensen, Cenozoic basin development and stratigraphy of the Faroese area , Geological Survey of Denmark and Greenland, Petroleum Geoscience, Vol. 9 (2003).
- Abbott, D: Chevron Dunes in Madagascar: The Most Spectacular Tsunami Deposits on Earth, Columbia University, New York City, NY; Aerospace Conference, 2007 IEEE, 3-10 March 2007.
- Adam Hadhazy, From Bountiful to Barren: Rainfall Decrease Left the Sahara Out to Dry - How a once-wet landscape became one of the world's great deserts. Scientific American, May 9, 2008: Quaternary International, Volume 195, 15 February 2009, Pages 69-87.
- Aharon Daniel: India History: Aryans and Dravidians - A controversial issue.
- Arrian : Indica, Anabasis Alexandri.
- Avesta , Yasna Avesta.
- Avesta, Khorda Avesta (Book of Common Prayer).
- Benton, RW: The Philistines and the Early Kingdom of Israel. Grace Theological Seminary, Grace Journal 8.1 (Winter 1967) 21-31.
- Bijal P. Trivedi: Genetic evidence suggests European migrants may have influenced the origins of India's caste system, Article in Genome Research, May 2001.
- Book of Enoch, Translated from the Ge'ez language (Ethiopic) by Richard Laurence, London, 1883.
- Brown, N: Pakistan and Western Asia.
- Bruce FF: The Book of Acts, NICNT (Grand Rapids, Mich.: Eerdmans, 1977).
- Chun Chang Huang and others, Extraordinary floods related to the climatic event at 4200 a BP on the Qishuihe River, middle reaches of the Yellow River, China, Department of Geography, Shaanxi Normal University, Xi'an, Shaanxi, People's Republic of China, 2010.

- Daniel, A: Aryans and Dravidians – A controversial issue. Website adaniels info site hosted by Tripod.
- Dares of Phrygia, History of the Fall of Troy.
- Dares Phrygius: The Trojan War. The Chronicles of Dictys of Crete and Dares the Phrygian. Translated by R. M. Frazer (Jr.). Indiana University Press. 1966.
- David Keys, Archaeology Correspondent, The Independent, Found: Europe's oldest civilisation, dated 11 June 2005.
- Dictionary of Greek and Roman Antiquities (edited by William Smith [1870]).
- Dollinger, A: Ancient Egyptian Didactic Literature. Lichtheim, M: Ancient Egyptian Literature, Vol. 1. The admonitions of Ipuwer.
- Dr D Margaret Avery , Journal of Archaeological Science (1995) 22, 343–353, Physical Environment and Site Choice in South Africa.
- Dr. Sander R. Scheffers and others, Tsunamis, hurricanes, the demise of coral reefs and shifts in pre-historic human populations in the Caribbean, School for Environmental Management and Science, Southern Cross University, NSW, Australia.
- Francisco Ruiz and others, Evidence of high-energy events in the geological record: Mid-Holocene evolution of the south-western Doñana National Park , Department of Geodynamics and Palaeontology, University of Huelva, Avda, Spain, , Palaeogeography, Palaeoclimatology, Palaeoecology, Volume 229, Issue 3, 20 December 2005, Pages 212-229.
- Geoff Carter, structural archaeologist, (http://structuralarchaeology.blogspot.com/2009/08/33-elsloo-32-neolithic-longhouse-made.html).
- H.A.C. Fermin and M. Groothedde, De Zutphense ringwalburg van de 9e tot de 14e eeuw. Zutphen Archaeological Publication No. 22.
- Haflidi Haflidason et al, The Storegga Slide: architecture, geometry and slide development [2004]).
- Hapgood, C: Maps of the Ancient Sea Kings; Evidence of Advanced Civilization in the Ice Age, 1966.

- Heather Smith: Celtic Clothing during the Iron Age – a very broad and generic approach.
- Herodotus of Halicarnassus (ca. 484 BC–ca. 425 BC): The Histories. Translated by George Rawlinson (1812-1902).
- Holy Bible : New Living Translation. 1997. Tyndale House: Wheaton, Ill.
- Homer (ca. 850 BC ?): Iliad, Odyssey. Translated by Samuel Butler (1835-1902).
- Hooker, R: Webpage on the Aryans.
- Julius Caesar (100 BC-44 BC): De Bello Gallico. Translated by W. A. McDevitte and W. S. Bohn (1869).
- Keller, W: Und die Bibel hat doch recht, Hamburg (1955). Translated by A.H. Jonker and J.J.J. Scholtz into Afrikaans: Die Klippe het dit Uitgeroep (1963) Haum Books, Cape Town.
- Kolbert, E: The Climate of Man - II .
- Laurence, Richard: The book of Enoch. Translated from the Ge-ez language (Ethiopic), 1883.
- Lucius Flavius Arrianus 'Xenophon' (ca. 86 - after 146): Anabasis of Alexander, Book VIII (Indica), Translated by E. Iliff Robson (1933).
- M. Lichtheim: 1973-80, Ancient Egyptian Literature, Vol. I, p.150, University of California Press.
- Mair, VH: Mummies of the Tarim Basin, Archaeology, vol. 48, no. 2, pages 28-35(March/April 1995).
- Martin Claussen (Prof. Dr.), Sahara's Abrupt Desertification Started By Changes in Earth's Orbit, Accelerated By Atmospheric and Vegetation Feedbacks. The Potsdam-Institut fuer Klimafolgenforschung (Potsdam Institute for Climate Impact Research), Germany. ScienceDaily, Washington, July 12, 1999.
- Murphy, E. F. 1997, c1996. Handbook for spiritual warfare. Thomas Nelson: Nashville.
- Murphy, James Cavanah: The Arabian antiquities of Spain, by, London 1813.
- Niroma, T: Website: The Third Millennium BC , (3100-2100 BC).
- Ottema, JG: Thet Oera Linda Bok (1872).

- Otto S. Knottnerus,, Sea Level Rise as a Threat to Cultural Heritage, Wadden Sea Newsletter 2000 (No. 2).
- P. Ovidius Naso, Metamorphoses, Book XII.
- Plutarch (c. AD 46 – 120): Lives of the Noble Greeks and Romans, (Parallel Lives) - Life of Demetrius, Translated by John & William Langhorne (1770).
- R Tewari, The Origins of Iron-working in India, Archaeology Online webpage, U.P. State Archaeological Department in India.
- Radford, A: From Goddess to King. Internet.
- Ranasinghage, P. N et al, Signatures of Paleo-coastal Hazards in Back-barrier Environments of Eastern and South-eastern Sri Lanka, The Smithsonian/NASA Astrophysics Data System: American Geophysical Union, Fall Meeting 2010, abstract #NH21A-1397.
- Richard Hooker: Ancient India, The Aryans.
- Sandbach, WR: The Oera Linda Book (1876).
- Smith, J. H. 1992; The new treasury of scripture knowledge Published in electronic form, 1996., Thomas Nelson: Nashville TN.
- Smith, W. 1997. Smith's Bible dictionary. Thomas Nelson: Nashville.
- Snyman, A: Die Oera Linda Boek (1998), Vaandel Uitgewers BK (Publishers).
- Petros Drineas, Associate professor of computer science and member of the Rensselaer Data Science Research Center and others, DNA Analysis Unearths Origins of Minoans, the First Major European Civilization, Nature Communications (14 May 2013).
- Strabo (63/64 BC – ca. AD 24): Geographica.
- Strong, J. 1996. The exhaustive concordance of the Bible: (electronic ed.). Woodside Bible Fellowship.: Ontario.
- Strong, J. 1997, c1996. The new Strong's dictionary of Hebrew and Greek words. Thomas Nelson: Nashville.
- Tacitus, Gaius Cornelius: The Germania (Latin: De Origine et situ Germanorum, literally: The Origin and Situation of the Germans) (c 98 AD). Translated by Thomas Gordon (1728).

- Tewari, R: The Origins of Iron-working in India. Webpage of Archaeology Online. U.P. State Archaeological Dept., India.
- The Bible: The New King James Version. 1996, Thomas Nelson: Nashville.
- The Geological Society of America: 2006 Philadelphia Annual Meeting (22–25 October 2006).
- The History of Herodotus,– CLIO, Translated by George Rawlinson, 1942.
- The Holy Bible : New Century Version, containing the Old and New Testaments. 1991. Word Bibles: Dallas, TX.
- The New York Times, 29 December 2008.
- The New York Times: Article: Ancient Crash, Epic Wave, November 14, 2006.
- The New York Times: Article: Meteorite Strikes, Setting off a Tsunami: Did It Happen Here? December 29, 2008.
- The Sciences, May/June 1996, p.34.
- Thompson, LG: Kilimanjaro Ice Core Records: Evidence of Holocene Climate Change in Tropical Africa. Science.
- Thucydides (c.460 BC – c.395 BC): History of the Peloponnesian War.
- Timo Niroma, Helsinki, Finland: The Third Millennium BC (3100-2100 BC).
- Titus Flavius Josephus (AD 37 – ca. 100): Jewish Antiquities, Against Apion. Translated by William Whiston: The New Complete works of Josephus.
- Titus Livius Patavinus (59 BC – AD 17), The History of Rome.
- Trivedi, BP: Genetic evidence suggests European migrants may have influenced the origins of India's caste system (May 2001) Vol. 298, 18 October 2002. UIUC McDonald Research Center: 1500 AD Y Haplogroups.
- Vartanyan SL: Radiocarbon Dating Evidence for Mammoths on Wrangel Island, Arctic Ocean, until 2000 BC. Geographical Research Institute, St. Petersburg State University, Sredniy Prospect 41, 199004 St. Petersburg, Russia.
- Weiss, H: Article in The Sciences: Desert Storm, May/June 1996.

Printed in Great Britain
by Amazon

17221057R00261